Ken Weber

Sheila Bennett

Special Education
in
Ontario Schools

Fifth Edition

Highland press

In Memory of Ron Forrester,
Publisher of Highland Press.
"Never a detail missed."

The authors of *Special Education in Ontario Schools* are grateful for the advice, assistance and support from many caring professionals in special education. Thanks are due particularly to John Amon, Bruce Drewett, and their colleagues in the Special Education Branch at the Ministry of Education, also to Don Dworet, Linda Fogolin, Andrea Jack, Susie Palumbo, Kelly Ann Russell, and Michael Walmsley.

Highland Press
Box 25, Palgrave, Ontario L0N 1P0
Telephone (905) 880-1277
Fax (905) 880-4134
E-mail hldpress@look.ca

Design and cover photo: Fortunato Aglialoro
Editor: Cecile King

Canadian Cataloguing in Publication Data
Weber, Ken (Kenneth Jerome), 1940-
    Special education in Canadian schools

5th ed., rev.
Includes bibliographical references and index.
ISBN 0-9693061-8-0

    1. Special education — Ontario.
I. Bennett, Sheila Marie, 1961-
II. Title.

LC3984.2.05W42 2004 371.9' 09713 C2004-901503-6

Printed and bound in Canada.

08 07 06 05 04   0 9 8 7 6 5 4 3 2 1

Table of Contents

Foreword

We first wrote this foreword in June, 1999 to introduce the Fourth Edition of Special Education in Ontario Schools. *While preparing the Fifth Edition we were pleased to note, individually and independently, that what we admired about special education five years ago still holds true today. Committed, professional teachers and educational assistants are still front and centre in their efforts to help exceptional students. Administrators continue to work to make the system effective, and the province's Ministry of Education continues to support special education to the fullest. We hope that after yet another five years has passed we will once more be encouraged in this way.*

Ken Weber, Sheila Bennett
May 1, 2004

Classroom practices, administrative procedures, and Ontario government policies in special education are built around the ideal that it is possible to respond to the strengths and needs of every special student. Legislation in the province guarantees access to public education for all students regardless of their needs. Further, it assures that exceptional students will have access to programs and resources to meet their special needs. Individual boards and schools are set up to deliver special education service and support, ranging through simple modification of a student's program to allocation of complex specialized resources, and even to changes in building design. Ministry regulations reinforce ideal professional practices such as the development and monitoring of individual education plans.

On the front lines so to speak, classroom teachers and educational assistants draw on training in special education, and on their own resources and talents and creativity to bring everything together for students with special strengths and needs. Ontario teachers have long been recognized, not just in their own province but elsewhere, for their leadership and commitment in matters relating to special students. These qualities are a main reason why special education has been implemented so successfully as a fully functional and vital element in the province's broader system.

Like all systems put together by human beings, Ontario's special education reveals occasional faults. But the system is dynamic. It responds to evolving needs and philosophies; it develops; it adapts. And most of the time it improves. In any case, special education will only be as effective as the people—at every level—who make it work. Ultimately, special education can only succeed as a concept, as a principle, and most importantly as a practice, through the actions of professionals who are committed to the belief that every student has a right to the best that schooling can offer. Ironically, the ideal of special education is to put itself out of business. The goal for which it strives is a system of education in which adaptation and accommodation for the needs of every student is automatic, and in which the very idea of "special" education is unnecessary.

CHAPTER 1

The Long Journey to Special Education

On December 12, 1980, Lieutenant-Governor John Black Aird signed Bill 82, the Education Amendment Act. Prior to the passing of this new legislation, Ontario school boards had been *allowed* to provide special education. Now they were *required* to. Disability would no longer be a barrier to the regular school system. Within a very short time, special education became an integral part of Ontario's system with such relative ease that it's tempting to believe Bill 82 was a law just waiting to be passed. From the perspective of the twenty-first century it may well seem so, but the long journey to special education as it is today was anything but simple and smooth. This chapter outlines a few of the bumps.

Dateline 1957 — The Case of Ruthie

It was not until she was almost eight years old that Ruthie began attending school. To begin with, her parents knew she was, in her father's words, "something behind the other young ones". Then there was the long walk down the concession and across the sideroad to the one-room school. She'd have to do it alone and everybody knew Ruthie had this habit of wandering off.

Even at age eight, Ruthie's future as a student was uncertain at best.

"We don't have to take this child in if you don't want," the chairman of S.S. #12 school board had said to the brand new teacher in August. "It's going to be hard enough in your first year without having a retarded child to look after. The regulations are clear. We don't have to take her. It's up to you."

But the teacher welcomed Ruthie and made her feel part of the tiny student body at S.S. #12. Two girls in grade eight took her outside to the toilet every day just before recess and noon hour. One of the older boys built her an extended desktop so she could more easily enjoy her favorite activity: colouring on the back of discarded rolls of wallpaper. The younger children, a bit perplexed at first because Ruthie didn't speak, soon learned to ignore her strange noises. And every day after lunch, Ruthie crawled happily into the teacher's lap for the reading of the next sequence in 'the afternoon story'. By the end of the school year, Ruthie could recognize her own name in print; she understood and followed routines, could count up to ten and, most important in the teacher's view, she no longer wandered away.

The next year might have shown even more development, but Ruthie got caught in a swirl of events that even her parents didn't quite follow. S.S. #12 was closed in June, along with all the other one-room schools in the township. Students were now to be bused to a brand new central school. Ruthie's teacher got married that summer and moved to the other end of the province. At 'Central', the school inspector told the staff in primary/junior that no one was obligated to take in Ruthie, but if anyone volunteered, she could be admitted.

There were no takers. Ruthie never went to school again.

In the Beginning

At First, Mere Survival

Disabled persons did not fare well in early times. This was true even in cultures like the Greek and the Roman, which we generally view as more enlightened and sophisticated. Under Solon's law, for example, the weak and disabled children of Athens were placed in clay vessels and abandoned. In Rome, disabled children were customarily thrown in the Tiber. And it was not unusual for wealthy families to keep a mentally handicapped person for entertainment. No less a personage than the moralist philosopher, Seneca, reported that his wife kept a "feeble-minded dwarf", ostensibly for that purpose. Even Aristotle, whose writings dominated western thought for more than a thousand years after his death, described deaf people as "incapable of reason, no better than the animals of the forest" and "unteachable". There were some exceptions to this quite universal attitude. The Talmud offered enlightened instructions regarding the blind and deaf, and Hippocrates' investigations into epilepsy and intellectual disability suggested that scientific curiosity about special needs was not entirely absent. However, the impact of these exceptions was very limited.

> "Every child has a claim on the community for the best means of moral and mental cultivation."
>
> *Harvey Peet, 1855*

In the Middle Ages, there were a few bright spots. Saint Nicholas Thaumaturgos, fourth century bishop of Wyre, became known as a protector of the feeble-minded but there is little evidence of what he accomplished. (He was also the patron saint of sailors and pawnbrokers — and the prototype for Santa Claus!) Some monasteries and other clergy established hospices but the superstitions of the day, along with a powerful belief in demonic possession and the sheer demands of mere survival, meant that persons with disabilities were very much on their own.

A few strides were made in Europe in the post-Renaissance Era, but they were isolated, short-lived bursts of change, the accomplishments of individuals with will and drive, rather than the product of a general amelioration in attitude. When these individuals died, the fruits of their efforts died with them. Most special educators today, for example, recognize the name Ponce de Leon (1529-82), the Spanish monk who taught deaf children to speak and read (although he is often confused with the explorer who visited Florida in 1513). De Leon's techniques were very successful apparently, but are lost and unknown to us largely because there was no general impetus after his death to continue their use.

Eventually, a Bit of Light

Three hundred years after de Leon, Louis Braille (1809-1852) had more lasting success with an alphabet for the blind he adapted from a cipher system invented by Napoleon Bonaparte's staff. But by Braille's time, attitudes were beginning to shift. British philosopher, John Locke (1632-1708) had impressed the intellectuals of the western world with his philosophy of 'sensationalism' which, among other things, took issue with the long held view that children are born with innate characteristics imprinted by God, nature, or the devil. Instead, Locke argued, they are a *tabula rasa*, a blank slate waiting to be written upon. Ever so slowly, this idea, given further impetus by scholars like Voltaire, Rousseau, and Goethe, began to chip away at the notion that disabled people are the unfortunate product of some Great Plan and should therefore be left alone.

Still, the march toward enlightenment was slow and innovation was actively discouraged. Jean Marc Itard (1775-1858) who discovered and tried to teach Victor, the wild boy of Aveyron, and Frederick Treves (1867-1923) who rescued John Merrick, the Elephant Man, are among the better known personalities who broke new ground, but their humanism was too radical for their contemporaries. The level of indifference, or perhaps just inertia, is evident in the fact that carnival shows continued to display physically unique persons like John Merrick, well into the mid-twentieth century.

In Canada, Some Real and Lasting Light

Louis Braille's alphabet was strongly resisted in the United States, but there was progress in education for the blind, and for the deaf, in Canada. A school for the blind opened in Toronto in 1872 and one in Halifax a year later. In Quebec, Ronald Mcdonald, a reporter with the *Montreal Gazette*, opened a school for the deaf in Champlain, in 1831, Canada's first formal special education project. Similar schools opened in Halifax in 1856, in Toronto (1858) and Winnipeg (1884). These were followed soon after by the first Canadian residential institution for the developmentally disabled which opened in Orillia in 1876. A few years before

that, and also in Ontario, the vigorous work of John Barrett McCann had brought about the founding of two residential schools: The Ontario Institution for the Education and Instruction of the Deaf and Dumb, at Belleville, in 1870, and the Ontario Institution for the Education and Instruction of the Blind, at Brantford, in 1872. In 1893, Children's Aid societies were formed in Ontario and became the model for such practice throughout North America.

By establishing such institutions, the Ontario government was reflecting the greater sense of social responsibility in the general population, as well as a developing interest in people with

Dateline 1965 — The Case of Leo

No one was more exasperated by Leo's lack of language skills than his mother. A former teacher, she had sent his two older sisters off to grade one so well prepared they both skipped a grade. Not Leo. To be sure, he appeared to be just as bright. Certainly he was charming, and so what if he had a few odd speech patterns? That was nothing unusual in a youngster. Yet no matter what she did, Leo's mother just couldn't teach him to recognize letters.

Not that she pushed him to frustration. She was too wise and experienced a mother and teacher. But Leo — she'd never seen anything quite like it. Take the letter 'A' for example. He'd willingly trace it, colour it, find 'A's hidden about the kitchen, and sing the 'A' song. Yet, though he'd then recognize the letter without a prompt for maybe two or three days, after a week on 'B' and 'C', the letter 'A' would be gone. And it would be really gone! That was part of the exasperation. Re-introducing 'A' to Leo was not a simple matter of stimulating recall. It was as though he'd never ever seen it before!

Of course, Leo's printing was disastrous. Nor did it improve as he got older. At the end of grade one, Leo's principal boldly left the 'Printing' mark blank on his report card so he could pass into grade two, but the problem was still there. So was his letter recognition problem and lack of progress in learning to read. Friends of Leo's mom tried to console her with the explanation that boys are almost always slower but Leo just didn't get any better. Nor did anybody have an explanation, although the grade four teacher had seen another boy like it once before, and he'd become a real problem because no one seemed able to do anything for him.

Still, the situation was not all bad. Leo's father ran a successful plumbing business where Leo helped out on Saturdays, and as long as the boy was given only one instruction at a time, no one worked harder or more reliably. In fact, it may have been the plumbing business that provided an out for everyone, because by grade five, Leo's behaviour was changing. He'd already repeated two grades, was facing failure again, and reading was still torture and writing an agony. By grade five, Leo was no longer getting headaches and stomach pains during language arts; he was now acting out in progressively alarming ways. That was the main reason Leo's mother reluctantly agreed to the arrangement that allowed him to leave school to work for his dad. Even so, one of her worst fears came true some years later. When Leo's dad retired, he had to sell the business, for although Leo was willing and handy, he never learned to read and write well enough to run things.

disabilities. Although some of the teaching methods used in the institutions seem odd today, and although the language and terminology make contemporary educators wince, the mere existence of residential schools was a striking development for the time, especially in light of the fact that educating the so-called "normal" population was still far from universal.

Still a Long Way to Go

Unfortunately, by reason of economics, not to mention Ontario's vast geography, comparatively few special children were served, relative to the actual needs in the population. Resources were aimed at the most overt and visibly obvious exceptionalities and the curricula were very much biased toward industrial training. The idea was, in the words of a contemporary, "to make something of the students" so they might find gainful employment. To be fair, that mission very much followed the wishes of the students' own parents and families who, perhaps understandably, felt that "making something of the students" at least offered them some hope of independence.

Not even this much was held out to the exceptional students whose needs were less obvious, and as a consequence, harder to understand or even acknowledge. Consequently students with a learning disability (the term did not even exist until 1963) or those with what we see today as behaviour problems, were usually

Dateline 1979 — The Case of Peter

On the agenda at the county school board meeting, item no. 5 appeared innocuous enough. It read

Approval of funds to install elevator, renovate main entrance, washroom, fire exits and classroom doorways as outlined in Report 995A.

To Pete and his family, and to three other families with sons and daughters who had severe physical disabilities, item no. 5 was full of implications. Pete had muscular dystrophy. Over his years in elementary school, the condition had developed to a point where he could no longer walk for more than a few metres without risking a serious fall. The walking itself was accomplished with the help of crutches which Pete used in alternating wide swings. Increasingly, he was spending longer and longer periods in a wheelchair, and now required some assistance when using the washroom. In a few months, Pete would be eligible to attend the secondary school in his community. But it was an old building where he would not be able to get around, much less get in or out, unless some major structural changes were made. There would also need to be some kind of arrangement developed for Pete's personal hygiene needs. Nothing in either education or civil law obligated the board to do these things, but because it was a fairly small community where Pete and his family were well known and active, the local trustees agreed to consider the matter.

The motion was defeated, but so narrowly that Pete's family was encouraged to press for another possibility. Since 1974, Ontario's Education Act had permitted school boards to provide special education services *if they chose to*, and by now, some boards in the province were doing that. A few had renovated some schools to accommodate students with physical disabilities. Thus Pete's family, supported by an advocacy group, began urging the local board to arrange — and bear the cost — for Pete to enroll at one of these. Once more the trustees listened carefully and sympathetically, but because there were a number of students in a situation similar to Pete's, they approached the proposal with caution. So cautiously, as it turned out, that the motion kept being tabled. Pete's parents, wary of the outcome, reluctantly sold their home, moved out of the community, and relocated in another part of the province near a school that was modified for students with special needs like their son's.

early dropouts. Right through to the final quarter of the twentieth century, dropouts were regarded — and also saw themselves — as poor educational material in any case. Assembly line industry absorbed them into fairly low-level employment and reinforced the perception.

As it was, even established schools were not always secure, especially if their faculties attempted to be innovative. The Ontario School for Crippled Children (now part of Bloorview MacMillan Centre in Toronto) had quickly established an international reputation for its programs. As early as 1890, faculty at the Orillia institution had developed quite advanced school programs for its clientele. Yet both had to struggle to keep their programs going in the face of widespread criticism. Students with serious profound needs were often seen as poor candidates for education on the premise that it served little purpose, and offered only minimal return to society. In light of that hypothesis, it is more than a little ironic that the societal benefit factor apparently played no role at all in discussions of special education for students who were especially able. Public education for gifted students was almost unheard of until the 1970s.

> "Individuals with disabilities should be served whenever possible in general education classrooms in inclusive neighborhood schools and community settings."
>
> *Council for Exceptional Children, 1993*

The Modern Era

There is little question that special education as we have come to understand it in Ontario today, is a comparatively recent phenomenon. Although as early as 1950, the Hope Commission had recommended expansion of special education programs, the watershed, the point at which the march to Bill 82 got under way, was in the 1960s. This decade saw things shift from episodic, disconnected attempts to somehow improve the lot of exceptional students, to a generally coherent movement aimed at educating them according to their needs. The change occurred around this time for a number of reasons.

A New Humanism

Key to a more sensitive and positive valuing of exceptional individuals was the decline and near-disappearance of the eugenics movement, a philosophy very much in vogue among intellectuals during the first part of the twentieth century. Eugenicists sought to protect society from genetic contamination, and argued that 'unfortunates' should be protected in institutions, thereby protecting society in the bargain.

In 1918, a coalition of medical doctors, social workers and influential citizens had formed the Canadian National Committee on Mental Hygiene to pressure the government to expand custodial facilities for the feeble-minded, whose spread was the result, in the Committee's opinion, of "procreation by unsound stock, the numbers of which were being accelerated by the government's admittance to the Dominion, of degenerate immigrants" (sic!). Under a principle of concern for the public good, and a seemingly well-intentioned concern for the less able, supporters of eugenics were successful in effecting a policy that not only segregated people with special needs, but in practical terms, isolated them.

By the end of the Second World War, what was already a trickle of doubt about eugenics became a flood because of the role it had played in Fascism. In the 1960s, a swell of concern for the individual rights of all persons led governments to enshrine those rights in law. Ontario, for example, established its first Human Rights Commission in 1962. By the end of the decade, any notion of racial or cultural superiority or indeed any kind of exclusive human purity had become anathema. Western culture was ready to listen to the idea that every human being has worth.

The Normalization Principle

Although separation *by ability* was still prominent well into the twentieth century, by the

A flurry of October transfers meant that Justin's grade three class acquired a new teacher only a week before his situation was scheduled for special review by an Identification, Placement, Review Committee (IPRC). The new teacher wisely allowed the full-time educational assistant in grade three to work with the school's resource teacher in putting together documentation for the IPRC. The assistant was experienced and held in high regard in the school, and she had worked with Justin for the past two years. More important, she was one of the few adults who understood and managed his behaviour effectively.

Over the past several years, Justin had been variously diagnosed as autistic, ADHD, learning disabled, cerebrally dysfunctional and mentally disabled, by a variety of clinical psychologists either in private practice, or employed by the school board. While Justin was still in kindergarten, an IPRC took the unusual step, for a student so young, of identifying him "exceptional: behavioural". Justin's mother signed on to the identification only because it would allow the school to bring in extra resources. However, she served notice she would appeal any move to take her son out of a regular class, and maintained that position through reviews in grades one and two in the face of growing evidence that a regular class might not be the best place for him.

The special review in grade three was arranged by the principal who, for everyone's sake, planned to make one more stab at modifying Justin's class placement. If that failed, she planned to initiate a rarely used process which could declare him 'hard-to-serve' and thereby excluded from the school. Fortunately, everyone, including the boy's mother, agreed to an adjustment. Justin would begin each day in the grade three class and then, with the assistant, join a small resource class. He would, depending on his mood and behaviour, return to the regular class as frequently as possible and for as long as possible. Above all, it was agreed that flexibility would prevail and both the assistant and the teachers would be free to make ad hoc decisions as necessary.

For Justin — and everyone — the long term outcome was very positive. He spent increasingly more time in the regular grade three class but there was always a friendly, secure home base to go to if the need arose. Perhaps most telling: the annual IPRC review in grade four lasted only ten minutes.

time Ontario enacted Bill 82, this notion was succumbing to the principle of normalization, championed in Canada by Wolf Wolfensberger through the National Institute on Mental Retardation (now the G. Allen Roeher Institute). In essence, normalization argues against institutionalization and contends that persons with special needs should be viewed more by the points on which they are similar to others, rather than by those on which they differ. The philosophy of normalization holds that once exceptional persons are integrated into mainstream society, they will take on the behaviours of the norm because they will have more normal models to follow. It is a concept that suggests unlimited growth and improvement instead of ceilings and limitations, and it struck a powerful chord, not just in Ontario, but throughout Canada and North America. In only about twenty years, government policies across the continent changed from building and expanding care-based facilities to strategies that saw these centres being closed and the residents being included in their communities.

Educators Take More Control

Educators in the sixties, and even more so in the seventies, began to set aside the then-popular medical model approach to students with special needs, a model which focuses on what is wrong with the students. What replaced it was a wider, more ecological view incorporating the whole person, a perspective that takes note of what an exceptional student can do in addition to what is hard or impossible to do. At the same time, teachers and paraprofessionals also began to recognize their own strengths, and the potential power of their own contributions to an exceptional student's case. Whereas in the medical model approach, a teacher or an educational assistant is expected to defer to some greater, outside expertise, the ecological focus grants them the right to exercise their considerable intuition, knowledge and experience. An important consequence of the latter approach is that students with special needs are seen as educable entities, not as custodial, medical cases for whom intellectual development and learning are secondary to coping with a handicap.

Deliver of special Ed. Perhaps more important, ultimately, is the effect of this perspective on the way special education service is delivered. In a medical model, expertise is visited upon the classroom from above and afar, but in a model that requires empiricism, hypothesis, flexibility and constant program modification, the decision-making and the delivery of service are likely to be much more current, not to mention appropriate, if they take place on site. By the time the Education Amendment Act was only a decade old therefore, the trend in Ontario was moving toward management of special needs in the local community school, and specifically in the regular classroom.

Advocates Flex Their Muscles

Social commentators frequently trace the origins of advocacy to the protest movements of the nineteen-sixties. Certainly, it was at this time when the parents of students with special needs found that they could achieve more for their sons and daughters by acting collectively rather than singly. The result was that political activism by parent and other advocacy groups began to have, and continues to have, a powerful effect on governments. The strength and sophistication of lobbying efforts by groups like the Learning Disabilities Association, the Association for Bright Children, the Association for Community Living, among many others, has been instrumental for decades now in motivating educational jurisdictions to improve the lot of exceptional students. In fact, there are many participants in the process that eventually gave birth to mandatory legislation in

Ontario, who acknowledge quite candidly that, were it not for the activity of advocates, it may not have come about as soon as it did. An important consequence of such powerful advocacy was that by the end of the twentieth century, it became accepted, indeed encouraged practice to involve parents or their representatives far more extensively in day by day educational decision-making.

What Ontario's New Legislation Provided

The Education Amendment Act was a major step for Ontario to take. Nova Scotia and Saskatchewan had passed mandatory legislation in the early 1970s, as had the U.S. in 1975, but the idea was not at all solidly established. Yet once the bill was passed, special education became a normal, functioning part of Ontario's education system with remarkable speed. Teachers still active today can point to a time only a decade before 1980, when the idea of sending students with special needs to a regular school was not even considered by most jurisdictions in the province. Yet within a decade *after* 1980, special education was as integral to the system as notebooks and chalk. Although the legislation itself is extensive, the elements most immediately affecting students and their families, and teachers and their schools and boards are these:

- Every school board in the province is required to provide special education programs and services for its exceptional pupils. If a board cannot provide programs and services, it must pay another board to provide them.

- School boards are to establish Identification, Placement and Review Committees (IPRCs) whose chief function is to identify whether a pupil is exceptional, and then decide upon a placement for him or her. (For more on the IPRC see Chapter 5.)

- Parents of an exceptional pupil are to be included in the IPRC process. An appeal process is available if they are dissatisfied with identification or placement decisions.

- Every school board is required to establish a Special Education Advisory Committee (SEAC) to advise on matters of special education programs and services.

- A comprehensive special education plan must be developed and maintained by each school board in which its programs and services are outlined for public and Ministry examination. The 'Plan' is updated and amended as necessary to meet the current needs of exceptional pupils.

- School boards are required to implement procedures for early and on-going identification of pupils' learning abilities and needs.

Meeting the Challenge

At the Board Office

Even critics of the legislation agree that the expectations it raised were met for the most part in the immediately ensuing years. When the bill was passed in 1980, the province's school boards were given five years to establish their plans and systems; yet in the majority of boards, special education policies and practices were fully operational well before the deadline. More subtle, but certainly crucial to rapid implementation was the relative ease with which special education became a natural feature in every school board. And it came about in the face of major challenges. Prior to the legislation, for example, separate school boards did not provide programs and services for what were called in 1980, 'trainable retarded pupils',

and thus most separate boards had to build services from scratch in a very short time. Many smaller school boards, both public and separate, had to develop special education systems with little or no existing base to build on. Even boards that already had some services before 1980, did not offer the comprehensive systems one could find almost anywhere in the province only five years later.

In the Classroom

Still another challenge was finding front-line staff to make the systems work on a daily basis. In 1980, very few teachers in the province undertook special education as a career path. Yet a combination of teachers' inherent skills and ready willingness to learn on the job, supported by a mass professional development drive on the part of the Ministry and of the province's universities, soon addressed this vital component. Within a decade, provincial authorities were able to point to a large cadre of teachers clearly committed to the field. Equally urgent was the need for resource and support personnel, most especially educational assistants, whose role soon took on ever more importance as schools began to deal with a variety of special needs never encountered before. Ontario's colleges were quick to show leadership in developing effective education programs for paraprofessionals, a response that paid dividends immediately, for the graduates soon proved their value in classrooms.

At Home and School

Although the idea of parent support for education was hardly a novel one by 1980, the manner and extent of parental involvement that grew as a consequence of special education, was a new experience. A few senior administrators found the experience more of a challenge than they were hitherto accustomed to, but for the most part, the outcomes proved to be positive. As everyone gradually came to understand through experience, parents can play a crucial role in educating children with special needs that is qualitatively and quantitatively different from the one generally required in supporting the education of other children.

The Special Education Plan

Under Regulation 306, each board of education must establish and maintain a master plan in which it sets out programs and services it will provide. The plan must be reviewed yearly, and every two years the board must prepare a report for the Ministry of Education. In 2000, the Ministry issued a policy document setting standards for these Plans.

Some Issues to Resolve

Clarity for Parents

Despite the fact that the IPRC process guarantees both the rights and specific involvement of parents, many were intimidated at first by its apparent complexity. The legislation very clearly requires boards to provide literature explaining the IPRC but, in the beginning especially, some were not quite successful at this. Over time, a combination of simple good will, along with cooperative effort on the part of boards, and some very effective work by parent associations and special education teachers, did much to mitigate this concern. The Ministry of Education too, reinforced the role of parents by first establishing, then strengthening SEACs, Special Education Advisory Committees.

Strengthening the SEAC

Each school board in Ontario is required to establish a Special Education Advisory Committee, usually with membership taken principally from various parent associations in the community. These groups play a key role in educating the public about special education in general. They have input in decisions about special education finances. They have strong involvement in all aspects of the Special Education Plan, and are often an effective liai-

---

Dateline 2000 — The Case of Onisa

Given that, in grade two, Onisa regularly brought clippings from the *Globe and Mail* and the *Economist* to 'show-and-tell', no one in her school was the least bit surprised when in grade six, she won a UN-sponsored trip to Geneva, Switzerland, for her essay on the meaning of democracy. Still, during the promotion and placement meetings that were held at the end of the school year, both Onisa's regular grade six teacher and her 'Challenge Program' teacher were uneasy.

Onisa had been identified 'gifted' for some time, and her academic achievements were remarkable, especially during her earlier years at the school. But a standardized achievement test administered just before the end of the year in grade six hinted at somewhat more modest abilities. Onisa still was clearly in the superior range, but if the language and general awareness categories were factored out, and only her results in math/science were presented, she was actually below the mean for her class. What intrigued both of Onisa's teachers was that this confirmed an unevenness they had noticed: a contrast between what appeared to be her giftedness in language, and her quite ordinary ability in math and science.

It was a dilemma for the teachers because in their board, all students left for new schools after grade six. For Onisa to continue in the 'Challenge Program' and be able to develop her unique abilities, her identification as 'gifted' would need to be confirmed by the annual IPRC review. However, whereas the 'Challenge Program' from grades one to six was an individualized, in-the-regular-class, enrichment offering, from grade seven on, students identified 'gifted' were generally placed in self-contained classes for an across-the-board enhanced curriculum (including advanced level math and science).

Happily, the school board's resources and the professionalism of its staff were brought to bear on Onisa's behalf. The head of the gifted program was aware of several other students with a similar math/science vs. language imbalance, students who shared Onisa's interests. Accordingly, they were each recommended for the same grade seven class. It would not be in a school designated for the specially enhanced curriculum, but Onisa and her peers would retain their identification so that if, in the future, it appeared any of them would be better off with the enhanced curriculum, then arrangements could be made with a minimum of fuss.

After six months in her new school, Onisa declined to make the switch when it was offered (although one of her peers accepted). After twelve months had passed, she was eligible once again to compete in the UN essay contest. This time her first step in the process was to write and request an appointment with the federal Minister for External Affairs.

son between parents and board in potentially difficult situations. Some boards in the province were already working with parent and advocacy groups as a matter of course, prior to the official setting up of these committees. Still, the fact that this very important role was enshrined in provincial policy suggests that parental involvement is conceived as beneficial in many ways.

In 1997, the Ministry of Education reissued its regulation governing SEACs (Reg. 464)* further strengthening their role. In 2003-4, the Ministry established information and training programs for SEAC members.

Adjusting the Appeal Process

The appeal process came under criticism early on. Parents dissatisfied with an IPRC decision can take their case first to an Appeal Board, and then if matters are unresolved at this level, to a Special Education Tribunal. Concerns about the fairness of Appeal Boards (which are put together on an ad hoc basis for each appeal) were raised on the premise that they were weighted in favour of the school board. Indeed, some school boards did not help matters by frequently appointing representatives who might be seen to lack objectivity. Although an early 1990s study of Appeal Board hearings showed that the process gives parents a fair and effective hearing, the province subsequently modified this stage of the process to minimize perceptions of unfairness.

The Tribunal stage too, weathered a rigorous examination in the 1990s in a legal action that ended in the Supreme Court of Canada. (See The Eaton Case, following.)

Pressure for Inclusion

At first it was fairly standard practice in most jurisdictions to place special education students in their neighbourhood schools in self-contained† classes according to their particular needs. This type of service delivery was not only considered normal but beneficial for all concerned. Enrolling exceptional students in the neighbourhood school was generally known as *mainstreaming*, or *integration*, while the philosophy driving the choice of classroom placement was called *least restrictive environment*. In only a very short time, however, the special education agenda was effectively overwhelmed by pressure from some parents and professionals to place exceptional students into regular classes, full time. They pointed out, with the support of quite powerful empirical evidence, that what happened in many if not most cases of mainstreaming was that schools hosted two parallel groups, a regular one, and those with special needs alongside it looking to get in. Exceptional students were *in* the neighbourhood school but not really *of* it.

In response, the Regular Education Initiative emerged in the mid-1980s. It was a metaphor more than a strategy but one that had considerable impact, and went a long way in shifting the educational mindset from the subtle parallelism of mainstreaming toward a fuller, more natural integration of students with special needs into the system. The next, almost simultaneous step was advocacy in favour of *inclusion* or *inclusionary schooling*. In many ways this too, was but a shift in vocabulary but it put even more emphasis on the principle of automatically placing exceptional students in the classrooms they would normally attend if they did not have a special need.

In tandem with the pressure for full inclusion was the shadow cast by legal concerns: whether or not a school board's decision to place a student in a separate, special class, can be a violation of his or her equality rights under the *Canadian Charter of Rights and Freedoms*. The 1997 Supreme Court of Canada decision in Eaton vs. Brant County did much to put this issue to rest.

• • • ——————

* The Ministry of Education periodically issues regulations which, essentially, have the force of legislation. These are numbered, with the year of issue following. The regulation dealing with SEACs, for example, is O.Reg.464/97. The Ministry also issues Policy/Program Memoranda which are more explanatory than regulatory but are still considered to have administrative authority. PPM 89/90, for example, describes the role and workings of the province's residential demonstration schools for students with learning disabilities.

† At one time, both special educators and advocates freely used 'segregated class' (and sometimes 'dedicated class') for the special, separated classes created for exceptional students, but this term was soon euphemized to 'self-contained', the term used in Ministry documents.

—————— • • •

The 'Eaton Case'

This lengthy case began when an IPRC determined that after three years in a regular class, experience and common sense made clear that the subject child, an eleven year old with extensive special needs, was not benefiting from inclusion and that her best interests would be served in a special class. The parents appealed this decision first to the civil court where the situation was directed back to the appeal process established by provincial legislation. The IPRC was then upheld by an Appeal Board and subsequently by a Tribunal. The Tribunal decision in turn was upheld by a judicial review, but then overturned by the Ontario Court of Appeal, which held that a placement without consent is discriminatory under Section 15 of the *Charter*.

The Ontario Court's position was emphatically rejected by the Supreme Court of Canada in a 9-0 ruling and the original decision restored, thereby making clear there is no Charter presumption in favour of inclusion. It also had the effect of affirming Ontario's special education legislation. In its written judgment, which quoted large parts of the Tribunal decision verbatim, the high court reinforced the notion that placement of children with special needs should be decided on a by-case basis, with the principal determiner being a child's best interests. This outcome did much to diminish the litigiousness that had been growing around special education legislation, and also had the effect of motivating parties on all sides to search for compromise and for "on-the-ground" solutions to the needs of exceptional students.

Achieving a Positive Balance

Accommodating Inclusion

Even before the 'Eaton case' began, the provincial government had taken steps toward accommodating the inclusion issue and amalgamating this point of view with other, usually more eclectic positions taken by many teachers, school boards and academics. While most people agree on the moral and philosophical merits of full inclusion as an objective, the practice does not always follow the principle with absolute success. Research to support the idea is, unfortunately, notoriously hazy. Perhaps more important, results in the classroom sometimes prove ambivalent at best. The ideal implied by inclusion is that when placed with regular students, an exceptional student will also be taught with them; yet irrespective of the effort and support brought to bear, it sometimes doesn't quite work out that way. As a consequence, although full inclusion remains a fundamental goal of special education, on the ground things are generally more fluid.

Thus as early as the spring of 1991, the Minister of Education declared to the Ontario legislature that integration of exceptional pupils into local community classrooms would be the norm wherever possible, but went on to assure the assembly that inasmuch as an integrated setting may not be appropriate for every child, school boards would be encouraged to offer a full range of alternative educational placements. It was a position that seemed at once reasonable, educationally sound, and politically astute, and has become, in effect, the way most special education works in the province today. The majority of exceptional students are in neighbourhood schools being educated with their peers, but because inclusion remains an adaptable concept, a minority continues to be accommodated in other ways.

Turning to Mediation

It is important to recognize that although appeals and litigation are popular avenues in Ontario, legal struggles have figured into just a very tiny number of situations since the passing of the Education Amendment Act. There have been thousands of IPRC decisions since 1980 but only a handful of Tribunals, suggesting quite strongly that the process does the job it was designed to do. Another more recent, and positive, trend, which as yet has no basis in the legislation but is actively encouraged by the Ministry, is the use of mediation to resolve impasses. Both parents and boards are finding this technique far less costly and time-consuming than formal appeals, and usually, one that minimizes post-adversarial residue.

"Reactive Attachment Disorder"

by 2 yrs.

early trauma

Dateline 2004 — The Case of Teodor (Teddy)

Until the day in late September when Teddy set fire to the hair of a girl seated in front of him, not one teacher in his new high school had paid attention to the special education department's description of 'reactive attachment disorder', and the advice that might counter its effects. The fire, however, raised Teddy's profile significantly, and when he vandalized several cars the very next day, staff awareness spread quickly.

Like most educators, few of Teddy's teachers had ever heard of 'reactive attachment disorder'. Among the paraprofessionals at the school, only one had knowledge of it; she had dealt with a similar situation at an elementary school. Teddy's case, everyone soon learned, was almost a stereotype. He had been born in Romania when *perestroika* came to that beleagured country and his first three years had been spent in an ill-kept, underfunded, and grossly under-staffed state orphanage. His adoptive parents — Canadians from Ontario — had devoted the next three years to helping him overcome the effects of severe malnutrition, and a mild but cor-rectable spinal deformity. Yet, by the time Teddy began senior kindergarten, the parents were painfully aware that the boy's problems went far beyond his stomach and his back.

Like many children with this syndrome, Teddy had never felt love or experienced bonding in his early, formative years; indeed his very survival day-to-day was uncertain. Had he been born in Canada, there is little doubt that similar treatment would be categorized as child abuse. Thus, despite the efforts of the loving and deeply caring couple who adopted him, Teddy's developing years were marked by low self-esteem, profoundly manipulative behaviour, aggression, defiance, and — a key element in the syndrome — a pronounced lack of capacity for remorse or of what our culture sees as moral perspective. *(conscience) psyc sociopath*

Although Teddy — not to mention his parents and teachers — had barely survived his ele-mentary school experience, his two years of senior public with the same teacher and under a very watchful and ready-to-intervene principal, had been, by comparison, relatively peaceful. But now, in high school, the worst of Teddy's behaviours were front and centre, a fact confirmed in a behavioural checklist his special education teacher asked staff to complete in advance of an IPRC review. Clearly, steps would have to be taken.

Accepting Alternative Implementation Styles

Some school boards in Ontario interpret parts of the Education Amendment Act somewhat independently. While all boards carefully accede to the Act's most important stipulation, the requirement to provide special education, a few do it with some variations. The most com-mon 'non-standard' practice is maintaining a full special education program without official-ly identifying students via the IPRC process. (There are also students receiving special edu-cation with the agreement and support of the parents even though the parents have refused an IPRC.) To date, however, it would appear that providing full special education programs, thereby meeting the principal requirement of

the Act, overrides much of the concern about variations in process.

Special Education Today: A Mature Force

Constant Fine Tuning

Given the sweeping changes effected by Education Amendment Act and its related regu-lations and policy memoranda, the amount of adjustment in the years since 1980 has been remarkably small. Indeed, much of what has been altered has gone barely noticed except by administrators, and by parents with a specific area of interest. Typical of the latter group were parents of developmentally disabled children in

1993, when the provincial government in what was known as 'Bill 4' removed the term 'trainable retarded' from the Education Act. The same bill removed the 'hard-to-serve' section. This was a complicated, never used set of clauses that allowed a board to exclude a pupil.

Significant modifications to official policy and practice were introduced in 1998 when the province re-issued the regulation concerning the IPRC process. The new regulation (Reg. 181) expanded the responsibilities of the committee in a variety of ways, required a written plan for the exceptional student, and generally strengthened the role and rights of parents. In the immediately ensuing years, the written plan, known as the Individual Education Plan (IEP) took on more and more importance and its development and use for exceptional students was subject to increasingly intense scrutiny, especially by the Ministry. In 2002, a voluntary template was made available by the Ministry, thus providing a theoretically ideal format against which individual boards and schools could compare their own.

Further developments include the Coordinated Services Unit set up in 2001 to establish improved service coordination across several provincial ministries, a pilot program on standards for autism in 2003, and the Ontario Disabilities Act, 2002, which placed specific accessibility obligations on public sector groups such as school boards. The Special Education Project (an ongoing venture) deals with development and implementation of policies and programs. Other fine tunings include the amount and quality of support materials now available from the Ministry of Education.

Irrespective of the activity outlined above, the fact that there have been relatively few major alterations in Ontario's official special education policy and practice, reinforces the impression that the system works well. When modifications become necessary, experience has demonstrated that teachers and individual boards and schools, with the support of the Ministry of Education and university and college faculties, are more than competent in bringing them about.

The Situation Today

For Ontario students with special needs, universal access to education is guaranteed. The definite first choice of placement is the regular class. And perhaps most important, students with special needs are just that: *students*. In short, special education has become a normal, integral and functional part of the system. Not that change and development and improvement will no longer be needed; adjustments will always be necessary and will continue to happen. But special education in Ontario is positioned now so that changes to it occur in the larger context of all educational development. As education itself adjusts to social change, to technology and to general needs, special education will adapt with it. In that context, future developments in special education are likely to be expressed in positive refinements of gains that have already been made.

READINGS & RESOURCES

For in-depth detail on provincial legislation, regulations, policy/program memoranda, funding guidelines, and a range of information and services from the Ministry of Education see *Special Education: A Guide for Educators (2001)* available from the Ministry's publications branch or downloaded at **http://www.edu.gov.on.ca/eng/general/elemsec/speced/guide.html**

Bunch, G., & Valeo, A. (1997). *Inclusion: recent research*. Toronto: Inclusion Press.

Carrier, J. G. (1986). Sociology and special education: differentiation and allocation in mass education. *American Journal of Education, 94*, 281-312.

Council for Exceptional Children (1991). "Code of ethics for the CEC", *Teaching Exceptional Children, 23,2*.

Council of Administrators of Special Education (1997). Position paper on delivery of services to students with disabilities. *Keeping in Touch.*

Eaton vs Brant County. SCC#24668, 7 Feb., 1997.

Foerter, J., et al (1991). *Special education: Bridging the centuries,* (Ontario Teachers' Federation).

Fullan, M. G. (1991). *The new meaning of educational change* (2nd ed.). New York: Teachers College Press.

Government of Canada (1997). *Directory of federal programs and services: persons with disabilities.* Ottawa, ON: Department of Human Resources Development, Minister of Supplies and Services.

Grossman, H. (1995). *Special education in a diverse society.* Toronto: Allyn & Bacon.

Hallahan, D.B., & Kauffman, J.M. (1994). *Exceptional Children: Introduction to special education.* Toronto: Prentice Hall.

Hardman, M.L.D., Clifford, J., Drew, B., & Winston, E. (1993). *Human exceptionality: Society school and family* (4th edition) Toronto: Allyn & Bacon.

Itard, J.M.G. (1806). *The wild boy of Aveyron* (G. Humphrey & M. Humphrey, trans.) (1962). Englewood Cliffs, NJ: Prentice-Hall.

Lieberman, L. (1991). REI Revisited… again. *Exceptional Children, 56,* 561-526.

Lupart, J. L.., McKeough., & Yewchuck, C. (Eds.). (1996). *Schools in transition: Rethinking regular and special education.* Toronto: Nelson Canada.

Malouf, D.B., & Schiller, E.P. (1995)."Practice and research in special education", *Exceptional Children, 61,* 414-424.

Oderkirk, J. (1993). Disabilities among children. *Canadian Social Trends,* pp. 22-25

Poirier, D., Goguen, L., & Leslie, P. (1986). The Canadian Charter of Rights and Freedoms and the right to education for exceptional children. *Canadian Journal of Education, 11,* 231-244.

Poirier, D., Goguen, L., & Leslie, P. (1988). *Education rights of exceptional children in Canada: A national study of multi-level commitments.* Toronto: Carswell.

Smith, D., Luckasson, R. & Crealock, C. (1995). *Introduction to Special Education in Canada.* Scarborough: Allyn & Bacon.

Smith, W.J., & Lusthaus, C. (1994). Equal educational opportunities for students with disabilities in Canada: The right to free and appropriate education. *Exceptionality Education Canada, 4,* 37-73.

Stainback,W. & Stainback S. (Eds.), (1996). *Controversial Issues Confronting special Education: Divergent perspectives* (2nd edition), Boston: Allyn & Bacon.

Winzer, M. (1993). *The history of special education: From isolation to integration.* Washington D.C.: Gaulladet University Press.

Wolfensberger, W. (1975). *The origin and nature of institutional models.* Human Policy Press.

Wood, M. (1998). Whose job is it anyway? Educational roles in inclusion. *Exceptional Children, 64* (2), 181-195.

Links

Canadian charter of Rights and Freedoms
http://canada.justice.gc.ca/Loireg/charte/consten.html

Ministry of Education
www.edu.gov.on.ca

Special Needs Education Network
http://schoolnet2.carleton.ca/sne/

CHAPTER 2

Continuing Issues in Special Education

"My kid's handicapped. He needs somebody to fight for him and that's me.
I'm a taxpayer too and if your kid can get an education so can mine.
I'm going to do what I have to do. Get used to it."

Laney G., parent of a child with multiple disabilities

Inclusion: Once Hot, Now Mild, But Still Alive

Teachers, educational assistants and principals in neighbourhood schools — the people who deal with inclusion on a daily basis — have pretty much discarded the notion that it is still a controversial issue. Even in academic journals, in administration offices, at professional conferences, and among advocacy groups, where the topic of inclusion was once guaranteed to brew up a storm, the winds are now relatively calm. There are a number of reasons for this, the most obvious being that inclusion today is a dominant reality. The vast majority of exceptional students are in regular classes, and in cases where alternatives are chosen, it is usually with the agreement of all parties involved. As an issue for debate therefore, inclusion no longer has much profile. What most educators are concerned with now is making inclusion *work*.

Among those for whom the issue still resonates, the arguments have pretty much reached a default stage

> "Why are we still arguing about inclusion? The first consideration for every child automatically is regular classroom. There are more urgent issues today. Like funding, delivering service. And keeping up — there's always something new in special ed!"
>
> *Patricia M., elementary school principal*

in parallax positions. One side tends to argue that *all* students with special needs, no matter how unique or demanding their needs, should be placed in regular classrooms of neighbourhood schools. To a significant extent, that position is argued as much from a stance of moral superiority as it is from one of superior educational outcomes. Ranged apart from this view are those who do not see the matter quite so unconditionally. This group contends that, whereas integration should indeed be sought as a first solution, some students might be better served if at least a portion of their program were delivered in a more specialized environment. Although this side leans toward practicality, its supporters, if pressed, will also claim that to deny such an option is in its own way, morally offensive.

Supporters of no-exception inclusion contend that the mere availability of alternative settings can make integration fail for the very simple reason that it does not have to work. Supporters of a range of settings, meanwhile, say that to be so rigid is unrealistic, that out of sheer practical necessity, certain cases demand at least some form of special placement from time to time. What has made the debate so enduring is that there does not appear to be any absolute answer. Research — a great deal of it over quite a long period of time — has been of regrettably little help, since for practically every research outcome demonstrating support for one view, an opposite result is readily available. Classroom experience is usually very case-specific, so it can be misleading to generalize from the success or failure of one, or even several situations. And empirical evidence demonstrates repeatedly that it is impossible to separate the success or failure of anything that happens in a school from the skill and commitment of individual teachers and assistants.

Fortunately, much has happened over the past decades to wind down the debate. The provincial government has long declared the integration of exceptional students to be the norm in the province's schools, a principle that continues to be affirmed by the Ministry of Education. Experience has taught both educators and parents that including students with special needs in regular classes is not as difficult as once thought, and usually produces significant benefits for all. Likewise, experience has demonstrated that there really are some students who benefit from an alternative setting, no matter how extensive the resources in a regular classroom, nor how adapted the curriculum, nor how allegedly ideal the setting. Ultimately, since proponents on both sides have always had the same objective: to achieve what is best for exceptional students, it is not surprising that the ardour which once prevailed has dissipated considerably.

The Power of Profile

The rapid expansion of special education in the final quarter of the twentieth century is marked by dramatic surges in awareness of certain special needs. No example serves better than that of learning disabilities. As recently as the 1970s, only a small number of teachers and parents, along with a sprinkling of academics were deeply interested in the type of student who

Arguments Used to Support Full Integration	Arguments used to Question Full Integration
➡ Less likely to stigmatize; more natural and reflective of the real world.	➡ Environment too manipulated to reflect the real world.
➡ Develops more positive attitudes and positive relationships.	➡ Student relationships are often unilateral, artificial, and in-class only.
➡ More opportunity for inter-action.	➡ Opportunities for intense instruction are reduced.
➡ Age appropriate models are more readily available.	➡ May not be able to teach and reinforce crucial special skills.
➡ Equal opportunity implies equal rights.	➡ Equal rights do not necessarily imply equal opportunity.
➡ Research says full integration works better.	➡ Research says range of settings works better.
➡ Teachers prefer full integration.	➡ Teachers prefer range of settings.
➡ Parents prefer full integration.	➡ Parents prefer range of settings.
➡ Students, exceptional and otherwise, prefer full integration.	➡ Students, exceptional and otherwise, prefer a range of alternatives.

seems to experience serious problems in school despite apparently normal intelligence. Although the number of concerned people was growing, and also by that time, the problem had acquired a name ('learning disabilities' was first proposed by Samuel Kirk in 1963) this special need still had a low profile in education and in the media. Only a handful of students in publicly supported schools were actually called, or even believed to be 'learning disabled'. By the end of the century, after a veritable explosion of awareness, approximately one-half of all students officially identified for special education in the province, were identified 'learning disabled'.

The raising of a profile for a special need seems to follow a pattern. Initially, an advocacy group, consisting mostly of parents with first-hand experience in dealing with the need, succeeds in getting the attention of the media and

— not always simultaneously — teachers and the school system. Usually, this is followed by a sharp rise in interest from academics. (Bureaucrats in education, interestingly, are often quite ahead of the game. For example, the learning disabilities issue had wide support among Ontario's Ministry of Education officials well before the school system at large came on side.) A final stage in profile development is to have the special need officially recognized administratively, thereby assuring it a permanent place on every school and school board horizon. The pattern does not end here for once a significant profile is achieved, the advocacy group instrumental in getting things started usually commits to a program of reinforcement through lobbying, information workshops, production of information literature, etc. An essential difference at this stage, however, is that the group now becomes more a partner in meeting

The Case of Parnell

On the surface, this case seems simple enough. Parnell lags behind his peers in achievement, by at least three grades. Most serious is his apparent inability to read. The problem might be accounted for by Parnell's own explanation that he "didn't go to school much" before coming to Canada three months ago, although the teacher of the grade 5-6 split class where he is placed, reports that the boy frequently manifests "learning disability-like characteristics", adding by way of illustration that he is frequently off-task, rarely follows instructions in proper sequence, seems easily confused, and regularly loses his personal property (and the school's). A preliminary assessment has only reinforced what everybody already knows: that Parnell can't read.

On the other hand, the (half-time) assistant in the class points out that when she is able to instruct Parnell one-on-one, in skills like phonics and letter/word recognition, he grasps the material quickly, and retains it. The teacher reinforces this. Unfortunately, neither has very much exclusive time available for Parnell, but time, along with the appropriate instruction, is available in one of the school's two special education classes. To benefit from it, Parnell would have to be identified as 'exceptional' by an IPRC, as the school board's policy is very strict on matters of this nature. A special reading program is not a viable option. The school's junior reading program was deleted two years ago owing to budget issues and staffing reallocation. The primary program is entirely over-extended and depends to a large extent on volunteers.

Parnell has not expressed an opinion one way or another about a shift to special education; nor has his father. (Parnell's mother lives in the Caribbean but plans to emigrate at some point in the future.) However, an intrusive issue of some delicacy must be dealt with in the case. Only a month ago, the senior public school that shares a campus with Parnell's school was the focus of obsessive media attention after an advocacy group accused it of "dumping" black children like Parnell into special education. A subsequent investigation agreed that the number placed in special education is indeed significantly disproportionate to the number in the general school population, and the school board has vowed to review all IPRC identifications carefully.

The IPRC will meet next week to discuss Parnell's case.

the special need than an agent for awareness.

Many educators acknowledge the necessity of intense lobbying to raise awareness of special needs. Yet an elevated profile is not without potential risks, especially for administrators and by extension, for the classroom. Cynics, with some basis, point to the possibility that intensive media fascination may actually create a "disability du jour", a charge that in the early years of this century, rightly or wrongly is directed at the number of students identified with forms of autism*. Further, there is always risk that a single issue may capture disproportionate space on the administrative agenda such as occurred over the matter of inclusion. As well, there is always strong potential that a high profile may cause an overreaction. For example, despite the fact that awareness of learning disabilities was long overdue and that the high profile has generated very positive results, there has never been an entirely satisfactory answer to a legitimate question: are there really *that many* learning disabled students in our schools, or is the identification convenient for administrators under pressure?

On balance, the benefits brought to the field by increased awareness outweigh the possible drawbacks, provided teachers, assistants, administrators *and* advocates behind the thrust keep in mind the need for a rational perspective. Education in general is extremely susceptible to cycles — *fads*, the cynics would say. Everyone involved with students who have special needs has a responsibility to guard against the backlash that invariably attends this phenomenon.

The Problem of the Purse

Concerns about funding for special education coalesce around several recurring issues, but the most basic one is, simply, *adequacy*: how much is enough? Unfortunately, no matter what funding is offered by the public purse, it will never be seen as enough. The need (demand?) always seems to outpace the number of dollars allotted. Governments have never managed to resolve this issue, which may be one reason why they pursue *accountability* with such rigor. While it is a laudable goal, not to mention one that attracts positive attention from taxpayers, accountability

is rarely achieved without significant impact on the system receiving the money. For example, a common method of funding special education, one that Ontario adopted in the late 1990s, is a system of incremental grants[†] based on documented needs of individual students.

Theoretically, such a system puts visible controls on the money, and guarantees that grants are used directly for the purpose issued. But there are downsides. One is that the extensive administrative effort it requires can make the path between grantor and grantee a torturously complex one. To get funding from a central source through several levels of management to an end user, is not an easy task even in simple situations, but the road twists even more when the amounts are based on documentation of individual need. The amount of paper a single special needs case can generate is intimidating, as is the amount of time and resource that might otherwise be devoted to instruction.

A paradoxical and potentially insidious element in incremental, documented-needs funding is that a school board, in order to get the best possible deal for a student, is tempted to present the most negative description possible: the worse the case, the higher the rate of support. A basic principle in special education is to build on the strengths of an exceptional student, yet to pry loose funds, a strategy that does the opposite seems more effective. On the other hand, allotting funds according to specific, individual cases does circumvent a risk in general

• • • ——————

* In the 1996-97 school year, Ministry of Education data reported 1,918 elementary school students identified in the category 'autism'. Five years later, in 2001-02, while the total elementary school population had increased by 3.8 percent, the number of 'autism' identifications had increased by 85.1percent. By comparison, in the same period, the increase in 'behaviour' identifications was 6 percent. Note that within this five year period expanded definitions of autism spectrum disorder were published in the Diagnostic and Statistical Manual of Mental Disorders (See chapter 10 for more.)
[†] In addition to a regular per pupil grant there is a second layer, the SEPPA (Special Education Per Pupil Amount). A further component, the ISA (Intensive Support Amount) is available at four different rates according to the nature and intensity of need of individual students. Beyond the ISA there is also the SIP (Special Incidence Portion) for exceptionally high needs. [**Note: funding policies are regularly reviewed and modified**. See the Ministry website **www.edu.gov.on.ca** for the most recent funding policy.]
——————— • • •

pool funding: namely that a blanket issue of monies without strings attached can possibly end up being used for other purposes.

Notwithstanding the inherent — and enduring — difficulties in funding special education, a positive side to the issue is that even when practically every government in the western world was cutting back educational funding drastically in the 1990s, Ontario continued to support special education. Although funding levels and funding methods will likely continue to be a source of friction between government and the governed, the thought that special education appears to have weathered the 1990s storm is at the very least, encouraging.

Labels, Categories and Definitions

Ultimately, the issue of labeling students is a factor of the importance of language in a culture, and that importance varies in intensity over time. There was a time when terms like 'idiot, 'imbecile' and 'moron' were not only acceptable usage but scientific categories.

Today there are school districts in North America that have already abandoned contemporary descriptors like "developmentally delayed" because of the gradual acquisition of negative connotations. It seems the need to search for ever more euphemistic vocabulary will never end, for as new and sensitive identifiers age, they take on overtones, thereby provoking need for yet newer ones.

There are indications that in this new century, the matter of labels and categories and definitions has declined significantly as an issue for debate. More and more generations are growing up with special people in their midst as a matter of course. Parents and professional educators recognize descriptors simply as a convenience for discussion and administrative procedure. Still, it is unlikely that the vocabulary of special needs will ever be entirely free of controversy for the simple reason that the meaning of words changes over time. Also, when categories of special need broaden, as they do from time to time (case in point: the field of autism at the turn of the century) a whole new battery of terms is added to the lexicon, any one of which can raise the level of debate, and provoke another round.

Against Labels	For Labels
⇒ A single label, like *gifted* cannot sum up the complexity of a human.	⇒ Academic discussion, professional development, teacher training, research, all need a common frame of reference to be effective.
⇒ Labels stigmatize by emphasizing weakness and dysfunction.	⇒ Specific vocabulary permits more precise communication in hands-on situations. Caregivers especially must work from the same text.
⇒ Labels often mislead; someone labelled *deaf* may only be hard of hearing. They propagate confusion and varied interpretation (as in *developmental disabilities)*.	⇒ Identification of a group's unique needs raises its profile.
⇒ A labeled person is seen in the label's terms, rather than as a human being with a special need, thereby provoking lowered expectations.	⇒ Differentiated categories facilitate differentiated responses.
⇒ Labels tend to be life long.	⇒ Accountability requires a mutually acceptable taxonomy of description.
	⇒ Experience shows that abolishing one set of labels simply produces another.

Of the five students still placed in 'junior resource class' at the end of the school year, Vanessa and one other have been deemed ready by an IPRC to spend part of the school day in a regular grade five class. The other three will remain in the resource class come September, where a teacher and two educational assistants will continue to emphasize appropriate behaviour and socialization.

Vanessa's gains after two years in the class have been considerable. She no longer screams at maximum pitch when dissatisfied. She has developed appropriate toileting skills (instead of using the floor, wherever and whenever). Biting, scratching, and hairpulling seem to have been discarded as communication methods. And experimental sessions in the regular grade four class indicate that, with a little help from her favourite EA, Vanessa can sustain an age-appropriate relationship with a peer group. Interestingly, what most pleases the adults dealing with Vanessa more than anything is that most of the time, with supervision, she can be trusted to take a regular recess without incident. Still, hers is a situation that will bear careful watching. A similar attempt at reintegration in grade three failed utterly, although all agree that this attempt was made too soon, and that the change was too drastic.

Two assessments suggest Vanessa is of average intelligence, and there is no indication of any physical or learning disability despite the experience of her early years. From the time she was a baby until age eight — when Children's Aid took over after her mother was jailed for voluntary manslaughter — Vanessa had moved seventeen times, had known six stepfathers, and had been treated for both TB and malnutrition. Her present school (from grade two) is the first one she attended with any regularity, although her behaviour was so extreme initially, that the principal had to arrange for a one-on-one supervision. (Three EAs, the school's full complement, spelled one another over the course of the day.)

A possible complication has recently developed. Vanessa's birth father, whom she had never seen until a few months ago, has applied to the family court for custody. Both the court and the Children's Aid Society agree that he is a responsible, mature individual (he is married with two other children) and a good parent. However, he proposes to enroll Vanessa in the same school as his other two children. This school is in a different board in a different community and has a full and absolute inclusion policy, with no designated resource or withdrawal classes. The family court judge has reserved a decision about custody until he receives an opinion from Vanessa's school as to whether or not the school change is serious enough to postpone the awarding of custody until she is able to make the change without risk.

Cultural and Socio-Economic Differences

Teachers wince at the accusation that special education is often a depository for the children of poverty and for the culturally different. They wince because over-representation of these groups in special classes is often the case, and that flies directly in the fact of everything education stands for. Yet for very real reasons, it is easy to see why the special class is often regarded as an appropriate placement. Children of poverty and some cultural minorities often have a high frequency of serious health and physical problems that affect their education. Conductive hearing loss (usually *otitis media*) among native children in Canada, for example, and eye infections affecting sight, occur at an average rate much higher than that of the general population. Children of minority groups sometimes experience linguistic difficulties that impinge on their learning in a major way. And assessment procedures that do not allow for cultural anomalies can have the effect of placing a child very restrictively in an education system.

It is not unusual for children from lower income families or from recently arrived immigrant families to have difficulties simply because they are confused by the demands of the school culture. Sometimes a family's lack of precedent for educational experience as well as lack of support for it can have a serious effect on a student's performance. Very often, heads of families do not manage a child's case by dealing with the school, the education system, and support agencies (or confronting them if necessary) either because they choose not to, or because they lack the sophistication.

In schools the issue is one of delicate choice. From an educational perspective, these are indeed students with very special needs. And very frequently the needs can be effectively met in a special education mode. However, the educational perspective must be illuminated by consideration of what is morally and socially appropriate. Identification and placement of a student in special education is a major step, one that can be taken with more certainty if the basis of the decision is strictly educational. When the basis is influenced by social, cultural and economic factors, there is inevitably commensurate erosion of that certainty. It is a hard nut to crack, and no jurisdiction in Canada has yet done so to everyone's satisfaction.

The Gap Between Assessment and Program

In theory, where perfection is always more attainable, the assessment of a student is conducted not just for the purpose of identification, but also for the purpose of program planning. In fact, inasmuch as many cases of exceptionality are broadly identifiable without formal assessment at all, it may be more accurate to say that the main goal of an assessment is to provide information from which program planning can be developed. Unfortunately, the practice often stumbles clumsily after the theory for several reasons. Chief among them is a strange combination of expertise and naiveté that seems to prevail on both sides of the assessment/program planning issue. Psychologists, psychometrists or other assessors, without actu-

al experience in teaching, often have either idealistic or simplistic notions of what actually occurs minute by minute in a classroom. Many classroom teachers, on the other hand, are cowed by assessments, and frequently have difficulty translating results into program.

To be fair to both sides, the number of professional, concerned, caring assessors and teachers who attempt to rise above this problem is impressive. Yet they are frequently obstructed by matters not of their own making, beginning with their own training. Traditionally, neither gets much opportunity to gain more than sketchy knowledge about the other. As well — and probably more important — both sides argue that the gap could easily be narrowed, even closed, by direct communication: that if the teacher(s) and educational assistant(s) of the student being assessed could communicate *directly* with an assessor, the questions that need answers will at least be put on the table. Yet in many jurisdictions, bureaucracy and systems management impede this very simple expedient. It is common policy for assessors to obtain and report data only to a third party (coordinator, committee, principal, etc.). Then, for a variety of reasons such as privacy regulations, work loads, or in some cases, inefficiency, these data come to the classroom, if at all, in a form that is altered or diluted or summarized to the point of irrelevance.

It is the student who falls into the gap this system creates. An assessment may well be competent; the teachers and paraprofessionals may well be effective. But unless there is opportunity for some form of direct communication, the whole point of the procedure is diminished. Fortunately, a very positive outcome of the continuing experience in special education is an increased emphasis on classroom observation and assessment. It stands to reason that competent teachers and educational assistants who are "watching it live" so to speak, are in a crucial position to make perceptive, realistic evaluations of a student's strengths and needs. The fact that their observations are being given increasing credence in many jurisdictions is a tribute to their professionalism and to common sense.

Special Education and Research

Drawing firm conclusions from research can be difficult at the best of times. In education, the matter can be especially challenging for the simple reason that the variables in studies involving human interaction — the type of study much pursued in special education — are extremely difficult to control. Unless a study is conducted under laboratory conditions, which paradoxically, would make it unreal at the very outset, researchers, not to mention end-users can never be absolutely confident about the reasons for an outcome. This weakness means educators are never entirely sure they are dealing with results that would have meaning in their own situations.

Ironically, the two most important components in all of education, students and teachers, are the two most difficult variables to control, a reality reflected in studies of inclusion. Simple logic forces acknowledgement that the personality, the commitment, and the training of classroom professionals have a profound impact on outcomes in their classes. Thus when a study compares outcomes in two classrooms where all conditions are matched except the element of inclusion, it is inherently flawed to the extent that it cannot account for the ever-so-crucial spirit and atmosphere that different professionals impart to a teaching environment. Nor can two classrooms ever be found where the collective personality generated by the students, is the same. If nothing else, this explains why there is so much contradictory research on inclusion.

Another problem lies in the improper use of results and data. (This is rarely a researcher's error.) For example, it has not been uncommon during the history of special education, for an advocate of one point of view or another to quite blithely use research results about children who are blind for example, to support a position on children who are autistic. A related abuse arises from the "gee whiz" stories that frequently appear in non-refereed journals and in newspaper columns, anecdotes in which success with a single subject is described in glowing terms. The implications are that a similar outcome can be expected in any student with a similar special need.

Ultimately, perhaps the most unfortunate issue is the reluctance of many teachers to attribute significant value to the role played by research. Many argue, with more than ample justification, that they simply do not have the time to "keep up". A good number insist, again with more than a little justification, that so much of the results are irrelevant in any case, at least to their own classrooms. As a consequence, the very people who might have the most to gain from research, and certainly the very people who should have prime responsibility for actually testing the relevance of results have, in fact, depressingly little involvement. This paradox has been a thorn in the side of education for a long time. Hopefully, given that special education is constantly facing new challenges, there may be possibility for new directions in the future.

Controlling the Paper

Special education generates a lot of record keeping. The students, to begin with, have special needs that often require a wide range of personnel who not only make their individual reports but must exchange these with the reports of others. Funding mechanisms tend to stir up a paper flurry, especially if unusual equipment or specialized instruction is necessary. Fundamental to teaching exceptional students is the need for extensive adaptations in curriculum and teaching methods, adaptations that need to be recorded for pre-post evaluation, and for dissemination to interested parties. And looming over it all is the need for a collating plan or file to make sure the

> It seems that no matter how much we tried to shorten the forms our board required in special education, they always took on a life of their own. And they always grew! Frankly, I don't recall a single form in my twenty-five years of special ed that ever shrank. Every one just got longer and longer until we chucked it as too unwieldy. Then the process would start all over again.
>
> *David C., superintendent*

various parts work together and toward the same purpose. The consequence is a great deal of paper, and for all parties, a serious task: just how much is necessary and who is responsible?

There is no question that written, education plans, have beneficial effects, especially if the plans detail students' needs and follow this with descriptions of how, where, and when the needs will be addressed, *and* with accounts of when and how the success (or failure) of these efforts will be evaluated. On the surface, the logic behind the practice is unassailable, for a specific plan brings focus and coordination to meeting a student's needs. It helps to satisfy the need for accountability: viz., if funds are being spent, personnel assigned, and effort expended, so at the very least, everyone involved can follow the tracks. A plan offers a common basis for discussion should the need for modification develop and, far from least in importance unfortunately, a documented paper trail should legal issues arise.

There are potential drawbacks, however. One is that a plan can easily become more important than the subject for whom it is designed. Once a plan becomes dominant, then flexibility diminishes and creativity disappears, and without these components, the very essence of 'special' education is lost. Granted,

the evaluation phase should preclude such an outcome, yet once plan supremacy is established, modifications become very difficult to bring about, especially if the exceptional student's needs are complex. The more complicated a case may be, the greater number of personnel there are to consult, the more resources must be shifted to effect a change — all with paper attached. Then there is the *professional time* taken up by record keeping. As valuable as the detailing of information may be, it is rarely more important than the time spent interacting with the student being recorded. Ontario boards, encouraged by the Ministry of Education, have tried to keep prescribed forms as brief as possible, albeit with mixed success. Experience suggests that forms and the supplements they seem to spawn, invariably grow in length and complexity over time.

Nevertheless, experience has also shown that to make a significant impact on an exceptional student's situation, coordinated and recorded planning is essential. Finding the elusive balance between the logical boundaries of a specific plan, and the art of creatively and intuitively responding to a student's needs, will always be a challenge in special education. The fact that teachers and administrators continue to search for it is to their credit.

READINGS & RESOURCES

Council for Exceptional Children (CEC). (1993). CEC policy on inclusive schools and community settings. *Teaching Exceptional Children, 25*(4), supplement.

Council for Exceptional Children (1991). "Code of ethics for the CEC", *Teaching Exceptional Children, 23,* 2.

Friend, M., Bursuck, W. & Hutchinson, N. (1998). *Including Exceptional Students: A practical guide for classroom teachers.* Scarborough: Prentice-Hall.

Fuchs, D. and Fuchs L.S. (1994). Inclusive schools movement and the radicalisation of special education reform. *Exceptional Children, 60*(4), 294-309.

Giangreco, M., Edelman, S., Dennis, R., & Cloninger, C. (1993). My child has a classmate with severe disabilities: What parents of nondisabled students should think about full inclusion. *Developmental Disabilities Bulletin, 21*(1), 77-91.

Gutkin, T.B. (1996). Core elements of consultation service delivery for special services personnel: Rationale, practice, and some directions for the future. *Remedial and Special Education, 17*(6), 333-340.

Harry, B. (1992). *Cultural diversity, families, and the special education system: communication and empowerment.* New York: Teachers College Press.

Inclusion Press/Centre for Integrated Education and Communication, 24 Thome Crescent, Toronto, Ontario M6H 2S5

Kliewer, C., & Bilkin, D. (1996). Labeling: Who wants to be called retarded: In W. Stainback & S. Stainback (Eds.), *Controversial issues confronting special education: Divergent Perspectives (2ⁿᵈ Ed., pp. 83-95)*. Boston: Allyn & Bacon.

Lupart, J. L. (1998). The delusion of inclusion: Implications for Canadian schools. *Canadian Journal of Education, 23(3)*, 251-264.

Minke. K.M., Bear, G.G., Deiner, S.A., & Griffin, S.M. (1996). Teachers' experiences with inclusive classrooms: Implications for special education reform. *Journal of Special Education, 30*, 152-186.

Palmer, D.S., Borthwick-Duffy, S.A., & Windaman, K. (1998). Parent's perceptions of inclusive practices for their children with significant cognitive disabilities. *Exceptional Children, 64*, 271-282.

Peterson, J.M., & Hittie, M.M. (2003). *Inclusive teaching: Creating effective schools for all learners*. Boston: Pearson Education.

Reynolds, M.C. (1991). Classification and labeling. In J.W. Lloyd, N.N. Singh, & A.C. Repp (Eds.), *The regular education initiative: Alternative perspectives on concepts, issues and models* (pp. 29-42). Sycamore, IL.: Sycamore.

Salisbury C. L., Palambaro, M.M., & Hollowood, T.M. (1993). *On the nature of change of an inclusive elementary school. 18*, 75-84.

Snow, J.A. (1989). Systems of support: A new vision. In S. Stainback, W. Stainback, & M. Forest (Eds.), *Education of all students in the mainstream of regular education* (pp. 221-231). Toronto: Paul H. Brookes.

Danforth, S., & Taft, S.D. (2004). *Crucial readings in special education*. New Jersey: Pearson Education, Inc.

Vergason, G.A., & Anderegg, M.L. (1997). The ins and outs of special education terminology. *Teaching Exceptional Children, 29(5)*, 35-39.

Vlachou, A. and Barton, L. (1994). Inclusive education: Teachers and the changing culture of schooling. *British Journal of Special Education, 21(3)*, 105-107.

Wood, M. (1998). Whose job is it anyway? Educational roles in inclusion. *Exceptional Children, 64(2)*, 182-195.

Ysseldyke, J.E., Algozzine, B., & Thurlow, M.L. (2000). *Critical issues in special education, 3ʳᵈ edition*. Boston: Houghton Mifflin Company.

York, G. (1990). *The Dispossessed: Life and Death in Native Canada*. Toronto: Little Brown and Company (Canada) Ltd.

CHAPTER 3

The Special Needs Population:
Categories and Numbers

Ontario Student Population		
Number of Students in Publicly Funded Schools[†]		Number Receiving Spec. Ed. Services
Elementary	1,448,270	176,352 (12.2%)
Secondary	714,838	100,508 (14.1%)
Total	**2,163,108**	**276,860 (12.8%)**

[†]All publicly funded schools exc. care & treatment facilities
Source: Ministry of Ed., School September Report, 2001-02

Table 3A

The Categories

Agreement on Generalities ...

Teachers, educational assistants and administrators in a school board usually share a common vocabulary when talking about special education. Sometimes their official terms are those promulgated by the Ministry of Education but it is not unusual for a board to popularize terms unique to itself. Academics may use a moderately differing special education vocabulary, especially if they have different fields of interest, say, psychology and bio-engineering. Advocates, especially if they are emphasizing softer terminologies for special needs, may have yet another set of words. Despite the potential confusion arising from these variations, the many branches of special education seem able to communicate nevertheless because there is a general understanding and acceptance of broad categories like these:

- *Intellectual differences:* includes students who are intellectually gifted and those who have intellectual delay.

- *Sensory disabilities:* includes the blind and deaf.

- *Communication disorders:* includes students with learning disabilities, and those with speech and language difficulties.

- *Physical and health difficulties:* includes students with genetic disorders, and problems that arise from birth trauma, orthopedic conditions, and disabilities caused by disease. Usually, students with neurological disorders are included here.

- *Behaviour disorders:* includes students with mental illness, those who are socially maladjusted, delinquent, emotionally disturbed, and those with conduct disorders.

- *Developmental disabilities:* includes students with pervasive disorders like autism or severe intellectual disability, and students with multiple disabilities.
- Combinations of the above.

... but Disagreement on Specifics

The terms above appear in the literature and they are used freely in discussions, but difficulty arises when it comes to defining the terms. After more than a quarter century of in-depth experience, special education has yet to establish a set of clear, standardized categories and definitions that everyone accepts and uses. Part of the difficulty lies in the varying purposes of different stakeholders. Administrators use definitions for identifying candidates, and for determining levels of funding and resource allocation. Parents, advocates and support associations, because they have more immediate remediation objectives, tend to emphasize extensive, symptom-based characteristics (although there are support groups that argue for no definitions at all because students with special needs simply do not fit into such confines).

Other stakeholders have very individualistic perspectives. Medical professionals have their own view, one that often has limited connection with education. Researchers may develop their own definitions to limit the variables in a study. Teachers want definitions to provide a practical guidance point for planning and practice. Then there is the very notion of special need itself. To anyone who reflects on the fact that *normalcy* is not defined, it is no surprise that departure from normal is hard to describe.

In the Classroom

For those who work with exceptional students on an active, daily basis—teachers, educational assistants, parents—the precision (or lack thereof) in categories and definitions of exceptionality is a minor issue in the grand scheme of things, but it's one that cannot be completely ignored. In the first place, if classroom professionals become involved with other professionals (medical, for example) over a student's case, it is important that each understand the other. Secondly, for better or worse there is an unavoidable underlay of politics in special education, so for understanding and productive dialogue, it behooves all parties to be tuned in to all positions. Finally, and perhaps most practically, official categories and definitions issued by a jurisdiction may well be the factor that determines which students are identified exceptional, and what resources can and will be made available for their benefit. For that reason alone, teachers, for example, must be sensitive to them.

Ontario's Official Categories and Definitions

When the Education Amendment Act made special education mandatory in Ontario, the Ministry of Education issued a set of quite detailed definitions of exceptionality. The idea was that boards of education would use them when identifying a student as exceptional and, initially, most boards did just that. Over time, some boards began to modify the definitions for their own use, and a few boards elected to discard definitions altogether. Others stuck to the Ministry list, but made additions and deletions. Still others created whole new ones. Partly, this was in response to the aging of the definitions; partly it was in response to parent advocacy; and partly, the changes were made because many boards felt that as special education matures, and as philosophies, scientific knowledge, and practices change, the categories and definitions should evolve as well.

The result was not the hodgepodge that one might expect from such independent forays. Granted, in some instances it became possible for a student to qualify for special education in one board in the province, but not in another. But most of the time these were unique cases that, conceivably, would have been problematic anyway. In effect, the relative independence of the province's school boards was simply a reflection of how difficult it is to accurately describe students with special needs. Many fit several definitions; others fall into cracks between definitions; still others resist the confines of qualifiers like 'mild', 'moderate', and 'severe'. Then, there is the reality of change. Exceptional students, like all students, grow and develop. Their special needs are not immutable.

Despite these difficulties, there are many useful reasons for maintaining a set of official categories and definitions in a publicly funded education system, not the least of which are issues in funding and other administrative factors. From the time special education first became mandatory in the province, Ontario has maintained an official set of categories and definitions. These are modified from time to time following extensive consultations. The current set, extant at publication, appears in the Appendix of this Fifth Edition.

The Numbers

In 1983, the Canadian Council of Ministers of Education issued data indicating that 15.5 percent of the school age population in the country is exceptional. That figure, developed at the time by less than rigorous science, became fixed in the consciousness of the general public, not to mention educators who usually have access to more accurate information. Despite the fact that both incidence data (number of new cases over a time period) and prevalence data (total number of existing cases) are notoriously difficult to collect and collate, there is sufficient experience in special education practice now, along with some useful studies, to suggest that the real figure is not that high. Table 3A, for example, offers a more optimistic perspective. As well, a look at placement data (See Table 4A in Chapter 4) implies that the majority of students receiving special education services, both elementary and secondary, is only mildly exceptional. The fact that large numbers receive special education services as modifications of their regular education, e.g., as resource support or withdrawal assistance, rather than as the central motif of their schooling, e.g., as in specialized fully self-contained settings, suggests that most special needs are neither profound nor severe.

Yet the Numbers are Growing

In 1986, by the end of the first year of mandatory special education in the province, Ontario's boards had identified 6.5 percent of the school population as receiving special education services. In these earlier days, many boards were still feeling their way through the process. By 1990 the figure was 7.9 percent and in 1997, the percentage was 9.24. Although the number of students identified exceptional in the province appears to have been steadily increasing, this rise in numbers is at least partly a consequence of improved procedures of identification, along with the expansion of special education in areas where it had not previously been offered. Still, the percentage figure of 12.8 for the school year 2001-02 appears to confirm a trend that has prevailed for some time: that the number of students receiving special education services continues to increase, and that the rate of increase is somewhat greater than the rise in the total school population. There are a number of explanations for this one of which in particular is peculiar to Ontario: the matter of the non-identified special education student.

Non-Identified Students Receiving Special Education Services

The majority of students who receive special education services in Ontario do so after having first been 'identified' by an Identification, Placement, Review Committee (IPRC). (In Ontario jargon, the process is often called 'being IPRC'd'.) Technically, according to officially mandated practice, it is the only way a student can become a recipient of service, but in practice, there are—and have always been— some students who receive service without being 'identified': hence the category 'non-identified'. (In Tables 3B and 3C, this is the category, SEG, Special Education Grant.). These include students whose parent/guardian refuses to agree to an IPRC, students whose IPRC is pending but who are receiving service in the meantime, and students who are felt to be at risk and receiving service but for the moment are essentially under observation. Significant contributors to the non-identified group are a number of school boards that interpret the legislation in a somewhat independent and modified way: viz., they offer full special education service but generally do not identify via the IPRC process.

In earlier years, data reporting the number of Ontario students in special education included only identified students, but more recently, the non-identified have become regularly included in provincial reports. Their number appears to be rising more rapidly than that of the identified. In the elementary panel, for example, between the school years 1998-99 and 2001-02, the number of identified students rose by 4.6 percent, whereas non-identified students increased by 16.6 percent*. Some administrators contend that forgoing the identification process allows for greater flexibility and fluidity and therefore, larger numbers may be reported as receiving service in their boards even though the service may be only temporary. As to whether the practice of not identifying will continue, the jury is still very much out. At the

● ● ● ───────

* Source: School September Reports. Note that data for 1998-99 above do not include hospital/provincial schools. These are almost invariably 'identified' students.

─────── ● ● ●

beginning of the new century however, the category appears to account for a significant portion of the students receiving service.

Why Steadily Growing Numbers?

Hard data to explain the rise in number of students receiving special education are difficult to come by. Accordingly, most explanations are based on empirical evidence, and to a significant degree, simply on speculation. Among teachers and administrators, for example, a sense persists that parents seem to have become more aggressive in demanding specific special education responses for their child. While this may be the case in individual situations, there are no data to support the notion as a broad trend. On the other hand, there is concrete evidence that provincial and federal courts—and Ontario's

The Case of Hobie

According to the special education teacher, Hobie is the most loved student in the entire school. No one is certain whether Hobie knows this but that does not matter to his classmates in grade three who, in the words of the teacher, "have become twenty-four willing caregivers". Hobie has severe multiple disabilities. He is blind, has no speech, and cannot move any of his limbs. His facial muscles respond to sound stimuli, a fact which convinces his parents—and the teacher and EA—that he can hear. No one has any firm idea at all of his mental capacities.

Hobie has outlived every one of the medical profession's dire predictions and despite initially grave misgivings about having him in a regular class, the school staff and especially the students, have received him enthusiastically. He spends much of his day on a modified skateboard-looking stretcher that can be raised and lowered, and a health aide takes him out every two hours to aspirate him and see to his quite extensive health and hygiene needs. No one has yet figured out how to communicate with him. The students, for their part, go out of their way for Hobie. They vie to roll him into every group situation. They take turns holding his hand during periods like "story time" and "the news". No one ever passes without patting his chest or gently putting a finger to his cheek, and instinctively, they speak to him in peer level language (no baby talk). Everyone interprets Hobie's facial reactions as proof that he is thrilled by what is happening (although recently, a visiting nurse wondered whether the reactions might possibly indicate discomfort or even pain).

Despite the very positive situation, a change looms. Hobie is in this class because the board's 'fragile health needs' unit is temporarily housed in the school. Next year it moves to a purpose built facility in a brand new school and all students currently in the unit move with it, along with the paraprofessionals and aides. When the grade three students, on their own initiative, asked the principal to keep Hobie with them next year in grade four, she was deeply touched, as was upper level administration and the board's trustees. Whether Hobie's thought-to-be-happy situation with the class should outweigh health, safety, and possibly legal considerations however, must first be resolved.

IPRC regulation—harbour great sensitivity to individual rights, and school boards tend to react in concert with this attitude.

There is also a public perception that science and medicine have significantly reduced the infant mortality rate, thereby saving the lives of some children who will need special education. Some of the data that might support this are tempting but hard to interpret with assurance. The number of students reported in the physical disabilities category in Ontario, for example, increased by 35 percent between 1996-7 and 2001-2*, but this dramatic increase is at least in part a factor of anomalies in data collection and reporting. (By comparison, the number of students reported in the behaviour category, which is regularly profiled in the media as accelerating, grew by 3.3 percent in the same period*.)

Yet there are instances in which a dramatic increase in numbers is undeniable and which cannot be explained away as a statistical artifact. The category 'autism' in Ontario, for example, shows an enrolment increase of 57.7 percent between 1996-97 and 2001-02*. Much of this, as special educators will attest, is a direct result of new and very broadening definitions of autism as promulgated in the Diagnostic and Statistical Manual of Mental Disorders.

Ultimately, the simple reality is that the number of Ontario students receiving special education service has indeed been increasing for some time and may well continue to do so if only because the field, relative to general education, is still very new. Irrespective of the fact that publicly funded schools have been offering a wide spectrum of special education for more than twenty years now, there is still much to be learned. Tying down the numbers and giving them meaning is certainly part of that.

Issues Affecting Special Education Data

The Inherent Risks in Comparison

Definitions of exceptionality vary and terminologies differ. Because some school systems

• • • ——

* Source: Ministry of Ed., School September Reports

—— • • •

classify a student's need in terms of the service required, while others do so in terms of a special need, designations like 'learning disabled' and 'mild intellectual disability' may be used in different schools for essentially the same case. Comparisons therefore must be regarded with wariness at least. In a classic comparison case in 1989, the province of Quebec shocked the field by reporting a prevalence of learning disabilities three times that of Ontario and *eight* times that of B.C. Only after sorting out the fact of differences in definition was the situation understood. (Even in the category Multiple Disabilities, which is theoretically subject to more rigorously controlled description, Quebec numbers that year were greater than Ontario's by a factor of 4.5.)

The possibility of misleading conclusions is even possible in *intra*-jurisdictional comparisons if the jurisdiction is large and complex. Ontario, for example now posts a website that allows for comparison of various data from the province's schools boards. (See **www.edu.gov.on.ca** and link to 'School Board Profiles'.) A comparison reveals that in 2001-02, for example, in the District School Board of Niagara, 14 percent of elementary and 19 percent of secondary students were receiving some form of special education program and/or service, while in the Catholic D.S.B. of Eastern Ontario, the data for that year are 20 percent elementary and 18 percent secondary. In the same year, Toronto D.S.B figures are 12 percent elementary and 13 percent secondary, the figures for the Avon-Maitland D.S.B. are 15 percent and 17 percent, and in Thunder Bay C.D.S.B, the numbers are 12 percent and 11 percent.

While these data may be instructive in some ways, interpreting them can be risky. Ontario is a large and populous province with large school boards that manifest no small degree of independence in their implementation of special education policy and practice. What qualifies as service or program in one board may not in another.

Blanket-Style Reporting

For obvious reasons, popular media tend to report data in as uncomplicated a manner as possible, often leaving issues unexplained, such as how the data were collected. In the early 1990s, for example, several major Canadian

[Handwritten margin notes: "Broadening" — "Autistic children enrollment increased to 57.7% between 1996-97 2001-2002 due to Broadening definitions"]

media sources reported that in the 1991 census, *StatsCan* (which has no vested interest in driving a popular perception of any kind) had uncovered the fact that about 3.2 million Canadians, 15 percent of the population, have some level of disability. What most media failed to reinforce was that census data are largely self-reported, and less trustworthy than that achieved through assessment by knowledgeable practitioners. Interestingly, the journal *Disability Today* (1995, *winter*, p. 7) using the same *StatsCan* data, stated that 390,000 Canadian children—those most likely to be counted in student populations— only about 5 percent had some form of disability!

Other Chronic Problems

Another concern that affects data collection and interpretation in special education is cases of co-occurring disabilities. In some systems, these situations are identified with terms like 'multi-handicapped' (as in Tables 3B and 3C) but there will inevitably be cases where, although 'multi' is an appropriate identification, for a variety of reasons the decision may be taken to classify the individual by what is determined to be a

Number of Students Receiving Special Education Services†
by Area of Exceptionality (Elementary)

Area of Exceptionality‡	Fully Self-Contained	Partially Integrated	Withdrawal Assistance	Resource Assistance	Indirect Service	Total
Behaviour	1,413	1,057	1,973	2,077	1,181	**7,701**
Autism	835	398	778	1,064	476	**3,551**
Deaf & H. of H.	227	200	413	323	342	**1,505**
Deaf (alt. prog.)~	36	23	84	25	21	**189**
Learning Disability	3,028	6,959	19,054	10,477	2,198	**41,716**
Speech Impairment	63	65	430	273	175	**1,006**
Language Impairment	961	1,007	2,842	1,833	370	**7,013**
Giftedness	4,352	1,687	3,436	1,523	1,515	**12,513**
Mild Intellectual Dis.	2,943	3,569	4,666	2,041	460	**13,679**
Developmental Dis.	3,083	767	822	684	238	**5,594**
Physical Disability	313	112	317	629	452	**1,823**
Blind & Low Vision	21	11	111	149	124	**416**
Deaf-Blind (alt. prog.)~	24	0	7	4	3	**38**
Multi-handicapped	1,909	1,116	1,646	1,297	505	**6,473**
SEG≠	594	755	38,234	19,940	13,612	**73,135**

† all publicly funded schools exc. care & treatment facilities

‡ categories/descriptions as in School September Report

~ alternative program: eligible for provincial school but receiving service in neighbourhood school

≠ (Spec. Ed. Grant) students receiving services but not identified

Source: Ministry of Ed., School September Report 2001-02

Table 3B

Number of Students Receiving Special Education Services†
by Area of Exceptionality (Secondary)

Area of Exceptionality‡	Fully Self-Contained	Partially Integrated	Withdrawal Assistance	Resource Assistance	Indirect Service	Total
Behaviour	443	294	1,042	1,458	1,043	4,280
Autism	180	103	112	154	29	578
Deaf & H. of H.	34	56	157	211	234	692
Deaf (alt. prog)~	0	8	4	9	6	27
Learning Disability	1,242	1,936	12,418	17,554	11,562	44,712
Speech Impairment	17	18	75	75	92	277
Language Impairment	86	234	946	1,895	1,173	4,334
Giftedness	1,102	2,238	1,725	4,508	4,305	13,878
Mild Intellectual Dis.	2,310	1,159	2,419	2,993	1,591	10,472
Developmental Dis.	1,898	544	225	238	96	3,001
Physical Disability	102	57	228	302	236	925
Blind & Low Vision	10	9	70	116	65	270
Deaf-Blind (alt. prog.)~	2	1	2	1	1	7
Multi-handicapped	1,043	578	643	755	477	3,496
SEG≠	347	328	4,839	4,281	3,764	13,559

† all publicly funded schools exc. care & treatment facilities

‡ categories/descriptions as in School September Report

~ alternative program: eligible for provincial school but receiving service in neighbourhood school

≠ (Spec. Ed. Grant) students receiving services but not identified

Source: Ministry of Ed., School September Report 2001-02

Table 3C

primary special need. (Note that the reported data in Tables 3B and 3C do not distinguish this—and probably could not in any case.). Yet another is the potential of certain needs to skew overall data pictures. Serious cases of special needs like blindness or severe developmental disability are usually identified and added to the data base early on, whereas something like a mild intellectual disability may not become apparent until the individual is in school, and even then, not necessarily until the individual begins to encounter difficulty. This individual may not even be added to a data base at all if it is decided that the need is not serious enough to warrant formal identification, or if the decision is taken to avoid identification in order to avoid stigma.

Nevertheless ...Benefits

Notwithstanding the cautions mentioned above, the data made available by the Ministry of Education's Information Management Branch such as that in Tables 3B and 3C, has significant value. These are data that confirm trends, the identifications in 'autism' being a

The Ministry of Education has direct responsibility for a number of very special schools in the province. The examples of longest standing, and certainly the best known, are the *provincial schools*. These are residential schools (with a few day students where feasible) geared to specific exceptionalities. The Ministry also participates in a number of *hospital schools* and *care and treatment facilities* at various key locations in the province, as well as schools in a number of *correctional facilities*. Unlike the provincial schools, where education is the primary mission, in these latter locations the 'school' aspect functions in tandem with other purposes.

Taken together, the population of provincial schools and facilities fairly consistently represents about half of one percent of the entire population of publicly funded schools in Ontario, and in most years, just under three percent of the population receiving special education services. (See more in Chapter 4 on Service Delivery.)

case in point. They force questions, such as why does the total number of students in the 'gifted' category increase from elementary to secondary school. The numbers are vital for both long and short range projection, for present and future allocation of resources. And are useful in confirming good news; the clear decline in Speech Impaired numbers as candidates progress through elementary to secondary school, for example, suggests very strongly that the remedial undertakings in this category have a positive effect. Data like these in the tables permit cautious comparisons and both verify and disprove polemical claims. They become especially valuable when compared with similar tables from other years. In short, irrespective of the problems inherent in data collection and presentation, and especially in interpretation, without the numbers, the system would be flying blind. Certainly a less appealing prospect.

READINGS & RESOURCES

Adelman H.S. (1992). LD: The next 25 years. *Journal of Learning Disabilities, 25,* 17-21.

Carrier, J.G. (1986). Sociology and special education: Differentiation and allocation in mass education. *American Journal of Education, 94,* 218-312.

Deno, E. (1994). Special education as development capital revisited: A quarter century appraisal of means versus ends. *The Journal of Special Education. 27,* 375-392.

Fujiura, G.T. & Kiyoshi, Y. (2000). Trends in demography of childhood poverty and disability. *Exceptional Children, 66*(2), 187-199.

Johnson, D.R., Stodden, R.A., Emanuel, E.J., Leuking, R., & Mack, M. (2002). Current challenges facing secondary education and transition services: What research tells us. *Exceptional Children, 68*(4), 519-531.

Lipsky, D.K., & Gartner, A. (1989). *Beyond Special Education: Quality for all.* Baltimore: Brookes.

MacMillian, D.L., Gresham, F.M., Bocian, K. M., & Lambros, K.M. (1998). Current plight of borderline students: Where do they belong? *Education and Training in Mental Retardation and Developmental Disabilities, 33,* 83-94.

MacMillian, D.L., & Reschly, A. (1998). Overrepresentation of minority students: The case for greater specificity of the variables examined. *The Journal of Special Education, 32*(1), 15-24.

Reynolds, M.C. (1991). *Classification and labeling.* Sycamore, NY: Sycamore.

Ysseldyke, J. & Bielinski, J. (2002). Effects of different methods of reporting and reclassification on trends in test scores for students with disabilities. *Exceptional Children, 68*(2), 189-200.

CHAPTER 4

Service Delivery
The Infrastructure of Special Education

We've got great teachers, great EAs—and our resources, well, you can always use more resources, but ours are okay. Really, as a principal, my most important special ed. job is getting the right people and the right resources to the right place. And fast.

Jackson T., principal

The Basics

The process by which a student becomes a beneficiary of special education service is basically the same in every school and school board.

Step one: identify a student's special needs.

Step two: develop an education plan to meet the needs.

Step three: place the student in the appropriate setting and implement the plan.

Step four: evaluate regularly and modify as necessary.

Although the sequence seems deceptively simple in a world of procedures and policies and staff shortages and scarce resources, these four steps, whatever the external influences, summarize how special education comes about for a student.

Step One: Identify a Student's Special Needs

A small number of students may come to a school with their special needs already assessed and with all or part of a program in place. Those with long established physical or medical needs are a frequent example. A few others may

come tagged so to speak, for "careful watching", to see whether suspected needs are serious enough to be addressed. Still others, especially the very young, will arrive with extensive information about their needs prepared by parents or a pre-school. Inevitably, there will be students whose special needs, perhaps for the first time ever, will become apparent only during the course of a school year.

Some or all of these students will become candidates for special education, a decision that will be made after an assessment and identification of their needs. Assessments vary in extent and formality, depending on the policy and the resources of the school board, and on the particular student being assessed. The purpose is to gain some insight into the subject's intelligence, strengths, needs, health and behaviour, to predict as much as reasonably possible the likelihood of success in school, and to gather information that will help in developing an individual educational plan should that be deemed necessary. For a few students, an assessment may indicate that special education is not really necessary, and the service delivery process may stop at this point. For candidates who are identified as potential beneficiaries, the steps below are what follow. (See Chapter 15 for more on assessments.)

Both Sheldon and Jean-Marc were accepted into a pre-school, regional centre day program when they were 4.4 years and 4.2 years old respectively. Although both boys presented almost exactly the same behaviours, Sheldon had been diagnosed as 'autistic' while Jean-Marc was diagnosed as having 'pervasive development disorder'. Both boys were totally introverted; they engaged in harmful self-stimulation; neither used intelligible speech, and both were instant run-aways if left unsupervised. Happily, the program at the centre was successful in quickly effecting some changes. After about three months, both began to use some meaningful speech, and as well, appeared to understand much of what was being said to them. By the end of one full year, their echolalic habits diminished significantly, and Jean-Marc (but not Sheldon) began to refer to himself in the first person (rather than calling himself "he" or "Jean-Marc") and would directly address his favourite educational assistant by name rather than as "she".

In their second year at the centre, Sheldon and Jean-Marc are now enrolled in what the staff calls the 'top' group. It took a psychometrist three tries, but she succeeded in completing a pre-school assessment of Jean-Marc and reported him to be of average to just below average intelligence, with speech, although delayed (at 6.4, he is at the norm for 4-year olds) improving at an accelerated pace. Jean-Marc makes eye contact spontaneously about half the time and when directed to "Look at me", will respond appropriately every time. He still exhibits some unusual behaviours (e.g., he will compulsively stroke any clothing that is red in colour, no matter who wears it; music of any kind will take up his total attention, not only during its playing but after. On occasion he will hum a melody over and over for the remainder of the day.) Staff at the centre point proudly to his ability to relate to others. On the thrice-weekly field trips (to shopping malls, parks, etc., anywhere that people gather) Jean-Marc follows directions, takes responsibility, and spontaneously assists with the group.

In Sheldon's case, the field trips are a weak point. Wide open spaces threaten him, as do large numbers of strange adults. While he copes with these situations as long as there is familiar adult support, he still turns to the comfort of repetitive, stereotyped behaviour at these times (alternately patting his cheeks and then his ears; another is spinning round and round, with eyes closed and arms extended; staff has noted several times that he can persist at this indefinitely without getting dizzy.) On the other hand, Sheldon's use of appropriate language has increased dramatically. Although he refused utterly to cooperate with the psychometrist who successfully assessed Jean-Marc, she reinforced—off the record—the opinion of staff that his language usage was at or just below age-appropriate level.

Now, notwithstanding a possible setback incident (After a fire drill, Sheldon was found inside a heating duct in a no-go area of the building; Jean-Marc imitated the alarm bell continuously for several days.) both boys are going to go to grade one classes in their neighbourhood schools. The receiving principals have asked for advice on how to best make the transition smooth.

Step Two: Develop an Education Plan to Meet the Needs

After an assessment confirms that a student is indeed a candidate for special education, the next—and very crucial—component is set in motion: the development and implementation of an individualized education plan tailored to meet his special needs. The individual education plan, or IEP, is a written plan of action that becomes a road map for everyone involved: student, teachers, educational assistants, parents and administration. Ideally, the needs highlighted by the assessment are addressed in the IEP. The plan not only summarizes the student's strengths, needs, interests, (and health and behaviour profile where applicable) it also sets out individualized goals and objectives. These may include simple modifications of the curriculum that everyone else is studying; sometimes they are entirely unique to the student. As well, an IEP offers ideas and strategies for instruction, elements of scheduling and other details as appropriate. For students fourteen years and older, a *transition plan* is also developed for post-secondary transition to work, community living and further education. (See Chapter 16 for more on IEPs.)

Step Three: Place the Student in the Appropriate Setting and Implement the Plan

An oft-debated matter in special education is just where to deliver the service, where to implement the plan. Most students with special needs are based in regular classrooms and receive all their special education in that setting. Some, especially those whose needs may be more profound, are placed in specialized settings. These may be anything from a school where the entire environment is devoted to a particular need (e.g., schools for the deaf) to separate, specialized classes in a neighbourhood school. A quite frequent placement choice will be a combination of the specialized, self-contained classroom, where a student will spend part of her day, while for the rest of the day she is in her regular class. ('Resource Room' and 'Learning Centre' are popular designations for special settings used in this way.) In some cases, the appropriate setting may be a regular classroom where resources are brought to the student. The permutations and combinations are considerable. Whatever the choice of setting for the student, it is *always*, within reason, subject to review and modification.

Step Four: Evaluate Regularly and Modify as Necessary

An essential component of an individual education plan is regular re-examination, for an IEP does not just delineate the student's program but is also a guide, an evolving benchmark for monitoring his progress and development. In most cases it is the baseline from which necessary additions and modifications are highlighted. For this reason especially, an IEP is effective in clarifying communication with parents and other significant figures in a student's life.

Where Service is Delivered: Typical Special Ed. Settings

Regular Class with Indirect Support

Very often, what becomes "special" about a student's education is a simple and straightforward adjustment in his or her program *within the regular class*. An example would be a student who has a condition like spina bifida and requires a wheelchair for mobility. If this student has learned to manage her own condition, as most do, she will participate in every aspect of the regular classroom in an entirely normal way, but at times, perhaps during a physical education program, there would likely be some accommodations made. E.g., the student may participate in calisthenics or basketball but would usually have a substitute activity for, say, cross-country running. Should she regularly need extra time for things like personal hygiene, a teacher would accommodate by trying to present new or difficult material at times when she is normally expected to be present.

Resource Assistance

'Resource assistance', sometimes called 'direct support' is delivered in a variety of ways, to the teacher, to the student or to both. In the case of a regular class where a deaf student, for example, is placed, there may be direct support to the student, ranging from special technical equipment to the presence of a signing interpreter. At the same time, a teacher or consultant with specialized knowledge about deafness may provide support to the classroom teacher in everything from program preparation to in-service training. Another typical example is the situation where an educational assistant will spend specific amounts of time in classrooms providing remedial support to students in, say, language development. Still another situation is that in which the assistant provides support to a student with behaviour concerns at times in the school day when those concerns tend to manifest themselves. (Resource assistance is sometimes mistakenly construed as

> I try not to resent the time I spend at meetings and writing reports, but every minute it takes to do that is another minute I'm not where I want to be: helping the kids.
>
> *Arlene Y., special education teacher*

relatively low impact but the assistance can be significant indeed. For example, it is not unusual for a student with intense special needs to have resource assistance in the form of an EA full-time or nearly full-time.)

Other resource assistance may be in the form of specialized equipment such as an FM transmitter system for a student who is hard of hearing.

Regular Class/Withdrawal for Assistance

For part of their program, some exceptional students may benefit from an individualized learning experience that is more effectively delivered in a setting less distracting or competitive, or in some cases more specially equipped, than a regular classroom. Thus a student may be withdrawn to a resource room, for example, where a different teacher or an educational assistant working in close concert with the regular teacher, will deliver the modified learning experience called for in the student's IEP. In this arrangement the student remains a member of the regular class, but part of his program is delivered elsewhere on a formally scheduled basis. A fairly typical example of a student who uses this type of placement is one with a learning disability for whom reading and writing

> Something you'll notice right away is there's a lot of teachers who don't know what to do with an EA! Not their fault really, any more than it's ours but it's an issue you have to work out.
>
> *Kana V. graduate of an EA program speaking to undergraduates*

pose extra difficulty. Often, the strategies that benefit the learning disabled as well as others with special needs, can be very effectively delivered in this type of resource arrangement. Taking a student out of a class for one-on-one instruction is by no means a novel idea, especially in the elementary grades. What distinguishes the practice in special education, is the specificity of the arrangement, and the guarantee of its regular delivery in a student's plan.

Part Time Regular Class/Self-Contained Class
(Partially Integrated)

As the designation would suggest, this is an arrangement whereby a student spends time in two settings. Unlike the withdrawal-to-a-resource room choice, this setup is somewhat more formal in that a self-contained classroom is usually more specifically dedicated and managed than a resource room. It is used frequently to help students who are making a transition from a full time self-contained class to a regular class (those gaining control of behaviour issues are a good example) and offers an effective combination of intensive instruction opportunity, together with a normalized experience. Note, for example, in Tables 3B and 3C of

---

Number/Percentage of Students Receiving Special Education Services by Type of Placement[†]

	Elementary	Secondary
Fully Self-Contained	19,802 (11.2 %)	8,816 (8.8 %)
Partially Integrated	17,726 (10.1 %)	7,563 (7.5 %)
Withdrawal Assistance	74,813 (42.4 %)	24,905 (24.8 %)
Resource Assistance	42,339 (24.0 %)	34,550 (34.4 %)
Indirect Support	21,672 (12.3 %)	24,674 (24.5 %)

† *Source: Ontario Ministry of Ed., School September Report, 2001-02;* all publicly funded schools exc. care & treatment facilities; includes non-identified students receiving service.

Table 4A

The Case of Cassie

Officially, Cassie is 15.2 years old although Family Services acknowledges she may be up to six months younger or as much as a full year older. There are no birth records; Cassie's physical appearance can be interpreted in a variety of ways; and nothing is known of her mother who is believed to have been a homeless person. Equally uncertain is the origin of Cassie's intellectual disabilities and behaviour problems. Fetal alcohol syndrome is one listed cause, but a large scar over her left ear with an adjacent depression in her skull has also led to a suspicion of acquired brain injury. Nevertheless, both administration and staff at Cassie's school are quick to point out that the cause of her problems concerns them far less than the symptoms.

Prominent among those are deep-rooted behaviour problems which follow a pattern that her teachers describe as "going on benders". Between episodes of relative calm, Cassie will become aggressive, often violent, for several days. Most recently, in a single day she scratched a teacher who (unsuccessfully) tried to stop her from beating another student; set fire to clothing in a change room; overturned her desk after failing a test, and then spent an impressive four consecutive hours crying in the arms of an educational assistant in the school's resource room. Academically, Cassie places in the very low percentiles except for mathematics in which she is rated Low Average.

Interestingly, the prime concern about Cassie at the moment relates to service delivery. At the beginning of the current semester, special education in her secondary school switched from a Fixed Resource model to a Mobile Resource model. In the Fixed version, over a four-period (plus lunch) day, identified students attended three regular classes and spent one specifically time-tabled period in a resource room with special education staff. In the Mobile model, identified students take four regular classes, often accompanied by special education staff, with the option to "drop-in" to a resource room as necessary. In theory, "drop-ins" occur after consultation among the student, the regular teacher and special education staff. In practice, students tend to "drop-in" at will.

Since the adoption of the Mobile model, Cassie has spent almost all her time in the resource room, to be in the company of an educational assistant assigned there. The EA is new but very popular with both students and staff and highly regarded for her skill in dealing with students who act out. Cassie's attachment to the EA and the resource room has generated a number of concerns. One is that sticking exclusively to the EA contradicts the goals of her IEP (not to mention that the EA has become unavailable for other duties). Another arises because the school board is very strongly and publicly committed to inclusion and sees the situation as a potential black mark. Regular teachers, understandably, are relieved that Cassie's presence in their classrooms is limited but that position puts them in conflict with the special education teachers. At first, no one wanted to stir the pot because Cassie has been undergoing an extended period of calm. Now, however, increasing numbers of identified students have picked up on the precedent and are following her routine. A response has become necessary.

Chapter 3, the relatively larger percentage of part time enrolments in areas like autism, speech and language, and developmental disability, where such a combination can be very beneficial. Students identified gifted are often seen in the part time setting, as these tables suggest.

Fully Self-Contained Class

In order to generate a very specific kind of learning experience, it may be deemed appropriate to place an exceptional student in a special setting full time. These placements are found in some, but by no means all, regular community schools. Ideally, exceptional students who take their entire program in such classes, participate in general school activities in the same way as other students. Students identified as gifted are sometimes found in these settings because it is simpler to arrange

Figure 4A

Figure 4B

the experiences that will challenge them productively. The fully self-contained class is also a carefully considered option for students whose special need relates to behaviour.

Special Schools

A number of dedicated-purpose schools in the province are run under the aegis of the Ministry of Education. In Brantford, the W. Ross Macdonald School, named after a former lieutenant-governor, has programs for blind and deaf/blind students. In London, Belleville and Milton, schools named after former Ontario premiers, the Robarts School, Sir James Whitney School, and Ernest C. Drury School respectively, offer programs for deaf students. The Ministry also maintains 'demonstration' schools at the latter three locations, for students diagnosed as having ADHD and/or severe learning disabilities. Each is a residential school with a fairly small population. They are known respectively as Amethyst, Sagonaska, and Trillium. In Ottawa, the Centre Jules-Leger offers programs for the deaf and severely learning disabled in French.

In addition to dedicated programs for their students, these schools also offer the standard Ontario curriculum; they are resource and

training centres for both teachers and the wider community, and play an important role in specialized teacher training. Both the provincial and the demonstration schools enjoy a well-deserved reputation for leadership and for excellence in education. Students are enrolled in the schools through an application process that involves the Ministry and the student's school board.

Specialized, Non-School Settings ("Section 20")

In situations where students are admitted to a care or treatment facility or to a custodial or correctional facility, special arrangements are usually necessary to address their educational needs. The educational program in these cases is part of a wider program of service that may include medical treatment or service from therapists, psychiatrists, social workers, etc. For the most part, the educational portion of the program is undertaken by a local school board under written agreement with the facility. Funding is a complex matter for usually several provincial ministries are involved, each with its own priorities, responsibilities and funding mechanisms. The Ministry of Education describes these as "Educational Programs in Government-Approved Facilities for Care, Treatment and Custodial or Correctional Purposes". In everyday parlance they are typically referred to as "Section 20s", this being the number and section of the funding regulation.

In terms of the placement continuum, specialized, non-school settings along with special schools are viewed as quite restrictive settings.

Range of Settings? Or Full Inclusion?

All school boards in Ontario treat inclusion of exceptional students in regular classes as normal practice. At the same time, it is Ministry of Education policy that a range of settings (such as those described above) should be available for students whose needs are best addressed under alternative arrangements. For most—but not all—school boards in the province this has been pretty much standard practice since special education was first established. The standard practice is based on variations of a long established placement model known by a variety of names such as Cascade, Continuum Model, etc. (see Figure 4A).

The distinguishing feature of this model is that a continuum of settings for exceptional students is available on a formal, more or less permanent basis. The settings, or learning environments, are progressively more specialized, and students, if it is deemed necessary and beneficial, may be placed in these alternative settings on a short or longer term basis. Important philosophical principles of the model are that students always be placed in the least restrictive environment, and that no restricted placement ever be regarded as permanent.

As one might expect, in a province the size of Ontario, geography has an influence on available placements. Geography and budgets. Thus in the case of a setting organized to deal with, say, extremely difficult behaviour, a board might arrange that only one school out of several in an area would offer this special environment. Another school in the area might be chosen to host a special setting for blind students. Still another might have a self-contained setting

for students with fragile health issues. Each school in the area, however, would likely have its own 'resource room' or similar, moderately specialized setting for part or full time placements. No matter how the school board arranges matters, theoretically—and for the most part in practice—in the range of settings model, all students in the board have access, if necessary, to the appropriate setting for their needs.

Placement arrangements built on the principle of inclusion, tend to be quite flexible and sometimes, quite ad hoc (note the looping arrows in Figure 4B). Very often, arrangements are created — and collapsed — entirely according to needs of the moment. In fact, there is good reason to conclude that placement arrangements are often so individualized, and so tailored on a by-case basis, that there really is no such thing as an inclusion model at all. Most school boards where inclusion is an underpinning philosophy, make at least minimal use of alternative settings nevertheless, if only informally. A board that has every single one of its exceptional students in regular settings, *full time*, is very rare. Still, the fundamental principle of inclusion is not diluted: an exceptional student, no matter where her special education service is delivered, is considered a full time student in her regular classroom. She is never administratively 'placed' elsewhere.

Debate over the moral and practical superiority of inclusion versus range of settings raged hotly for several years, but has very much diminished in the light of experience. Most educators in Ontario, even before provincial policy was clarified, were operating from the position that regular class placement, should be a first choice as a matter of course. And over time, even the most vociferous supporters of inclusion have acknowledged the accumulating evidence that some students with special needs do indeed benefit from specialized settings. Today, in most schools, it is difficult for an untrained observer to distinguish between the two positions, so similar have they become in practice. What seems to have taken place then, in the debate over inclusion and range of settings is an amalgamation of the best of both.

Getting Special Education Under Way

In the earlier days of Ontario's special education history, boards of education tended to rely quite exclusively on formal procedures to get the process going. Hence most decisions were made by officially constituted Identification, Placement and Review Committees (IPRCs). A committee would make a determination of exceptionality (if appropriate), decide on a placement, in some cases make recommendations regarding program, and then if the parents agreed, the student's special education program would begin. As systems and practice matured, schools began to adopt simpler procedures for some students, reserving the time-consuming and demanding formality of the IPRC for the more complicated cases. The models shown in Situations I and II are reasonably typical examples of the less formal, in-school variety. The model shown in Situation III (Figure 4E) is considerably more formal.

Situation I (Figure 4C) presents a type of case that occurs frequently. It begins when the teacher and/or educational assistant or parent becomes aware of a student's special need(s). When it is possible to bring about appropriate modifications to meet the needs in the classroom without bringing formal processes to bear, a matter can be resolved quickly, simply, and with reasonable hope of immediate benefit. In Situation I, it is very likely that assessments would be informal and carried out by the teacher, perhaps with assistance from in-school personnel. The individual education plan in this case, as well as the continuing evaluation, may be less formal. In this case, the student is usually not officially identified exceptional, although for school purposes and for data reporting, he or she may be considered so.

Situation II (Figure 4D) is somewhat more complex in that it will likely involve more personnel. This procedure does not formally identify the student as exceptional, but will likely call for somewhat more standardized actions than in Situation I. The assessment of needs will usually be more detailed, and may even be supported with formal test results. Likewise, an IEP is likely to be more fully developed and maintained, with more specifics in matters like amount and nature of resource support, the date for a review of progress, etc. As with Situation I, the student may now be considered part of the school's special education population. Situation II, incidentally—and Situation I—in fact any model that

Figure 4C

Figure 4D

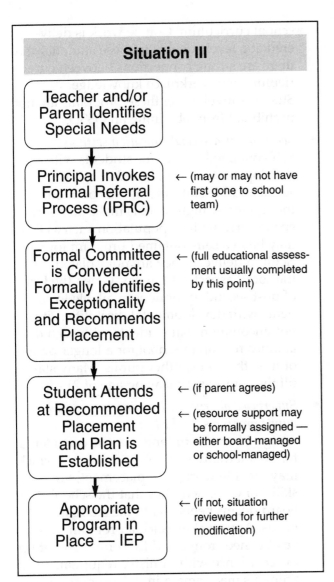

Situation III

Teacher and/or Parent Identifies Special Needs

↓

Principal Invokes Formal Referral Process (IPRC) ← (may or may not have first gone to school team)

↓

Formal Committee is Convened: Formally Identifies Exceptionality and Recommends Placement ← (full educational assessment usually completed by this point)

↓

Student Attends at Recommended Placement and Plan is Established ← (if parent agrees)
← (resource support may be formally assigned — either board-managed or school-managed)

↓

Appropriate Program in Place — IEP ← (if not, situation reviewed for further modification)

Figure 4E

incorporates resources like a 'school team', is a reflection of how a school approaches special education philosophically.

As Figure 4E implies, Situation III is more complex. It reflects provincially regulated practice in the province, and is the approach necessary to have a student formally identified exceptional. Naturally, it is more time-consuming than Situations I and II, and is subject to standardized procedures required by provincial regulations.

Procedures used by individual schools and boards will differ. These are examples only and have no official status. In some cases, in order to maintain flexibility and a policy of by-case response, a school will not use standard procedures at all. All schools, however, pay heed to

Ministry regulations, and invariably try to proceed with the student's best interests as the top priority.

Service Delivery in Secondary Schools

Because of the structure of a typical high school, special education service delivery is quite different from that in elementary settings. The number of teachers, other students, courses, diploma requirements and scheduling options that an individual with special needs encounters in a secondary school setting is much greater than in the elementary experience. Secondary schools have complex timetabling; most are organized on a semester system, and fundamental to the structure is the completion of credits, the basis on which diplomas are awarded. Matching the typically large number of course options with the special needs of an exceptional student means the role of a special education teacher in a high school frequently involves more coordination and consultation than direct intervention.

For a majority of students receiving special education services at the high school level, considerations such as course reduction, careful and strategic course selection, and scheduling of resource room time are common practices, and these must be monitored. Regular teaching staff and other school personnel need information about students with special needs along with effective practices for instruction, all of which requires extensive collaboration and much of which comes under the secondary school special education teacher's purview.

Diplomas and Credits

Currently in Ontario, successful completion of a high school program leads to an Ontario Secondary School Diploma (OSSD). This diploma requires completion of 30 high school credits, 40 hours of community involvement, and successful completion of the Ontario Secondary School Literacy Test. For those students who fail to meet the requirements of the OSSD, an Ontario Secondary School Certificate, which requires 14 credits, may be issued instead.

How does Service delivery in secondary schools differ from that of elementary schools.

A small number of students unable to meet the certificate requirements may be issued a certificate of accomplishment or some other type of recognition for work completed during their time in secondary school.

Aside from diploma matters, a student with special needs in an Ontario high school is required to have a transition plan in place to assist in program planning. All students with special needs aged 14 or older, except those identified gifted, are required to have such a plan, the goal of which is to assist them in the successful transition from school to the workplace, to post secondary education and to community living. (For more on transition plans, see Chapter 16.)

Modifications

It is certainly the goal of all high schools across the province that as many students as possible successfully complete the high school requirements for graduation. With this in mind, a number of programs and options are available to assist the student. While specifics may vary, most high schools offer the following types of services and programs.

- *Program accommodation and modification within the regular classroom:*
  A large number of students are accommodated through arrangements made by the special education department. These students may spend a portion of their day receiving extra assistance in a resource room setting, scheduled either as a regular, daily item, or on an as-needed basis. The same students often have modified programs in the regular classroom. Achievement based on these modified learning expectations is assessed in light of provincial requirements and a decision is made by the principal as to whether to grant a high school credit in the subject area.

- *School – work transition programs:*
  Students at risk for failure and those identified with learning problems have an opportunity to participate in school-work programs. These programs vary from board to board and consist of a body of course credits developed to deliver adapted high

school curriculum. Course work is delivered at a level suitable to these students and there are strong connections between curriculum and workplace knowledge. Students involved in these programs are not prohibited from obtaining an OSSD.

- *Self-contained special education settings:*
  Self-contained classes for students with developmental disabilities that focus on social and life skills are not uncommon, though many high schools make an effort to ensure that, while a population such as this may be in a self-contained program for curriculum delivery, they are not isolated for the social aspects of the day. Given the lack of post secondary options available to students with developmental disabilities, it is not uncommon that students with such disabilities remain in school for a longer period of time than most other pupils. Many stay till the compulsory leaving age of 21.

- *Supervised alternative learning for excused pupils programs (SALEP) :*
  At age 14 or 15, students may be considered for an alternative school environment which may include workplace placement, life skills, or other activities that the school board deems beneficial to the student's needs. Approval for such a program must be obtained from a SALEP committee set up in accordance with Ministry requirements. Students may remain in this program until the age of 16. During that time these students are considered registered in school and may apply any credits obtained toward an OSSD.

The Service Providers

The number and type of personnel involved in delivery of service to exceptional students usually depends on the nature and extent of the needs. Naturally, service can only be delivered if personnel are available, if the system is organized to flow the service to the need, *and* if the ever-so-crucial element of cooperation prevails. Fortunately, the combination of professionalism among educators and members of related fields, and the natural disposition to ameliorate the situation of students with special needs, means that most of the time, the right things happen.

The list of personnel — *of service providers* — who work with exceptional students in an exceptional setting can be as varied as there are variations among students. By far the most deeply involved in every educational situation are combinations of the following:

- classroom teacher
- educational assistant
- special education teacher. (There are many local terms for this role.)
- special consultant

with input from:

- principals
- parents
- school teams
- advisory groups
- advocacy groups
- social agencies
- specialists

"Outside" people typically become involved when a response to special needs requires a particular expertise. They include members from fields like psychiatry, psychology, psychometry, social work, health, speech, physical and occupational therapy. Some boards of education, particularly larger ones, employ members of these professions directly. This is most frequently the case with professionals in the speech area, and with what is often called 'psycho-educational services' (or a variation thereof) usually people who specialize in assessment and counseling. The latter are more involved at the assessment and program planning stages, although sometimes they will also participate in ongoing delivery of service in situations where exceptional behaviour, for example, is a factor.

The Impact of Funding

As discomfiting as it may seem, there are times when decisions about the type of setting for a student or the style of service delivery are affected by funding matters. There may well be situations where school board or Ministry policy supports funding for a setting that is not necessarily ideal for a certain student, yet it may be only in that setting where the needed personnel and resources are found. The level of formality in a special education track can be affected too, for if allocation of funds is based on clearly establishing the intensity of a student's need, and on accountability, it is not inconceivable that decision-makers would choose to follow a formal route principally because it will loosen the purse strings.

Deploying The Personnel

An abiding concern of administrators is to get the appropriate resources into the appropriate settings as efficiently and effectively as possible, all with a view to cost, cooperation and availability. To accomplish this, schools and boards generally organize deployment models, or service models, schemas for managing the various elements in delivering service, for once it has been decided that a student is exceptional and is to receive support there are management factors that must be decided such as

- How much support will be needed?
- Are the needed resources available?
- Who is providing support?
- How long will it continue?
- Where does the support take place?
- Who has primary responsibility for the student?
- When and with what frequency will the case be reviewed?

Who Controls the Resources?

Although resource management policies differ across the province, the most common style is a combination of board-wide control of service delivery, and individual school responsibility. Schools within a board will typically have a number of resources allocated, often according to a formula based on population but which also recognizes unique school needs. Thus within a school, one or more special education teachers will have responsibility, under the principal, for allocating available resources and personnel as needed. If there are needs that go beyond a school's allocated resources or unique situations demanding a response, the board will—ideally—enhance the allocations (an outcome, however, that is inevitably shaped by availability and funding). School-based management, because it circumvents time-consuming bureaucracy, can bring service to bear quickly and flexibly, along with a greater likelihood of informal but immediate cooperation and approval from parents. Special needs that require very specialized expertise — blindness for example — is often more effectively managed at the board level, even though the resources will likely be delivered in a neighbourhood school. The combination of board-wide and individual school service delivery, seems not only fiscally reasonable and responsible, but also addresses issues of immediacy, flexibility, accountability and optimum use of resources.

The School Team

A most significant development in the late 1980's and early 90's was the gradual realization that the mystery of educating students with special needs is not all that different from the mystery of educating any student. Experience has taught that many educational matters which at first glance imply an elaborate response, can actually be addressed 'in-house'. No one denies that expertise continues to be important, and there is no question that dealing with certain types of exceptionality such as, say, hearing or blindness, often requires specialization of some kind. Nevertheless, the needs of most exceptional students can usually be met through a healthy application of common sense, the kind of approach that effective teachers use in all of educational practice. At the same time, teachers have found that cases of special need are almost always more effectively addressed when they are the focus of broad concern, of general cooperation and support, rather than the sole responsibility of a single individual. In many schools, this combination of insights has borne fruit in a more or less formal arrangement known as the School

Assistance Team, or the In-School Team or Teacher Support Team or School-Based Support Team or similar title.

The School Team Concept

A support or assistance team is a committee of staff members organized to advise and consult with individual teachers who request assistance regarding students perceived as having special needs. *The team neither precludes nor replaces formal special education nor diminishes it in any way.* Rather, it supports special education, and helps it function more effectively in a school, and more efficiently. In many schools, the team is a forum of first resort, to which teachers and parents may bring concerns about the special needs of particular students, without formally invoking special education procedures. This practice not only tends to keep students in the mainstream, but also, by offering this pre-referral opportunity, a team helps to free its school's special education personnel to bring resources to bear where needs are greatest. A team can also enhance service delivery simply by offering broader involvement. Perhaps most important — to teachers and students equally — a team can be a vital instigator of professionalism: the kind of drive that leads a staff to seek solutions. (For more on the school team see Chapter 16.)

The Multidisciplinary Team Concept

For particularly demanding exceptional cases, service delivery is sometimes managed by a multidisciplinary team on which educators share membership with professionals who have specialized expertise. The situation, for example, of an exceptional student with multiple needs such as severe physical disabilities along with fragile health and possibly behavioural or developmental problems, may require the services of a variety of personnel. For this student, a multidisciplinary team may come together only once or twice on a more or less ad hoc basis, usually in an advisory capacity and most often at the initial stages when the student's placement and programming are being established. Ongoing delivery of service will usually be the responsibility of only certain members of the team.

The Expanding Role of Educational Assistants (Paraprofessionals*)

When special education first became mandatory in Ontario, support personnel, if any such existed at all in a school, were usually found in self-contained classrooms or in a special school where students with extensive needs were placed. Rarely were they found in regular classrooms. That reality changed dramatically over time so that today, educational assistants play a role in regular classrooms as a matter of course and indeed, are much sought after as important contributors in the delivery of service. Their role expanded significantly once inclusion became established as the normative style in the province's schools so that it is not unusual now for both teachers and parents to expect that if students with special needs are placed in a class, an EA will be there too.

What Do EAs Do?

Both the assistants themselves and the teachers they work with, as well as principals and parents, tend to answer this question with "Anything and everything!" A central role, or at least an ideal one, is active teaching of special education students under guidelines established by the teacher and the instructional plan. The teaching takes many forms from direct instruction to remediation to supervision of repeated practice. Very often an EA's instruction of a student with special needs is one-on-one in order to expand or reinforce a concept or skill that other students in a regular classroom have grasped more readily. This will be the case especially in larger, busy classes where demands on the classroom teacher are multiple.

Assistants may observe and record data for a variety of purposes, particularly for assessments wherein recorded observation plays a key role. They may be involved in things as complex as helping develop an IEP, or as straightforward as responsibility for classroom supplies. Among other contributions, EAs tutor, help manage general classroom conduct, modify educational materials, become part of a school team, provide health needs support, and—often a very important role—provide behaviour management support. What they do is, in short, anything and everything.

Growing Pains?

Because the practice of teaming teachers and educational assistants is fairly new, and the EA role still rather undefined, it is often left to both professional and paraprofessional to establish working relationships in a classroom as best they can. The situation can be fraught with all the risks found in any human interchange. Anecdotal evidence, for example, is reported from time to time of EAs being given (or taking) ownership of a special needs case, particularly a behaviour issue, or of EAs "wasting away" because a classroom teacher—who is highly unlikely to have received any pre or post-service preparation in working with another adult in the classroom—is reluctant to share or delegate responsibility. Fortunately, the vast majority of teacher/EA relationships work out positively. It takes time and experience to establish that the purpose of the educational assistant role is not to replace the teacher but to support what goes on in the classroom, as well as time and experience to appreciate that by working cooperatively, two committed adults can fulfill the ultimate goal of all educators: helping students to learn and grow.

Qualifications

At time of publication, Ontario had no legislation precisely addressing the qualifications of educational assistants, although many school boards have their own prerequisites, a policy strongly supported by the Ontario CEC (Council for Exceptional Children). A number of colleges in the province offer impressive pre-service programs.

• • • ———

* As a professional designation, support personnel in classrooms are sometimes described as 'paraprofessionals' like their counterparts in medicine and law, 'paramedics' and 'paralegals'. In education, the term 'educational assistant' (EA) continues to be popular.

——— • • •

An area of difficulty with the multidisciplinary team approach in educational settings is management and organization. Since the approach is used almost exclusively in cases of extensive need, there is sometimes disagreement over priority in meeting the needs (education? social? physical well-being?). Also, the mere task of bringing together a team of otherwise occupied, diverse professionals is awkward and time-consuming, and usually requires the authority (i.e., for budget, for freeing personnel from other obligations, etc.) of someone in an upper-level administrative role. As well, because there is such wide involvement, ultimate responsibility for the student—even legal responsibility—may become an issue. Difficulties like these often force serious consideration of a quite restricted placement like special day school or residential facility simply because the situation is easier to manage in such a setting.

READINGS & RESOURCES

Demchak, M., & Morgan, C.R. (1998). Effective collaboration between professionals and paraprofessionals. *Rural Special Education Quarterly, 17*(2), 10-16.

Dworet, D., & Bennett, S. (2002). A view from the North: Special education in Canada. *Teaching Exceptional Children, 34*(5). 22-27.

Fisher, D. (1999). According to their peers: Inclusion as high school students see it. *Mental Retardation, 37*(6), 65-69.

French, N.K. (1998). Working together: Resource teachers and paraeducators. *Remedial and Special Education, 19*, 357-368.

French, N.K. (1999). Para-educators: Who are they and what do they do? *Teaching Exceptional Children, 32*(1), 65-69.

Hunt, P. & Gotez, L. (1997). Research on inclusive educational programs, practices and outcomes for students with severe disabilities. *Journal of Special Education, 31*, 3-29.

Jones, K. H. & Bender W.N. (1993). Utilization of paraprofessionals in special education: A review of the literature. *Remedial and Special Education 14*(1), 7-14.

Lusthaus, E. & Lusthaus, C. (1992). From segregation to full inclusion: an evaluation. *Exceptionality Education Canada, 2*, 95-115.

Minke, K.M., Bear, G.G., Deemer, S.A. & Griffin S.M. (1996). Teachers' experiences with inclusive classrooms: implications for special education reform. *Journal of Special Education, 30*, 152-186.

Morsink C.V., & Lenk L.L. (1992). The delivery of special education programs and services. *Remedial and Special Education, 13*, 33-43.

Pickett, A.L., & Gerlach,K. (1997). *Supervising para-educators in school settings: A team approach.* Austin, TX: Pro-Ed.

Smith, W. & Lusthaus, C. (1993). Students with disabilities in Canada: What rights do they have? *Education Canada, 5*(9), 45- 46.

Thousand, J., Rosenberg, R.L., Bishop, K.D., & Villa, R.A. (1997). The evolution of secondary inclusion. *Remedial and Special Education, 18*(5), 270-284, 306.

Wang, M.C. Walberg, H. J. & Reynolds, M.C. (1992). A scenario for better – not separate- special education. *Educational Leadership, 50*, 35-41.

Authors' note: Many Ontario school boards have developed modified programs for exceptional students, especially in secondary schools. The substance of these programs, along with descriptions of service delivery methods, can usually be found on board websites. School board websites can be accessed via **http://sbinfo.edu.gov.on.ca/**

CHAPTER 5

Identification and Placement
How the IPRC Works

This schema outlines main features of Ontario Regulation 181/98, Identification and Placement of Exceptional Pupils, which came into force on September 1, 1998 (amended by Ontario Regulation 137, in 2001).

Step One

Every school board is required to appoint one or more IPRCs.

> **Student is formally referred to an IPRC by the school's principal.**

Principal may initiate referral (notifies parent*). Must initiate referral if asked by parent in writing.

IPRC has minimum of three members. One must be a principal or supervisory officer of the board (or designate).

Step Two

School board must publish a detailed Parents' Guide (see Note 1).

> **IPRC obtains and considers educational assessment. May interview student with permission of parent*. Receives information put forward by school and parent. Shares all written information with parent.**

Medical and/or psychological data may be requested, subject to Health Care Consent Act (1996).

Teacher interview and/or input not required by regulation, but most school boards will include these.

* *Parent* here includes *parent(s) and guardian(s)*. Wherever *parent* appears, note that students 16 years and older may be part of the process, along with parent.

Step Three

IPRC must consider all information and proposals for special education programs and services.

Parent may present proposals in addition to those from school board.

Parent entitled to have a representative of choice present.

Parent and representative may participate in all discussions except decision making.

Step Four

IPRC decides student is not exceptional.

Process ends, unless parent appeals, or requests follow-up meeting.

or

Decision statement must list placement, category(s) and definition(s) of exceptionality, and student's strengths/needs.

Written decision of IPRC goes to parent, referring principal, school board.

IPRC identifies student as exceptional, and decides on a placement.
May make recommendations (but not decisions) regarding programs and services.

Placement to be regular class if it meets needs, and if parent wishes. IPRC must give reasons if special class is chosen.

Parent may request IPRC meet again to reconsider.

Step Five

*Within 30 school days principal of school where student is placed must see to development of IEP and
for 14 year olds and older, a Transition Plan. (See Note 2.)*

If parent signs consent
or
if consent is not signed, but parent does not appeal.

Student is placed according to IPRC decision. IEP is developed and implementation begun.

- - - - - → Step Five stayed if parent appeals.

Review

Rights and requirements as in Steps One to Five.

Student's situation to be reviewed at least once every school year by an IPRC. Parent may request review after three months.

Reviews confirm existing situation, or may make changes. Principal to review and update IEP.

In Cases of Appeal

(handwritten annotation: chose a chair { one selected by parents / one member selected by Board)

Step One (A)

Parent may appeal identification as exceptional, or placement or both.

School board convenes a three member Appeal Board to review the IPRC material and decisions.

One member chosen by board; one by parent; the two select a third as chair (in case of disagreement, chair is chosen by MoE).

Step Two (A)

Parent and/or representative entitled to participate in all discussions except decision making.

Appeal Board agrees with IPRC and recommends its decisions be implemented,
or
disagrees with IPRC and makes recommendation to school board about identification or placement or both.

May interview anyone whom Appeal Board chair feels has information to contribute.

Written recommendation to parent, principal, school board and chair of IPRC.

Written reasons must accompany written statement of recommendation.

Step Three (A)

School board considers recommendation and decides what action to take.

School board is not limited to recommendation of Appeal Board.

Step Four (A)

Written decision of school board goes to all parties.

School board decision is implemented.

If parent signs consent
or
if consent not signed but parent does not appeal.

Step Four (A) stayed if parent appeals.

Final appeal stage is to Special Education Tribunal (see Note 3).

Note 1: Each school board must prepare a parent's guide explaining all elements of the IPRC process including rights of appeal and the steps involved. The guide must be available at every school in the board, and if requested by a parent, must be made available in braille, large print, or audio form. The guide will also identify organizations and associations from which parents may seek advice and help.

Note 2: The Transition Plan requirement does not apply to students who are identified 'Gifted'. See Chapter 16 for a full explanation of IEPs and Transition Plans.

Note 3: The Special Education Tribunal (Section 57 of the Education Act) is a provincially appointed body that hears appeals from decisions of IPRCs upheld first by an Appeal Board and then by the school board. Tribunal hearings are complex, adversarial in structure, and are conducted under the Statutory Powers Procedure Act of Ontario. A Tribunal decision is final and binding. *The vast majority of IPRCs end at Step Five. Appeals are infrequent and Tribunals are rare. Where either is imminent in a student's case, the Ministry of Education encourages parents and school boards to attempt mediation before going forward.*

Also of note...

- The regulations set specific time limits on steps in the IPRC procedure; e.g., appeals, response periods, etc.

- With a parent's agreement, adjustments are sometimes made to an identified student's situation without a formal IPRC meeting. Also a formal Review is generally not convened to modify a student's IEP unless major change is requested or expected.

- IPRCs were governed originally by Regulation 554, issued in 1981. The procedure was modified by Regulation 305 in 1990. Fairly significant modifications were made in 1998 by Regulation 181, its current form. Regulation 137 in 2001 made a small change to Step Five, specifying a time frame for an IEP and Transition Plan. There have been no other changes.

- For the complete versions of the IPRC regulations and other documents, see **www.edu.gov.on.ca**, or the Ministry publication: *Special Education, A Guide for Educators* (2001), available in government bookstores, public libraries, school board offices.

The Case(s) of Luis and Estella

Although Luis and Estella are almost nine years old, their mother continues to dress them in clothes with matching material and designs. It is her contention, as she explained to an IPRC, that the more Luis and Estella are perceived as "cute", the more readily they will be "welcomed by normal society." The two children are fraternal twins and are developmentally disabled. Luis has Down syndrome, while Estella sustained serious brain injury at birth. Although both speak in a baby talk style, they are otherwise quite socially adept. Their mother has devoted her life to their care and to integrating them into society. The twins attended nursery school. They were enrolled in clubs and sports; and from kindergarten to grade three were placed full time in the same regular class in their neighbourhood school.

No one has questioned their placement until now. With two months to go in grade three, the school has requested an IPRC review. Although the majority of their class reads and writes at an age-appropriate level, neither twin writes his or her name as yet. Luis can recognize his, but Estella does not. Luis can identify about half the letters of the alphabet; he counts to one hundred by rote but does not appear to associate numbers with amounts or quantities. Estella, when asked, will count to five or six and then, as she always does when challenged, will produce a totally engaging smile. The school board psychologist feels that Luis especially, but Estella too, has far greater ability. Experience shows that both learn from very structured teaching and frequent repetition. However, the regular grade three class does not provide much opportunity. It is a large, busy class, with one EA who also shares responsibility for the health needs of a girl with cerebral palsy.

Next year presents even more concerns. The school's junior division places several classes into one large, pod-style room, where individual study is emphasized and small group projects prevail. Some, but not all, of the school team believe it would be a disservice to place Estella here, and possibly Luis too. The alternative, at least part time, would be placement either in the school's primary resource room, or the junior one. Current enrolment in the primary room is six. There are three children with severe developmental disabilities, two with physical disabilities, and one child identified autistic. Only one of the six has normal speech. The resource teacher and full time EA emphasize language development. The junior room is almost a mirror image of the primary. The twins' mother objects to placement in either setting.

CHAPTER 6

Students With Learning Disabilities

"His whole week is a disaster! On Monday, he's Mr. Eager Beaver; the first one finished with everything— and all wrong. And I mean wrong! Like he was doing a completely different exercise! Tuesday, he's on another planet; can't focus, can't remember, loses everything. Wednesday's hyper day 'cause there's gym in the morning. On Thursday—well, you name it. We've rotary timetable so we have to go find him at least once. By Friday he's discouraged, poor kid. Most Fridays he gets into a scrap."

Susan B., a first year teacher, describing Jordan, age 11.

Misconceptions About Learning Disabilities

1. 'Learning disability' is a social invention that excuses failure in middle and upper class children.

A large body of research and an even larger catalogue of experience make clear that a learning disability is a genuine special need, and one that knows no social class barriers. As with any exceptionality, however, the effects of a learning disability can be aggravated by socio-economic factors.

2. Heredity plays no role in learning disabilities.

Although the strength and nature of the connection are unclear, evidence points to a pattern of learning disabilities in families. This seems to be the case particularly in the matter of reading acquisition and fluency, where contemporary genetic research has identified linkages with specific chromosomes.

3. Learning disabilities only show up in schools and are therefore a 'school problem'.

Certain disabilities may remain hidden until the demands of school-based learning reveal them (e.g., language skills, mathematics skills) but other specific disabilities (e.g., memory and attention; perceptual-motor processing) will become obvious independent of schooling.

4. The main cause of learning disabilities is bad teaching.

Not long after the term for this exceptionality was first developed, its critics offered 'dyspedagogia' (bad teaching) as the real cause of the syndrome. Although ineffective instruction has negative consequences for all students, decades of experience, careful observation, and research have demonstrated clearly that learning disabilities are a pre-existing set of special needs, independent of the quality of instruction (although the effects of disabilities are usually made worse by poor instruction).

5. Most children will outgrow a learning disability.

With effective instruction, the majority of learning disabled children manage their needs, but disabilities usually endure into adulthood.

6. Learning disabled students are highly intelligent.

Although many students with a learning disability develop clever coping strategies and what is sometimes called substitution or diversion behaviours, there is little evidence to substantiate the claim of above-average intelligence. In fact, the weight of evidence suggests that on IQ tests, their scores run across the same range as the general population, with what seems to be a tendency to fall in the average to below-average categories.

7. Left-handed students are more likely to be learning disabled.

"Lefties" are sometimes over-represented in classes devoted to the learning disabled, but no hard data exist to connect the disability with left-handedness.

8. Hyperactive (AD/HD) students are learning disabled (and vice versa).

Hyperactivity and learning disability have become very much interwoven over the past several decades. The connection, however, is not absolute. A person with AD/HD is not always learning disabled, or vice versa.

9. Learning disabled students are more likely to become delinquent or criminal.

This claim originated in the 1960s and, if nothing else, contributed to the high profile that learning disabilities acquired after that time. Some research shows a slightly higher incidence of learning disabilities in prison populations, but definition problems weaken those findings.

10. It is possible to detect the presence of a learning disability by testing.

No test yet available can detect a learning disability in the same way that a hearing test, for example, can specify the nature and seriousness of a hearing loss. A learning disability is identified through teamwork by educators, parents, and sometimes other professionals, using observation, curriculum-based assessment, informal tests, and to some extent, standardized, formal tests.

What Is a Learning Disability?

This is the most elusive of all areas in special education. In the first place, it is not a global impairment in which all elements of a student's performance are affected. Nor is it a consistent, easily measured and clear special need. The only criterion that all learning disabled students seem to share, is loosely described as a difficulty in dealing with information, particularly language-based information, despite apparent freedom from any intellectual or sensory handicap or cultural difference. The difficulty may be in taking in the information, or, in integrating it with what they already know and understand, or, in expressing what they now know as a result of taking in and integrating the information. Or—and this is where the elusiveness begins— it may be a combination of the previous three elements (or just two of the three!). Learning disabled students may be disorganized, unable to focus attention, forgetful, and disoriented. They may be hyperactive—or *hypo*active. They may be highly resistant to changing counter-productive behaviours, or, so compliant that they are easily led astray. One student may manifest all of these characteristics; another student, while functioning at the same low academic level, may manifest only one of them. And either student may demonstrate some of these characteristics on one day, and on another day, show absolutely none of them. Or all of them!

In effect, the special need, 'learning disabilities' is a syndrome of a number of behaviours. Unlike students with intellectual disabilities, in which case the impairment seems to be global, affecting all elements of an individual's performance, students with learning disabilities usually have more specific issues to cope with.

Defining the Indefinable?

When the late Samuel Kirk proposed the term 'learning disability' to a conference of parents seeking information about their "mystery kids" in the early 1960s, the response was immediate and positive. The fact that the term became wide spread very quickly indicated the extent to which large numbers of concerned parents were seeking an explanation why their children did not succeed in school, despite what they, the parents, knew was not lack of intellect. (And it was parents, far more than academics, who were responsible for placing learning disability front and centre, in education.) The new term was non-pejorative and all-encompassing. It avoided implications of low intellect and ineptitude, and successfully replaced a variety of unsatisfactory general descriptors like *dyslexia, perceptual handicap, minimally brain-injured, maturational lag,* even *slow learner.* The dark side, however, is that 'learning disability' is loose enough to permit a variety of interpretations, and although it offered a sense of focus and direction, and put a consensual face on an issue that had been running in all directions, making the next step to a clear and widely accepted definition, proved then—and still does today—a challenging task.

A Variety of Explanations …

Many notions and ideas about how to view learning disabilities have enjoyed periods of popularity since the 1960s. Because they continue to crop up in the literature, and because none of them have been effectively and clearly disproven, they are briefly summarized here.

- *IQ Score/Achievement Discrepancy:* Supporters contend that a difference of two years or more between the mental age obtained on an intelligence test, and the grade-age equivalent obtained on a standardized achievement test indicates a learning dis-

The Case of Cory

After his parents' separation, Cory lived with his mother in an inner city area. For a period of about four years, she regularly obstructed the father's visiting rights, contravening a string of court orders. On the day Cory entered grade one, his father picked him up from school at lunch hour and the two disappeared. Eighteen months later his maternal grandparents appeared at Pearson Airport with the boy in tow, claiming they had rescued him from an abusive situation abroad. Children's Aid Society (CAS) intervened and placed him with foster parents for six months, after which his mother was again awarded custody. One year later, Children's Aid again intervened and Cory was returned to the foster parents who had maintained him previously. Meanwhile, Cory's father returned to Canada and applied for, and was denied, permanent custody. But contrary to the recommendations of the CAS, the court granted him weekly visitation rights. At about this time, Cory's mother suddenly remarried, abandoned her suit for restoration of custody, and moved to South America. Her parents (the maternal grandparents above) have now applied for custody, and CAS has entered an application to make Cory a permanent ward.

Cory is now almost ten. He is in a split grade three/four in his eleventh school, and has missed about a full year of schooling. He takes medication for TB, and he has a slight hearing loss. Cory reads very poorly. Both his printing, and the language and content of his stories can be easily mistaken for that of a much younger child. His math skills are inconsistent. Although his teacher suspects he may have an articulation problem, a speech consultant feels his odd way of talking is a product of mixing English and Spanish early in life. Everyone agrees that at least part of his learning problems is the result of timidity. A psychologist described Cory's manner as "juvenile shellshock".

The social worker responsible for Cory (a former teacher) believes the evidence clearly indicates a learning disability and that if he is so identified, he'll get some of the help he so obviously needs. The School Team believes Cory's status is a result of his personal history and that what he needs is love and above all stability. To identify him as learning disabled, they argue, will add yet one more change. The principal is strongly opposed to what she calls "using the learning disability category as a dumping ground for problems that have alternate solutions." The IPRC considering the case says it will listen to any argument that clarifies whether or not Cory has a learning disability, and will consider any and all recommendations.

ability. Its flaw is that it reduces the complexity of an individual to numbers. Also, a two-year discrepancy has different meanings at various age and grade levels.

- *Presumption of CNS Disorder:* Much of the early work in learning disability grew out of central nervous system and brain injury research of the 1930s and 40s. Researchers, because they noted similar behaviours between children known to have brain injury and those in the new subject pool, tended to make a leap of attribution so that learning disabled students were seen to have CNS disorder. Although by the 1980s, special education had generally retreated from the belief in brain anomalies as a cause of learning disabilities, new technologies like magnetic resonance imaging (MRI) have now shown subtle differences in the brains of individuals thought to be learning disabled. Although the connection remains vague, and its value to education unclear, that finding has kept the file open.

High Tech Shows Nothing New?

In 2003, an American study by Aylwards used MRI technology to show differences in the brain activity of 'normal' children when reading compared to the brain activity of students identified 'dyslexic' when reading. By using teaching methods with the 'dyslexics' that stimulated brain activity similar to that observed in the 'normal' subjects, researchers were able to bring about significant improvement in the 'dyslexics'' reading ability within a relatively short period. Interestingly, the teaching methods used to bring the 'dyslexics' up to speed were all techniques that classroom professionals have been using for decades: intense drill, phonics, word games, summarizing, and repeated readings. Although there is scope for cynicism about research like this, especially since the study was blessed with funding and personnel support rarely found in a typical classroom, at the very least it reinforces what effective teachers are already doing.

- *Impairments in Psychological Processing:* Psychological processing includes such cognitive functions as memory and attention, perceptual-motor processing, language processing, visual-spatial integration, etc. A strengthening conviction that diminished capacity in one, some, or all of these processes distinguishes the learning disabled, led a very important support group, the Learning Disabilities Association of Ontario, to give this hypothesis prominence in its definition published in 2001.

- *Exclusion of Environment, Culture, Mental Retardation, Sensory Impairment, Emotional Health:* If a learning problem is related to one of the above, that problem is usually not considered a learning disability. Unfortunately, the connection between such factors as emotional health and low, generalized academic achievement is well established, so that separating them from the fact of a learning disability is difficult. (In its "Special Education Guide", published 2001, The Ministry of Education includes this element in the definition of learning disabilities.)

- *Classification:* Educators have favoured classifications of *degree* in dealing with learning disabilities, applying descriptors like 'mild', 'moderate' and 'severe', as well as classifications of *type*, usually 'specific' for those cases where a student's need tends to be singular (e.g., has special needs in language; does well otherwise) and 'general' where a student lags behind peers in most areas. Unfortunately, the lack of an adequate, objective testing instrument for learning disabilities usually means that these classifications become pretty much subjective evaluations. As well, the terms transport poorly. What is 'moderate' and/or 'specific' in one school may not be in another.

... and a Variety of Definitions

- (Learning Disabilities Association of Ontario, adopted 2001)

Learning Disabilities refers to a variety of disorders that affect the acquisition, retention, understanding, organization or use of verbal and/or

Learning Disabilities are global T.F. - and they are distinct from intellectual disabilities.

non-verbal information. These disorders result from impairments in one or more psychological processes related to learning in combination with otherwise average abilities essential for thinking and reasoning. Learning disabilities are specific not global impairments and as such are distinct from intellectual disabilities.

Learning disabilities range in severity and invariably interfere with the acquisition and use of one or more of the following important skills: oral language (e.g., listening, speaking understanding) reading (e.g., decoding, comprehension) written language (e.g., spelling, written expression) mathematics (e.g., computation, problem solving). Learning disabilities may also cause difficulties with organizational skills, social perception and social interaction. The impairments are generally life-long. However their effects may be expressed differently over time, depending on the match between the demands of the environment and the individual's characteristics. Some impairments may be noted during the pre-school years, while others may not become evident until much later. During the school years, learning disabilities are suggested by unexpectedly low achievement or achievement that is sustainable only by extremely high levels of effort and support.

What are the causes of Learning Disabilities

Learning disabilities are due to genetic, other congenital and/or acquired neuro-biological factors. They are not caused by factors such as cultural or language differences, inadequate or inappropriate instruction, socio-economic status, or lack of motivation, although any one of these and other factors may compound the impact of learning disabilities.

Frequently, learning disabilities co-exist with other conditions, including attentional, behavioural and emotional disorders, sensory

The Case of Tino

Resource Room before   *self-contained*   *High School*

A multi media literacy program in the self-contained learning disability class at Tino's secondary school has had a major impact on him. The program uses video and audio tapes, and some single sheet print material, but its centrepieces are a software program, items downloaded from the internet, and a "chat line". Tino gives full credit to this program for the fact that he now can read the TV guide, and billboards, and can "get" the jokes that show up on the chat line. Two weeks ago, the second part of a standardized assessment instrument, administered in split-half form, showed that Tino has learned to note periods at the end of sentences; he can identify the correct spelling of previously learned words after three days (but does not yet write the words). And he can follow directions that tell him how to complete geometric figures. Tino could not do any of these things six months ago.

Progress.

These are the first indications of progress for Tino in a very long time. He was identified 'learning disabled' seven years ago (he's now 15) and has been placed mostly in resource classes since that time. According to reading assessments, Tino has never been able to read above a grade three to four level. Prior to starting on this new program, Tino had been a regular visitor to both the vice-principal and the counseling office, but for the past while he has avoided demerit points.

Has helped his behaviour

8 years in resource classes.

Tino's situation comes up for annual review in a month, by the IPRC. Although reviews in the past have pretty much rubber stamped a continuation of his identification and placement, Tino's parents have served notice they want a "serious discussion" this time. The problem, they feel, is that the multi media program, while beneficial, is too much fun and too unrealistic. They argue that clicking responses on a screen to gradually produce a finished product of some sort (e.g., a math problem, a string of short, connected sentences, a drawing—the program also prints out a certificate of accomplishment each time) will achieve nothing in the long run. The parents want some evidence that Tino either can now, or will soon be able to, manage independently. The situation is not without irony, for Tino's teachers have also wondered about this. Yet they are more aware than most that for the first time, he seems to be getting somewhere. The issue is how to wean him from the program, or perhaps even more basic: whether he should be.

immediate feedback

You need to show that I can produce something

Can some of the program strategies be incorporated into class work.

impairments or other medical conditions. For success, persons with learning disabilities require specialized interventions in home, school, community and workplace settings appropriate to their individual strengths and needs, including: specific skill instruction; the development of compensatory strategies; appropriate accommodations.

- (Ont. Ministry of Education, as published in *A Guide for Educators*, 2001)

Learning Disability is ... A learning disorder evident in both academic and social situations that involves one or more of the processes necessary for the proper use of spoken language or the symbols of communication, and that is characterized by a condition that:

a) is not primarily the result of: impairment of vision; impairment of hearing; physical disability; developmental disability; primary emotional disturbance; cultural difference;

b) results in a significant discrepancy between academic achievement and assessed intellectual ability, with deficits in one or more of the following: receptive language (listening, reading); language processing (thinking, conceptualizing, integrating); expressive language (talking, spelling, writing); mathematical computations; and

c) may be associated with one or more conditions diagnosed as: a perceptual handicap; a brain injury; minimal brain dysfunction; dyslexia; developmental aphasia.

- (National Joint Committee on Learning Disabilities (USA) as presented, 1988)

Learning disabilities is a general term that refers to a homogeneous group of disorders manifested by significant difficulties in the acquisition and use of listening, speaking, reading, writing, reasoning or mathematical abilities. These disorders are intrinsic to the individual, presumed to be due to central nervous system dysfunction, and may occur across the life span. Problems in self-regulatory behaviour, social perception, and social interaction may exist with learning disabilities but do not by themselves constitute a learning disability, Although learning disabilities may occur concomitantly with other handicapping conditions (e.g., sensory impairment, mental retardation, severe emotional disturbance) or with extrinsic influences (such as cultural differences, insufficient or inappropriate instruction) they are not the result of these conditions or influences.

Characteristics of Learning Disabilities

Processing Language

Many learning disabled students are challenged by the task of processing language. At the *receiving* stage (when the student is hearing language or attempting to read it) or at the *sending* stage (speaking or writing), or at the *elaboration* stage (when the student attempts to integrate some language with what he already holds), a learning disabled student often has real problems. For some students it's only at one of the stages; for others, difficulty arises at two or all three stages. For example, a younger student may not be able to process an incoming set of instructions like: "Use your red crayon to colour the robins, and then your yellow one to draw a line under the 'r-r-r-r' sound." He will *hear* the instruction all right, but all the linguistic information: robins, crayons, red, yellow, 'r-r-r-r' sound, not to mention the activity, may be too much to process. He may miss the instruction altogether, or miss a piece of it, or confuse red and yellow, or interchange pieces of information. The result will likely be a poor performance or a non-performance.

An older student may have an equally difficult time with something like this from, say, a geography teacher: "If you refer to your maps of West Africa, you'll notice a good example of how Africa was fragmented by decolonialization. Notice how Gambia is literally inserted into Senegal, and then further down the coast you'll see even more examples with Guinea-Bissau, Guinea, Togo, and Benin all sitting side by side." The older student may have more sophisticated language ability than the one colouring robins,

but then he is expected to deal with more sophisticated language, and relatively, is going to have just as much or even more trouble.

It is not unusual for an adult working with a learning disabled student to confuse the student's weakness in processing of language with weakness in visual or auditory discrimination. For example, unless she has a vision or hearing loss, this student will have no difficulty visually discriminating the letter A from a picture of a teepee, or the sound of "book" from the sound of "hook". Where she will manifest difficulty, however, is recognizing the letter A as such, and giving its name (or recalling the word teepee and saying it). It is not distinguishing between the sounds of "book" and "hook" that is hard; it is recognizing the words and the meanings; or, giving the right answers even if she knows them. A learning disabled student may also have difficulty in *producing* the letter

The Case of Raghubar

Raghubar's mother is fully involved with the stress of learning to live in a new country and a new culture, but even though she has no other children on whom to base a comparison, she has not been too preoccupied to notice that her little boy does things differently. Not that he is hard to control; and he definitely is not deaf, but somehow, he never seems to hear her. Well, not quite that way either. He hears her, but does perhaps half of what he's asked, or starts the task and then wanders away, or more often than not, does it backwards or leaves out a step. Raghubar almost never gets anything exactly right. Except in soccer. In soccer he is so good that older children in the community park stop to watch him. Still, that too is a mixed blessing. Raghubar is a natural athlete, a gifted one, probably. But he also has no fear. He puts himself at such risk that his mother is certain that one day he'll injure himself permanently. And that concern ties into another one. Raghubar never seems to learn from the experience of a bad fall or a banged shin or painful cut. The very next day, he'll go out and do the same thing that led to an accident the first time.

Although she has a fairly limited education herself, Raghubar's mom had the good sense to visit her son's teacher-to-be, well before his formal schooling began. As a result, the teacher was on the lookout for what sounded to him like a learning disability, a suspicion that was reinforced when Raghubar lagged the rest of the class when it began to learn letters. After six months now, in the first grade, it is clear the boy is not picking up what his classmates get. He recognizes only six letters, and in counting, gets to ten and becomes confused. Over half his class is already reading more or less independently.

When the teacher suggested to the principal that an IPRC might be in order, he got the two responses he expected: one, that Raghubar is far too young and undeveloped for such a major step; and two, that at this early stage the best strategy is to revise the boy's program. The teacher has now turned to his colleagues for help. Is a six year old too young and undeveloped to be called 'learning disabled', he wants to know? And, what program steps can he take right away, for a boy who does not count past ten, and recognizes only six letters?

A on paper (or the words "book" or "hook"). He may draw a teepee, but it may be disproportionate. On the other hand, he may be able to draw a beautiful teepee but when instructed to add a campfire at the left and a horse on the right, will have to guess at these juxtapositions.

Variations in Ability

What makes the language processing deficiency above so insidious is that it is so variable. If there are three students in the geography class who have learning disabilities, one of them might be entirely confused by the concept of "decolonialization" and miss everything else as a result. A second, unless there is a map right before him will be overwhelmed by all the verbal details of the countries mentioned. The third may understand the point perfectly and even be able to hypothesize on it, but three days later on the examination, she may be entirely unable to put together the language that will explain what she thinks.

The English Language is a Factor

The subtleties of English may pose a barrier for the learning disabled. A teacher for example, who says to a student, "I don't see your answer" may mean a number of different things. She may mean the answer is simply not visibly apparent, or that the answer was not completed, or that she does not understand the answer, or that she disagrees with it. Because some learning disabled students not only have difficulty with language, but even further difficulty in reading between the lines of communication situations and social contexts, they may respond incorrectly to "I don't see your answer" or, respond undiplomatically, or just not respond at all.

Language that attempts to capture time and sequence is another of the many stumbling blocks, in part because the language itself can be very complicated, and in part because chronology and sequence are problems all on their own. For example, in the sentence "Only after it first sprouts blossoms, can the tree bear fruit", the

---

Dyslexia versus Learning Disability ✍️☝️

The term 'dyslexia' was first used by a German ophthalmologist in 1877 to describe a phenomenon in which otherwise normal individuals seem to have great difficulty extracting meaning from print. Around the same time a pair of British doctors noted the disability but called it 'word-blindness', a term that was soon discarded. Over the decades since, a combination of genuine academic research, pop psychology and media fascination* have done much to fix 'dyslexia' in the public consciousness. An American organization with international affiliates, the Orton Dyslexia Society, named after neurologist Samuel Orton (whose work dates to the 1920s and 30s) has done even more to carry the idea forward, so that 'dyslexia' has become completely familiar in our culture.

For teachers and EAs, the issue is not so much whether dyslexia is real. Most professionals agree there are individuals who, although otherwise physically and intellectual-ly normal, are unable to extract meaning from print or to produce written text in a manner that is age appropriate. But confusion arises because 'dyslexia' is regularly used as a synonym for general learning disabilities (as is frequently the case in England, for example). Although for Canadian educators, 'dyslexia' usually means a specific difficulty—i.e., processing the printed word—such use of the term is not universal, so confusion may occur. The simple reality is that 'dyslexia' and 'learning disability' are not really one and the same inclusive term. The former describes a specific special need associated with language development. The latter has a far broader application, incorporating both language difficulties and other, non-language based learning problems. To use the two terms interchangeably does a disservice.

* Popular press items on 'dyslexia', regularly trot out a list of "famous dyslexics" like Alexander Graham Bell, Pablo Picasso, Jay Leno, Cher, John Lennon and others.

words and the syntax used to describe the sequence, set up real complication. The phrase, "only after" is at the *beginning* of the sentence. Yet it sets up a condition and presents a time frame for the rest of the sentence, which then describes what in effect must happen *before* "only after "! Efficient language users can usually comprehend such a sentence. Students with learning disabilities often do not. Still another barrier exists in the pronoun "it". Not only must "it" be held in short term memory until its referent ("tree") surfaces, the listener/reader must perceive that "it" refers to "tree" and not some other idea! (Research shows that the difficulty with pronouns normally experienced by young language learners, aged four and five, is experienced by the learning disabled well into their teenage and adult years.)

Difficulties like those above are compounded by learning disabled students' problems in relating one sentence to others in a passage, or in relating passages to passages, or even stories to stories, whether written or spoken.

Are We On the Same Wave Length?

One of the more unsettling aspects of the problem in processing language, for teachers, parents, and certainly for the students themselves, is the frustration of discovering that a communication which appeared to be successful, has been partly or even completely misunderstood or misinterpreted. (Admittedly, this is a common trait in all children, but what distinguishes the learning disabled is the consistency with which this occurs.) Because teachers, parents, and students often engage in a communication knowing that the potential for confusion is high, all parties often take extra care to be sure that the communication has meshed in a way that

what was *sent* is also what has been *received*. It is not difficult therefore, to imagine the stress that results when what appeared to be a successful interchange, was really two separate tracks of communication that overlapped from time to time but never bonded into that stage of information interchange we like to call *understanding*. The implications of this problem for life in general, and for the classroom especially, are significant. Whether it occurs solely because of faulty language processing or because of memory problems has yet to be clearly established. All that is known for sure is that it happens. Often.

Problems Remembering

An apparently poor memory for learning and for new information is another characteristic that distinguishes many students with a learning disability. They may, at the moment of instruction, learn a technique or an idea, or acquire information, or memorize a sequence or a formula at the same pace and in the same depth as their non-learning disabled colleagues. But unlike the latter, they will have difficulty retrieving it next day.

Accounting for this supposed memory problem has generated considerable speculation. One hypothesis is that the students forget because they cannot transfer learning and information from short term to long term memory, or at least, cannot do so easily. Another is that it is strictly a result of poor language processing: not a case of simple forgetting but of not getting a correct grasp of the material in the first place. (More recently, there has been argument, particularly from audiologists, that the faulty processing results from imperfections in the central auditory nerve.) None of the explanations is entirely

> In high school they put all us LDs in one class and that's the first time I ever felt comfortable. Nobody laughed if what I said made no sense because we were all in the same boat. See, if you're LD what you want to say isn't always what comes out. Sometimes only half comes out. Sometimes you even say the opposite of what you want to! Don't get me wrong, elementary was O.K., but there were times I thought I was on a different planet. So did the other kids! You see, I never understood anything first time. If two things came at me, I always missed the second one. (Still do!) Order is still a problem too. And jokes. I never got jokes! Pretended too, but... In high school, when we were all LD, then we could work on that stuff. Saved my life, I think. Still don't get jokes, though.
>
> *Moira M. (at her community college grad banquet)*

satisfactory. If the students cannot transfer from short to long term memory, then why can teachers and parents cite examples of phenomenal long term memory retention in learning disabled students? If the central auditory nerve is the culprit, why does the forgetting occur just as frequently with written language? And if language processing problems are the sole cause, why do learning disabled students so often make the same *social mistakes* time after time? (Learning disabled students frequently have difficult peer relations because of a seeming inability to gain from social experience. They continue to repeat social gaffes, seemingly not remembering what happened when a similar situation cropped up previously.)

Whatever the cause, it is essential to be aware that learning disabled students may not have retained what everyone else thinks they have — or should have. It inevitably shapes how we relate to them.

Poor Executive Function

In the matter of understanding the self, of being aware of the mind's activity, and of being sensitive to the strategies available for learning a task and of understanding the regulatory mechanisms needed to complete it, students with learning disabilities have another grave problem. Teachers and educational assistants can readily attest to the difficulty a learning disabled student has in taking on a project and organizing it through to completion. He or she finds it extremely difficult to know *how* to begin and *where* to begin. Finding information — the research component — is as problematic as is dealing with the information if it is found. And putting it together is overwhelming. Consequently, a student will almost invariably fail to complete an assignment without some very specific direction, not because he is avoiding or rejecting it (although by adolescence, avoidance does tend to be habituated) but because he simply does not know how to go about pulling it together. He needs *executive* help. (Parents particularly, are often frustrated observers of this characteristic in day-to-day living. Such matters as organizing one's own room, or hockey equipment, or toys, or hobby materials are managerial challenges for learning disabled children that go far beyond "just being a kid".)

An Upside to LD

In 2003, Tulip Financial Research Inc., an organization based in England, published a study which found that millionaires are significantly more likely to suffer from dyslexia. (In England, 'dyslexia' is generally used as a term rather than 'learning disabilities'.) About 40 percent of the 300 subjects in the study had been diagnosed with the condition. The researchers speculated that 'dyslexics' (i.e., the learning disabled) tend to be poor with details and compensate by grasping the big picture. Further, because they are not bogged down in detail and standardized procedures, they often produce original ideas.

Difficulties With Sequence and Order

Students with learning disabilities miss steps in a sequence, get them out of sequence, reverse the sequence, and as often as not, may simply ignore a sequence. Research has not been able to demonstrate clearly whether this is a cognitive or an affective characteristic but the weight of empirical evidence is in favour of the former interpretation.

Satisfaction With a Peripheral Understanding

An adolescent seeking a credit in chemistry, when asked what is Boyle's Law, might typically answer "Oh it's about pressure and that." The likelihood is he knows more: probably a definition of Boyle's Law, perhaps even an understanding of how to apply it in a problem. If this adolescent is learning disabled the answer "Pressure and that" may well constitute the sum total of his knowledge of the law. *Yet he will quite likely believe he has a thorough grasp of it*, and proceed comfortably in that self-assurance until confronted by a request to apply Boyle's Law to a problem. This is the same student who in grade two wrote three lines in his journal while the rest of the class averaged twenty. And who likely responded indignantly to a comment about such a slim output with something

Some Day-to-Day School Problems Associated with Learning Disabilities

Coordination/Cooperation

- may have difficulty lining up
- often confused or anxious over taking turns
- may bump, trip, or spill far more frequently than peers

Writing Skills

- may confuse letters in writing and in recitation
- mixes upper and lower case letters
- mixes manuscript and cursive styles, or will continue to use manuscript long after age and grade peers use cursive
- frequently distorts letter size and shape
- attempts at continuous text are scratchy, barely legible
- often mirrors or reverses letters
- awkward, even unnatural movement of the pen or pencil

Personal Organization

- forgets, misplaces things
- needs constant reminding (and often has successfully trained others to do this)
- frequently late or in the wrong place
- poor notion of chronological order
- may confuse instructions especially if there is more than one step

Copying/Note-Making

- careless, often reproduces inaccurately
- loses place often
- far-point copying very slow and inaccurate
- overprints, telescopes, omits
- may have difficulty reproducing a shape from memory
- ignores sub-headings and organization cues

Arithmetic

- reverses numbers
- careless about columnar structure
- may not remember rote matters (multiplication tables)
- carries or borrows wrong digit
- skips or omits steps in problem solving

Reading/Language

- loses place regularly
- makes many flying guesses
- does not attempt a new or strange word
- ignores punctuation and other cues
- makes up words, telescopes
- reverses and transposes
- loses meaning of a sentence from beginning to end
- gets events out of sequence
- infers content that is not there
- forgets details
- does not seem to retain a basic stock of spelling words
- often uses creative, phonetic spelling

Work Speed

- very often does not finish
- works slower than age and grade peers
- frustrated under time pressure

Social

- may relate poorly to peers
- often repeats a social error
- may fail to "read" the wishes of others
- often has difficulty keeping friends
- frequently on the fringe of groups

---

like "I *did* my journal." or "That's all I have to say!" The key feature is the student's satisfaction with a vague, incomplete, peripheral piece of work, *and* his conviction that it is adequate. This is a crucial behaviour for educators to recognize. It's not defiance; it is not shirking; and it is not an utter lack of ability. It is a misinterpretation of what constitutes completeness.

Poor Time Management

It is not surprising that a student who rarely plans ahead and even more rarely accommodates her activity to due dates and timetables, is frequently late, or in the wrong place, or in conflict with some time-specific requirement, or is just chronically off-task. Many learning disabled students seem to be unaware of time, or at least of time as a concept organized into sequentially discrete units. This page in the LD catalogue accounts for a significant portion of their trouble in school. Because schools are so time-driven, so inflexibly organized into chronological chunks — sequenced, hierarchical, chronological chunks — the student often feels entirely out of place. School bewilders her not just because of its emphasis on language (and its commensurate de-emphasis of non-language elements like music and art and athletics where she may shine) but also because of its apparent obsession with time in specified units. Regrettably, the outside world is equally passionate about time, and learning to deal with that is a necessary prerequisite in all of education. It is not unusual for a student with learning disabilities to perform better, both generally and academically, in an environment where she is liberated somewhat from the demands of time.

Inconsistent and Episodic

What is at once tantalizing and frustrating for anyone who tries to view the field of learning disabilities objectively (viz., teachers, paraprofessionals, parents, academics, medical professionals, et al.) is the knowledge that a learning disabled student's profile is never the same day after day, and that a single characteristic of learning disability is never universal. A student with this disability may regularly write "on" for "no" and "b" for "d", yet in the same sentence use all four elements correctly. He may use "on" for "no" consistently for three weeks, and then suddenly and spontaneously use them correctly while simultaneously begin writing "was" for "saw", even though those had been correctly used hitherto. This is the adolescent who cannot remember a single irregular verb in French, or the formula for calculating the area of a circle, or the definition of alliteration but who, on a warm Saturday, can strip down, clean, repair, and completely reassemble a mountain bike. This is the child who bumps into everyone in the queue, whose shoes are untied and whose shirttail hangs out, but who is the first in his age group to earn Red Cross badges for swimming excellence. This is the one who forgets where he put his clothes, his books, and his lunch, who confuses his telephone number and his address, but can recite without error, a T.V. ad or the lyrics of a song.

It is an acknowledged fact by all associated with the learning disabled that no one student will be the same as another, and that no one student's own pattern will ever be consistent and regular. This phenomenon, among other things, makes learning disabled students almost completely resistant to positive identification by formal standardized tests. It bears equally important weight for the classroom teacher who must be ever prepared to adjust to the episodic nature of their performance. And of course for parents, it is yet one more arrow in the quiver of confusion.

Difficulty Paying Attention

That learning disabled students do not attend as well in class as their more academically successful colleagues is a given. What is less clear is the cause. Do they fail to attend because years of confusion have taught the value of avoidance? Or is the habit innate? The question is a continuing debate in the field. Whether the characteristic is inherent or learned, the simple fact is that most learning disabled students do not concentrate in school (and often at home) in sufficient depth or for sufficient time to learn or acquire new information or receive instruction effectively. This attention problem is expressed in forms that vary from simple daydreaming to pervasive, counter-productive activity.

Very Low Self-Esteem

Of all the commonly occurring traits in the learning disabled, this one is not inherent but acquired. And the cause, at least as far as school is concerned, is fairly obvious. In a system, in a tradition that not only rewards but celebrates academic achievement, it is easy to understand that a student who consistently fails to achieve at anywhere near the expected standards, will develop serious doubts about his whole persona. What makes this characteristic so damaging is that it feeds a continuous loop. A student with a learning disability who has become accustomed to low achievement, also becomes accustomed to putting out minimal effort on the quite understandable premise that there is no point if there is no payoff. Therefore the achievement level decreases even further, both because it may have been affected in the first place by the learning disability, but also by lack of effort. As a result, neither teacher nor parent, nor the student gets to see how good the results really could be. Even worse, both sides become so accustomed to poor achievement that on the rare occasions of success they often look first for the fluke that brought it about!

The next link in this chain is invariably behavioural. Students develop personas to divert attention from their disability and their failure and to attract attention to other matters. The class clown, the victim, the super-competent, the I-don't-care, the bad-guy — these are all popular masks that learning disabled students wear.

Assessment and Identification

By Standardized IQ and Achievement Tests

IQ tests and standardized achievement tests are too narrow to capture the complexity of a learning disability, at least in ways that would bene-

fit the student or his teachers. Most of the time, these instruments simply offer a number that reveals what everyone knows already, although a number may have purpose if it is needed to pry loose funds, or to set the table for an administrative action. Another weakness in the use of these tests lies in the episodic nature of learning disabilities, for very often the same instrument will produce an entirely different result on consecutive days, thus diminishing its reliability. Even more important, at least in the classroom, tests do not point to practical, helpful, strategies that classroom personnel can use.

Nevertheless, extensive formal testing to uncover learning disability continues, possibly because it is a long established practice (or perhaps because it offers at least a feeling that something is being done!). Therefore, in situations where this type of instrument is used, it is important that the results be seen as only one of several clues.

By Teacher-EA-Parent Teamwork

Experience shows that classroom professionals, working cooperatively with parents, and often with the input of other professionals, are in the best position to establish the presence or absence of a learning disability with considerable certainty. In fact, this kind of teamwork,

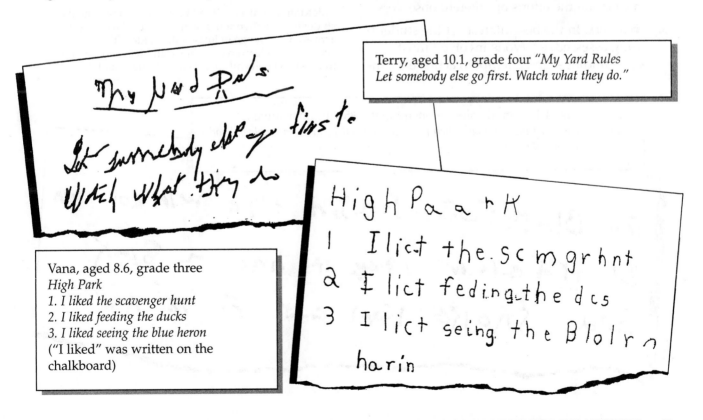

Terry, aged 10.1, grade four *"My Yard Rules Let somebody else go first. Watch what they do."*

Vana, aged 8.6, grade three
High Park
1. *I liked the scavenger hunt*
2. *I liked feeding the ducks*
3. *I liked seeing the blue heron*
("I liked" was written on the chalkboard)

shaped by a few prerequisites, may be the only way to make a diagnosis with confidence. The prerequisites are disarmingly simple.

1. *Understand the exceptionality.* To diagnose and identify a learning disability, one must be clearly aware of the characteristics that make up this special need. Because a learning disability does not yield to a definable set of criteria in the same way that a hearing loss, for example, does to an audiometric assessment, to uncover the presence a learning disability, one must first know what to look for empirically.

2. *Observe carefully.* Armed with the knowledge of what to look for (and sufficiently informed by that knowledge to go looking) it follows that the an effective way of making the identification is to watch for clear evidence of some or all of the characteristics.

3. *Take time.* Since a learning disability is episodic by nature, it is a given that observation must take place over a period of time. Learning disabilities are not revealed in a one-shot assessment.

4. *Use informal aids.* Rating scales, questionnaires, informal reading inventories and the like can be of assistance, especially in providing specific focus on a student's needs, and in collating the efforts of different observers.

5. *Teamwork.* In the best interests of the student being assessed, everyone involved must share findings, and attempt to achieve a consensus. A team is more likely to impose caution on the identification process. Because the presence of a learning disability is difficult to pin down, and because every human being exhibits some LD characteristics some of the time, the broader view available to a team helps to keep things in perspective.

Some Issues in the Field

◆ *Universal acceptance of a definition* of learning disabilities continues to elude those who care about this special need. Nor do the many extant definitions, both official and otherwise seem to be coalescing around key points in any noticeable way.

◆ *Assessing* the presence and extent of a learning disability in a manner that produces clear, indisputable results does not seem to be possible.

◆ *Co-occurring disabilities*, most commonly AD/HD and behaviour disorders are a constant challenge. Not only is the presence of other special needs difficult to identify and assess*, the very notion is a challenge to administrators charged with service deliv-

• • •
* McKinney et al. (1993) in "Educational assessment of students with attention deficit disorders" reported that across a wide range of jurisdictions, identification of co-occurrence of learning disability and behaviour varied from 9 to 80 percent! *Exceptional Children*, 60, 125-31.
• • •

Cameron, aged 15.3, grade nine — opening of a 95 word narrative …
"A black robe faced the window. When it turned around I saw it had a black hood. Snakes came out of the hood."

a BlaK roB FaSid tle windol wn
It trd arun i say it had a BlaK
hod Snaiks Kam cut cF th hod

ery and to those who must address the situation day to day in the classroom. Interestingly, empirical evidence seems to suggest that the issue is a far greater concern at the bureaucratic level, where formal identification, funding and placement are matters of daily importance. In the classroom, teachers and educational assistants tend to find themselves addressing co-occurring disabilities in a manner similar to that in which they approach students with (presumably) only one special need.

✦ *Integrating* learning disabled students into regular classes or educating them in self-contained classes, is always up for discussion. The principal advocacy group in the field, the Learning Disabilities Association (LDA) is generally supportive of the idea that schools should maintain the option of self-contained resource placement for some students. Because the trend toward inclusion continues, however, and given the numbers of students identified as learning disabled, teachers of regular classes should always expect to have one or more — usually more — such students in their classes.

✦ *Gender representation* has been a niggling concern for years and is no closer to being explained than it ever was. Data show that males outnumber females by at least two to one in the category of learning disability. Yet, examination of data from any typical Canadian jurisdiction will show that this phenomenon is equally true of almost every category of exceptionality, and these have never been explained either.

✦ *Overidentification?* Available data show that learning disabled students outnumber their peers in any other category of special need. (This is not an Ontario phenomenon; these data are similar to those in other provinces and in the U.S.) Such numbers continue to provoke accusations of gross misidentification, and of excessive "dumping", viz., underperforming students are simply called learning disabled because that relieves the school system, the parents, and the students themselves of any blame for doing poorly. While there are few educators who would deny that this kind of escape indeed takes place, the accusation is very much unwar-

ranted. Awareness of learning disability is relatively new in education and it follows that there may well have been a rush to identify students who fit so ideally into the category. Evidence that current numbers of identified learning disabled students are probably realistic can be found by examining prevalence and incidence data over the past thirty years. The sharp rise in numbers over the late sixties and through the seventies began to slow in the mid-eighties, and numbers have remained quite consistent since.

✦ *Quackery or experimental science?* Even before the term learning disability became popular, there were many unusual therapies, techniques and teaching methods available to deal with students who, despite apparently normal ability, spoke incomprehensibly, or wrote in most unusual ways, or generally performed in ways that are off the mark for their age. (See the writing examples in this chapter.) It would have been fairly common practice at one time, for example, to engage students like Vana and Terry in extensive calisthenic exercises to—theoretically—develop their "visual-motor integration skills". Very often, popular support for these unusual techniques blossomed as a result of endorsements and "gee whiz" articles in non-refereed journals. Usually, the popularity of a technique declined after it was submitted to careful scrutiny.

Still, it is unfair to dismiss unusual teaching methods out of hand, if only because, given the uncertainty over just what constitutes a learning disability, any response demands at least rational consideration. An example of an idea that met with derision and later, more serious reflection is "scotopic sensitivity", first broached by the Irlen Institute in California, which advanced the theory that a type of visual flaw impairs some students' reading ability, and can be treated by having them wear coloured lenses. While the idea quite understandably challenges educators' common sense, evaluations reported in the *Journal of Learning Disabilities* (1990, 23,10) makes clear that the Irlen approach merits consideration in some cases.

Ultimately, a resolution to this issue rests in professionalism. Educators must, first of all, be open to examination of apparently unusual or even radical means to address a learning disability, an openness that presumes, secondly, they will stay abreast of the literature.

✔ STRATEGIES FOR THE CLASSROOM

(1) Empathy and understanding are prerequisite qualities in any person hoping to offer instruction to the learning disabled (although this point is likely redundant to an effective teacher). Once one "gets inside" the particular nature of learning disabled students, making the necessary steps of accommodation follows naturally. A teacher must set up a warm, supportive climate, without pandering to, or making excuses for, or drawing unnecessary attention to the students' particular needs. The older the students are, the more difficult this task tends to be, for they will likely have well-established and annoying avoidance behaviours, developed over years of practice. Yet, unless a teacher has an appreciation of what his or her students are contending with, and unless there is some sensitivity toward that, all efforts will eventually degenerate into despair and conflict. An environment of mutual trust is crucial for teaching all students with exceptionalities, but for the learning disabled there is an added, subtle layer. These students usually do not appear at first to be handicapped in any way; in fact they often seem as though they should be especially successful. But they are not, and most of the time, they do not understand why, any more than the adults in their lives do. Such is the insidious nature of a learning disability. It is why empathy and understanding on the part of the teacher are so important.

(2) Positive, frequent feedback as quickly as possible, especially on academic matters, is crucial. This helps practically, by keeping the student on task, and more abstractly, by reinforcing momentum, the component so necessary for continuing academic success and achievement. A learning disabled student, especially if he has had a history of failure, is not willing to defer gratification as successful students do. He needs reassurance and reinforcement to build self-esteem to a point where he'll put forth his best effort. Fortunately, this kind of feedback does not have to be dramatic (although an occasional "celebration" can work wonders). Simple attention to even modest achievement is often all that is necessary to develop self-esteem.

(3) A consistent, systematic approach will help the learning disabled student eventually learn to interpret and accommodate expectations. Part of this approach will be a firm insistence on on-task behaviour and thoroughness. Perhaps a more encompassing term would be *structure*. The very nature of the learning disabled student's day-to-day cognitive function means that not only classroom instruction but such apparently simple things as classroom regulations and expectations must be clearly outlined, with the parameters firmly established. Teachers must remember that a learning disabled student not only does not learn or manage himself as effectively as he might, he usually does not know how. If his teacher establishes the boundaries and points out the steps, both self-management and learning become easier. (And once a structure is established, it is also easier for the teacher to be empathetic and supportive because an operating context has been established which both parties understand.)

(4) Graphic and visual support benefits learning disabled students significantly. Use of the blackboard, overhead transparencies, pictures, maps, and other concrete supports, helps them to comprehend what might otherwise be a mass of confusion. In fact, many successful teachers assert that it is impossible to teach otherwise. A positive note here is that while graphic and visual support are essential for the learning disabled, they are also helpful techniques for all students.

(5) Help in sequencing is important. Teachers must emphasize steps and stages in the proper order as a lesson progresses. The same applies to all assignments, projects, homework or any other item that requires independent and individual completion. Without guidance in where to begin, and what organization to follow, the learning disabled student will become con-

fused and likely as not tune out or give up. Learning disabled students need 'maps'.

(6) Help in dealing with print is important for many learning disabled students. Reading, as well as producing legible and coherent text, can be a difficult and time-consuming procedure, so not only must a teacher recognize that challenge and make allowances in time, he may well have to modify the challenge, by simplifying instructions, for example.

(7) Awareness of time constraints, one of the realities of school that regular students pick up quickly, is yet another factor that teachers must factor in for their learning disabled students. Many do not forward plan, and it may well take their entire school careers before they learn the responsibilities inherent in due dates, appointments and scheduling. Yet they can and do eventually acquire these skills, however imperfectly, and for that reason it is essential that their teachers persist. (Both parents and teachers attest that this issue is one of the most frustrating, and one that offers the strongest temptation to simply give up.)

(8) "Staying-on-top of things", for lack of a more professional-sounding phrase, may be an apt way of describing all those apparently superficial, but in reality, fundamental behaviours, that a teacher must help her learning disabled students to exercise. Drawing the student's attention to signal words, counseling about sequence and about time, reminding him to bring and take, cueing things by saying "Watch for the change here." and "This is important." — all these seemingly small things go together to help the student cope with daily life in the classroom. It is part of developing his sense of 'executive function'. Software programs are particularly useful here, and for suggestion #9 also.

(9) Making allowances for those skills which the learning disabled never ever seem to master, is another part of the teacher's role. Correct spelling, for example, is an expectation many almost never meet, and to pursue it relentlessly is counter-productive. It is far more

effective both in short and long term to teach them how to use a dictionary effectively, or to get help via software. Similarly, since they never seem to master the memorization of multiplication tables, it makes sense to forgo the memorization requirement. Other matters, simple on the surface to most of us, frequently escape learning disabled students. Multiple choice questions for example, so time-honoured and so commonly used, often have a subtlety that totally confounds. So does convoluted syntax. An attempt to persuade, for example, by saying "Inasmuch as the field day is on Monday and the movie on Wednesday, wouldn't you be better to get the project done this week?" will not succeed like this will: "Finish the project this week, because next week we have a field day and a movie. There will be no time to do it next week".

(10) Simplifying the environment. Within the boundaries of what is practical and sensible, simply by removing distractions, a teacher can make a difference. Sometimes the seating arrangement in a room or the adjacent surroundings of a learning disabled student can be modified to his benefit.

(11) Finally, as evanescent as **hope and optimism** may seem, they are the glue, along with **trust** and **encouragement** that hold the relationship of teacher and student together. A learning disabled student, usually far more than his peers, will respond to a stimulus, not so much because of a vague awareness that it is part of his education, but rather, because his teacher, the one he trusts and respects, has asked him to. It is a reality that imposes a heavy responsibility on the teacher, but then, without that reality, the art of teaching would not be as exciting. Or as rewarding. It is trust and encouragement and hope and optimism that lead to the extra steps, the extra efforts, the one-more-times, and ultimately, to the breakthroughs. Realistically, breakthroughs are not all that frequent. What is far more common is plodding progress, but then progress of any kind is worth the effort.

TWO SIMPLE ESSENTIALS: Time & Drill

Special education is especially susceptible to allegedly novel instructional concepts often hailed as quasi-'cures'. Most of these flare up and dominate the stage for a time before being abandoned or else incorporated into regular classroom practice, usually with more than a little modification. Most of the time, these leading-edge teaching strategies (and the lofty vocabulary that typically accompanies them) are simply elevated re-castings of time-honoured, sound classroom practice. When teachers take a moment to analyze techniques like 'scaffolded instruction' or 'metacognitive training', or 'mnemonic keyword method', for example, they often recognize methods they have already been using, albeit modified to their own purposes. One positive outcome of these models of instruction, is that they give special education practices an elevated status. A drawback is that they tend to divert attention from the merit of simple ideas that experience has proven valuable. Two of these simple ideas, long known to be effective with students who are learning disabled, are *expanded instruction time* and *drill*. We draw extra attention to them here, lest they are ignored for lack of apparent sophistication.

Time: Learning disabled students take longer to learn, and teaching them a concept, a technique, a set of facts, therefore, simply takes more instructional time. As any experienced teacher will attest, learning disabled students often need to be re-taught, or taught the same lesson in a different manner, or with different materials. And they need time to redo and review on their own until the lesson is firm. The following formula illustrates the point.

$$\frac{\text{quality of}}{\text{instruction}} \times \left(\frac{\text{time spent}}{\text{time needed}}\right) = \frac{\text{degree of}}{\text{learning}}$$

For example, if quality of instruction is represented by an arbitrary factor of '5', and if the time needed by the student is also '5', but time spent is '1', the results are modest.

$$5 \times {}^1\!/_5 = 1$$

Notice that even if the quality of instruction is doubled (to a factor of 10) the effects are still modest if the time spent does not match the time needed

$$10 \times {}^1\!/_5 = 2$$

But if the time actually spent equates more closely to the time the student needs, the results are significantly different

$$5 \times {}^5\!/_5 = 5$$

Like any formula laid over something as abstract and individual as learning, this one is guilty of oversimplification. Yet it illustrates the potential impact when a profound need of the typical learning disabled student—*enough time*—is addressed.

Drill: A logical correlate of time is *drill* (or "opportunity to reinforce by practice" if a more elevated description is preferred). Both through research and empiricism, teachers know that practice—drill—plays an important part in learning. Can it be less than reasonable to assume then that learning disabled students, who find learning difficult, require more opportunity to practice until they have something down pat? Granted, going over previously traveled ground is tedious, but no procedure has yet been found, scientific or otherwise, that equals the effect of repeating something often enough until it becomes part of a student's repertoire.

The sentence by Cameron below is the fifth rewrite of the item that appears on page 68. A resource room EA assisted Cameron with rewrites 2, 3, and 4. This is an independent effort.

A black note fas faced the window. When it turned arond I saw it hada had a black hood. Snakes came out of the hood.

Attention Deficit Disorder Not here.

READINGS & RESOURCES

Aylwards, E.H. (2003). Instructional treatment associated with changes in brain activities in children with dyslexia. *Neurology, 61*(2).

Deshler, D.D., Ellis, E.S., & Lenz, B.K. (1996). *Teaching adolescence with learning disabilities: Strategies and methods.* Denver: Love Publishing Inc.

Dyson, L.L. (1996). The experiences of families of children with learning disabilities: Parental stress, family functioning, and sibling self-concept. *Journal of Learning Disabilities, 29*, 280-286.

Dyson, L.L. (2003). Children with learning disabilities within the family context: a comparison with siblings in global self-concept, academic self-concept, academic self-perception, and social competence. *Learning Disabilities Research and Practice, 18*(1), 1-9.

Ferretti, R. P., & Okolo, C. M. (1996). Authenticity in learning: Multimedia design projects in the social studies for students with disabilities. *Journal of Learning Disabilities, 29*(5), 450-459.

Gersten, R. (1998). Recent advances in instructional research for students with learning disabilities: An overview. *Learning Disabilities Research and Practice, 13*(3), 153-172.

Gresham (1997 November/December). We need a better way to identify students with learning disabilities. *CEC Today*, p.14.

Hallenbeck, M. J. (1996). The cognitive strategy in writing: Welcome relief for adolescents with learning disabilities. *Learning Disabilities Research and Practice, 11*, 107-119.

Higgins, E. L., & Raskind, M. H. (1995). Compensatory effectiveness of speech recognition on the written composition performance of post secondary students with learning disabilities. *Learning Disability Quarterly, 18*, 159-176.

Hinchelwood, J. (1917). *Congenital word blindness.* H.K.Lewis.

Hughes, C.A. (1996). Memory and test-taking strategies. In D. D. Deshler, E. S. Ellis, & B.

K. Lenz (Eds.), *Teaching adolescents with learning disabilities* (2nd ed.). Denver: Love.

Huntington, D. D., & Bender, W. N. (1993). Adolescents with learning disabilities at risk? Emotional well-being, depression, suicide. *Journal of Learning Disabilities, 26*, 159-166.

Jitendra, A.K., Edwards, C.M., Choutka, C.M., & Treadway, P.S. (2002). A collaborative approach to planning in the content areas for students with learning disabilities: Assessing the general curriculum. *Learning Disabilities Research and Practice, 17*(4), 252-267.

Levy, N.R. (1996). Teaching analytical writing: Help for general education middle school teachers. *Intervention in School and Clinic, 33*(2), 95-103.

Mavis, L., Donahue, M.L., & Pearl, R. (2003). Studying social development and learning disabilities is not for the faint hearted: Comments on risk/resilience framework. *Learning disabilities Research and Practice, 18*(2), 2003, 90-93.

McKenzie, R. G. (1991). Content area instruction delivered by secondary learning disabilities teachers: A national survey. *Learning Disabilities Quarterly, 14*, 115-122.

Raskind, M. H., Herman, K. L., & Torgeson, J. K. (1995). Technology for persons with learning disabilities: Report on an international symposium. *Learning Disability Quarterly, 18*, 175-184.

Rea, P.J., McLaughlin, V.L., & Walther-Thomas, C. (2002). Outcomes for students with learning disabilities in inclusive pull out programs. *Exceptional Children, 68*(2), 203-222.

Richardson, S. (1992). Historical perspectives of dyslexia. *Journal of Learning Disabilities, 25*(1), 40-47.

Salend, S.J., & Hofsetter, E. (1996). Adapting a problem-solving approach to teaching mathematics to students with mild disabilities. *Intervention in School and Clinic, 31*(4), 209-207.

Sherman, G. F. (1995). Dyslexia: Is it all in your mind? *Perspectives, 21*(4), 1.

Speece, D.L., & Shekitka, L. (2002). How should reading disabilities be operationalized? A survey of experts. Learning Disabilities Research and Practice, 17(2), 118-123.

Strong Scott, M., Fletcher, K.L., & Stoyko Deuel L.L. (1998). The effects of intelligence on the identification young children with learning disabilities. *Learning Disabilities Research and Practice, 13*(2), 81-89.

Swanson, H.L. (1993). Executive processing in learning disabled readers. *Intelligence, 17*(2), 117-149.

Welch, M. (1992). The PLEASE strategy. A metacognitive learning strategy for improving the paragraph writing of students with mild learning disabilities. *Learning Disability Quarterly, 15,* 119-128.

Wong, B. (Ed.) (1995). *Learning about Learning Disabilities* (2nd Ed.). California: Academic Press Ltd.

Links

Learning Disabilities Association of Canada **http://www.ldac-taac.ca/**

LD on line **http://www.ldonline.org/**

National Council for Learning Disabiities **http://www.ncld.org/**

Learning Disabilities Association of Ontario **http://www.ldao.on.ca/**

CHAPTER 7

Students With Behaviour Disorders
Students with AD/HD

*"He turned 22 yesterday, Alvin did, and I still don't find this easy to talk about.
Right from kindergarten he was in trouble: punching, kicking, fighting. I bet he missed
two years in elementary sitting on the VP's bench. The worst part is he didn't care!
About anything! And nothing worked—rewards, punishments, you name it.
Then in high school the bullying and the stealing started. Makes me sick thinking about it.
Thank God for that music teacher. Her and the special ed teachers. They're the ones started
the turnaround. I still worry but... I don't know...at least it seems better now."*

Marilyn, mother of Alvin, identified with a behaviour disorder at age 7.

Misconceptions About Behaviour Disorders

1. Youth violence has increased significantly since the mid to late twentieth century.

Educators, legal authorities and community workers find it to difficult to establish whether the increase is real, whether data collection is more rigorous, or merely whether perceptions have changed. (A 1999 Canadian study* found that while 56.4 percent in a sample of secondary school administrators believed violence in schools had increased, only 28.1 percent believed this was true in their own schools!)

2. Developments in mental health science have made the identification and classification of behaviour disorders simpler and easier for educators.

The dominating schemata for clinical description and classification is the American

Psychiatric Association's *Diagnostic and Statistical Manual of Mental Disorders†*. The DSM, however, classifies disorders as either present or absent. To most classroom teachers and assistants, behaviour problems are far more subtle.

3. Bullying is an age-old, natural schoolyard phenomenon and students learn to deal with it as part of growing up.

While educators have long been aware of bullying as a reality of the schoolyard, it is now known that the phenomenon can have long-term consequence for both the bully and the victim.

• • • ————

* Dolmage, W.R. (1999). Lies, Damned Lies and Statistics: The Media's Treatment of Youth Violence. *Education & Law Journal, 10*, 4-46. (The article describes misconceptions created by media on the issue.)
† At time of publication of this text, the Diagnostic and Statistical Manual of Mental Disorders was in Revised Fourth Edition (2000), or DSM-IV-R. It is usually referred to simply as the DSM.

———— • • •

4. Behaviour disorders are neither age nor gender related.

Most studies show identified cases of males outnumber females by ratios of up to 5 to 1. In the last decade of the twentieth century, however, new data began to show significant rate increases for girls over boys, in identified behaviour and in crime.

5. There is no relationship between single-parent families and behaviour problems.

Statistics Canada reported in 1998, that children in single-parent families have behavioural, emotional, academic or social problems at a greater rate than children of two-parent families.

6. Behaviour disorders are manifested in patterns of aggression and frustration.

There is no doubt that outward-directed behaviour is noticeable and may well be disordered. However, symptoms of behaviour disorder can also be expressed by reticence and withdrawal. The latter is not as easily noticed, particularly in large classroom groupings.

7. Very often a behaviour disorder indicates a student who is bright but frustrated.

Available data suggest a correlation between behaviour disorders and average to low IQ test scores, with the more severe cases even lower.

8. Difficult behaviour is an external manifestation of something deep-rooted.

There is no sound evidence that all the causes of behaviour are rooted deep in a student's psyche, or even necessarily connected to emotional disturbance. Especially in school, inappropriate behaviour is often spontaneous and temporary.

9. A permissive atmosphere that allows students to develop understanding and acceptance of the self, is the most effective way to change inappropriate behaviour.

Evidence suggests that a highly structured, ordered, and predictable environment brings about the greatest change in students with a behaviour disorder.

What is a Behaviour Disorder?

To most people, disordered behaviour is behaviour that varies markedly and chronically from accepted norms. In a general way then, the notion is quite widely accepted and understood much in the same way that a general notion of *normal* behaviour is widely accepted and understood. It is from this point that differences develop, for there seems to be remarkably little agreement as to exactly where on the continuum from normal to otherwise, behaviour

Bullies and Their Victims ✍

Bullying behaviour varies among individuals but three behaviours appear to be common: it is a repeated action over time; it takes place in relationships where there is an imbalance of power; and it is unprovoked. While research—and schoolyard observation—suggests that more boys than girls engage in the behaviour, many teachers insist that more rigorous investigations will inevitably reveal that girls tend to use more subtle, less visible methods to accomplish their ends. Very often, the act of bullying is part of a wider set of behaviour problems. Bullies are often in conflict with authorities, tend to be depressed, are prone to a life style that compromises their health, and often have problems with peer relationships.

Victims tend to have lower self-esteem and some manifest rather disturbed behaviour, although it is not clear whether this is a condition that arises from the bullying or is pre-existing.

Although a prevailing perception in the early twenty-first century is that bullying has become rampant, it is extremely difficult to establish hard data to support that belief because bullying has become a treasured subject of the media, and also because most schools have enacted rigorous policies that may of themselves elevate incidence statistics. Based on other studies of chronically violent individuals, the long term prognosis for bullies does not appear to be good.

becomes aberrant. Social and cultural conditions, are influencing factors. Certain cultures, for example, have very permissive ideas about child rearing, and when the children of that culture, the young particularly, encounter a dominant group where child rearing values are more structured and restrictive, it is not hard to see why the different values may lead to perceptions of behaviour disorder.

Other factors too, influence perceptions of what is disordered behaviour. Even within a single social setting such as a school there can be wide differences, for the same behaviour may be seen as disruptive by one teacher but normal by another. Then there are the realities that all children display varying behaviours and that behaviour patterns increase and decline over time within a single individual. Special educators are especially aware that patterns of conduct are affected by disabling conditions. Students with hearing problems can become extremely frustrated by their inability to comprehend; the same is true of students with visual abilities (especially younger ones whose condition has not yet been diagnosed) and equally true of those with developmental or learning disabilities.

In order to create a common ground of understanding, mental health professionals particularly have attempted to organize behaviour disorders by classification (as in the DSM). Unfortunately consensus among this group is still limited. Interestingly, educators seem to have less difficulty with the issue, possibly because they have a more unified perspective and a more clearly delineated set of common objectives. Immediately following is a brief description of the more popular views held by mental health professionals, and of the general view held by educators.

The View From Mental Health

Mental health professionals tend to view behaviour disorders from a particular perspective or theory or enveloping concept, a tendency that affects the research they do, their treatment styles, and the way they attempt to educate others. Listed here is a very brief summary of the more widely held theories.

- *Environmental* Factors in the environment, including diet, air pollution, metals, etc. lead to behaviour problems. (Note that this concept is often held in concert with one or more of the others listed below.)

- *Psychodynamic* People with behaviour problems are experiencing deep-rooted inner turmoil and their deviations are a manifestation of this.

- *Psychosocial* (sometimes called *Ecological*) An individual's relationship with family and peers may bring on inappropriate or unacceptable behaviour.

- *Psychoeducational* A student's behaviour may be owing to a combination of circumstances that are brought about in school.

- *Behaviourist* Deviation from normal is the result of having been taught the wrong things or by following inappropriate role models.

- *Biophysical* Deficiencies in genetics, neurology, biochemistry, along with disease and malnutrition cause deviant behaviour.

- *Combinations* Some or all of the above theories appear in combination.

The View From Education

Most teachers, educational assistants, child care workers and others responsible for the students with behaviour disorders, accept the value of classifications for mental health purposes, but do not find them very practical on the front lines. Thus, while the classifications used by mental health professionals may be informative, or may have some administrative value, or may possibly be used by a multidisciplinary team, the prevailing style in education is to approach the notion of behaviour disorder without terminology. In determining whether or not a student might be behaviour disordered, an assessment team will almost always consider exclusionary factors: whether or not the behaviour can be traced to specific sensory, social or health-related causes. Nevertheless, even if a student's inappropriate behaviour can be explained as a direct outcome of some specific, explainable factor, he or she might still be identified as behaviour disordered, for the simple reason that no matter what the cause, it is still the behaviour — the effect — that the educators must deal with.

When educators identify a student as having a behaviour disorder, they generally do so on the basis that he or she:

✓ deviates in a significant manner from the behaviour that is normally expected in the situation;

✓ breaks social or cultural norms that are usually well established for the age level;

✓ shows a tendency toward compulsive and impulsive behaviour that negatively affects learning;

✓ has poor interpersonal relationships, and low self-esteem;

✓ has low academic achievement owing to conduct;

✓ (perhaps the most important) manifests any or all of the above characteristics intensely and consistently over a period of time such that special education is likely required.

Behaviour Disorders: on the Rise?

Behaviour that deviates from the norm attracts a disproportionate amount of attention from the media, an interest which leads to a perception that the prevalence of disorders is on the increase. The increase may indeed be real. Or not. Most of the time, research data simply confirms what teachers and educational assistants already know: that boys outnumber girls, particularly in aggression and hyperactivity; that prevalence rates are highest in the upper grades of elementary school and first grades of secondary school, and lowest in the primary grades; and that there tends to be a higher rate of aggressive behaviours among children from lower socioeconomic groups. Yet the value of data collection should never be disregarded. It is widely believed, for example, even by teachers, that students are being identified 'behaviour' in Ontario at a very rapidly increasing rate. Yet between 1998-99 and 2001-02, while the total student population in the province increased by 2.9 percent, the number of students in the behaviour category grew by 3.7 percent.* Hardly a rapid increase, especially in a time period that saw

great attention focused on bullying and zero tolerance. The relatively contained rate of increase in this climate is a tribute perhaps, to special educators in Ontario and their ability to manage, but certainly it is an indication that the popular perception differs somewhat from the reality.

Causes of Behaviour Disorders

Biophysical

The majority of students who have behaviour disorders appear to be physically healthy. Nevertheless, recent theory and research suggest possible links between biological makeup and behaviour. Sometimes the connection is clearly, if also distressingly, apparent. Children born with fetal alcohol syndrome or fetal alcohol effects are a case in point (see chapter on intellectual disabilities). The causes of pervasive development disorder (autism) have become an area of extensive research —and speculation — inasmuch as biology is concerned. Research in genetics is provoking a continuing reassessment of disorders like schizophrenia. As recently as 2003, an Ontario judge sentenced a fourteen year old girl to two years probation, after she had pleaded guilty to aggravated assault on a teacher. The sentencing was very much affected by testimony that the girl's behaviour was influenced by a particularly powerful premenstrual syndrome. Biology, it seems, is now being considered in cases of behaviour disorder, almost as a matter of course.

Allergies

Allergies too are being re-evaluated as causes of disordered behaviour. While the physical effects of allergies on some students are readily acknowledged, a more recent conception of allergies incorporates the thesis that allergenic reactions can generate learning and behaviour problems in a far deeper and more subtle way than the very obvious physical reactions. A widely accepted notion now, is *total load*: the idea that an individual has a capacity to tolerate only so much substance in the environment,

• • • ─────

* All publicly funded schools. *Source: Ministry of Ed., School September Report.*

───────── • • •

and in some individuals, say, a student in a classroom, a combination of stale air, chalk dust, moulds and fungi in the carpet, and perfume or shaving lotion on the teacher, may exceed that student's tolerance (total load) and cause an allergic reaction expressed both in a physical way (e.g., a rash or watery eyes or sneezing) and in her behaviour. These reactions are often far more subtle yet profound than may be immediately apparent.

Speech and Language

Researchers have consistently found a higher incidence of behaviour disorders among students with speech and language impairments than is found in the general population. While there is some debate in the field over whether language impairment is a cause or an effect of behaviour disorder, it seems logical to conclude that a student who has difficulty expressing his needs —or his frustrations — may choose to act

them out. Either way, it is certainly a point which classroom personnel must heed.

Psychological

Psychological explanations for behaviour vary by perspective (e.g., a psychoanalyst sees things differently from a behaviourist) and by setting (e.g., the home, the community, the school, etc.). Two very powerful influences on a child's behaviour are the home and the school. A child's relationship with parents is crucial to development, particularly in the early years. In homes, for example, where discipline is inconsistent and sometimes harsh, and where there is little reinforcement for affection, children often learn to be aggressive. Empirical evidence, supported by research, has consistently shown that the style of child rearing used by parents will have an impact on the behaviour of their children. Still, teachers, especially those who are parents, realize that the causes of a child's behaviour may well be a two-way

New. Problem Solving #2

The Case of Scott

With the cooperation of the district school board, an arrangement worked out by a social worker, the crown attorney, and the family court will keep Scott in custody for the remainder of June, and for July and August. In September he will go to a different school from the one he attended for the past two years. The school will be in a different neighbourhood for Scott will live in a secure group home until it is decided he can be placed with foster parents. Scott is thirteen.

The board has two possible schools for him. One school has a full rotary timetable and a behaviour resource class called the 'drop-in room' where students may or may not be counseled depending on need, or work on their academic program, or just relax. If Scott goes to this school, he will be enrolled in a regular grade six class. An IPRC has confirmed his 'behavioural' identification, and he will be eligible to go to the drop-in room when he feels the need, or, he can be sent there by any of the teachers. The principal of this school, and the staff, openly espouse a nurturing and personal development philosophy. The second school does not have a drop-in room; in fact, it has no designated class for behaviour, and has only a very limited rotary timetable. If Scott goes here, he will be enrolled in a regular grade six class and spend most of his time with the teacher of that class. Whereas the three educational assistants in the first school are assigned to specific classes full time, the three in this school move as needed. The principal here believes strongly in academic achievement and the development of self-reliance, and she too, has attracted a staff with similar beliefs.

Because of privacy laws, no one knows why Scott is presently in custody. However, it is known that he has a history of aggressive behaviour, especially toward girls, and that the current brush with the courts is the latest in a string. What is also known is that Scott's full scale IQ score is Average; there is no evidence that he has a learning disability, and that on a standardized achievement test, he was one grade below the age appropriate level in math and three grades below in language skills. The director of the board has asked for a recommendation as to which school should receive Scott.

street, with parents responding to the behaviour originated by the child, rather than the latter simply becoming a product of what she is taught. Unfortunately for those who work directly with a student, the cause of disordered behaviour is less of an immediate issue than the effects, and is in any case, something they are somewhat powerless to modify: one reason why a multi-disciplinary team, which usually has a member working with the family, can be effective.

Some mental health professionals maintain that schools are a major cause of behaviour disorders but there is no clear evidence to support this. Yet since schools are where students spend a major portion of their wakeful day, it is logical to conclude that what goes on in the classroom, under the direction of the adults there, has a major influence on behaviour. The relationship therefore, between a student and a teacher, between the student and peers, and between the child and the school at large, can have a significant impact both in causing and correcting disordered behaviour.

Reactive Attachment Disorder (RAD) ✍ NEW

A recent addition to the list of disorders in the DSM-IV-R is a condition that is believed to arise from an individual's failure to bond with other humans very early in life. RAD (a.k.a. AD) may develop in the very young because of the lack of nurture and attention in places like shelters for abandoned or orphaned children during wars or other crises, or because of deliberate abuse, or even, as some would have it, because modern parents are too involved and time-driven to provide the necessary emotional support for a newborn. According to the description, "RAD Kids" develop a protective shell against what they believe is an unsafe world where no adults can be trusted to care for them. Among the extensive list of symptoms these "unbonded" children are said to present are rage and destructiveness along with frequent lying, cheating and stealing. They are said to be obsessive, manipulative, unaware of (or unconcerned with) consequences, and have no or limited empathy.

Unfortunately, RAD is easily confused with bipolar disorder, AD/HD, Tourette syndrome, even learning disabilities. Advocates of the syndrome insist this occurs simply because RAD is still poorly understood. Critics argue it may be because RAD is not really a separate disorder at all.

Assessment of Behaviour Disorders

Unless a student comes to a school already diagnosed and identified, the first step in an assessment is usually taken by a classroom teacher, who calls upon nothing more technical than experience and common sense to recognize behaviour that departs from the norm seriously enough and often enough to be distinguished. In fact, informal screening by teachers and teaching assistants has been established throughout education as a fairly reliable first measure.

In most jurisdictions in Canada, what follows formally after this initial phase is governed by a school board's particular plans and procedures. These would include formal assessments, which in turn may be governed by the availability and the expertise of personnel, and the current conceptual model for dealing with behaviour disorders. The teacher and assistant, and often the parents and possibly a social worker or other community service worker, will usually be asked to complete some form of observation instrument like a behaviour checklist or rating scale. A declining practice in the assessment of behaviour disorders, although it is still used in some jurisdictions that favor the psychodynamic approach, is the administration of projective tests, instruments that purport to reveal the intra-psychic life of the subject. (These tests have come under fairly heavy criticism for their questionable validity and potential for entirely subjective interpretation.) Once sufficient information is gathered, the next phases, program and placement are decided, sometimes by a school team, sometimes by special education teachers, or even by administrative fiat.

Since there is fairly convincing evidence that students who have serious behaviour problems in later grades often had difficulties in kindergarten, there is pressure to identify behaviour disorders early. This is not always possible, however, since disorders often do not emerge until the later grades when personal responsibilities and social and academic demands increase in complexity. Ultimately, the identification of a student as behaviour disordered is best accomplished by teamwork, by the collaboration of classroom personnel, parents, and where available and helpful, mental health professionals, operating in an atmosphere of mutual respect and understanding.

Some Issues in the Field

✦ *Agreement on an acceptable term* for this exceptionality has long been hard to achieve. Among the more popular identifiers, some of which are still current and overlap several fields are: *socially maladjusted, emotionally disturbed, mentally ill, predelinquent, delinquent, emotionally handicapped, socially handicapped*, and of course, most frequently used in education: *behaviour disordered*. In the past, labels developed at what seemed to be the discretion of whoever was writing on the subject. *Emotionally disturbed*, for example, first appeared (without precise definition) at the beginning of the twentieth century. Other terms have cropped up at other times. Educators have not always been helpful either, for one jurisdiction will choose a term, often without reference to any other jurisdiction. Thus across Canada there are a variety of descriptors all more or less the same in intent but sometimes markedly different in substance.

The term *behaviour disordered* has acquired a steadily strengthening credibility among educators because it is conceptually inclusive of a variety of problems that war-

<table>
<tr><td>

Expertise in Behaviour: a Myth?

In 1988, a comprehensive study published in the distinguished journal *Science* traced individuals whose future behaviour had been predicted by psychiatrists and psychologists as part of 'expert' testimony in U. S. courts. The followup study shocked both the judicial and behavioural science professions by showing the expert predictions wrong more than half the time! Faust, D. & Ziskin, J. (1988). "The expert witness in psychology and psychiatry", *Science*, 241, 4861, 31-35.

</td></tr>
</table>

rant professional attention; it is less negative and stigmatizing than many of the other terms in use; and it tends to circumvent the suggestion of legal identification. Above all it is sufficiently comprehensive to have wide applicability.

✦ *Developing a useful definition* has proven just as difficult, for it follows that if the names for an exceptionality are elastic and capricious, describing it would be just as problematic*. Definitions are vulnerable to their authors' theoretical perspective: behavioural? psychodynamic?; to their discipline: teacher? psychiatrist? lawyer?; and to their purpose for writing a definition: for research? for education? The effect of these differences is a serious block to practical communication, especially in light of the fact that a multi-disciplinary approach is often necessary, especially in the more serious cases.

On the other hand, there may be merit in the argument that this exceptionality, more than any other, should perhaps not be defined at all, that rather, a statement of needs should suffice. Inasmuch as there is no definition of normal behaviour—which would therefore be the referent for behaviour that is not— it is only reasonable that

• • • ——————
* E.g. The DSM has included Conduct Disorder as a classification for some time, but in the fourth edition it separated out 'Oppositional Defiance Disorder' (ODD). According to the description, an individual with ODD regularly argues with and defies authority, throws tantrums, and is generally resentful (something teachers encountered daily, long before it had a formal name!).
——————— • • •

behavioural exceptionality cannot be defined either. Even though behavioural disorders are distinguished by frequency and degree rather than by their nature, disorders cannot be measured quantitatively. There is no system analogous to the IQ test. And to add to the murkiness, people who exhibit disordered behaviour also behave normally! Above all, behavioural anomalies are exclusive to an individual; there is really no set of symptoms common enough to permit a description, much less a definition, that would be applicable to all cases, and be helpful to those who work with the individuals in question. Thus the likelihood is that the lack of a useful, universally accepted definition will continue.

♦ *Are needs being met?* An area of concern is the discrepancy between the percentage of the school population that is behaviour disordered and percentage that is actually being served. A Canada-wide study by Dworet and Rathgeber (1990) found that not only are the needs of large numbers of behaviour disordered students going unserved, this population is getting even less attention than it did in 1981! Hallahan and Kauffman (1994) conclude that over two percent of the school population exhibits disordered behaviour. Yet data show that typically, less than one percent is being served. Ontario data show a fairly consistent rate of 'behaviour' identifications by IPRCs at around .53 to .56 percent of the school population. Recent U.S. Office of Education data show about 1 percent identified as 'seriously emotionally disturbed'.

♦ *School standards too high?* There is some evidence that schools illuminate behaviour as unacceptable because they have unrealistic and unnatural standards. Some theorists refer to this as *iatrogenic disorder*: i.e., the behaviour arises as a consequence of the way the student is treated, and not out of a natural predisposition at all. Other theorists advance the idea of *psychonoxious* behaviours or attention-getting styles that, over time, accumulate a large pool of resentment in peers and teachers so that the student in question is treated as behaviour disordered, whether he or she actually is so or not.

♦ *Socioeconomics and class distinctions* come into play in this exceptionality. Particularly in the case of adolescents, students from lower income families report a greater number and variety of penalties for their behaviour. Moreover, certain behaviours by lower income students are more likely to be regarded as disordered, whereas similar behaviours by students from high-income families are more likely to be seen as legitimate responses to stimuli. A study by Brantlinger (1991) suggests this phenomenon may be owing to inequities in school conditions for lower income students. Her study was conducted in the U.S., however, and in Canada there is ample reason to argue that poorer school conditions in lower SES areas are uncommon, and that in fact extensive resources are committed to preventing such inequities. Nevertheless, this is not to deny that different *attitudes* toward the behaviour of students from lower social classes may well prevail here.

♦ *The stigma* of behaviour disorder creates a lasting impression. It affects the opinion of teachers and peers, and it can contaminate matters for the student identified. Once placed in the 'behavioural' category, exceptional students often find their history hard to escape, and must contend with an atmosphere where expectations govern the way others respond. As a consequence administrators are often reluctant to apply a behavioural identification, so that some genuine cases of behaviour disorder may not be getting the appropriate intervention.

♦ *Legal requirements* regularly complicate the education of a student who has become involved in crime. One of the more significant issues is the disruption of a student's education if he or she is moved through a variety of settings while a case is being decided and a sentence is being served. It is not unusual for an adolescent particularly, to experience a variety of custodial settings through both the court hearing procedures and subsequent serving of a sentence. These settings will invariably have different educational approaches — if any — and usually, little effort is made to coordinate them. To a student with a behaviour disorder such a lack of continuity can aggravate the problem. Another issue that arises out of the legal side is the rigorous privacy stipulations in Canadian law* which in some cases preclude a teacher's being informed of circumstances surrounding a student's involvement in crime, or even of being informed

• • • ─────
* In April, 2003, the much debated Young Offenders Act was replaced by the Youth Criminal Justice Act. The new legislation purports to strengthen the options for dealing with young offenders but has retained many features of the previous act, including stringent privacy regulations. ───── • • •

about a transgression at all. While this may have no immediate bearing on educational planning, it may require the withholding of information that in some cases could be important not just to the student's program, but also to the well-being of the teacher and other members of the class.

✦ *The use of drugs* to manage behaviour has provoked debate among educators and mental health professionals from the time the very first pill was swallowed. Initially, much of the argument clustered around

---

Video Games and Behaviour ✍

Teachers and parents have long suspected that the violence portrayed in some video games has a negative impact on the behaviour of children and adolescents. Although there is inherent logic in that perception, and although it appears to be supported by empirical evidence in the hallways, playgrounds and even in the classrooms of our schools, it has taken some time to reinforce the suspicion with solid research. In part, this is because the level of extreme violence in some video games is a fairly recent phenomenon, and research that might reveal a potential impact (or not) on players' behaviour must necessarily follow some time after.

It would appear, however, that the research gap is now being filled. A review of the literature at publication of this Fifth Edition of *Special Education in Ontario Schools* shows that about forty peer-reviewed studies have been published to date, every one, without exception, concluding that playing violent video games has an impact on the behaviour of children and adolescents. Several well-executed studies published in the February 2004, issue of the *Journal of Adolescence* (vol. 27, no. 1), make the case with particular clarity. One study, for example, (Gentile et al) conducted on a population of over 600 students in grades eight and nine, concluded that compared to controls, children and adolescents who play violent video games:

• see the world as more hostile;

• get into more arguments with teachers;

• have more fights;

• achieve lower grades.

One of the strengths of this study is that it controlled for gender, for amount of time spent playing (average was nine hours per week), and for the possibility of pre-existing hostility in the subjects being studied, all of which adds to the credibility of the results.

Other studies consistently demonstrate effects on violent video game players such as lack of empathy for victims, de-sensitization to violence generally, and a greater tendency to condone violence as an acceptable response.

It is important to highlight here, the fact that the research work, most particularly the studies conducted since the beginning of the current century, has focused on violent video games that have become available only in the past few years. Teachers and parents who have not reviewed contemporary game materials should realize that the relatively innocuous *Pac-Man* and *Pong* type games of earlier generations pale in comparison to more recently available programs that portray indiscriminate mass killings and offer intensely graphic displays of violence. Clearly, video game violence is a phenomenon that will raise concerns in schools and homes for some time to come. For special education, the problem will be determining to what extent the games may be a contributing or possibly an obfuscating factor in situations where a student is thought to be behaviourally exceptional.

...chool board that expelled Suzette six weeks ago has a zero tolerance policy on vio-
...given several chances before the expulsion occurred. On one occasion she pushed
...ed a teacher. Action on this incident was shelved by mutual agreement, when
...she had reacted "when he grabbed me". Three student witnesses and one teacher
...contradict that claim but the teacher asked the principal to drop the matter because, innocent or not, he refused to be, in his words, "dragged through media mud". On another occasion
Suzette scratched another student seriously enough to leave a scar, but an investigation of the incident gave Suzette the benefit of the doubt on the basis of self-defence. The precipitating event for
the expulsion was another fight. This time Suzette beat up another girl very badly.

Suzette's exasperated parents have prevailed upon a personal friend, the principal of a large secondary school in a neighbouring board, to accept Suzette, but now he has a dilemma: whether or not
to place her in the school's behavioural resource class. This is an exceptionally successful unit with a
highly competent teacher who places almost all her emphasis on academic achievement. There is no
scheduled counseling in the class, and despite the fact that all but one of the students has a social
worker, she has managed to ban every one of them. The students work hard on a full program, go on
field trips, and participate in school events, but their entire program is delivered in this class.

Suzette is sixteen and was designated 'behavioural' four years ago. She had been an excellent,
high achieving student until, as her mother said to an IPRC "she went teenage-nuts!" Suzette is
articulate and has a very powerful personality. At one of her several court hearings, a judge
remarked, "After five minutes with you, no one would ever say 'Suzette who?' the next day." What
the principal is worried about is a struggle for power if Suzette goes to the behavioural class. He
knows her potential for success is very high there, but if a power struggle erupts, the results could
be very harmful to both Suzette and the other students.

moral and ethical values that may be violat-
ed by chemically altering an individual's
makeup and natural function. The debate is
unlikely to diminish as long as drugs are
used. Other oft-voiced sentiments prevail as
well, despite the fact that empirical evidence has weakened many of them. The
belief that administering drugs to a child
will lead to later drug addiction has not
proven demonstrably true. And the argument that drug therapy is an opportunity
for parents (and even teachers) to turn their
responsibilities over to chemicals, while it
may be a fact in isolated, individual cases,
has also not found support over time. On
the other hand, the jury is still out on the
issue of psychological effects: i.e., what
impact does regularly taking a pill have on
a child's self-esteem? And the accusation
that teenagers especially, with quantities of
mood-altering drugs available, are often
tempted to take illegal advantage of the
fact, has evidence to support it.

Overall, however, supporters of psycho-
pharmacology as a method of behaviour
management can now point to some positive outcomes. Relatively long term experience has demonstrated that many children
respond positively to medication, most
particularly those who are given drugs to
reduce impulsivity and improve concentration. There is also fairly clear evidence that
drugs are crucial in the treatment of psy-
chotic illnesses like childhood schizophrenia. Yet critics respond that this alleged (and
rather narrow) success is a double-edged
sword in that it is rapidly accelerating the
rate at which drugs are prescribed at the
expense of other, drugless therapies. The
comment has much evidence to support it.
In 1997, for example, Health Canada estimated that over the previous six years,
Ritalin consumption had increased by some
460 percent! There is ample reason in fact,
to accept that drug therapy had become a
standard treatment regimen, if not *the* standard. (See also Drug Therapy Approach and
Medications in Popular Use, in this chapter.)

Intervention Styles and Their Educational Implications

Although academics and mental health professionals tend to subscribe to a particular, and usually narrow school of thought when it comes to treating behaviour disorders, emphasis on a singular view of behaviour is far less common in the classroom. However, it behooves teachers and educational assistants to be aware of some of the current approaches in the mental health field.

Psychodynamic Approach

Although it is a declining force among educators, psychodynamics continues to attract attention in television shows and popular literature. This perspective views behaviour disorders as being within the individual. Thus when this treatment approach is used, the teacher is usually part of a mental health team that seeks to develop a warm supportive atmosphere in which the student will hopefully overcome his or her inner turmoil. Emphasis is placed on acceptance and toleration, somewhat at the expense of direct instruction and acquisition of academic skills. A variation of this style is called the *psychoeducational approach*, in which more effort is directed to practical classroom outcomes. One of the reasons for the decline of the psychodynamic approach is an accumulation of evidence that it does not improve academic achievement, and at the same time, limited evidence that it helps to improve behaviour.

Biophysical Approach

This style emphasizes the organic origins of behaviour, and postulates a direct relationship between behaviour and such things as physical defects, illnesses, diet, and allergies. Advocates of this view have generated a multiplicity of causation theories each with a responsive therapy. Some examples include megavitamin therapy, diet control, symptom control medication, removal of offending substances (like carpets) etc. In the classroom this approach is often combined with a structured, behaviour-based style that emphasizes routine, daily scheduling, frequent repetition of tasks presented in careful sequence, and the elimination of environmental

stimuli that are perceived to be extraneous. Available data on the results of this treatment have difficulty separating which aspect, the therapies or the style of instructing, has the most impact.

Environmental Approach

Supporters hold that individuals are a particular collective in a particular space and time, and as such, must be regarded as the product of an ecological unit made up of themselves, their family, school, neighbourhood, and community. Educational response to behaviour disorder therefore must necessarily involve the whole of the ecological unit. Where this theory is followed in schools, teachers are expected to instruct the student in social and interpersonal environment skills. At the same time, attempts are made to modify the school's environment to meet the needs of the individual. Family counseling, and in some cases, counseling of the student's classmates may be part of the program. The key element is to create in all parts of the unit, an awareness of its reciprocal relationships, and an impetus toward monitoring these relationships to the ultimate benefit of the behaviour disordered student. Classroom teachers and educational assistants with experience in this approach, while they attest to its efficacy at least initially, also point out that the amount of coordination necessary to make it work well, is almost impossible to bring about.

Behaviour Modification Approach

Still seen as the dominant intervention style from an educational point of view, this approach follows the assumption that all behaviour is modifiable by principles of reinforcement. (It is worth pointing out that the dominance of the behavioural approach is at least partly owing to the vast amount of published material it spawns, much of it from American colleges and universities where the theory does indeed dominate. The Canadian view, and especially Canadian educational practice, does not favour behaviourism quite as heavily.) Educators who adhere to this approach believe that behaviour is controlled by impinging stimuli and that it is possible to:

i) create behaviours that presently do not exist;

ii) maintain and generalize behaviours already established; and,

iii) eliminate inappropriate behaviours.

What happens practically, is that first, a desirable behaviour or set of behaviours is established. Then, using a potent reinforcer at the appropriate time, teachers and assistants intervene when these behaviours appear. Educators who use behaviour modification — and many do to a degree, even those who would deny being 'behaviourist'—regard every student as a candidate for learning, irrespective of whatever psychopathology may be at the root of behaviour.

Drug Therapy Approach

This treatment essentially means that a student with a behaviour disorder is administered psychotropic drugs, most often in pill form, to control his or her behaviour. Research over the past thirty years suggests fairly emphatically that

The Case of Logan

On just her second day in office, the (acting) principal spotted Logan under the secretary's empty chair after morning recess. He was pale, and shaking, and appeared to have been crying. Logan is a month away from his seventh birthday and is in grade two. The principal, suspecting a playground incident, deliberately ignored Logan for a few minutes, but intervened fifteen minutes later, when he had not moved and began crying hard. In her office, Logan said his grade two teacher "touched me here and here and put his hand inside my pants", adding that it had happened several times. When the principal moved to follow board policy by notifying authorities, the school secretary, who had only just returned from an errand, suggested she first call both of Logan's parents. The parents are divorced and have joint custody of Logan. Last year, he told each of them, on consecutive days, that the other was abusing him sexually. Before the accusations were exposed as completely false, Logan's mother was asked by her professional association to voluntarily suspend her practice (she practices pediatric psychiatry). His father, an attorney with a prominent firm, was asked to take a leave of absence, although the firm denied the request was connected to an interview that Logan gave—on his own initiative—to the tabloid press. The principal decided to follow the secretary's advice and after both parents independently insisted the teacher was almost surely innocent, she did not pursue the matter further. But the teacher was under a cloud of suspicion for several weeks.

After deeper investigation the principal learned that in grade one, Logan had convinced a girl in the class that her parents were separating. She is now in a different school, but according to her parents, still has anxiety attacks even if the two of them leave for work at different times. Also in grade one, until the teacher discovered it, Logan was quietly talking classmates into destroying their work because it was no good. The same teacher suspects, but cannot prove, that Logan is responsible for a spate of missing materials, and that it was he who ruined the controls of a powered wheelchair used by a disabled boy in the class. At the same time, she acknowledges that Logan is academically superior, that she has never actually seen him do anything remotely improper (The second grade teacher agrees) and that in terms of completing work, obeying routines, and in helping others, Logan appears to be a model student. The acting principal's instinct is to call for an IPRC which would likely identify Logan 'behavioural'. Still, she wonders what that would accomplish.

the medication does indeed succeed in this purpose, implying therefore, a positive or at least an improved outcome for both the student and others in his school and personal life. Classroom professionals often become involved in this therapy, first of all to administer the medication during the school day, and secondly—particularly if a drug is being used for the first time with a student—in the monitoring of its positive and negative effects. In the ideal situation, no medication is ever given to a student without its effects being carefully noted and duly reported, so that modifications in the dosage can be made—an outcome that is often necessary. Regrettably, a challenge for teachers and assistants is that necessary modifications which are always under the control of parents and medical professionals, are not always forthcoming in a timely way. Of possible interest both to parents and educators may be the claim by practitioners of naturopathic medicine that they can treat attention deficit and hyperactivity by means that do not involve administering potentially invasive chemistry.

The Classroom Approach:

Flexible Common Sense

Teachers and educational assistants who study behaviour theory often find it difficult to be entirely faithful to only one of the approaches above when they apply it in the cold (or hot!) reality of the classroom. Most combine a variety of approaches and apply them on a by-case basis. For example, all teachers of all students—not just those with behaviour disorders—espouse the value of a warm, supportive atmosphere. All teachers recognize the interplay of environmental stimuli, and all are aware of the importance of these phenomena in both learning and social development. Teachers and assistants universally modify behaviour in their students but only some will actually call it behaviour modification. And the view of each student as a dynamic, individual entity is at the very heart of teaching as a profession. Taken together, the practices followed by most educators most of the time, could best be collected under the expression: *flexible common sense*. While the term may not have definitive intellectual reverberations in the field of behaviour theory, it describes pretty much the route that is followed in the classroom: doing what is effective at the time and what makes sense at the time.

New Section - With Behaviour Disorders, / With the Past it was with Learning Disabilities

Students with AD / HD

Throughout the final years of the twentieth century and on into the next, a confusing and controversial condition has taken a very high profile front seat in special education: Attention Deficit/Hyperactivity Disorder (AD/HD). The condition is being diagnosed with ever-increasing frequency by psychiatrists and psychologists especially in North America. As well, AD/HD has captivated the popular press, become a regular subject of educational research, and has been almost completely—and rather uncritically—accepted by the teaching profession. Unfortunately, it is the subject of considerable debate, not just as to the nature of the special needs it represents, but also whether it requires or even deserves distinctive status. Ontario, like most educational jurisdictions, does not list AD/HD as a distinct category of exceptionality. Nor is it included in the Individuals with Educational Disabilities Act (IDEA, 1997) in the U.S. Yet irrespective of its (un)official status, and of the controversy it continues to generate, AD/HD has become a factor in special education today. The following section attempts to present a perspective for educators and parents.

Medications in Popular Use

The chart below offers a brief, non-definitive overview of some of the more frequently prescribed medications for younger individuals.

Medications	Intended Effect	Some Possible Side Effects
Stimulants		
methylphenidate hydrochloride (Ritalin) & dextroamphetamine (Dexadrine)	reduce hyperactivity and enable increased attention	sleep disruption/appetite loss rebound effect[†]
magnesium pemoline[‡] (Cylert)	as above	weight gain, may affect liver
Tranquilizers		
thioridazine (Mellaril) & chloropromazine (Thorazine)	calm aggressive and/or disturbed behaviour	constipation drowsiness/dizziness nasal congestion
haloperidol (Haldol & Serenace)	as above	blurred vision, muscle spasms
Antidepressants*		
imipramine (Tofranil)	treat childhood depression	headache/nausea weight gain (increased appetite)
amitriptyline (Elevil)	as above	fatigue, dizziness sensitivity to sunlight
Antihistamines		
hydroxyzine (Atarax &Vistaril)	treat childhood (anxiety)	drowsiness muscle tremors

† Critics of drug therapy argue that stimulants particularly, may cause a user's behaviour to worsen when the pharmacological effects wear off.

‡ Claims are made for Cylert that it does not have the side effects of a typical stimulant.

* Some medical practitioners assert these medications have no effect on children.

Note 1: Dosages of the various medications may vary considerably (Ritalin, for example, is usually administered in 5,10, or 25 mg doses;) and are administered at differing frequencies. (Ritalin is usually administered twice or three times a day, although there is also a single dose, slower release form now available.)

Note 2: The side effects shown above are but some of those commonly reported. The literature has accounts of other, albeit rare, dramatic side effects such as blackouts, tardive dyskinesia, etc.

Note 3: A relatively new *non*-stimulant for managing AD/HD is a drug called *Straterra*. It must be administered daily and some weeks may be necessary before its best effects are seen. The long term effects of Strattera, both positive and otherwise, are still uncertain.

What Are the Symptoms of AD/HD?

There is fairly substantial agreement on three primary symptoms, the first being *inability to sustain attention at age-appropriate level*. The student cannot screen out irrelevant stimuli, does not concentrate on tasks long enough to complete them, does not sustain the thought processes necessary to do school work. The second is *impulsivity*. The student does things without considering consequences, and often repeats the behaviour (does not learn from experience). Work patterns are erratic and scatter-focused. Often perseverates with counter-productive behaviour.

Hyperactivity is the third characteristic. The student engages in non-purposeful movement and activity that is usually not age appropriate, and often at an accelerated level. This usually continues despite intervention. (Interestingly, teachers can often see many of their students in a description like this, or members of their family, or even themselves!)

What is The Difference Between ADD and AD/HD?

As the absence of an 'H' would imply, ADD is identical to AD/HD without the presence of hyperactivity. ADD was first classified in the DSM in 1982, five years before AD/HD, and almost immediately, the attempt to distinguish two conditions as one *with* hyperactivity and the other without, was vigorously debated. Subsequent research suggests that the composite syndrome, AD/HD, is far more common. As well, both educators and parents found that term more useful, so that over time, AD/HD seems to have taken over and is by far the most frequently used.

Are AD/HD Symptoms the Result of Other Factors?

Disruptive or unresponsive behaviour may be the result of anxiety or depression. Regular lapses in attention might be evidence of absence (*petit mal*) seizures. Fetal alcohol syndrome sometimes produces hyperactive behaviour. An uncooperative student, especially a younger one, may be uncooperative because of a hearing loss, the result of chronic inner ear infections or an undetected hearing problem. In short, there are many things that can cause the symptoms. To further confuse the matter, AD/HD is most often a medical diagnosis arrived at, supposedly, on the evidence of these symptoms; yet professional educators see the same symptoms every day in students who are not identified this way! Supporters of the condition as a separate entity, argue—often with good evidence to support them—that the distinguishing criteria of AD/HD symptoms are *high frequency* and *severity*, and that they are seen repeatedly *over extended time*.

What Causes AD/HD?

Advocates argue that AD/HD has been around for a long time under other titles like 'hyperkinesis' and 'minimal brain dysfunction' and 'moral deficit'. They posit further, that what makes it real is a biological or psychological basis, or both. As for psychological cause, proponents argue that there are some individuals who, through no fault of their own, cannot use their human will and self control to manage themselves from within, and that the pace of modern life aggravates this lack of a central control mechanism. The majority of advocates for AD/HD, however, see it as a neurologically-based medical condition. Among the causes identified, but not yet widely accepted by both the medical and educational communities are faulty regulation by a neurotransmitter called norepinephrine, and genetic factors owing to anomalies in certain chromosomes. More recently, the National Institutes of Mental Health (NIMH) in the U.S. has sponsored research which suggests a relationship between attention and the level of glucose used in the brain. Ultimately, the cause of AD/HD—if any—is still unknown.

Just a Confusion with Other Special Needs?

AD/HD has long been associated with learning disability because of the inattentiveness factor. They are not, however, the same thing. Estimates vary, but the literature generally suggests that about one-third of learning disabled students may have some degree of attention disorder. Alternatively, the rate of learning

After only a month in nursery school, Hannah was being secretly called 'Beagle' by the staff, because of her penchant for running flat out until something or someone stopped her. It was a habit she continued over the next several years. Kindergarten passed fairly smoothly for Hannah's teacher was a completely unruffled person, committed to letting her students express themselves as much as they wished. Grade one, however, was a disaster. Not entirely Hannah's fault; the grade one teacher was having a difficult year. She had two pre-school children of her own, one of whom was chronically ill, and a husband who worked shifts. But Hannah didn't help things. By this time, running about during story time, quiet time—any time—was an established habit. She regularly blurted out whatever was on her mind during instruction, and seemingly could not keep from interfering with others in the class when they teamed up for an activity. Hannah regularly "borrowed" material without asking, never returned it unless told to, and did not seem remotely aware of how annoying she was to others.

Grade two was marked by a field trip crisis when, because of Hannah, the class was asked to leave a petting zoo. Following this trip, Hannah's mother agreed to accompany excursions as one of the parent volunteers supervising a group. Nevertheless, because of some more incidents, and because of an extensive list of complaints from other parents, Hannah's mother eventually kept her daughter at home during all subsequent field trips. Unfortunately, the residue of this move carried into grade three, when several other parents used it—unsuccessfully—as a precedent for requesting that Hannah be removed from the class altogether.

In grade three, a pediatrician diagnosed AD/DH and prescribed medication (Ritalin), but Hannah turned out to be one of the minority for whom the side effects, especially sleeplessness, made it impossible to continue. Hannah's mother, a nurse, ruled out a second medication, Cylert, because she'd heard it may cause liver damage. Throughout grade three, Hannah's impulsive, annoying behaviours worsened. By then it was also evident that she was lagging her peers academically.

Hannah is now in grade four. Her mother reports that she had a "good summer" at a camp for children with AD/HD. Both mother and daughter have new hope because Hannah learned some self-control skills at camp, and because the grade four teacher has a reputation for competence in dealing with AD/HD. In spite of this, there has already been an incident. The class is forming groups to put together material for a 'time capsule' to be opened in June. Because no group would accept Hannah, she had a tantrum, and then for the first time any one can remember, she began to cry in a deeply heartfelt way. The teacher sees that as a sign the time is ripe for renewed effort to address Hannah's case. An In-School Team meeting has been called to come up with ideas.

high rate of LD in AD/HD

disabilities is high in students who are diagnosed AD/HD, possibly because lack of attention and off task behaviour are detrimental to mastering basic skills. One special need, however, does not absolutely and automatically imply the other. (The same caution applies to commingling AD/HD with other behaviour disorders, and with Tourette's syndrome.)

Another "Modern Day" Phenomenon?

Not entirely, although it did not capture the public eye until the late twentieth century. A German doctor, Heinrich Hoffman first described hyperactivity in 1845. In 1902, George

Still, a British physician added a moral overlay, a notion that unproductive hyperactivity is somehow associated with evil, a notion that still dogs the issue. (He described 'sick' children of average or higher intelligence who had an "abnormal deficit of moral control". Hence the term 'moral deficit'.) AD/HD was classified clinically in 1968, and acquired its current designation in 1987 (both times an initiative of the medical profession).

When matched against other, more recent types of special need, the time frame in which AD/HD achieved its high profile seems reasonable enough, yet there continues to be intense, sometimes vicious disagreement over whether it should be seen as a distinct clinical entity, or even stronger, whether it really exists! Critics contend that AD/HD has become a *label du jour* in North America, an invention of a culture that has cast aside its obligation to parent well and now needs an excuse for the result. While such statements are unquestionably harsh, and may be offered more for effect than polemic, they have a powerful impact in the light of two very real factors. One is the accelerated rate of diagnosis. In 1997, the *Globe and Mail* newspaper reported that an estimated half million Canadians, mostly students, had been diagnosed, an extraordinary number for a condition that only got its name a decade before! Subsequent revelations in 2003 and 2004 indicate that the accelerating rate continues.

The other factor is the failure—so far—of the field of psychiatry to achieve general agreement or even establish clarity in the matter. In fact it is possible that psychiatry has muddied the issue further with the "new" behaviour disorders that continue to appear in the DSM. It is difficult for teachers and educational assistants to have confidence in medical literature, and even in educational literature, when one can find classifications in addition to AD/HD such as ADD (attention deficit disorder), ADD-WHO (without hyperactivity), AD/HD-HI (hyperactive-impulsive type), AD/HD-NOS (not otherwise specified), and still other variations such as ODD (oppositional defiance disorder).

An entirely separate area of controversy, but one of consequence, is the use (and possibly, abuse) of medication and other as yet unsubstantiated methods like biofeedback, visual training, restricted diets, etc., to control AD/HD.

What does AD/HD Mean to the Classroom?

Teachers and educational assistants have long been used to "antsy" students, particularly younger ones, who find it hard to sit still. And in most classrooms the behaviour is managed successfully most of the time. But where a strongly suspected case of AD/HD is present, teachers can expect a high level of physical activity, inappropriate responses, low frustra-

tion tolerance—the list goes on. And each of these behaviours *repeat*, despite intervention. Whereas it is the student's parent who must bear the ultimate costs emotionally and physically, teachers have a burden all their own, for a student with AD/HD has a concentric effect. *having a common centre* His lack of restraint and his acting out will invariably draw in his peers, or distract them, or cause conflict, or interrupt their work, or…

Regrettably, there is no sure remedy in the *Remedy* classroom. Certainly there is no universally accepted way to deal with AD/HD in school. *No sure remedy.* Behaviour modification is often tried, but offers no guarantees. Isolating the student with AD/HD may be beneficial for her peers, but is not a solution for the student herself, at least not long term. Ultimately, the most effective management techniques usually turn out to be those that the teacher and educational assistant work out creatively, often with the parents' help, and these techniques, most of the time are uniquely successful for that particular student. Chances are slim the same methods will work with the next candidate. Nevertheless, most teachers do find through experience that there are a few common threads in successful management. One is flexibility. There is not much point in banging heads with a student who seems predisposed to repeat wrong behaviours in the first place. Another is setting modest goals, objectives the student has a realistic chance of attaining. Still another is diversion. And all of these must be supported by, for lack of a better phrase, "kind firmness".

Classroom Strategies for Students with Attention Problems

Manage the Environment:

Seat the student away from distracting stimuli like doorways and traffic areas. Try to seat him so that particularly stimulating students are not in his natural line of sight; if possible seat him near stable peer models. Periodically utilize a special stimulus-reduced study area like a carrel. Encourage parents to do the same. Experiment with natural light vs. fluorescent.

Some teachers have reported that natural light is superior.

While instructing:

Be simple and concise. Offer one instruction or task at a time, after you are confident you have her focused and ready. Limit the use of subordinate clauses and embedded phrases, and welcome questions of clarification. Help the student to feel secure by being nearby when she starts her work. While instructing a large group or the whole class, position yourself near her frequently. If school policy permits, and if you and the student are comfortable with the practice, use BRIEF, reassuring physical contacts once in a while (like a hand on the shoulder).

Managing the Day:

Prepare him for shifts in topic, setting, schedule, etc. (Again, a teacher's or educational assistant's proximity when these are about to happen, can be very important.) Meet and greet with a few positive one-on-one seconds at crucial points during the day, points when the potential for hyperactivity increases: e.g., returning from lunch, gym, recess, etc. When in-class activity is assigned (homework too) help him get started and then, at first, check back as frequently as you can. Help the student organize his output (into notebooks, files, etc.)

so that he gradually accumulates a visible, concrete, cumulative record of his efforts.

Other Support:

Enforce classroom routines and procedures *consistently*. And have only a few! Too many rules invites disaster! Since planning is never this student's long suit, the adults in his life must compensate by planning for him, and building in extra time. When a disagreement arises *do not argue!* You cannot win. Reinforce "good" chunks of time such as on-task behaviour with just-for-her, positive eye-contact or other supportive expressions. When your experience tells you an impossible-to-resolve situation is developing, try 'antiseptic bouncing': i.e., send her on an important errand out of the room, or provide some other task that 'needs doing now'.

Think Momentum:

Not motivation but *momentum*. A teacher who only motivates is forever pushing from behind. Eventually he or she wears out, or runs out of patience or ideas or most likely, desire. On the other hand, a teacher who tries to build momentum in students, who works at developing in them a sense of personal responsibility, this teacher will not only have a greater and lasting impact on the students but will last longer herself.

✔ STRATEGIES FOR THE CLASSROOM

Teachers and educational assistants who work with the behaviour disordered are the first to acknowledge that there is no pedagogical magic, no secret formula for teaching success in this area of exceptionality. And those who think there is one and go looking for it are bound to be disappointed. Still, there is one truth, an abiding one that all educators recognize, as do students, parents, and anyone else who bothers to take a second look at classrooms. This is the truth that a teacher who is effective with 'regular' students, is usually more effective with 'behavioural' students. It follows then that to emulate what effective teachers do is at the very least, a practical beginning point for all classroom professionals.

An Effective Teacher's Attitude

There are many human strengths needed to teach effectively. Traits like patience, flexibility, creativity, a sense of humour, a capacity to see all sides of an issue—these are elements that, in the heat of a teaching moment, will outweigh intelligence and scholarship. Effective teachers manifest these characteristics most of the time. However, what they manifest all of the time is not a characteristic at all, but an attitude, a perspective, namely: respect. When teachers', or educational assistants' abiding view is built on respect for students—and on self-respect—the atmosphere in their classroom immediately reflects that attitude in a variety of ways. A place where students feel respected is a safe place to make a mistake, and therefore, an ideal place to learn and grow. Where respect prevails, students recognize that in the eyes of the significant adults there, they have value. Once students feel respected themselves, they are far more likely to show it toward others. And respect for others is fundamental if students are ever to modify their behaviour.

From the instructional end of things, respect, quite simply, infuses everything a teacher does. It smoothes rapport, supports flexibility and patience, and fuels the vitality of faith and hope. A teacher who respects students, plans better, prepares better and instructs better. A teacher who respects students, instinctively avoids those spontaneous but regrettable and damaging management errors from which recovery is so difficult. Above all, if a teacher establishes genuine respect as the central idiom in a classroom, then everyone shares a behavioural reference point. Mutual respect offers both a stage from which to begin, and an objective to keep in sight.

An Effective Teacher's Style

(1) Recognizing where students are "at". Students with a behaviour problem are often burdened by a history that shapes the expectations that others have of them. And they know it. A second burden, one that reinforces the first, is in-the-classroom helplessness. So many of them do not know how to set about academic tasks, or, how to conduct themselves socially in any way other than in the manner that brought on their problems in the first place. An effective teacher is very much aware of this fact, and begins much of his or her work from inside the student's view. It is a delicate undertaking, for one must purposefully go to where the student is "at", while at the same time continuing to be a separate, adult mentor, with all that the role implies. For a teacher or

educational assistant to become a buddy is a deadly mistake. Students don't want that. What they want is an adult who is open, who listens, and who will attempt to understand what they know and do not know, and who will then help them in a face-saving way that produces results, however modest.

(2) Realizing the importance of personal conduct. The manner in which teachers and assistants present their professionalism is a crucial factor in preventing inappropriate classroom behaviour. Ideally, adults who deal with behaviour disordered students are role models who don't react defensively to challenge, who have the skills to divert a troublesome situation until stability is restored (and then deal with it) and who employ fair and realistic consequences in a consistent way. These are also the people who get to class ahead of time, who are present and visible, responsible and proactive. They are role models of adulthood that communicate to students the possibility that the world does have some sense to it. Naturally, things do not always work out this way, but even the students (or perhaps especially the students, unfortunately) don't expect things to work right every time. Yet classroom professionals must strive to model this type of conduct if there is to be any hope of modifying their students' behaviour.

(3) Establishing a realistic, consistent and predictable learning environment. This is the sine qua non of an effective teacher's style. Students with a behaviour disorder already have trouble making sense of the world, not to mention school. And they are notoriously poor at reading between the lines to determine what is expected of them. These are not students who know how to, much less want to, play the game of school. Teachers and assistants can make things much easier for them—make it more possible for them to behave appropriately—if procedures and expectations are clear, uncomplicated and predictable. Particularly in the beginning, and until the students develop some confidence in

themselves and in their teachers, a predictable pattern is crucial.

This sense of stability and consistency in the classroom develops naturally out of the behaviour of the teacher, but also out of the day to day organization. Effective classrooms are not hamstrung by a long list of ironclad rules that students will invariably break, and for which some disciplinary response then becomes necessary. Structure, organization, sequence—these are the important features, and a minimum number of simple, reasonable procedures and routines, not rules, for ensuring that these obtain, makes sense even to students with behavioural problems. There will be some bona fide rules, of course, but most of these are the ones established by the school or the board or other more global entity. And what distinguishes them from classroom procedures and routines is that consequences are applied for breaking them. In the classroom however, teachers and assistants who organize from a perspective of respect, and who model that attitude themselves, not only have a standard to refer to, but have some room for flexibility when a student pushes against it.

(4) "Catching a kid doing something good." It may be a very challenging task sometimes, but looking for positives and discreetly praising them will pay dividends. "Discreet' is an operative word here. Behaviour disordered students, especially older ones, often harbour a profound cynicism that walls them in and protects them from positive reinforcement that they are convinced is insincere. Many of them have had unsatisfactory experiences with so-called 'positive reinforcement programs' and as a result have well-developed detectors. Praise is important, but it must be proportionate to the accomplishment, sincere, and utterly free of excess. Effusiveness will only embarrass the students and may provoke them into negative behaviour just to restore the balance.

(5) Treating democracy as a very fine line. If given the opportunity, students quite natu-rally wish to contribute to a classroom's plans, procedures, and even curriculum. Understandably, this is more often the case with older students. The issue is a difficult one for teachers. Anyone who has ever experienced the exchange ["What do you want to do?" "Nuthin!"] is naturally wary of a suggestion that students should be consulted. And it is a healthy wariness. To expect students who have been identified behaviour disordered to involve themselves in productive interchange about procedures and curriculum is something that happens more often in movie scripts than in classrooms. Still it's worth a try. Most effective teachers would never begin a term or a relationship this way, if only because students with a behavioural problem are looking for leadership and order, whether they realize it or not. After some time has passed, however, and once an atmosphere of respect is established, eliciting and then acting upon a behaviour disordered student's suggestions can produce real benefits, if only because he has thereby taken on some responsibility. At bottom, teachers and assistants must keep in mind that they are dealing with an exceptionality where almost always, chaos in various forms has prevailed. That reality must infuse all democratic decisions.

(6) Establishing momentum is more important than motivating. A teacher who constantly seeks to motivate is soon exhausted by the effort it takes to always push from behind. Any teacher who operates solely on a principle of motivation quite naturally runs out of ideas over a long school term because the responsibility is always his or hers. Not that motivating is counter-productive or a waste of time, but it is only superficial, and while it may pay temporary dividends, motivation rarely has a lasting impact because it is always the teacher's responsibility (a fact which doubles the potential for an all too common teaching trap: the teacher becomes an entertainer).

More effective is to plan, organize, and teach with a view to getting students rolling on their own. Each teacher or educational assistant will accomplish this in different, personal ways, but establishing momentum has a few absolutes. One is beginning where the student is "at" and then setting achievable goals so that he can have the delightful (and hitherto unusual) experience of success. Part and parcel of establishing momentum is making those goals short term so the success can come soon. Another is arranging, even manipulating, the goal—especially at first—to make certain the student does succeed. Then, as soon as there is a success, set up opportunity immediately for another, so that the first one can be reinforced and momentum can begin. Still another absolute, a very simple one on the surface, is arranging one's planning and teaching so that students accumulate visible products, like notes, every day. Most behaviour disordered students have never had the sense of accomplishment that comes from accumulating a set of notes, or of accumulating anything. (Worth pointing out here, is that teachers who are successful in establishing 'momentum' in their students, report that they are then much easier to 'motivate'!)

(7) Keeping academics front and centre. With the possible exception of cases where the mental health of a student is clearly established as a serious issue, the premier classroom focus should always be on academic learning. Even if the development of social skills is a vital feature of a student's educational plan, the student's own perception should always be that he or she is "here for education". A student with a behaviour disorder already feels singled out. To devote the major part of a program to the development of social skills in a transparent, obvious way, only reinforces the distinction. Social skill development can continue to be a principal objective, but its realization should be achieved not just by direct social skill instruction itself, but by learning it during the process of studying what all the other kids are studying. (See Fergie's enlightening comments below.)

(8) Working hard is better than sitting around. Fergie, a fifteen year old student in a regular grade nine class with a 'reputation', and in which five (sic!) students were identified behavioural (including Fergie) presents this argument much better than we can. See the comment below.

"Some teachers, they don't get much work ready for us 'cause they think we don't care about nothin' right? And they think we don't notice. But how many crossword puzzles do they think we gotta do before we figure it out, right? Don't know why they do that. I mean, we're in school, so why not give us schoolwork? But that's not everybody, now. You take Mrs. P…. Now in her class do we ever have to put out. I mean, she's got work and everything every day! Like there's always stuff on the board for us, and then we get a lesson-thing. And then more work. And we got this huge ton of notes!

What's cool is nobody messes around in Mrs. P.'s class. And like, it's not just that she's OK and all that. I mean, she really is but she teaches math! Who wants to do math? But I mean—like—it's like you're really doin' something in that class, man. It's—it's like you're learning something!"

Fergie S., aged 15, on audio tape.
(Mrs. P was in her first year of teaching.)

Some Habits of an Effective Teacher

- Establishes and then maintains consistent routines for entering the classroom and beginning the session (the point at which much of the tone for what follows is established). E.g., an effective teacher is always at the doorway to greet, manage, intervene if necessary.

- Sets up and insists on specific, seating arrangements (which are then altered as deemed useful in order to reduce or increase opportunities).

- Is highly visible. Interacts with students outside the classroom. Tries to attend anything in the school in which a behavioural student is involved.

- Uses 'antiseptic bouncing' when a student is worked up or aggressive. Give him an errand to run outside the class, or some other activity that may let off steam.

- If demerits are used in the school or class, allows for merits to be earned too.

- Uses proximity control and stands nearby when it appears a situation may develop. Proximity also works in the sense of being available to help and being available to interact. Effective teachers never spend the whole day at the front of a classroom.

- Rarely if ever, makes the dread mistake of being sarcastic, and always avoids yelling (a profoundly counter-productive behaviour if it's used more than once a term!) or other behaviours that shred dignity.

- Never uses corrosive discipline techniques, e.g., writing out lines, class detentions, using curriculum content like math or spelling drills as a punishment.

- Avoids confronting behaviour disordered students in front of peers. And does not get into arguments.

- Uses diversions. Younger students especially can be distracted from a counter-productive path by giving them alternate activities and goals.

- Lets students know there are high expectations. If necessary, on occasion, an effective teacher will quite willingly manipulate the components of a task to ensure a positive outcome for a student who needs a boost.

- Sets short term goals for students who have not yet learned to defer gratification.

- Makes use of visible reward systems like progress charts, and ensures that students accumulate notes and other visible, physical evidence that the time spent in school is producing something of consequence.

Aust, P. (1994). When the problem is not the problem: Understanding attention deficit disorder with and without hyperactivity. *Child Welfare, 73*(3), 215-227.

Barabasz, M., & Barabasz, A. (1996). Attention deficit disorder: Diagnosis, etiology and treatment. *Child Study Journal, 26,* 1-38.

Carbone, E. (2001). Arranging the classroom with an eye (and ear) to students with ADHD. *Teaching Exceptional Children, 34*(2), 72-81.

Caseau, D., Luckasson, R., & Kroth, R. L. (1994). Special education services for girls with serious emotional disturbance: A case of gender bias? *Behavioral Disorders, 20*(1), 51-60.

Clarke, S., Dunlap, G., Foster-Johnson, L., Childs, K.E., Wilson D., White, R., & Vera A. (1995). Improving the conduct of students with behavioral disorders by incorporating student interests into curricular areas. *Behavioral Disorders, 20*(4), 221-237.

Cole, E. (1995). Responding to school violence: Understanding today for tomorrow. Canadian *Journal of School Psychology, 11,* 108-116.

Coleman, M. (1992). *Behavior disorders: Theory and practice (2nd ed.).* Englewood Cliffs, NJ: Prentice-Hall.

Colucci, S. (1993, May). Peer mediation: Creating opportunities for conflict resolution. *Communiqué,* pp. 25-27.

Danforth, S., & Boyle J.R. (2000). *Cases in behavior management.* Upper Saddle River, NJ: Merrill/Prentice Hall.

DePaepe, P.A., Shores, R.E., Jack, S.L. & Denny, R.K. (1996). Effects of task difficulty on the disruptive and on-task behavior of students with severs behavior disorders. *Behavioral Disorders, 21*(3), 216-225.

Dworet, D.H. & Rathgerber, A.J. (1990). Provincial and territorial government responses to behaviorally disordered students in Canada. *Behavioural Disorders, 15*(4), 201-209.

Epstein, M.H. (1999). The development and validation of a scale to assess the emotional and behavioural strengths of children and adolescence. *Remedial and Special Education, 20*(5), 258-262.

Epstein, M.H., Foley, R.M., & Polloway, E.A. (1995). Homework problems: A comparison of students identified as behaviorally disordered and nonhandicapped students. *Preventing School Failure, 40*(1), 14-19.

Faber, A., & Mazlish, E. (1996). *How to talk so kids can learn.* New York: Fireside.

Frey, K.S., Hirschtein, M.K.., & Guzzo, B.A. (2000). Second step: Preventing aggression by promoting social competence. *Journal of Emotional and Behavioural Disorders, 8*(2), 102-112.

Furr, D.L. (1996). Now I understand the rage. *Reaching Today's Youth, 1*(1), 9-12.

Henley, M. (1997). *Teaching self-control: A curriculum for responsible behavior.* Bloomington, IN: National Education Service.

Gentile, D.A., Lynch, P.J., Linder, J.R., & Walsh, D.A. (2004). The effects of violent video game habits on adolescent hostility: Agressive behaviour and school defiance. *Journal of Adolescence, 27*(1), 5-22.

Jenson, W. R., Rhode., & Reavis. (1994). *The tough kids toolbox.* Longmont, CO: Sopris West.

Jones, F. (1994). *Positive classroom discipline.* Santa Cruz, CA: Fredric H. Jones and Associates, Inc.

Kauffman, J.M. (1999). How we prevent the prevention of emotional and behavioral disorders. *Exceptional Children, 65,* 448-468.

Kauffman, J.M. (2001). *Characteristics of emotional and behavioral disorders of children (7th. Ed.)* Columbus, OH: Merrill/Prentice Hall.

Koplewicz, H.S. (1996). *It's nobody's fault: New hope and help for difficult children and their parents*. New York: Times Books.

Landau, S., & McAnich, C. (1993, May). Young children with attention deficits. *Young Children, 48*(4), pp. 49-57.

Lantieri, L., & Patti, J. (1996). Waging peace in our schools. *Reaching Today's Youth, 1*(1), 43-47.

Lewis, T.J., Heflin, J., & DiGangi, S. (1991). Teaching students with behavior disorders. *Basic questions and answers*. Reston, VA: Council for Exceptional Children.

Lewis, T.J., & Sugai, G. (1999). Effective behaviour support: A system approach to practice school wide management. *Focus on Exceptional Children, 21*(6), 1-24.

MacDonald, I.M. (1997). Violence in schools: Multiple realities . *Alberta Journal of Educational Research, 43*, 142-156.

Maag, J. W., & Reid, R. (1994). Attention deficit hyperactivity disorder: A functional approach to assessment and treatment. *Behavioral Disorders, 20*(1), 5-23.

Maté, G. (2000). *Scattered Minds: A new look at the origins and healing of attention deficit disorder*. Toronto: Knopf.

Mendler, A.N. (1992). *How to achieve discipline with dignity in the schools*. Bloomington, IN: National Education Service.

Miller, D. (1994). Suicidal behavior of adolescents with behavior disorders and their peers without disabilities. *Behavioral Disorders, 20*(1), 61-68.

Moore, R., Cartledge, G., & Heckman, K. (1995). The effects of social skills instruction and self-monitoring on game related behaviors of adolescents with EBD. *Behavioral Disorders, 20*(4), 253-266.

Murray, F.R. (1996). You think you have animals in your class? *Beyond Behavior, 7*(3), 10-13.

Oseroff, A., Oseroff, C.E., Westling, D., &

Gesser, L. (1999). Teacher's beliefs about maltreatment of students with emotional/behavioural disorders. *Behavioural Disorders, 24*,(3), 197-209.

Reid, R. (1999). Attention deficit hyperactivity disorder: effective methods for the classroom. *Focus on Exceptional Children, 32*(4), 1-20.

Rhode, G., Jenson, W.R., & Reavis, H.K. (1992). *The tough kid book: Practical classroom management strategies*. Longmont, CO: Sopris West.

Safran, S.P., & Oswald, K. (2003). Positive behaviour supports: Can schools reshape disciplinary practices? *Exceptional Children, 69*(3), 361-372.

Shippen, M.E., Simpson, R.G., & Crites, S.S. (2003). A practical guide to functional assessment. *Teaching Exceptional Children, 35*(5), 36-44.

Sprague, J., & Walker, H. (2000). Early identification and intervention for youth with antisocial and violent behaviours. *Exceptional Children, 66*(3), 14.

Wright-Strawderman, C. Lindsay P., Bavarette, L, & Flippo, J.R. (1996). Depression in students with disabilities: recognition and intervention strategies. *Intervention in School and Clinic, 31*(5), 261-275.

Links

Children and Adults with Attention Deficit Disorder
www.chadd.org

Mental Health
http://www.hc-sc.gc.ca/hppb/mentalhealth/ problems.htm

Gov. of Canada bullying
http://www.prevention.gc.ca/en/library/ publications/children/violence/

Government of Canada /anxiety
http://www.hc-sc.gc.ca/hppb/mentalhealth/ pubs/anxiety/

CHAPTER 8

Students Who Are Gifted

Gifted kids were dealt a bad hand by Galton* with his theory that cream will rise to the top no matter what. That was a century ago and my guess is a century from now we'll still be selling the gifted short, and for the same reason—the silly notion that because of their talents they don't need help. That is utter nonsense. The gifted need support as much as any other exceptional group.

Paul T., teacher of gifted students

Misconceptions About Giftedness

1. Gifted students always outpace their peers.

A gifted student's level of achievement does not always reflect true ability. While some fare well at school, other gifted students may underachieve. Cultural differences, gender and disabilities may affect performance. Some students express giftedness in non-academic ways, or in ways not necessarily curriculum-related.

2. They work harder than their peers.

One of the accepted markers of giftedness is strong task commitment but the trait is not automatic. Commitment may not become evident until it is stimulated by the appropriate conditions.

3. Gifted students are bored with school, disruptive, and antagonistic.

Usually they enjoy school, are well adjusted and get on easily with peers and teachers. They react to neglect, inequity, etc. like any other students.

4. It is common for emotional instability to accompany giftedness.

Gifted students usually enjoy good mental health and tend to have fewer emotional problems than the norm. Empirical evidence suggests they may be exceptionally sensitive to matters like injustice, world issues, etc.

5. Gifted students are physically inept, self-absorbed and narrow-minded.

For the most part, they look and act like any other students, although teachers generally report them as above average in health, moral responsibility, and social adeptness.

6. Giftedness is a stable, absolute characteristic.

The evidence, particularly empirical evidence, seems to show that while a highly developed ability in a student seems to be relatively constant, it will express itself with varying intensity over time.

7. Gifted students are easy to identify.

They do not necessarily stand out in a group of age peers. Theoretically, a gifted student performing at age level is underachieving. Although IQ tests are a frequent means of identifying gifted students (and they may often score very high) these instruments are far too narrow as a sole criterion, for they are unable to

● ● ● ——————

* Francis Galton, a nineteenth century English scientist, eugenics advocate, and one of the first to examine giftedness, proposed that genius would surface no matter the circumstances.

—————— ● ● ●

measure or even highlight characteristics like artistic ability or creativity, for example. Reliance on IQ measures may also discriminate against culturally diverse or disabled populations.

8. Normally a school system will find 3 to 5 percent of the population gifted.

The percentage identified usually depends on the jurisdiction's definition of the gifted, and on its conception of giftedness. (Many Ontario boards interpret giftedness quite generously, as the data in Chapter 3 imply.)

Defining Giftedness

How an education system defines students who are gifted not only influences identification rates but the design of organizational models for instruction. Ironically, for an exceptionality that on the surface would seem to be easily described, giftedness is defined in many different ways. At the research level, the use of "gifted" prevails in spite of a strong push by a U.S. Department of Education task force report in 1993, to delete the word and substitute 'exceptionally talented' and 'outstandingly talented'. In Canada, the term "developmentally advanced" enjoys some popularity. Provincial policy in Ontario, however, has stuck with 'gifted'. The dominant advocacy group, Association for Bright Children (ABC) has long maintained a distinction between 'gifted', a concept oriented toward intellectual ability, and 'bright', a wider notion that encompasses intellectual, creative, musical, artistic, athletic and leadership abilities.

No matter the approach taken, any attempt to describe the characteristics of gifted students reveals just how interwoven are matters like ability and desire in the human psyche, and how crucial are the matters of opportunity, environment and circumstance. Every classroom teacher, for example, will notice in many of her students, from time to time, any or all of the characteristics that appear in the list opposite. At the same time, she will inevitably reflect on whether the characteristics are situation-related and temporary, or whether they have always been genuinely present in the student, just waiting for exposure by the circumstance. There are other concerns too, like distinguishing high verbal ability (a commonly accepted identifying

characteristic) from mere artfulness and facility; or, distinguishing truly inherent abilities from those that show up in school as a consequence of the student's life at home. The end result is a large body of literature and a wide range of views on just what constitutes giftedness.

Defining by 'Characteristics'

Gifted students appear to have characteristics and abilities that stand out from the general run of things. What follows here are many of those most cited by both educators and parents. These are but one way of defining gifted students and their use may well prevail more out of tradition than scientific method. However, they are at the very least a beginning point. The challenge, for educators especially, is to determine not just the presence and the stability of these characteristics in a student, but to decide on their relative importance as standards qualifying a student for specialized instruction.

- wide range of abilities both academic and otherwise
- well developed attention span, and a deep curiosity; ability to grasp, retain, synthesize, and act upon information
- ability to work independently, and to take responsibility
- capacity to adjust easily to new situations and demands
- superior vocabulary and reading ability;
- considerable energy and above-average health
- well-developed capacity for abstract, complex, logical and insightful conceptualizations
- more interested in questions than answers
- enjoys learning
- self aware and reflective
- creative and imaginative
- ability to generalize information across settings
- highly developed sense of consequence and forward planning
- motivated and goal oriented
- able to see unusual diverse relationships
- advanced sense of moral/ethical judgment

- thought processes accelerated

Note that along with the positive characteristics above, students who are gifted may also demonstrate attributes that can be considered negative in a learning environment. These include:

- bored and inattentive, particularly when the subject area is not of interest to them
- highly sensitive
- extreme perfectionism
- difficulty changing tasks
- stubbornly prefer certain ways of learning
- overly self-critical and will strive for perfection unrealistically
- unwilling to listen to other perspectives
- insists on dominating discussion

Defining by 'Interactions'

Most educators recognize that giftedness is a dynamic exceptionality, really too complex to be confined to a list of static, observable characteristics. Consequently, it has become regular practice now, to define giftedness in terms of fluid, overlapping constellations. According to this approach, giftedness is the result of a number of characteristics interacting to achieve a purpose, rather than being present in the individual in a kind of parallel isolation. One of the first and still very much accepted presentations of this style of identification was offered by Renzulli (1977), which he called the Enrichment Triad Model.

Renzulli, J.S. (1977) *Enrichment Triad Model: A guide for developing defensible program for the gifted and talented, Creative Learning Press. (The model has been embellished slightly in subsequent editions.)*

Enrichment Triad Model

Sometimes called the 'three-ring model' because it is presented as three overlapping circles, giftedness in this schema is seen as an interaction among a high level of general ability; a high level of task commitment; a high level of creativity. Within the model all three attributes must be present but will not necessarily be equal.

Students who are gifted, according to Renzulli, are those capable of developing this composite set of traits and applying the composite to any potentially valuable area of human performance. What is significant in this approach is the recognition of both human dynamism and the interplay of key qualities. There are times, quite naturally, when the degree of task commitment glows or fades in an individual. Everyone is more (or less) creative at some moments than at others. And abilities may well be relative to the nature of a task. The Enrichment Triad Model accommodates all of this, which probably explains why it gained very rapid acceptance among educators. Yet it has not led gifted education entirely out of the woods. Renzulli himself, in subsequent publications, argued that general ability is less important than specific performance in an operational definition of giftedness. (Which means, of course, that everyone can be gifted at some time: another major consideration for those responsible for definitions.)

Defining by 'Multiples'

An increasingly popular way of looking at giftedness is to recognize that enriched abilities in a human being not only take many inherent forms, but also can be expressed in a variety of ways. Such a point of view is eminently satisfying to educators who accept that academic achievement by itself, and the traditional view of intelligence as measured by an IQ number, are entirely inadequate representations of giftedness.

Triarchic Theory of Intellectual Giftedness

Robert Sternberg (1997) who has published extensively on the nature of creativity has offered special education two multiple views of what giftedness means. In the first, his triarchic

Kyle is an only child of professional parents, both very successful lawyers, and both very caring and nurturing to their son. A nanny brings Kyle to the school's day care when it opens, but one or sometimes both parents pick him up (at varying times) from day care after school. Their home and their life style is very much intellectually and culturally enriched. That influence was very obvious when Kyle entered grade one with a vocabulary and linguistic ability very much beyond the norm for his age. His identification as gifted was immediately and smoothly effected. (The parents had requested an IPRC prior to his enrolment.)

Throughout grades one and two, Kyle's school performance was equal to that of his also-identified-as-gifted classmates, although there was a glitch in grade one. Kyle began the year in French immersion, but it became obvious immediately, that it was a most unsuitable program for him. The parents demurred at first, but after extensive consultation with a psychologist they retained privately, they accepted the school's recommendation and Kyle was withdrawn. Early in grade three, a more serious problem developed. The gifted group, although nominally in regular class, was doing more and more study on a self-contained basis and Kyle had trouble keeping up. By the end of grade three, the gap between him and his classmates had widened.

It is now June, and the crunch has come. The regular IPRC review requested a full assessment of all students in the gifted primary group, because board policy shifts placements at grade four to either full time special class or full time regular with enrichment. Kyle and one classmate are below criterion for special class on all markers but one (parent nomination). Board policy gives the IPRC latitude to withdraw Kyle's identification as gifted. The committee declined to do that but did place him in a regular class, His parents are appealing now, on two bases: one that assessments of children Kyle's age (7.9) are unreliable; and two, that separating him from his peers of the past two years is not in his best interests, especially since it was the board that grouped him thus in the first place. The school board says that by its widely accepted standards, Kyle's abilities do not merit special placement. The Appeal Board must now make its recommendations.

theory, Sternberg posits three kinds of intelligence as necessary for giftedness:

analytic: particularly analytic reasoning and reading comprehension (the intelligence more likely to be measured by traditional IQ tests);

synthetic: creativity, intuition; response to invention, novelty and coincidence;

practical: ability to apply one or both of the above pragmatically.

Most people have all three kinds of intelligence in their makeup but a central part of giftedness in this theory is the act of coordinating the three and knowing when to use which one. A gifted person then, is a competent self-manager. Such an individual not only knows what and how better than most, he also knows better where and when to use what and how. One reason for the positive reception of Sternberg's position among teachers is its appeal to the notion that creativity, adaptiveness and old-fashioned common sense and shrewdness play a major role in gifted behaviour.

Pentagonal Implicit Theory of Giftedness

Sternberg presents another theory of giftedness which offers criteria held as implicitly valuable in a culture. The five criteria are excellence, rarity, productivity, demonstrability, and value. (See Figure 8A.) Educators who give credence to this theory are led to consider first what their culture holds dear before they propose to set out a definition of giftedness. If nothing else, this is a theory that goes a long way toward answering a frequent criticism of gifted education: namely, that it ignores gifted potential in minorities because of a prejudice in favour of the dominant culture. It also adds background light to the charge that most people interested in gifted education, both implicitly and explicit-

A Summary Adaptation of the Pentagonal Implicit Theory

Criterion	Explanation	Example
Excellence	Superior in some way to age peers	Writes narrative fiction much better than peers with same schooling
Rarity	Ability infrequent at age/peer level	Not just better fiction but usually superior
Productivity	Individual produces	Other writers recognize superior skill
Demonstrability	Proven in a public way	Wins awards of consequence
Value	Ability is valued by society	Recognized by the culture in public ways

Figure 8A

ly limit that interest to elements our society values most. That is to say: in our education system, to be gifted as a writer of poetry, or to be a virtuoso violinist, has more value than to be a gifted cabinet-maker, because that reflects the dominant cultural view.

Multiple Intelligences: The 'Gardner Theory'

In *Frames of Mind*, Howard Gardner (1983, 1993) proposes a theory of multiple intelligences: linguistic, musical, logical-mathematical, spatial, bodily-kinesthetic, interpersonal, intrapersonal and naturalist. (See Figure 8B.) The theory holds that each of these intelligences is independent in function, and that if one intelligence is more powerfully developed than another, it will take over for a weaker or less developed one. (He originally developed the theory while studying stroke patients.) Gardner's very persuasive writings, supported by interesting research, emphasize the multifold aspect of human intelligence, illuminating yet again the inadequacy of IQ testing with its implied notion of intelligence as a single, internal construct. His work has been instrumental in expanding the view that there is considerable development and plasticity in human growth. Further, even though this plasticity may be modulated by genetic constraints, humans are predisposed to certain intellectual operations and styles of operation, all of which can be addressed by education. The Gardner theory has particular appeal to teachers, perhaps because it reflects much more than other notions, the wide variety of abilities they see in a classroom full of students. Not only that, a theory of multiple intelligences reinforces the natural disposition of teachers to promote self-esteem in their students by recognizing that the world has room for many kinds of talent. On the other hand, the theory has also been criticized as a first step in the demise of gifted education for, as the definition becomes broader and more all-encompassing, it has the effect of eliminating any distinction giftedness may have.

Emotional Intelligence

A view advanced by Daniel Goleman (1995, 1997) concludes that star performers owe their superiority to what he calls emotional intelligence. According to Goleman, this intelligence is found in people skills: social radar, political sensitivity, trustworthiness, empathy in personal relationships, and team-building ability to create opportunity out of diversity. The theory was developed out of a survey of personnel in over 500 organizations worldwide. Although it enjoys an exceptionally enthusiastic reception in business and industry, the theory does not have the same appeal to education. Some argue that educators' reticence is owing to the fact that the theory appeared first in the popular press instead of acquiring official sanction by exposure in academic publications first.

The Importance of a Balanced View

The varied explanations of giftedness (there are others beyond those summarized above) both plague and enrich the attempts of educators and parents to define giftedness and properly

A Summary Adaptation of Multiple Intelligences (Gardner Theory)

Type	Manifestation
1. Linguistic	Exceptional ability to use words, often prolific
2. Musical	Uncommon sensitivity to pitch, rhythm, timbre, often without training
3. Logical/ Mathematical	Rapid problem solving, grasp of underlying principles of causal systems, extraordinary ability to handle long chains of data
4. Spatial	Transforms easily among elements, superb mental imagery, very highly developed perception of pattern
5. Bodily/ Kinesthetic	Poise and control of body and movement evident even before training
6. Interpersonal	Capacity to 'read' people even without language
7. Intrapersonal	Very mature sense of self
8. Naturalist*	Sensitivity to nature and ability to recognize and classify natural things

*A recent addition. It has not been accepted as enthusiastically as the initial seven

Table 8B

identify its candidates. Nevertheless, because these views tend to lead away from the notion of giftedness as a single construct (the IQ notion) toward a view of giftedness as an expression of several contributing factors, students are beginning to be more fairly identified. Above all, the idea of giftedness as a construct standing on a number of foundations, gives more credence and importance to creativity, to commitment, and to the expression of ability in ways other than the narrow confines allowed by academic achievement alone.

Some Issues in the Field

✦ *Discrimination and gifted identification?* Researchers and educators alike are becoming increasingly concerned about the under representation of particular groups within the category of giftedness. Persons with disabilities, students who are culturally different, females, and students who have low socioeconomic status are often excluded from gifted classes in part due to the narrow identification procedures employed by some school boards. Heavy reliance on IQ measures for example, can present difficulties for students who have learning disabilities, as well as for those with sensory impairment. The lack of instruments normed on such groups suggests that the scores obtained by students with disabilities may not be representative of their actual ability.

✦ *Separate Classes?* How to deal with students once they have been identified as gifted is a continuing debate. At one time, the heat arose primarily over whether or not the students should be placed in separate schools. Proponents of this approach argue that a totally separated (but not totally isolated) environment can offer a much more enriched experience where the students are challenged by interchange with others like themselves, by special teachers, by an atmosphere of intellectual ferment, and by the momentum of exclusivity where elevated goals will obtain. The argument goes further to posit that a congregated environment will offer role modeling less likely to be available in the mainstream. There are reasons to accept the validity of this position. Empirical evidence particularly, has long demonstrated the stimulating power of high expectations in a specialized, highly charged, intellectual environment.

On the other hand, there are also strong arguments in favor of inclusion. A principal tenet holds that although segregated environments may be successful, they are so specialized as to be unrealistic, and therefore counter-productive. By extension, experience in a rarified environment may mean the gifted student will be ill prepared to perform effectively in the real world. Ultimately, like most arguments over this issue, whether to congregate gifted students in special schools, or include them, will never be fully resolved, not least because of the politics involved.

♦ *How to program?* When decisions have been taken to maintain gifted students in an integrated environment, a next stage of issues inevitably arises over how to provide the proper program. One camp argues for enrichment: providing special activities within a regular class setting for selected students. Proponents say that this keeps the gifted student rooted in reality, and that given the premise that every one exhibits giftedness from time to time, there is less risk that potential giftedness will be ignored.

Detractors state that enrichment really does not qualify as gifted education because gifted students in regular programs suffer under the myth that they can easily teach themselves and that what passes for enrichment often means just giving more of the same work, utilizing gifted students as tutors, or providing busy work such as crosswords.

A next, more specialized style, *ability grouping*, is also offered in an inclusive environment where the gifted are selected out for differentiated instruction in more or less homogeneous groups. Supporters of this style usually advance the separate classes argument described above, while detractors say ability grouping fosters elitism. A third style, *acceleration*, despite a great deal of uniformly supportive evidence in favour of

The Case of Lydia

At a professional development day, one of Lydia's former primary teachers (grades one and two) met the girl's grade eight teacher in her new school and was surprised to hear that Lydia, one of her brightest ever students, was "just getting by".

"Lydia can certainly handle the curriculum," the grade eight teacher said, "and she's truly a pleasant young person—wonderful with the little children in our tutoring program; a natural who teaches as well as we do—but yes, just getting by. The work's always done, and on time. Adequate but not much more than that.

"I've always felt she could do better," the teacher continued, "but I've got a big class. The truth is, I'm in my first year and I'm having a busy time. I just can't get around to her as I'd like to, especially with some of the demanding students I've got."

The conversation piqued the grade eight teacher's curiosity, however, and he soon uncovered the fact that Lydia had been identified gifted in grade four in her former school, but neither her placement nor her program changed upon instructions conveyed by the family's parish priest. Lydia's family had emigrated to urban Ontario from a mountain village in southern Europe when she was a little girl. Her parents still do not speak English, and until now their parish priest has been their interlocutor with schools and other officialdom. Lydia's older sister had also caused a minor flurry at the school when she left school after grade six to marry a man to whom she had been betrothed by her parents. The grade eight teacher was also told that Lydia's grade four teacher, a committed feminist, had been transferred to another school after she had defiantly attempted to enrich the girl's program.

Without authorization or permission, the grade eight teacher informally administered an achievement test to Lydia and discovered that, according to the test, she was capable of grade 11-12 work in language and even in math, although she had not yet been exposed to the subject in a any significant way.

"A waste," he said to the primary grade teacher a few weeks later. "A shame and a waste. Lydia should be in a gifted class, or at least, deserves enrichment. Isn't there anything that can be done here?"

"Termites" ✍

Lewis Terman, sometimes referred to as the father of gifted education, did much to develop the founding knowledge base for this population. Between 1922 and 1928 Terman and his colleagues, utilizing standardized intelligence testing, identified approximately 1500 children as gifted. Researchers tracked these children (in later years known as "Termites") for three-quarters of a century. The results did much to dispel the myth of the weak, fragile, brainy child. The findings of the long term studies indicated that while being intellectually superior, the subjects were also superior socially and psychologically, and were more physically healthy.

it, is one of the least used programming methods, usually because of the fear of negative social and emotional consequences for the accelerated student.

Most school boards tackle the program issue by offering a variety of styles for students identified as gifted, on the quite reasonable premise that variety of program is necessary to satisfy a variety of superior abilities.

✦ *Limits to the category?* Advocates of gifted education wince at the fact that despite the broadening of the concept, programming for *talent*, unusual ability in, say, music, or athletics, or drama, or the visual arts, continues to be a poor relative in most school boards. Because these abilities are not necessarily accompanied by superior academic achievement, the issue is first: whether to classify them as examples of giftedness; second, and likely far more important: how—even whether—to offer programs aimed at developing talents. An increasing practice in larger jurisdictions now is to develop 'arts schools' for talents that come under this rubric. However, admission to these excellent academies is often tied to superior academic achievement. Also distance means students in rural areas may have little

opportunity to avail themselves of these specialized settings. (It is an interesting comment too, on our culture, Sternberg's theory notwithstanding, that exceptional ability in areas like carpentry or design or other trades receive little or no accommodation under the title of giftedness.)

✦ *Survival?* Education for the gifted regularly endures accusations of meritocracy and elitism, no matter how egalitarian admission prerequisites may be. For this very important, if somewhat insidious reason, special education for gifted students is often in jeopardy. It is not unusual therefore, for the continuing existence of specialized programming to depend on the vigour and determination of parent advocacy groups, acting in support of determined educators who feel this kind of special education is not just a practical but a moral obligation. On the other hand, it is impossible to ignore the uneasiness raised by the overly high number of students identified as gifted.

✦ *Gifted education for primary?* An enduring argument in the field thrives over the issue of offering programs for the very young. Many boards of education are reluctant to formally identify students in the primary grades as gifted, and equally reluctant to authorize special classes, or formal, differentiated program for them. This attitude has taken hold, first of all, because the developmental elasticity so typical at ages 4-5 to 8-9 can make confident identification difficult. Secondly, since primary education is usually very adaptive and flexible, and more individualized, the gifted can be easily accommodated in the main stream. Further, in primary education there is an importance attached to social skills that in some schools takes precedence even over the development of academic and cognitive skills.

✦ *Gender?* More males are identified for gifted programs than females, and both educators and parents have had difficulty finding concrete and agreeable explanations for this. There is no conclusive research that points to biological difference as an explanation. Yet, explanations that point to traditions of male dominance in our culture have equally sparse research support. While some efforts have been made to examine whether the learning needs of gifted females require a different view of gifted education, consensus in the field is that too little has been done to address this discrepancy.

◆ *Building a labyrinth?* The field of the gifted is regularly accused of burying itself in complexity, with inordinately interwoven and complicated models for identification, equally intricate models for program, and constant, complicated self-examination. There is empirical evidence to support this. Some boards in Ontario, for example, while recognized for their commitment to educating the gifted, have such amazingly intricate and time-consuming patterns of identification—and programs to match—that it is conceivable some students may not be receiving appropriate program for the sim-

ple reason that they (or their parents) lack the will or the means or the stamina to crawl through the bureaucratic web.

How Students are Nominated for Gifted Programs

All school boards in the province, whatever their respective policies regarding the nomination of candidates for gifted education, use a number of different methods for making determinations. Usually, a board relies on a combination of elements like the ones listed here.

1. Despite the acknowledged weaknesses of IQ tests, they continue to dominate as a screening device. What is administratively attractive about IQ tests is that they produce a quantified statement, a number, irrespective of whatever else they offer, and in most jurisdictions this

---

Gifted Underachievers? *New*

These are students whose potential is implied by significant achievement, or by high IQ test scores, but whose apparent abilities are not realized. Not that they are failures, necessarily. They may well work at grade. However, if an individual is truly gifted, yet produces at an average level, then it may be reasonable to conclude he is an underachiever. On the other hand, lest students who are thought to be superior become tarred with the brush of underachievement, it is important for their parents and teachers to evaluate a number of factors before making a judgment.

Has he learned to learn? Many very able students 'coast' in the early grades because they master classroom demands effortlessly. Then, as the level of challenge increases and more is required, they may not rise to the occasion, either because their confidence is eroded, or more likely, because they have not learned consistent, effective work habits.

Do the social factors permit success? Some children deliberately underplay their potential because they do not wish to be singled out.

Gifted underachievers also tend to have low self-esteem and peer problems, which only exacerbate the underachievement.

Are expectations realistic? Learning is not automatically easy for children who are bright. Sometimes the expectations of the adults in their lives, especially parents, do not match what the children are capable of doing at particular points in their development. Flexibility, communication, addressing skills deficits and creative programming can greatly assist gifted underachievers in realizing their potential.

Is there a good 'fit' between the child and the classroom? An overabundance of busywork, inflexible teaching, low expectations, and an overly competitive classroom environment are factors that contribute to poor achievement by gifted students. Some gifted children do not fare well in structured environments. Others find it difficult to conform even to the simple demands that are necessary to make a school run efficiently. Such students may well underperform as a result.

By the end of the second grade, Colin's pranks had already made him a legend in his school. At first, most of the staff were willing to see the funny side. The upset he caused with his first major foray, for example, by putting what appeared to be soiled facial tissues (he used camembert cheese) on the tables at the school bake sale, was forgiven with chuckles. So was the time he upped the ante with seemingly used toilet tissue in his classmate's lunch boxes. However, everyone was less than amused when, during the return from a fire drill, Colin somehow convinced the entire junior kindergarten class to hide in the janitor's storeroom. Nor was the principal too pleased when Colin attached an inflated condom to the parents' notice board in the entrance hall.

Inevitably, the litany of mischief gradually became more serious. Colin discovered he could bring police to the school by activating the overnight security system with a handheld laser pointer. On one occasion he pulled the fire alarm at dismissal time and in the ensuing chaos, disabled two school buses by plugging their tail pipes with styrofoam. It was a carefully planned endeavour, for the plugs were precut to size and the chosen vehicles were at the very front and very back of the bus lineup. When a large order of pizza arrived at the school during the first week of school in grade three, it was widely concluded that Colin was warming up for another year, and something would have to be done.

Serendipity intervened at this point, in the combination of an educational assistant with three year's experience in a class for the gifted, and a teacher with a passion for Renaissance art. In response to a group project they devised for the class, Colin produced a mural which duplicated Da Vinci's *The Last Supper*, but from a ground level perspective. Thirteen very large pairs of feet exactly paralleled the positioning in Da Vinci's famous work! Among the reactions to this mural was the educational assistant's strong push to have Colin assessed as a candidate for gifted class. The outcome confirmed her intuition. He was found to be off the scale in creativity and very superior in IQ test results. As well, Colin became caught up in the "Renaissance passion", and the pranks stopped, or at least went on hold.

Where things stand now, Colin qualifies for the highest level of gifted placement in the board's Special Education Plan. That would mean a transfer to a nearby school, but both Colin and his parents are opposed to any placement that would take him away from his current teacher and educational assistant. Unfortunately his present school is not designated for in-class gifted resource, and the EA is soon to be heavily involved at the other side of the grade three pod with two students who have severe multiple disabilities including chronic health problems. Everyone is concerned that if Colin is unchallenged, the ever more serious pranks will return.

number becomes an entry-level border for admission to programs. The established figure varies from one school board to another (Figures of 140 and 130 Full Scale score on the Wechsler Intelligence Scale for Children are typical). The work of such people as Sternberg and Gardner notwithstanding, faith in tradition has not yet been seriously shaken. Rationales for the continued reliance on a number include the presumed fairness of using an objective measure, the high correlation between IQ testing and academic strength, and good old fashioned test mystique! Detractors argue that IQ tests discriminate against students who are culturally different and students with disabilities.

2. Tests of creativity are sometimes used to identify gifted especially in jurisdictions where creative behaviours are given credence as a major cluster. However, because the validity of these tests is so much in question, their use has less impact, generally, than IQ test scores, and teacher, parent and peer nominations.

3. Achievement tests are used as initial screening mechanisms for giftedness much in the same way as in the assessment of retarded performance. In typical practice, the student who scores significantly above his or her age level (usually two or more grades) is a potential candidate for gifted programming.

4. Teacher nomination is a popular method of

screening in the very early grades. Many boards require teachers to use a clearly defined rating scale, or inventory checklist to substantiate a nomination. One problem with this method is that scales usually correlate the academic behaviour of students with what is expected of them academically in the succeeding years (inevitably raising the concern that students who "play the game" are most likely to have an advantage).

5. Parent nomination is used by many school boards, on the quite reasonable premise that parents have the best knowledge of their child's development. Although parent nomination is clearly a beneficial factor in the process of selection, educators must keep in mind that parents often lack opportunity for the wider view when assessing their own child's current and potential success in school. What seems gifted ability at home may not seem so when compared to abilities across a whole class. Interestingly, parents from lower socioeconomic groups seem more likely to report giftedness than parents from higher socio-economic areas.

> The most gifted members of the human species are at their creative best when they cannot have their way
> - Eric Hoffer

6. Peer nomination is yet another method for initiating referral. Although experts in the field have been favourable in their attitude to this style, there is still a serious lack of research to support it.

7. Self nomination has developed as a recent practice. Very often a self-nomination accompanies a nomination by teacher or parent, and more often than not is presented because the student has been asked to do so by one or both of the latter.

Organizational Models

Organizing the Students

It is quite common practice for boards to organize students identified as candidates for gifted education into levels, most commonly three

levels. Given names like 'mode' or 'plateau' or 'level', these groups are usually differentiated by ability so that the majority will likely be identified as Gifted: Level I (or Mode or Plateau 1). A smaller number will be designated Level II and even fewer will be in Level III.

The largest group, Level I, will likely spend most of its time in the regular classroom, but will receive some enriched or differentiated curriculum. This may be in the form of a theme study undertaken independent of, but in addition to, the regular curriculum. The classroom teacher may be helped by a resource teacher, or the latter may have responsibility for the venture entirely on her own. (Many schools encourage the teacher and resource teacher to co-operate, and to involve all the students in the class as much as possible, whether they are designated Level I or not.)

Level II students may also be assigned to a regular class, but may be withdrawn more frequently for independent pursuits under the guidance of a resource teacher. These students may also be somewhat more involved in projects that involve several schools at once, and that culminate in special presentations, workshops, etc. Level III students are more likely to be in separate classes where the entire curriculum is differentiated.

Organizing the Programs

School boards invest considerable time and effort in developing organizational models to fulfill programming requirements for the gifted. One immediate outcome is that the programs are thus established on a broad basis, so that there can be a good deal of interaction among schools, with sharing of resources, expenses, etc. To a greater extent too, than in most other areas of special education, there tends to be more board-wide excursions, cooperative projects, and involvement with what the community at large has to offer. Whether or not a board formally divides its gifted students among levels as described above, it usually designs the delivery of program service around a particular style or model. Following is a list of some of the models that continue in popular use in Ontario. Almost without exception, they are implemented with local variations.

The Enrichment Triad

With modifications, the Enrichment Triad (Renzulli, 1977) is very widely used in the province, indeed throughout Canada. It proposes three levels of activity:

General Exploratory Activities: designed to expose pupils to exciting topics, ideas, and fields of knowledge not ordinarily covered by the regular curriculum. There are extras like visiting speakers, field trips, demonstrations, and interest development centres.

Group Training Activities: methods, materials, and instructional techniques designed to develop thinking processes, research and reference skills, and personal and social skills.

Individual or Small-Group Investigations: students investigate real problems and topics using appropriate methods of inquiry.

An important modification of the Enrichment Triad is the *Revolving Door Identification Model* (Renzulli, et al., 1981)). In this model, the resource room teacher is a consultant and the classroom teacher is directly involved in the students' special projects. Students are not permanently in or out of the program, but can apply for special consideration to work on projects of their own choosing. The resource teacher helps the student to frame the area of interest into a researchable problem; suggests where he can find appropriate methodologies for pursuing the problem like a professional enquirer; helps him to obtain appropriate resources, provides assistance and encouragement, and helps find appropriate outlets and audiences for the creative work.

Both styles above enjoy more popular use than a third notion developed by the same author called the *Multiple Menu Model* (Renzulli, 1988) which focuses on ways to teach content in efficient and interesting ways.

The Autonomous Learner Model

This is a program developed by Betts (1986)* principally for the secondary school. It adapts to the departmentalized structure of high schools, and anticipates that students will be withdrawn for single periods at specified times of the week. The student progresses through five stages:

i) orientation;

ii) individual development: learning the attitudes and concepts necessary for life-long learning;

iii) enrichment activities: exploring outside the curriculum; becoming aware of resources;

iv) seminars: presenting results of personal pursuits and findings to larger groups for evaluation;

v) in-depth study: opportunity to pursue an area of interest on a longer term basis.

The Purdue Three-Stage Enrichment Model

This is a half day or full day withdrawal program (Feldhausen & Kolloff, 1986) used mostly in elementary schools. The Purdue type of program is quite popular (under names like "Challenge", "Upward Bound", etc.) because it offers enrichment and opportunity without taxing the already scanty resources that typify so many elementary schools. Needless to say the quality of these programs varies dramatically according to the teacher in charge.

There are three basic components:

i) divergent and convergent thinking, in which the program concentrates on problem solving, decision making, forward planning, etc.;

ii) creative problem solving, which offers strategies and techniques in creative problem solving of real problems;

iii) development of independent learning, which requires the student to engage in the development of a product through learning and investigation and then share it with an audience.

Other Styles

Other responses to the need for educating the gifted use more time-honoured approaches.

✧ Enrichment in the classroom: A differentiated program of study offering experiences beyond the regular curriculum. This model

• • • ――――――

* Note that almost all of the models listed here continue to undergo modest revisions (with later publication dates) but in all cases their basic structures are the same. As it is, very few schools or school boards adopt a model without making further adaptations.

――――――― • • •

is delivered by the regular classroom teacher, with or without assistance from a consultant or resource teacher.

❖ Consultant teacher program: Differentiated instruction is provided within the regular classroom by the classroom teacher with the assistance of an educational consultant or specialist. (Occasionally delivered by the specialist.)

❖ Community mentor program: Students interact on an individual basis with selected members of the community to study topics of special interest.

❖ Independent study program: projects supervised by a qualified adult.

❖ Learning enrichment service: Generally, this is a networking system that combines many of the above ideas in an organized way.

Although the content and methods in the styles immediately above do not differ widely from those of the more formal models (assuming they are well-run) they are not as well received, principally because, their defenders say, they lack the aura that attaches to a program with an impressive title and a more apparently formal design. Critics, on the other hand, say that less formalized structures are much more susceptible to casual, ad hoc programming, and are at greater risk of arbitrary cancellation.

✔ STRATEGIES FOR THE CLASSROOM

"Achieving potential" is admittedly a buzz-word in all of special education, but its use requires no apology for it identifies what special education is all about. The phrase has extraordinary personal and societal significance in the case of the gifted.

A program for gifted students must be based on the idea of achieving potential, and from that premise alone proceed to accommodate their unique needs. Part of that program—in some cases perhaps all of it—will be met in the role played by the classroom teacher. Each individual teacher of the gifted brings to a program, or a class, or a student, his own unique nature, as well as his own unique talents and interests and skills and background, all of which in the right circumstances, go a long way toward fulfilling the notion of achieving potential. In other words, as with any teaching-learning situation the teacher is the key.

There are however, certain absolutes to which teachers should subscribe, irrespective of their own preferences, styles, and areas of interest. These are planning goals which include the following:

(1) Establish an environment which shows clearly that intelligent thought, analysis, and creativity are valued.

(2) Encourage students to discover and develop their special abilities. Provide the time, space, materials and opportunities for them to do this at the sacrifice, if necessary, of the laid-on curriculum. (In this sense the teacher is much more of a facilitator than an instructor.) Arrange learning experiences that go beyond the normal acquisition-of-knowledge level. Gifted students need to go higher, deeper, and wider in their pursuit of a subject, pushing past the usual limits. Very often the teacher acts as a consultant, using maturity and experience to help the student find a productive critical path, or a method of investigation.

(3) Provide opportunities for students to interact with adults, other students, and with various experts so that they will be challenged, not just to know about things, but about people, and so that they will learn to see their own place and their responsibility in the human connection.

(4) Create an atmosphere where risk-taking, speculation, and conjecture can be undertaken safely. The teacher recognizes that trial and error are part of learning and that the only real failures in a classroom are those which erode self-esteem. If the teacher herself takes risks, and fails, the student invariably will learn from this too.

The Characteristics of the Teacher

More than in any other area of special education, the literature on the gifted goes on at great length about the ideal teacher. Most texts spin out lists of desirable characteristics that include such things as having a broad general knowledge base, being a good facilitator, good questioning skills and confidence. Viewed cynically, one might be forced to conclude that truly effective teachers of the gifted are a composite of genius, encyclopedic information, intuitive splendor, and sainthood.

Realistically, truly effective teachers are effective no matter what their responsibilities. And one would hope that all teachers are effective. Yet common sense dictates that the gifted and talented will naturally respond better to teachers with broad interests, extensive information and abundant creative energy. Not that students who are, say, learning disabled or behaviour disordered would not benefit from such teachers as well. The difference may be in the horizons implied by achieving potential. The needs of a student with a learning disability or a behaviour disorder, for example, are usually more immediate and more focused. But for the gifted, achieving potential provokes images of more distant horizons. The "miles to go before I sleep" of Robert Frost's famous poem, Stopping By Woods On a Snowy Evening, simply seem more numerous, and more significant in the case of the gifted, and therefore generate more concern about the teachers who will show the way.

READINGS & RESOURCES

Allen, D. (1995). Encouraging success in female students: Helping girls develop math and science skills. *Gifted Children Today Magazine, 18*(2), 44-45.

Ambrose, D., Allen, J., & Huntly, S.B. (1994). Mentorship of the highly creative. *Roeper Review, 17*(2), 131-133.

Betts, G.T. (1986). *Autonomous learner model for the gifted and talented.* Autonomous Learning Publications.

Blythe, T., & Gardner, H. (1990). A school for all intelligences. *Educational Leadership, 47*(7), 33-37.

Clarke, B. (2002). *Growing up gifted: Developing the potential of children at home and at school* (6th ed.). Upper Saddle River, NJ: Merill/Prentice Hall.

Colangelo, N., & Davis, G.A. (1997). *Handbook of gifted education* (2nd ed.). Needham Heights, MA: Allyn & Bacon.

Davis, G.A., & Rimm, S.B. (1998). *Education of the Gifted and talented.* (4th ed.) . Needham Heights, MA: Allyn & Bacon.

Del Prete, T. (1996). Asset or albatross? The education and socialization of gifted students. *Gifted Child Today, 19*(2), 24-25, 44-50.

Dorry, G. (1994). The perplexed perfectionist. *Understanding our gifted, 6*(5), 1, 10-12.

Feldhausen, J.F., & Kolloff, P.B. (1986). The Purdue three-stage enrichment model for gifted education at the elementary level. In J. S. Renzulli (Ed.) *Systems and models for developing programs for gifted and talented.* Mansfield Centre, CT: Creative Learning Press.

Feldhausen, J.F. & Moon, S. (1992). Grouping gifted students: Issues and concerns. *Gifted Children Quarterly, 36*, 63-67.

Feldhausen, J.F., Van Winkle, L., & Ehle, D.A. (1996). Is it acceleration or simply appropriate instruction for precocious youth? *Teaching Exceptional Children, 28,* 48-51.

Feldman, D. (1993). Child prodigies: A distinctive form of giftedness. *Gifted Child Quarterly, 37,* 188-193.

Fetzer, E.A. (2000). The gifted/learning disabled child: A guide for teachers and parents. *Gifted Child Today, 23*(4), 44-50.

Flint, L.J. (2001). Challenges of identifying and serving gifted children with ADHD, *Teaching Exceptional Children, 33*(4), 62-69.

Ford, D.Y., & Harris, J.J. (Eds.). (1999). *Multicultural Gifted Education.* New York: Teachers College Press.

Friesen, J.W. (1997). The concept of giftedness in First Nations context. *Multicultural Educational Journal, 15,* 26-35.

Gardner, H. (1983). *Frames of mind: The theory of multiple intelligences.* Basic Books.

Gardner, H. (1993). *Multiple intelligences.* Basic Books.

Gardner, H. (1999). *Intelligence reframed: Multiple intelligences for the 21ˢᵗ century.* New York: Basic Books.

Goleman, D. (1995, 97). *Emotional Intelligence. Why it can matter more than IQ.* Bantam Books.

Louis, B. & Lewis M. (1992). Parental beliefs about giftedness in young children and their relationship to actual ability level. *Gifted Child Quarterly, 36,* 27-31.

Maker, J.C., Nielson, A.B., & Rogers, J.A. (1994). Giftedness, diversity and problem solving. *Teaching Exceptional Children, 27,* 4-19.

Masse, L. (2001). Direction of gifted education in the first decade of the 231ˢᵗ century: A step back, continuity, and new direction. *Journal of Secondary Gifted Education, 12,* 170-173.

Montgomery, W. (2001). Creating culturally responsive inclusive classrooms. *Teaching Exceptional Children, 33*(4), 4-9.

Pirto, J. (2001). *"My teeming brain": Understanding creative writers.* Cresskill, NJ: Hampton.

Reis, S.M., & Westberg, K.L. (1994). The impact of staff development on teachers' ability to modify curriculum for gifted and talented students. *Gifted Child Quarterly, 38,* 127-135.

Renzulli, J.S. (1988). The multiple menu model for developing differentiated curriculum for the gifted and talented. *Gifted Child Quarterly, 32,* 298-309.

Renzulli, J.S., & Reis, S.M. (1986). The enrichment triad/revolving door model: A school-wide plan for the development of creative productivity. In J. Renzulli (Ed.) *Systems and models for developing programs for gifted and talented.* Mansfield Centre, CT: Creative Learning Press.

Shaywitz, S.E., Holahan, J.M., Freudenheim, D.A., Fletcher, JH.M., Makuch, R.W.., & Shaywitz, B.A. (2001). Heterogeneity with the gifted: Higher IQ boys exhibit behaviours resembling boys with learning disabilities. *Gifted Child Quarterly, 45,* 16-23.

Shore, B. M. , Cornell, D.G., Robinson, A., & Ward, V.S. (1991). *Recommended practices in gifted education.* New York: Teachers College Press.

Silverman, L. K. (1994/1995). To be gifted or feminine: The forced choice of adolescence. *Journal of Secondary Gifted Education, 6*(2), 141-156.

Sternberg, R.J. (1997). A triarchic view of giftedness: Theory and practice. In Colanelo, N. & Davis, G. (Eds.) *Handbook of Gifted education* (2ⁿᵈ ed.). Toronto: Allyn & Bacon.

Winner, E. (1996). *Gifted children: Myths and realities.* New York: Basic Books.

Links

Association for Bright Children
http://www.abcontario.ca/

Goverment of BC resource guide
http://www.bced.gov.bc.ca/specialed/gifted/

Roeper Review
http://www.roeperreview.org/

Kids Source
http://www.kidsource.com/kidsource/pages/ed.gifted.html

Teaching Gifted Children
http://www.canteach.ca/links/linkgifted.html

MENSA
http://www.mensa.org/

CHAPTER 9

Students With Developmental Disability, and Students With Mild Intellectual Disability

*"When I cared for these kids back in the sixties, the goals were so limited.
Teach them to feed themselves, how to go to the toilet ... Stay out of sight! ... that was
a big one. 'Course that's when we had 'em at the home. Easy to aim low when you shut
them away. Today—well, it's just amazing. There's so much retarded kids can do now.
No wonder we don't call them that any more."*

Terry B. (retired institutional care worker)

Misconceptions About Intellectual and Developmental Disabilities

1. Developmental disability is a condition like an illness.

It is not something one *has*, like a heart condition, or big feet, or schizophrenia, but rather a state of functioning characterized by limitations in both intelligence and adaptive skills.

2. An intellectual or developmental disability puts a cap on learning.

An individual's intellectual functioning is not a static thing. (If it were, the role of education would be much different!) Especially for a person with mild disabilities, intensive instruction can make a major difference.

3. The disabilities occur equally across class and gender.

Data collected over decades by the American Association on Mental Retardation (AAMR) and others show that, for a variety of reasons, the number of boys identified is greater than that of girls by factors of five to ten. The disability also has a significantly higher prevalence in children from lower socio-economic classes.

4. Developmental disabilities are reflected in physical appearance.

Certain groups of students, including many with Down syndrome, do appear physically different from their peers, but the vast majority of students with intellectual or developmental disabilities look just like any other students.

5. Students with intellectual problems always learn more when they are included with/separated from other students.

It is not possible to lump all special students into a learning environment classification. If they learn much like everyone else as the evidence suggests, it must be granted that — just as with everyone else — no one environment is consistently and universally superior.

6. A low IQ test score is evidence of at least borderline disability and means the subject's adaptive skills are below normal.

An IQ test may predict academic or school matters, but an individual's level of adaptive skills are more a factor of training, motivation, and social environment, and generally are not tapped by IQ tests.

7. Students with intellectual or developmental disabilities are always compliant/difficult.

Like everyone else, they experience both happiness and emotional stress and react accordingly.

8. Certain racial groups have a higher rate of disability.

This notion has developed in part because a severe, genetically based condition, Tay-Sachs disease, occurs almost exclusively among Eastern European Jews. The situation is very unusual and offers no scientific basis for racial or ethnic attributions.

Changes in Definition and Classification

Changes Over Time

For the first half of the twentieth century, when significant numbers of people with intellectual and developmental disabilities were housed in large institutions, the prevailing definition was one established by American psychologist, H.H. Goddard, in 1910. Goddard divided the exceptionality into four categories of declining ability, beginning with *feeble-minded*, followed by *moron, idiot*, and ending with *imbecile*. By the 1950s, Goddard's categories were overtaken by the general term *mental retardation*, with adjectives of degree like 'mild', 'severe', etc. added to differentiate. Although in the minds of those who advocated for the term, the change represented the best science of the time (and was less offensive than the Goddard terminology) 'mental retardation' was nevertheless loaded with implication for it suggests an incapacity that is both permanent and comprehensive.

By the end of the twentieth century, 'mental retardation' was pretty much replaced by the terms 'intellectual' and 'developmental', usually in combination with a follower: either 'disabilities' or 'challenged'. This change occurred in part out of a gradual realization that classifying people as retarded is a gross over-simplification that ignores the importance of adaptive behaviour, and in part out of passion for political correctness. The result has been, by and large, positive. Although there is some confusion, even among professionals, as to whether terms like 'intellectually disabled' or 'intellectually challenged' are most appropriate—or whether either term is as comprehensive as 'developmental', the language reflects a clear shift in attitude. Not just educators and medical professionals but the public at large, now generally view persons with this disability as equal citizens in the community, capable of learning, and deserving of an education.

The State of Things Today

Regrettably, there is still no universally accepted definition of intellectual disability, but a large body of research, along with intense advocacy by interested parties, and thoughtful application of empirical evidence by educators has led to a more or less general acknowledgement that three inter-related factors describe the exceptionality. These are:

1. sub-average intellectual functioning,
2. problems in adaptive behaviour,
3. both of the above occurring during the developmental period.

1. Sub-average Intellectual Functioning

This aspect is usually addressed by using IQ test scores to indicate levels. Prior to 1973, it was common practice for school boards to follow the policy of the dominant professional body in the field, the American Association for the Mentally Retarded (AAMR) which recommended an IQ test score of 85 and below as the cutoff for identification as 'mentally retarded'. This is only one standard deviation below the mean, or norm, of 100. In 1973, the AAMR recommendation was changed to an IQ test score of "approximately 70 to 75", or *two* standard deviations below the mean, thus significantly lowering the barrier. The change recognized the importance of other factors, and reinforced the

The annual review of Christina's case took longer to complete this year because she is in grade eight and the committee requested a full psychometric assessment. It was the first such undertaking since she was in grade three, five years ago, and confirmed the assertions of the special education resource teacher in the school: that Christina is not only an improved but an improving student. Her IQ test score (both verbal and performance) on the Wechsler scale is Low Average to Borderline (as it was in grade three). But standardized achievement scores show significant gains in academic skills. Christina reads grade four/five material comfortably. (She has had a particularly rewarding experience this year as a "reader" in the kindergarten class.) Creative writing is still a challenge, although this may be a physically related issue; Christina has a disabled left arm and is naturally left-handed. Even with the classroom's several computer programs to help her, however, she has trouble writing even minimally coherent prose. Math gains are significant and measurable. Five years ago, she could not do any basic arithmetic. This year she is working one-on-one with the EA out of the fourth grade textbook.

All the adults who have immediate contact with and responsibility for Christina—her mother, the grade eight teacher, and the educational assistant who has known her since grade six—confirm independently that she has had "a very happy year". Everyone agrees this is very much a result of efforts to manage her occasional bursts of unusual behaviour, and the fact that Christina's classmates now accept her so completely.

In light of this, and given that next year's placement must be decided, the IPRC has offered two options: one, that Christina be promoted to grade nine and go with her classmates to the neighbourhood secondary school (She would have an integrated program as in grade eight), or two, that she spend another year with the grade eight teacher and educational assistant. Christina's mother has mixed feelings on the matter. Christina herself is quite passive and expresses no opinion at all. The IPRC has asked the teacher and assistant to indicate which of the two placements, in their opinion, would work best.

notion that IQ tests are only an aid, not a diagnostic magic wand.

Although there is no "official" set of scores, school boards that use test scores to classify intellectual and developmental disability generally apply the following ranges, each with its own set of general expectations or needs*.

IQ Score	Expectations
Below 25	Student may learn basic self-care and communication skills. Full time ed. assistant or tech. support (or both) likely.
25-40	Part to full time support may teach limited independence. Some life long assistance likely needed.
40-55	With support may learn independent self care and basic academic skills. Supervised independence possible.
55-70	Academic achievement to grade five or more is possible with intermittent support. Secondary school may challenge.

2. Adaptive Behaviour

Generally, adaptive behaviour refers to how well an individual is able to meet — to adapt to — demands made by his or her environment. It is a dynamic construct, one that is influenced by factors like cultural norms, the demands of a particular situation, and the age-group to which an individual belongs. Including adaptive behaviour in the assessment of intellectual ability, a practice that began in the 1970s, has proven to be instrumental in shaping a more positive view.

• • • ——————

* Some jurisdictions correlate IQ ranges with 'classification by degree'. The four most frequently used terms are *mild, moderate, severe, profound.*

—————— • • •

Taking adaptive behaviour into account recognizes that many individuals who might score poorly on an IQ test can actually live and learn quite well in a variety of environments. As well, it encompasses recognition of an individual's strengths, not just weaknesses.

3. The Developmental Period

This is the period up to the chronological age of 18.

Defining by Support Needed

In 2002, the AAMR made yet another major revision to its definition of mental retardation, a change which still includes the intellectual functioning, adaptive behaviour and developmental period factors, but places new emphasis on the importance of *supports*. A primary purpose in describing an individual's limitations, the association insists, is to develop a profile of needed supports which, over time, will improve that person's life functioning. Rather than classifying an individual according to a pre-existing diagnostic category—usually one tied to available models of service—a supports approach evaluates the person's needs and then tries to find strategies that address those needs.

Although skeptics say there is nothing new in this approach except the name, and that it is exactly what effective teachers and educational assistants do when they are given the freedom to act in the name of good, common sense, advocates point out that at the very least, it puts the student ahead of the program and the paperwork.

Ontario's Definition

The categories and definitions of exceptionalities as published in the Ministry of Education's, *Special Education: A Guide for Educators* (2001) presents two levels of disability: 'mild intellectual' and 'developmental', the difference in degree being implicit in the terms. (See Appendix for the complete definitions.) By using both the 'intellectual' and 'developmental' terms, rather than confuse matters the distinction makes the issue of classification administratively simpler. At the same time, the expansion of each term is worded in a manner that anticipates practical response *without* adding undue complexity. Such a positive accomplishment is relatively rare in government literature.

Some Issues in the Field

✦ *Terminology.* An abiding concern is what to call an intellectual disability — or whether to call it anything at all! Part of the tension arises out of the desire of administrators, researchers, clinicians and academics to have a neutral, scientific, and widely accepted term to identify a consonant group for their various purposes. Balanced against this is the far less scientific but equally important desire of parents and advocates to expunge terminology from the field for the simple reason that descriptive terms for this exceptionality, no matter how carefully they are chosen, invariably seem to imply limitations, and very rapidly are adopted for pejorative use in popular parlance.

There appears to be no simple way out of this dilemma. To professionals, terminology is part and parcel of scientific, educational practice. But what terms are appropriate, and how can they be kept from degenerating into insult? No serious professional today would dream of using discarded terms like 'feeble-minded'. Yet so much of the new, semantically gentler terminology seems only to generate its own black humor. ('Developmental' in particular has generated

> My first year and I get not one, but *two* developmental kids in my class! I have to be honest; at the end of September I was going to quit. Sure glad I didn't though. Now that I've had some time, well … it's no different from having any other kids in your class. Not really. But then, these two were pretty good kids. I sure could have used more time on special kids in my teacher training. We never talked about them enough, and well … They're the *real* challenge.
>
> *Alexandra P.*

some unfortunate schoolyard epithets.) This is made especially ironic in light of the fact that 'mentally retarded', the long-accepted term, had pretty much shed its pejorative connotations as society at large developed a more enlightened and balanced view of intelligence, ability, and individual worth. Still, at least in Ontario, advocates have been generally successful in removing 'mentally retarded from the special education lexicon.

◆ *Normalization.* The argument that people should be seen for their similarities to, rather than their differences from the population at large, and that they should be allowed to thrive in the larger society to the maximum possible extent, has provocative implications. In the nineteenth century, the gradual development of institutions to care for the intellectually and developmentally disabled was regarded as a major step forward. And no doubt it was, for institutions which offered care when the alternative was often abandonment, reflected a degree of social and moral responsibility hitherto unknown. But institutions have a potentially insidious nature. For reasons of economy, ease of management, and sometimes ignorance, the environment in an institution is often impoverished in terms of stimulation and opportunity. Given what special educators now know about human development, it is apparent that many of the behaviours historically associated with a disability are consequences of institutional living.

The Case of Robyn

At age seven, Robyn spent several months in a day program at a development centre, but then became ill (she has severe respiratory problems) and remained at home where she was visited daily by a Special Services At Home worker. At age eight she attended her neighbourhood school in a regular grade one for three weeks, but with the agreement of her parents, was transferred to a special resource class, full time. This placement continued until grade four, when she was gradually integrated into a regular class. Robyn moved with her classmates to Grade five and spent that year with them. She is now in grade six.

Robyn is identified as seriously developmentally disabled. Her language abilities are below age norms. Her speech is babyish and mostly in the third person "E.g., *Teacher:* Hi, Robyn! How are you today?" *Robyn:* "Robyn O.K." She does not seem to be able to read, but very much enjoys being read to. She does not participate in any meaningful way in the curriculum; however, she likes to be part of a group when it pursues a task, and very much enjoys being paired with other students when seat work or other individualized tasks are assigned. Attempts to present "parallel curriculum" have been singular failures. Since grade four, Robyn has never once worked on her own. She seems content only when she is part of others' endeavours. An occasional exception to this behaviour is her willingness to spend time at an art table, colouring with crayons and magic markers, but tends to have temper tantrums when tired of this activity if she is not immediately diverted. Robyn destroyed a keyboard when she became bored with a computer program.

Until now (February of grade six) the fact that there is no assistant available to this class (and will not be) has been blunted by the willingness of two classmates, both girls, to befriend, guide, and patiently assist Robyn. But almost simultaneously, the two—in the words of their teacher—"have just discovered boys!" and now actively avoid Robyn, not just inside the classroom but outside too. Robyn's tantrums are now frequent and severe, and her skills have regressed. Motivated at least in part by complaints from parents of other children, the principal has called for an IPRC review. At the committee's first meeting, Robyn's mother made it clear she will not agree to a special class placement. The committee has asked the school, as a first step, to prepare a new IEP for Robyn, working within the present resources available.

The overwhelming impetus in the field therefore, has been toward de-institutionalization, and inclusion in mainstreamed society. The impetus has been driven more by advocacy groups than by governments and educators, but the response of the latter, although late, has been very positive. The reality today therefore, is that very large numbers of disabled people are living in the mainstream, many of them on their own, or with some supervision, many with gainful employment, and acquiring and enjoying the benefits of education.

♦ *Inclusion.* Including intellectually and developmentally disabled persons without reservation in mainstream society is an issue, in large part because of conflict that seems to arise out of the impatience of its supporters, and the guarded hesitancy of the larger society. At the most liberal end of the spectrum are those who argue that *all* persons should be fully included in society immediately, and most especially in schools. The view is that total inclusion at once is the only possible position that a society can morally and ethically adopt. Regrettably,

this position often forces an adversarial context, particularly when educators argue that that for some students, empirical evidence suggests a modified school environment may produce better results.

It is not that the educators reject inclusion but rather that some prefer a cautious approach, arguing that students should be considered on an individual basis, for not all students are ideally suited for immediate inclusion, and that consequences can be potentially disastrous for everyone involved. Unfortunately, the different perspectives often harden because instead of being able to simply recommend this position, educators are made to defend it, and find themselves using arguments that can be interpreted as pro-segregation, whether or not this is indeed what they believe. The risk for students is that the significant developments of the past few decades, are sometimes jeopardized by hasty decisions, emotion, polemics and blanket policies.

Empirical evidence shows that generally, children who begin their school lives in inclusive classrooms treat that environment as natural. And most of the time, the inclusion is successful and continues to succeed for all children as they grow. Where success is not universal is in those situations where the inclusion does not start until later grades, and where it is *arbitrary*.

♦ *Time to learn.* Early theory held that a developmental or intellectual disability implied an absolute limit to potential. This notion was handily reinforced by supposed empirical evidence (especially bizarre behaviours which often turned out to be institutional behaviours) and by notions of incurability. Especially since the success of the normalization movement, it has become evident that with stimulation, support, and direct instruction, there is literally no limit to students' learning capacity. However, the process for some students takes longer. They are learners but they are slower learners. The time factor becomes an issue because many jurisdictions make school enrolment terminal (usually tied to chronological ages of students) either through funding limitations or simply by decree. While continuing

---

Prerequisites to Successful Inclusion

A lucid and comprehensive article in the *American Educational Research Journal*, by Scruggs and Mastropieri (1994) offers both a summary of useful research and their own findings on this issue, concluding that seven factors are crucial to successfully integrating students with special needs.

⇒ Administrative Support

⇒ Support from Special Education Personnel

⇒ Accepting, Positive Classroom Atmosphere

⇒ Appropriate Curriculum

⇒ Effective General Teaching Skills

⇒ Peer Assistance

⇒ Disability-Specific Teaching Skills

education programs go a long way toward circumventing this problem, it is still an issue that has not yet been satisfactorily resolved by school boards and governments.

✦ *Employment and vocational training.* Some disabled adults have paid employment in industries described as 'sheltered workshops', where they are paid for relatively simplistic and repetitive industrial tasks. On one side of this issue is the thought that they are thus given opportunity to contribute to their own support by gainful activity that is within their capacity under supervision. On the other side, there is opinion that such employment is exploitation, and simply an unsubtle extension of institutionalization. The issue is an awkward and difficult one to resolve in a free economy, and proponents of both sides are able to refer to many practical examples that support their respective arguments. For educators the disagreement is uncomfortable, since they must resolve for themselves the importance of this potential employment when determining learning objectives for their students.

✦ *Modern medicine.* Techniques in medical science have introduced whole new areas of uneasiness and controversy. One such, developed in Europe, involves surgery that may alleviate the respiratory complications often suffered by children with Down syndrome. It has become fairly common practice to include facial surgery in the procedure — some argue it is necessary — in order to enhance speech abilities, and to alter the allegedly mongoloidal appearance of the children so that they will look "normal". Its advocates support it largely on the premise that if the children appear normal, they will be treated normally, and grow into a better life as a result. Its detractors hold that normal appearance will raise false and unattainable expectations.

✦ *Greater Challenge in the Classroom.* Changes in definition, especially the lowering of the 'IQ cutoff', changes in placement, especially including students in classrooms rather than institutions, and the steadily growing awareness that intellectually and developmentally disabled people are learners,

mean that teachers and educational assistants today encounter greater numbers of special needs students in their classrooms. Although few would disagree with the premise that these changes have been positive, at the same time the shift has not been without impact. For example, Ontario once had a category of disability called 'trainable mentally retarded' (usually with an IQ test score two standard deviations below the mean) and students identified this way were almost always segregated in separate classrooms with separate, dedicated programs. Today, almost all the students who once might have been classified in this way, are placed in regular classrooms, thereby expanding dramatically the demands on the professionals who teach in those classrooms.

✦ *Other changes too challenge educators.* The uncertainty over just what constitutes intellectual or developmental disability sometimes makes it difficult for schools boards to acquire the extra funding that is often necessary for appropriate support. The reluctance to apply the term 'intellectually disabled' has meant an increase in the number of students identified 'learning disabled' in some jurisdictions, for the latter term is generally seen as less pejorative. Students with fragile health or extensive physical needs, factors that frequently accompany developmental disability, are more often included today in regular classrooms. Taken together, these changes present a level of challenge to educators that has never been experienced before. The fact that teachers and educational assistants are successful for the most part, even though in many cases they are breaking new ground, is a tribute to their professional expertise.

Should Cause Be a Concern for Educators?

Although insight into the reason for a particular student's disability may satisfy intellectual curiosity and the natural desire to know as much as possible about a student in order to support him effectively, several factors diminish the value of this knowledge.

The amount of hard science in the field, not to mention theory and speculation, is extensive and bewildering even to medical specialists. Causes range from trauma (e.g., anoxia at birth) through chromosomal abnormality (e.g., Down syndrome, tuberous sclerosis, Klinefelter's syndrome) to metabolic (e.g., phenylketonuria, Prader-Willi syndrome) and infectious/toxic conditions in the pregnant mother (e.g., rubella, syphilis, alcohol, cocaine). More than one name is used for some conditions (e.g., *epiloia* for tuberous sclerosis), and very often they are poorly or incompletely described, or presented in language that is comprehensible only to the thoroughly initiated. Not only can this create confusion, it is also rare in any case, that a practical educational response can be inferred from a description of cause. Even worse, it is not unknown for a child's case to be given up as educationally hopeless on the basis of a scientific description of cause. For these reasons, some educators argue that causes, therefore, should be tendered only for very compelling reasons. (Boards of education in Ontario, as a matter of practice if not official policy, do not state the cause of a student's disability on the record unless it has treatment implications.)

The Special Case of Down syndrome

One area of disability in which cause may have significance for educators is the chromosomal difference called Down syndrome, estimated to account for 5-6 percent of all cases of intellectual retardation. Students with Down syndrome are often recognizable because of certain common characteristics like a generally smaller stature, thick epicanthal folds in the corners of the eyes, and a smaller oral cavity that results in a protruding tongue. (Less easily noticed but typical, are speckling of the iris, a wide gap between the first and second toes, and a single palmar crease on short, broad hands.)

These physical factors provoke an issue of importance when they are juxtaposed with a typical factor that is non-physical. Most persons with Down syndrome are in the mild to moderate range of retardation, and have generally been shown to have what is called 'trait plastic-ity' (malleable intelligence). Research suggests their early development is normal, particularly in infancy, although it seems to slow as they age. Thus, because the physical aspects of Down syndrome are quite recognizable, it would be a mistake to assume automatically, as many uninformed people do, that a child with the syndrome is intellectually retarded and *ipso facto* incapable.

A second issue accruing to Down syndrome is the physical health factors of which teachers and assistants should be aware. Persons with Down syndrome are at greater risk for congenital heart defects and upper respiratory infections. Many have hyperflexible joints with a high potential for orthopedic injury. Taken together or singly, these characteristics have implications for what goes on in a classroom or schoolyard.

Some Implications for the Classroom

Physical

Milestones like learning to walk, toilet, etc., tend to be attained up to nine months or a year later than the norm. There is also a tendency to perform below age-related standards in motor areas, and frequently, features of height, weight and skeletal development are often at the extreme ends of age norms. Persons with moderate (as opposed to mild) disabilities often show even more complex physical differences, and tend to be markedly less able motorically. Very often severe mental handicaps are part of a multiple set of disabilities with the consequence that simple locomotion and other basic activities become an issue.

Learning and Memory

Problems here, as with other areas, become more marked and more easily observable in tandem with levels of severity, but in almost all students with the disability, learning and memory problems are usually significant. Specific areas of difficulty include ability to pay attention, verbal communication, motivation, ability to generalize, and the ability to understand similarities and differences. Quite typical is difficulty with short term memory. The students

◉ Consumption of alcohol by an expectant mother, even small amounts, can damage a developing fetus, leading to an organic disorder generally known as *fetal alcohol syndrome* (FAS). The disorder very often has a major impact on the child after birth, and by extension, on his or her parents and teachers.

◉ FAS usually manifests itself in a combination of physical, behavioural or intellectual problems ranging from minor to very serious. The condition is life long.

◉ A number of other terms for the syndrome are in use, *Fetal Alcohol Spectrum Disorder* (FASD) and *Alcohol-Related Neuro-developmental Disorder* (ARND) being more recent examples. Perhaps most germane for educators is that medical science now tends to distinguish the full blown syndrome, FAS, from less severe cases by describing the latter as *Fetal Alcohol Effects* (FAE).

◉ Characteristics associated with FAS, and to a lesser extent with FAE, are extensive and usually have a major impact on the individual's education and general life style. Physical anomalies are often skeletal, showing up in deformed limbs and growth deficiency, and may appear in a range of heart and urino-genital problems. Individuals born with FAS also have a high rate of epilepsy, especially in the early years. Very often, the more severe cases will have a facial appearance not unlike that associated with Down syndrome.

Severe learning difficulties and even the ability to live independently as an adult are possible outcomes of FAS. The learning problems typically found in students are similar to those usually classified as developmentally disabled (poor visual scanning, reading problems, inattentive to or unable to absorb detail, difficulty generalizing and deducing, etc.).

Indeed, FAS is now considered to be the second major cause of mental retardation in western countries. In addition, significant behavioural problems such as hyperactivity, indiscriminate forming and severing of bonds or attachments, difficulty expressing emotions, poor inner control, low rate of task completion, are common.

◉ A significant body of opinion, yet to be clearly substantiated by research, holds that the incidence of FAS among homeless people is much larger than that in the general population. Supporters of the thesis contend that FAS is a cause of disabilities that lead to homelessness and a factor that leads to continuation of the life style.

◉ Medical science has been certain of the effects of alcohol on an unborn fetus only since the 1970s. Research into FAS, therefore, and experience with the syndrome as a separate condition is still fairly slim. Nevertheless, strong evidence already suggests that for an individual with FAS or even FAE, the manifestations of the condition intensify rather than lessen as the individual grows older.

◉ Although conclusive data on the prevalence of FAS are still being developed, there is a consensus that the numbers are rising. The impact of increasing numbers has sharp relevance for special educators since it is in their hands where most of the individuals with the condition may end up. Even more frustrating to professionals like teachers and educational assistants who must deal with the effects of FAS is that the syndrome is not a genetic accident but an entirely preventable condition.

◉ For the most part, practical classroom response is similar to the methods applied in the case of other students with developmental disabilities (See Strategies for the Classroom).

do not tend to use memory strategies spontaneously, although they will learn to use mnemonic strategies if explicitly taught to do so. It is important to point out that once a thing is learned and filed in long term memory, the students will recall it as well as anyone else when conditions are appropriate.

Learned Helplessness

Poor short term memory combined with an apparent lack of motivation and a tendency to be off-task, often leads to a passive pattern wherein the student allows a significant adult (or sometimes a fellow student) to manage everything. Viewed from the other side, so to speak, the disabled student manages to train a significant adult to do everything for her, simply by being universally passive. Educational assistants in particular, report this as a recurring problem.

Speech and Language Problems

Frequency of speech defects are considerably above the norm. Mutism and primitive speech are quite common among the severely disabled. Typically, the language level, both oral and written but especially the latter, is below commonly accepted age norms.

Social Adjustment

Many of the students experience difficulty in social interaction because they do not find it easy to 'read' a social setting. It is not uncommon for them to participate inappropriately, perhaps by being too loud or too ebullient for example. Some students in an inclusive setting may at first function in what is called "parallel existence". That is, because they do not know how to naturally ingratiate themselves with their peers, they simply go along in their own world, without really becoming a part of the general social environment. This occurs most frequently, when disabled students and so-called normal students interact with one another for the first time, especially if there has been no preparation. (It is very encouraging however, to observe a class of very young children. The mutual acceptance one invariably sees, forces the conclusion that interaction like this can be natural if inclusion begins early.)

Perseveration

Some individuals develop behaviours that the rest of the world may look upon as bizarre, and tend to indulge in these behaviours repetitively in times of stress or discomfort. As a consequence, a large part of educational planning is sometimes devoted to teaching self-control. Proponents of inclusion argue — with considerable empirical evidence to support them — that inappropriate behaviours are eliminated more easily and quickly in the mainstream.

Self-Injurious Behaviour

Perseveration that leads to harm of a subject's own body is not infrequent, especially among those with severe developmental disabilities. These behaviours cover a wide range such as head-banging, scratching, pinching, hitting and rectal digging. Unfortunately, research has yet to shed light on the causes of these behaviours

---

Genetic Research and the Future

Persons with Williams' syndrome are usually mildly to moderately retarded (Typical IQ test scores are about 60), and have profound difficulties with spatial relationships, abstractions and logical sequences. They typically have elfin-like facial structure, an above-average incidence of heart problems and very often, hyper-sensitive hearing. At the same time, persons with Williams' syndrome have strikingly developed vocabularies, are often warm, compassionate and outgoing, and—what intrigues researchers most—many have prodigy-level talent in music. What is believed to be the cause of the syndrome was discovered in 1993: the loss of some genetic material on Chromosome 7. Researchers believe this site also influences concentration levels and visual and spatial skills. Discoveries in this type of research may one day revolutionize education.

The Case of Blaine

Blaine has just completed his first year at secondary school. He is 18. Although the school is committed to inclusion, three self-contained classes are available on an ad hoc basis. No one is officially placed in these classes full time, but during the past year four students have spent their entire school time there. For the final quarter of the year Blaine became the fifth, mostly because of his overwhelming moroseness and his apparent unwillingness to do anything for himself.

In Blaine's medical report, *fetal alcohol syndrome* is noted as a primary cause of his disability. He also has chronic health problems and spent three years in a hospital school. Academically, Blaine works at approximately a 9-10 year old level, but every teacher who has had responsibility for him insists that he is significantly more capable than his output indicates. They are unanimous in the belief that the academic performance gap is a product of attitude which—also unanimously—they call 'learned helplessness'.

The school's physical education department has proposed to the In-School Team (IST) that next year, the senior football team make Blaine one of the school's 'inclusion pals'. He would be made an honorary player, attend all practices, and be at all games, dressed in equipment and uniform. Although he would not actually compete, he would be part of every other activity. Football team members would also be expected to invite Blaine to their social events and involve him after school. The coach did this once before with a special student, Mel, and the project was so successful it attracted enthusiastic reviews from the media. Blaine's parents, however, are aware of a dark side. When the football team graduated and scattered to universities, colleges, and employment, Mel was, in effect, suddenly abandoned. So traumatic was the experience that he has still not recovered. Mel was then 22 years of age and he too left the school but now his guardian (a grandmother) reports that " … for nigh on a year now he sits, and eats, and stares. Won't talk. Won't look at me. Won't do anything."

Blaine's parents are willing to do anything for their son but want some assurance from the IST that the football team's undertaking will not end up the way Mel's case did.

or the keys to remediation. Empirical evidence suggests a lack of stimulation and stress as possible causes.

Academic Achievement

It requires little effort to recognize that academic achievement is an issue. Achievement deficits seem to be most pronounced in reading comprehension and in arithmetic reasoning and problem-solving. Nevertheless, a steadily growing body of research evidence suggests that time is an important factor. The students pass through the same phases of cognitive development as non-disabled students, particularly childhood phases, but pass through more slowly and often attain lower levels of achievement. Accordingly, it's safe to infer that many disabled students can indeed learn much of a standard school curriculum, but will do it more

slowly and likely with less efficiency. This makes time and *regular practice* crucial items in the educational planning process.

The Importance of Self-Help Skills

For obvious reasons, the most immediate of which is physical health, an important part of an education program deals with items like hygiene, eating and dressing, use of the toilet, physical appearance, etc. While this aspect will be part of an educational plan only to the extent necessary, and that necessity will vary according to the degree of need, learning these culturally significant skills is nevertheless crucial to a student's sense of well-being and sense of self. For intellectually and developmentally disabled students there is much truth in the old adage that connects feeling good to looking good.

Self-Esteem

Self-esteem tends to be low. A combination of discouraging social experience and of repeated failure often leads to self-expectations of poor performance. When this is overlaid with learned helplessness, it is easy to understand why disabled students avoid or ignore challenging tasks. The 'if-at-first-you-don't-succeed-quit' syndrome is tempting and comfortable. Educators must avoid the trap of becoming a controller — the easy route — and instead, by judicious encouragement and behaviour modification, demonstrate to a student that he can do an assigned task and should feel proud because of it.

Assessment and Placement

Although IQ tests continue to play a role, their use has declined significantly. In practice, a student may only be assessed with this type of instrument should an unique situation arise (e.g., the need to settle an issue for funding.) Anecdotal reports by parents, teachers and EAs play an important part in completing a picture of needs. So do a range of instruments known as Rating Scales, Achievement Inventories, Personal Checklists, etc. These vary in length and in nature of information sought, but are similar in principle. They are completed by adults who have been able to observe the student in different situations and are able to judge her skills in a number of areas.

> I think we accepted early on, my wife and I, that this was a lifetime commitment. Our Sammy's retarded, but he's ours and we don't love him any less. Probably a bit more. Still it's scary when we wonder what will happen to him when we're not around any more. The schools … they've done a good job. Really, they have. But he won't be in school forever. And if his mother and I aren't here, what then?
>
> *Hank. S.*

Usually, the skills are rated on a comparative basis (fair, good, excellent, etc.). And most often, the questions deal with areas of general performance like family, community and peer relations, self-care skills, cognitive abilities, and so on. Although these instruments are usually quite informal, and are often constructed locally to meet local needs, there are published adaptive behaviour scales available (e.g. Vineland Adaptive Behaviour Scales, 1984, American Guidance Service). In practice, an IPRC will quite regularly accept almost any information about a student with developmental disabilities when it is making determinations regarding identification and placement.

As the tables in Chapter 3 indicate, relatively more students in this area of special need are placed in full time and part time self-contained classes, despite the vigor of advocates who favour inclusion. Nevertheless, compared to the days before the passing of the Education Amendment Act in 1980 when it was rare for a disabled student to attend a regular school, there have been very great changes. Specially dedicated schools for the 'mentally retarded', where these students were enrolled—if they went to school at all—have almost all become regular neighbourhood schools. Disabled students, even though some may be placed in special classes, are part of those neighbourhood schools now, and the majority of students by far, are placed in classes on the basis of what their teachers and their parents together believe is in their best interests.

✔ STRATEGIES FOR THE CLASSROOM

(1) For teachers and educational assistants working in this area of special need, there is a prerequisite to individual education plans, instructional strategies, curriculum—all the trappings that gather nominally under "education". The prerequisite, quite simply, is a positive attitude: recognition and acceptance that these are students like any other, with strengths and needs and likes and dislikes and idiosyncratic behaviours and a capacity to learn. What distinguishes them, perhaps more than any other trait, is that they tend to learn more slowly. The implications of that slower learning speed (perhaps learning rate is better) are significant, but the students can and do learn. Classroom professionals, by nature, accept this, but when they have such students in a class, they need just a bit more of that faith: that quality reflected in the patience, the effort, the flexibility, and the sense of humour that together with enlightened instruction make classrooms successful. Without these intangibles — in liberal quantities — no amount of tactic or technique can be effective. The teacher, as always, is the key.

(2) It is common administrative practice to assign educational assistants in classrooms where one or more disabled students are enrolled. A principal reason for the popularity of the practice is that time and again, assistants have proven their immense value. However, doubling the number of adults in a room does not double the achievements automatically. Whether an assistant is assigned to a whole class or specifically to a student (this latter option has come in for serious criticism as a form of de facto segregation) it is crucial that both teacher and assistant work together in an atmosphere of mutual respect and appropriately shared responsibility.

(3) In a similar vein, teachers and assistants recognize that when students with special needs are in their classes, they are expected to cooperate extensively with other professionals, and certainly with parents. In the case of students with developmental disabilities, this support circle often widens considerably. Very active involvement by advocacy groups for example, often leads to the development of a team of key players in a student's life, who share information, ideas and concerns about that student and then take some wider responsibility for promoting his inclusion in the life of the community. Since school is a major part of a student's community, it is only natural that such a team will often involve and overlap the classroom role. Thus in addition to their responsibility for individual instruction, teachers and assistants often find themselves part of a larger circle of action that includes other students, parents, and interested members of the community.

Sometimes the teams are organized under relatively formal structures (one such is MAPS*); at other times the situation is informal, often the result of the will and dynamism of a key player in the student's life. Either way, classroom personnel should expect involvement that often goes way beyond the walls of that classroom.

(4) Careful attention to structure both in direct individual instruction and in the general learning environment is another important factor. Experience in both integrated and modified environments suggests that the students are much more comfortable when classroom routines and expectations are regularized. In this case, familiarity breeds not contempt but comfort, and the security engendered by this comfort can usually assure more effective learning. Establishing a structured environment may mean that the teacher or assistant arranges for and continually repeats certain sequences until they are fully assimilated by the students. It may mean temporarily reducing the number of choices a student is expected to make. Very often a great deal of effort is expended on what, in the grand scheme of

● ● ● ──────

* Forest, M., & Lusthaus, E. (1990) "Everybody belongs with the MAPS action planning system", *Exceptional Children*, 22, 4 (36-39).

────── ● ● ●

things, may seem relatively trivial: colour-coded notebooks, for example, with red for one purpose, green for another, etc. Yet these are precisely the kind of arrangements that protect the students from confusing and overlapping demands and allow them to bring their available cognitive strength to bear on a learning task. Without a carefully established structure in which to learn, students tend to expend a prohibitive amount of energy trying to establish it on their own. In an unstructured environment it is easy to seek the comfort of learned helplessness or perseverative behaviour.

The challenge is finding the right balance of structure and flexibility so that organization does not become more important than learning. An additional challenge is finding this balance in an inclusive classroom, where there are many students whose need for a structured and carefully sequenced instruction may not be the same. Professionals in this type of classroom can argue with considerable authority that such a placement for a student with serious developmental disabilities, despite its benefits, may also mean having to forgo some of the vital learning support that occurs in a carefully arranged structure.

(5) *Interestingly,* just as advocates have tried to find a more palatable term for 'mental retardation', educators have tried to upgrade the vocabulary for a time-honoured and effective practice for all students and especially for those with mental handicaps: namely, 'drill' and 'repetition'. Whatever the currency of suggested replacements, the simple fact is that all students seem to need the opportunity to go over material a certain number of times until it is taken in, and students with this disability perhaps more so.

(6) *Momentum, or commitment* within the individual is another concern. Students with a disability regularly and successfully invite oth-ers to do their work for them, and equally regularly, back away from challenge and opportunity. Encouragement by significant adults is very important therefore. In fact, a teacher who establishes a sense of commitment in a student has usually led him or her through one of the most important steps of development.

(7) *Using the Task Analysis Method.*
Task analysis is a method of breaking down a general concept or skill into its component parts. The component parts are then presented in a logical sequence. Particularly for students whose needs are fairly extensive, the method has proven very successful because it is based on sequencing and operant conditioning, and offers a sense of accumulating success.

An example follows. Teaching begins at baseline: the level where the student is functioning prior to instruction (or possibly, one step below, so that success is assured). Each step is taught in a variety of ways until 'overlearning' has taken place. Overlearning means practicing the concept beyond the point of original mastery because the instructor cannot assume a student has mastered the concept on the basis of a single correct response. Instead the instructor should present the concept on numerous occasions over a time period, expecting the student to respond correctly most of the time before being satisfied the concept has been mastered. (Some instructors determine in advance the criteria for mastery, e.g., four correct responses out of five consecutive trials.)

1st step: state behavioural objective; e.g., tell time to ¼ hour,

2nd step: list all steps, operations and prerequisite skills necessary to do step 1.

3rd step: order these in hierarchy or logical teaching sequence.

4th step: find out where in this sequence the student is functioning (baseline).

An Example of Task Analysis: (Steps 1-3)

Objective: Student can count a handful of coins correctly (pennies and nickels)

1. verbally identifies penny and nickel
2. states nickel = 5 pennies
3. counts rows of pennies — straight line
4. counts pennies scattered on desk
5. counts one nickel and several pennies — placed in straight line
6. counts, when arranged in a straight line, one nickel and several pennies when nickel is not first
7. same — scattered fashion
8. counts by 5's
9. counts rows of nickels (straight line)
10. counts nickels (scattered)
11. counts rows of several nickels and pennies when all nickels are placed first
12. counts (same as 11) but all nickels are not first
13. counts handful of nickels and pennies (the stated behaviour objective).

READINGS & RESOURCES

Beck, J., Brores, J., Hogue, E., Shipstead, J., & Knowlton, E. (1994). Strategies for functional community-based instruction and inclusion for children with mental retardation. *Teaching Exceptional Children*, (1994, Winter) pp. 44-48.

Brigance, A.H, (1995). *Life Skills Inventory*. North Billerica, MA: Curriculum Associates.

Carnevale, A.P., Gainer, L.J., & Meltzer, A.S. (1990). *Workplace basics, The essential skills employers want*. San Francisco: Jossey-Bass.

Cipanni, E., & Spooner, F. (1994). *Curricular and Instructional approaches for persons with severe disabilities*. Needham Heights, MA: Allyn & Bacon.

Crealock, C., & Bachor, D. (1995). *Instructional strategies for students with special needs* (2nd. Ed.). Scarborough, ON: Allyn & Bacon Canada.

Cronin, M.E., & Parron, J.R. (1993). *Life skills instruction for all students with special needs: A practical guide for integrating real life content into the curriculum*. Austin TX: Pro-Ed.

Drew, C.J., Hardman, M.L., & Logan, D.R. (1996). *Mental retardation a life cycle approach* (6th ed.), Upper Saddle River NJ: Merrill/Prentice Hall.

Feldman, M.A., & Walton-Allen, N. (1997). Effects of maternal mental retardation and poverty on intellectual, academic, and behaviour status of school age children. *American Journal on Mental Retardation, 101*, 352-364.

Freeman, S.F.N., & Alkin, M.C. (2000). Academic and social attainments of children with mental retardation in general education and special education settings. *Remedial and Special Education, 21*(1), 3-18.

Graziano, A.M. (2002). *Developmental disabilities: Introduction to a diverse field*. Boston, MA: Allyn & Bacon.

Grossman, H.J. (1992). *Special education in a diverse society*. Boston: Allyn & Bacon.

Hankin, J.R. (1994). FAS prevention strategies: Passive and active measures. *Alcohol Health and Research World, 18*(1), 62-66.

Helmke, L.M., Havekost, D.M., Patton, J.R., & Polloway E.A. (1994, Winter). Life skills programming: Development of a high school science course. *Teaching Exceptional Children*, pp. 49-53.

Herr, S.S., & Weber, G. (1999). *Aging, rights, and quality of life: Prospects for older people with developmental disabilities*. Baltimore, MD: Paul H. Brookes.

Kozma, C. & Stock, J. S. (1993). What is mental retardation? In R. Smith (Ed.), *Children with mental retardation* (pp.1-49). Rockville, MD: Woodbine House.

Meyer, L.H., Peck, C.A., & Brown L. (1991). *Critical issues in the lives of people with severe disabilities*. Baltimore, MD: Paul H. Brookes.

Reiss, S. (1994). Issues in defining mental retardation. *American Journal of Mental Retardation, 99*, 1-7.

Sands, D.J., & Wehmeyer, M.L. (Eds.). (1996). *Self-determination across the life span: Theory and practice*. Baltimore: Brookes.

Scruggs, T., & Mastropieri, M. (1994). Successful mainstreaming: A qualitative analysis of three representational cases. *American Educational Research Journal, 31*(4), 785-811.

Snell, M.E. (1993). *Instruction of students with severe disabilities* (4th ed.). New York: Macmillan.

Weaver, H.R., Adams, S.M., Landers, M.F., & Fryberger, Y.B. (1998). Meeting the life skills of students with developmental disabilities in integrated settings. In A. Hilton & R. Ringlaben (Eds.), *Best and promising practices in developmental disabilities* (pp. 87-106). Austin TX: Pro-Ed.

Links

Ontario Association for Community Living
http://www.acl.on.ca/

Canadian Association for Community Living
http://www.cacl.ca/

Canadian Down Syndrome Society
http://www.cdss.ca/Home.html

Canadian Centre for Substance Abuse (FAE/S)
http://www.ccsa.ca/fasgen.htm

New

Students With Autism Spectrum Disorders

*"Once Danny starts talking to me about trains or NHL teams or black holes—
whatever his latest obsession—I can walk out of the room, pick up my mail in the office,
stop off in the washroom, whatever ... When I come back he'll still be holding forth.
And still talking to the spot where I was standing."*

Laila B., Danny's grade five teacher

Misconceptions About Autism Spectrum Disorders (ASDs)

1. **ASDs are a kind of mental illness.**
Although autism appears in the list of mental disorders presented by the DSM, there are no known psychiatric causes.

2. **ASDs are untreatable.** Intensive intervention, especially if begun early, can often make a significant impact on an individual's development. Not all treatment styles, however, are effective for all children with ASDs.

3. **Preoccupied, career-oriented parents are most at risk for causing ASDs.** Although this was once a popular theory, there is no concrete evidence to substantiate it.

4. **ASDs are the result of our socially disconnected urban culture.** The nexus of relationships once regularly present in families and communities may indeed be disappearing, but the effects have not been connected to ASDs.

5. **ASDs can be caused by vaccinations.**
The study that led to this belief, published in *Lancet* in 1998, was retracted by most of its authors and by the journal, in 2004.

1943 - We had single term Autism
But that is too narrow so now we have the word Spectrum implies a range

Is it Autism? Autism Spectrum Disorder? Pervasive Development Disorder?

— used as a shorthand
To take into account the varied type - DSM identifies 5 different

Autism is a severely incapacitating disability that can affect all aspects of an individual's development, and if not treated, can be life long. People with the disorder are believed to have anomalies in both the structure and the chemistry of the brain.

For several decades after autism was first described in 1943, it was customarily known by that single term. By the end of the century, 'autism' was seen as too narrow to encompass the many manifestations of the disorder, so that both professionals and public alike began to acknowledge a range or spectrum. Hence the more or less accepted term today is 'autism spectrum disorders', although in general discussions, in symposia, and even in academic papers, 'autism' is regularly used as a kind of shorthand. A further development must be noted in that the Diagnostic and Statistical Manual (DSM) now presents five different distinctions of autism, under the heading 'Pervasive Development Disorder' (PDD) so this term too is now part of the mix.

— There are too many manifestation of the disorder to use one term.

1. What should teachers and E.A.'s be aware of when dealing with the terminology used to describe autism?

A simple caveat for teachers and educational assistants is to be aware that terminology used to describe autism is somewhat elastic, and that explanations of cause, characteristics and prevalence are evolving as well.

The DSM and

Pervasive Development Disorder

Recent editions of the Diagnostic and Statistical Manual of Mental Disorders, divide ASDs into five separate categories, under the main heading 'Pervasive Development Disorders'. The five are briefly summarized here. (In each category, the manual specifies characteristics that must be present both in quantity and type.)

Autistic Disorder includes impairment in social interaction, communication and imaginative play prior to age three, with restricted interests and repeated behaviours.

Asperger's Disorder (Syndrome) is usually applied to individuals with speech and average to above average intelligence, but who are impaired in social interactions and have unusually restricted or specialized interests.

Childhood Disintegrative Disorder is characterized by the presence of a range of autistic behaviours that appear after normal development for at least two years.

Rett's Disorder is progressive and so far seen only in girls. There is a period of normal development followed by the loss of acquired skills. A key symptom is replacement of purposeful hand movements with repetitive movements between ages 1-4.

Pervasive Developmental Disorder – Not Otherwise Specified is also called 'atypical autism'. This is a somewhat vague category that picks up individuals otherwise not classified but who nevertheless have severe impairments of an autistic nature.

Typical Characteristics of Autism

Whatever definition of autism eventually prevails, a reality in the classroom is that students who have the disorder generally present certain characteristic manifestations or symptoms. These vary in style and intensity from individual to individual in one or several of the following clusters.

- *Social interaction.* May find relating to others difficult or even impossible, reflected in anything from lack of eye contact to total withdrawal. May show little interest in making friends or in shared play and will spend inordinate amounts of time alone. Seeming unawareness of social interplay and an absence of intuition are typical (e.g., student does not read body language of others; talks but does not listen; seems unaware of protocols).

- *Communication*.* Speech may be delayed, diminished or entirely absent. May use gestures rather than words; often uses words without attaching their usual meaning.

- *Behaviours.* The descriptor 'bizarre' is often applied. May become obsessed with a theme (e.g., hockey scores) or object (spinning objects are frequent examples among children). Will often engage in repeated ritualistic actions (e.g., rocking in place) and demand absolute adherence to routines.

- *Responses to sensory stimuli.* Reaction to sights, sounds, conversational buzz, the development of a crowd (e.g., as at recess or an assembly) etc., often varies dramatically from what would usually be anticipated in other students; responses may range from extremely acute to nothing at all, and are often bizarre.

- *Responses to Change.* Modifications in standard classroom routines may be extremely upsetting (e.g., shifting to group work after quiet seat work). Shifts into and out of recess or lunch hour or dismissal time are often difficult.

- Although it is not a characteristic, current evidence suggests that autism spectrum disorders typically appear in the first three years of life, especially between the ages of two to three, and so far, is four times more common in males.

• • •

* The Ministry of Education includes autism under Communication in its definitions (see Appendix).

• • •

Raven, age 15, has spent the past three years in a self-contained classroom with four other severely autistic students, where she has made great strides under a dedicated teacher and very patient educational assistant. Because school board officials repeatedly point to this classroom as proof of 'what is possible', it has become a popular spot for visitors. Curiously—or perhaps *not* curiously—despite all the positive features in the setting, what visitors remember most is the sight of Raven's palms. Both her left and right hands have thick scars that match the concentric rings of electric stove elements. One day when she was nine, Raven turned the elements on and put palms down until they—quite literally—cooked!

Six years later, Raven still has an inexplicable insensitivity to physical pain. (She nearly died at age 12 from a burst appendix; an abcessed molar went unnoticed until huge swelling made it obvious.) Yet she is extremely sensitive to other, seemingly innocuous stimuli, especially sounds. Only in the past year, for example, and only if warned in advance, can she tolerate the sound of paper being shuffled or folded. Although music is an important part of her program—the EA discovered some time ago that Raven's tantrums can be calmed by soft classical music—the classroom piano had to be removed because just one note would send her into a frenzy.

Raven still does not have—or does not use—speech, but she will now mouth certain nouns softly if she wants something. She still rocks when bored or stressed or faced with change in her routine or surroundings, but no longer pulls out clumps of hair. She has stopped throwing her food, and waits her turn for the classroom "en suite". Recently, she undertook responsibility for the aquarium. Raven has also learned to acknowledge the presence of others, even strangers, although she will not make eye contact. She now sits in 'circle' after lunch each day without prompting. In sum, a comparison of Raven's profile today with the base line established three years ago, shows major, continuing progress.

A potential crisis threatens. Raven is native. She was raised as a foster child in a non-native family, and now one of her long time caregivers has developed multiple sclerosis. Last year, Raven's birth mother located her, and with the support of the band council has undertaken to have her returned to the mother's community. There is no professional support in this remote community for someone like Raven but the mother argues that her people have always been far better at accommodating differences like autism than non-native, urban cultures. Raven's caregivers counter that to remove her now, from a setting that is obviously so beneficial for her, will make her regress to a point from which she may never recover. Before taking a position on the matter the school board wants to hear the recommendation of the teacher and the assistant.

Exploding Numbers: The Exceptionality That Grew

Obscure Beginnings ...

In 1943, American psychologist, Leo Kanner, published a paper identifying what he called 'autistic children'. Not that the exceptionality suddenly appeared in the mid-twentieth century; rather, what Kanner did was separate out a small group that to this point had been classified as either emotionally disturbed or mentally retarded, or both. Kanner pointed out that the group he called autistic (borrowing the term from Eugen Bleuler, who also coined the term 'schizophrenia' in 1912) was not as slow learning as the mentally retarded, and did not fit the pattern typical of the disturbed.

A year later, in 1944, Austrian psychologist, Hans Asperger, independently published what was essentially a similar hypothesis but unlike the group Kanner described, the people Asperger identified all had speech. Hence 'Asperger's Syndrome (or Disorder) came to be used to distinguish autistic children who used language.

... and Small Numbers

As recently as the 1980s, prevalence rates for autism were held to be one in every ten thousand. And for the most part, few people had any awareness, much less understanding of this exceptionality for many identified cases were institutionalized, often for life. At the end of the twentieth century, prevalence rates were being revised sharply upward to ranges of around one in every one thousand births. By 2004, Autism Canada was citing a prevalence rate of one in every 286 births! If accurate, that figure means the rate has nearly quadrupled in only a very few years!

Why the Rapid Acceleration?

Although such a profound increase in prevalence rate challenges credibility (an issue that will likely confront the field for some time) there are a number of explanations for it, some satisfactory, some otherwise. Once the DSM included autism, there was an increase in the number of diagnoses if only because a wider range of medical professionals became more enlightened. Educators, faced with the presence of vastly increased numbers of special education students in the 1980s and 90s, became far more sensitive to the reality of ASD. Increased publicity led to greater awareness in the public at large. With more awareness has come more

> Having Asperger's is like being a coyote in a city park. You survive but it's the wrong environment. You just don't fit.
>
> *Jon K., age 19, diagnosed with Asperger's Syndrome*

Red Flags for Parents ✍

Children do not attain developmental goals according to a timetable. Yet it may be important for parents to seek medical advice if they notice that their child

- ◆ does not babble at 1 year,
- ◆ hears but does not respond to his name,
- ◆ avoids eye contact and cuddling,
- ◆ begins developing language then stops,
- ◆ does not point to things or seek attention.

---

research, greater attention to empirical evidence, more elaborated definitions and more informed diagnoses.

Still, just as the field of learning disabilities once had to struggle for recognition and then deal with the diluting effects of over-identification before achieving clear status, the potential for a similar pattern in the field of ASD is obvious. Only time—and more research* and experience—will tell.

Have the Causes Changed?

Typical of a burgeoning interest in disorders for which no cause has ever been clearly established, explanations for ASDs are plentiful and—so far—mostly theoretical. Some theories have appeal, based as they are on attractive empirical evidence, a good example being the current dominance of the genetic cause. Indeed, much of the current research leans heavily toward discovering a genetic basis, the hypothesis reinforced by apparent patterns of ASD in families. Other, harder-to-substantiate theories posit the impact of the physical environment, with the finger pointed at industrial/chemical pollution[†]. Still other theories point to the alleged unfriendly social structure of modern urban families. (Teachers with long memories may recall the "refrigerator mother effect", a widely accepted theory in the 1960s and 70s advanced by Bruno Bettelheim.) Yet another, most intriguing idea is the so-called 'Geek Syndrome'.

Is the "Geek Syndrome" a Factor?

Between 1987 and 1998, the state of California recorded a 19 percent increase in demand for

• • • ———

*What is predicted to be a watershed piece of research is under way at publication of this text, headed by Dr. Jeanette Holden of Queen's University. Among other objectives, the study will examine the biological basis of ASD, and attempt to develop methods for identifying infants at risk.

† One of the highest prevalence rates in the world (one per 125 births) is in Brick N.J., where residents fear an unknown toxin is the cause.

——————— • • •

treatment of autism. In the Silicon Valley area, the increase was a staggering 273 percent! More recently, educators, medical professionals and advocates (albeit without truly hard data as yet) are pointing to a similar pattern in other geographic areas where computer science is a dominant employer, areas such as Ottawa, Dublin (Ireland), Cambridge (England) and Boston's Route 128. The theory—it is only that for now—supports the genetic factor hypothesis for it argues these areas bring together like-minded "geeks" who marry and have children. Since both preliminary data and empirical evidence point to a significantly above average incidence of ASD, especially Asperger's Syndrome, in these communities, the possibility that this theory has merit is difficult to deny. (Bill Gates of Microsoft is well known to be prone to rocking, monotones and temper tantrums, all symptoms of Aspergers. Although such behaviours in a well known figure is not a supportive argument *per se*, observers report an above-average level of social unawareness among similar "geeks".)

Diagnosis …

It follows that since there is no certain explanation of what causes ASD, diagnosis—and treatment—consequently share an element of uncertainty. There is no medical test to diagnose autism but because there might be co-occurring disabilities, a battery of medical and quasi-medical tests is often administered. A logical choice, for example, is a hearing test since the behaviour of children with ASD might well

Since diagnosis is unclear so too is the treated

The Case of Larry

Because his mother has been offered a major career opportunity, Larry's family is considering a move to another community and the stress of relocating is exacerbated by Larry's situation. He is eight years old and has Asperger's Syndrome. Although the parents insist he is not a savant, Larry does things that other eight year olds do not. He can, for example, recite an entire weather forecast verbatim, having heard it only once (provided weather is his current *passion du jour*). When he became interested in the Korean War, he could cite the regimental names and personnel numbers of every country contributing to the UN forces. At the moment, Larry is obsessed with astrolabes, sextants and compasses. He can describe their origins, history, function and construction with a degree of accuracy known to only a few scholars.

What are Characte

Larry is also afraid to use any bathroom except the one in the basement of his family home. He has yet to master tying shoelaces and, to prevent anxiety attacks must be escorted to and from the school bus by an adult he trusts. Although he has an impressive vocabulary and clear speech, Larry cannot—or does not want to—converse with others. And he does not get on well with his peer group. As the EA explained, "It's not so much that his peers can't *understand* him; it's more that they can't *stand* him!" Larry, it seems, prefers his own world and actively excludes others from it.

Yet his current situation in a regular grade three class shows marked improvement. According to his principal, Larry is placed where both the teacher and the educational assistant are not only qualified in special education but have taken a particular interest in autism spectrum disorders. Together, they have made extensive, if uphill, efforts to create an atmosphere of positive acceptance and community in the class. (Larry is not the only special needs student included here.) They have been successful in generating a feeling among the other students that human differences are a matter of degree and that "we're all different". They have also made strides in "softening Larry's corners" as the EA puts it, teaching him to respect the feelings of others.

It is apparent that Larry will continue to develop important social skills in this environment. The question is: what can be done to transplant this momentum into a new classroom if Larry's family moves?

suggest they are deaf. (The fact that they experience deafness at a rate no greater than the general population implies that a high level of skill, not to mention an understanding of ASD, would be important in the audiologist doing the testing.)

Ideally, a child should be evaluated by a multidisciplinary team, the members of which are familiar with autism in its various manifestations. Again ideally, the conclusions of the team will be reached only after extensive observation—the sole diagnostic technique with any solid history—and after a collation and comparison of the various results, and then after informed discussion. Needless to say, unless the subject child's case is managed aggressively, an ideal evaluation is less than frequently achieved. In practice, a diagnosis that actually places a label like PDD or Asperger's Syndrome on a child is ultimately in the hands of a medical professional.

> I still remember in the delivery room I had visions of flooding the back yard, skating, shinny. He'd be a right winger; that was my dream. But when Kev stopped talking to us—stopped *looking* at us—and started all that strange stuff, I knew hockey was going to be the last thing on the agenda.
>
> *Alf R., parent of a child diagnosed with 'childhood disintegrative disorder'*

Once that label is attached to a student, the education system may go forward with its own approach to both a placement and a program that accommodates the student's needs.

The Triad of Impairments

Among both academics and practitioners on the front lines there is a growing consensus that the presence of a triad of impairments (as posited by Wing, 1988) identifies the presence of ASDs. These are impairments in:

1. *social and emotional understanding;*
2. *communication and language;*
3. *flexibility of thinking and behaviour.*

While the way these impairments are expressed or manifested will vary from one individual to the next, according to the hypothesis the presence of all three elements is indication of ASD. As with most ideas in a relatively new and developing field, the acceptance of Wing's triad is not unanimous but it has attracted widespread attention and constitutes another element of which educators should be aware.

... and Treatment

There is no standard, universally accepted treatment for ASDs; in fact the range of responses is mind-boggling and rife with controversy, tributes, and half-truths. Because of the ease with which "gee whiz" anecdotal literature is picked up by popular media or posted on the internet, parents and educators need to be somewhat wary.

Taken generally, treatment approaches fall into four principle categories: *biochemical* (vitamin supplements, medications, food allergies); *neurosensory* (over-stimulation and patterning, sensory integration techniques, facilitated communication, auditory training); *psycho-dynamic* (holding and body contact therapy, psychotherapy); *behavioural* (intensive behaviour intervention, aversive therapy, and various other forms of behaviour modification).

For every treatment style there are vociferous supporters and equally vocal critics although comparatively few styles are actually backed (or claim to be) by scientific studies. One such is Intensive Behaviour Intervention (IBI), also called Applied Behaviour Analysis (ABA)*.

IBI: the "Gold Standard"?

Intensive Behaviour Intervention is a highly structured program designed to develop age-appropriate skills and independence in a child with ASD (or other disability). Originally, IBI was conceived for and applied to children from the ages of approximately two to approximately five or six, but there is pressure from advocates to expand that target group. The program follows behaviour modification principles and is

• • • ───────

* The treatment is also called Discrete Trial Training(DTT) and 'The Lovaas Method'. Professor I.O. Lovaas is regarded as its founder, although the principles are very much those long established by B.F. Skinner.

─────────── • • •

very intensive and hands-on, typically involving 20 to 40 hours per week of direct service from professionals. Parents and/or caregivers are crucial to its implementation and are expected to follow the regimen faithfully and precisely.

An IBI program is individualized and built around needs in communication, daily living and safety skills, social skills, motor skills, pre-academics, self-management and attending skills. It is formally administered, supervised and evaluated by qualified service providers, typically a clinical psychologist in tandem with other qualified personnel. (At time of publication, the province of Ontario sponsored nine regional providers of IBI programs.) IBI is claimed to be very effective with young children and when the intervention is early, is said to produce dramatic, positive results.

Examples of Other Treatment Programs

Behavioural programs in various forms are not new in the treatment of autism. *Aversion therapy*, for example, has been in use for several decades, although it has generally been applied only in institutional settings, and often experimentally. Mild electric shock, rarely applied any more, was once considered effective in curbing self-injurious behaviour. Other aversion methods still in occasional use include water spraying, pinching, and denial of food treats.

A program in the neurosensory category that attracted a rash of front page media attention during the 1990s is *facilitated communication* (FC). This idea operates on the premise that an autistic (or other) person who does not use speech, can peck out words or symbols on a keyboard if an 'assister' gently props that person's arm above it. FA continues to be used although it is heavily criticized for lack of validation. Another treatment example is the *Tomatis Method*, an auditory integration training concept, in which an individual spends hours a day listening to specially created sounds and classical music, particularly that of Mozart, with the low frequencies filtered out. Over time, the frequencies are added back, along

with voices and other everyday sounds. A premise is that children with autism may overcome extreme oversensitivity to certain sounds, and may be sufficiently soothed to decrease hyperactivity. Like FA, the Tomatis program is criticized for lack of validation.

There have been reports, although poorly substantiated until now, of using highly intelligent animals such as dogs and pigs to help children with autism become able to bond, show affection and communicate. A research trial ongoing at University of Guelph at time of publication would have interesting implications for the classroom if its results were to suggest a form of positive treatment. In the trial, children are being paired with assistance dogs, a method used successfully in a variety of other situations. Initial indications, although anecdotal and individualized at this stage, report improved behaviour, calming effects, and displays of affection on the part of the children. *The TEACCH program (Treatment and Education of Autistic and Related Communication Handicapped Children)* established in 1972 by Dr. Eric Schopler has a positive profile in the field, its continuing use after more than thirty years being a tribute to its efficacy. This program begins with an exceptionally detailed assessment to uncover the individual's potential for acquiring communication skills and competencies for independent living. TEACCH is not behaviour modification in that it does not work on behaviours directly (except in the case of endangering behaviours). Rather it tries to give the student a better understanding of his environment to reduce anxiety (and the reactions that develop from that) and emphasizes communication skills so that the student can deal better with the world around him.

Do the Treatments Work?

An enduring problem for both professionals and parents is true validation of the many methods proposed to treat ASD. For parents

> You want *real* security at those airport scanners? There's three autistic kids in our special unit class who can process detail in micro-seconds. *Nothing* would get by them once it's showing on the screen.
>
> *Alysia Van T., educational assistant*

Facilitative assister

who, understandably, are interested in almost any proposal that may offer help to their child, whether or not to adopt a particular treatment program can be a real dilemma. Very often they learn of a program through enthusiastic anecdotal tribute, and the impetus to try it becomes almost irresistible. But once launched into a program, they typically face significant costs in time, effort and money (very few programs produce immediate or even early results) and the ever-present worry that they may not have chosen wisely.

Professionals too face concerns for they would like to be able to recommend a *proven*, research-validated method. Unfortunately, there is enormous discord in the research literature. Many studies lack robust, vigorous investigation and far too often the results are ambiguous at best. Even when initial research points to positive outcomes in a program, it is not uncommon for that program to receive enthusiastic support well before it is truly tested. The much-lauded IBI method, for example, depended heavily at first on a 1987 paper by Lovaas, and even though a careful reading of the paper might leave the impression that his quite small experimental group did not represent truly autistic children, IBI spread far, fast and wide, well before replication could reinforce his findings. (See also Issues, following.)

Implications of Specific Treatments for the Classroom

Very often, a student identified with ASD comes to the classroom with a treatment program already in place. The teacher—and the educational assistant if the classroom is fortunate enough to have one—is then expected to adhere to the tenets of that program, and sometimes even be in charge of implementing it whether or not she agrees with its principles or has received training in it. This can be a particular problem because of the amount of time and resource the program may require, not to mention its potential for disruption. Even more troubling to many teachers is that a predetermined treatment program may well deny them opportunities for creative response. As well, in inclusive classrooms especially, a method with laid-on requirements has the potential of denying the purpose of inclusion by isolating the student, however unintentionally.

On the other hand, teachers can be just as confused and challenged by a student with ASD as anyone else, and the clear plan of response typically outlined in a treatment program may well be a relief.

Empathizing versus Systemizing ✍

British psychologist, Simon Baron-Cohen, has stirred a flurry of interest with a thesis that autism is essentially an imbalance between two kinds of intelligence: the kind used to *understand people* ('empathizing') and the kind used to *understand things* ('systemizing'). Studies consistently show females are better at empathizing while males have a stronger knack for systemizing. Baron-Cohen suggests that autism is basically an exaggerated version of this male profile: an extreme preference for ordered, rule-based, and detailed systems, together with a diminished ability to intuit people's feelings, reactions and intentions.

The thesis may have some merit. Studies continue to show that most males (all ages) do indeed have a dominant "System-style" while most females (all ages) have a dominant "Empathy-style". As well, the detached, obsessed-with-detail patterns common to various components of ASD, appear in males at a rate of about four to one over females. Whether the thesis will sustain over time has yet to be demonstrated, but it reinforces a trend to see autism as a mental *style* or difference that can be accommodated, rather than a disease that needs to be cured.

Some Issues in the Field

♦ It is not unusual for a *bandwagon effect* to develop around a treatment. Many programs, particularly the more esoteric ones, tend to be supported by anecdotes about quasi-miraculous outcomes. While rational doubt should be enough to make most people view these accounts with caution, a strong wish to believe on the part of some parents, together with a lack of information can easily subvert natural wariness. A bandwagon effect even accrues to programs where positive results are supported more scientifically. For example, both empirical evidence and investigation now leave little doubt that for the most part, IBI can improve matters for a child with ASD, particularly if that child is very young and if the treatment begins early. Yet there is still no absolute certainty that it works significantly better than other treatments. As well, evidence continues to demonstrate—no surprise—that IBI is more effective with the less severe cases. Yet by the beginning of the millennium, the program was being vigorously pursued by parents irrespective of the type of ASD with which their child was diagnosed. And by the middle of the decade, there was an added twist. The apparent success of IBI with very young children had led parents to advocate for its extension beyond the time (age 5-6) at which the program has typically ended.

♦ The *cost* of implementing a program continues to beleaguer both parents and governments. Not that ASD is unique on this issue, but the intensity of need that distinguishes autism usually requires a response of equal intensity—with heavy expenses attached. The delicacy of the issue lies not in whether the program is worth the price, but in who will pay it. A program like IBI which requires 20 to 40 hours of service a week from qualified personnel, along with training, travel and other supplementary expenses is way beyond the income of most Canadian families. Although government funding is available in most provinces, Ontario included, those monies are not unlimited. The demand by parents for greater funding and expanded programs has thus led to an increase in litigation and human rights appeals.

♦ The *media* have had a powerful impact on the public impression of autism over the past decade or so, and as usual, the impact comes as a mixed blessing. The performance of actor, Dustin Hoffman, in the popular 1988 Hollywood movie, *Rain Man*, did much to create awareness of an exceptionality hitherto known only vaguely. Yet the same movie did much to create a false impression. The autistic person played by Hoffman is typically obsessive, but not so typically, he has competent language, is very charming, and is also a savant. As any special educator can quickly attest, neither charm nor language are always present in people with ASD, and those with savant characteristics represent only about 10 percent of the autistic population.

♦ To *include* in the regular classroom—or not—is, as ever, an issue that continues to roil, although in the case of students whose ASD is reflected in self-injurious or bizarre behaviours, the debate tends to get hotter. All the standard arguments on both sides of the question apply, although even strong advocates of inclusion acknowledge that the intense needs of severe cases of ASD are a major challenge to the support usually available in a regular classroom, and quite possibly an unreasonable challenge to classroom personnel who do not have special training. This may be the reason why the degree of advocacy for inclusion is not as powerful on behalf of students with ASD as it is for students with other special needs. As well, programs requiring the degree of intervention in IBI are usually more efficiently administered in a special setting.

> If you let your students pick their own groups we'll always be picked last. Defeats the purpose of having groups, doesn't it?
>
> *Jon K., age 19, diagnosed with Asperger's Syndrome*

Note 1: Students manifesting quite severe characteristics of ASD are likely to be placed in special classrooms for at least part of their school day. Typically, teachers and assistants in this setting will implement a predetermined program.

Note 2: With ASD, perhaps more than any other exceptionality, there is less commonality from case to case and what "works" in one situation often will not translate to another. Thus in the regular classroom especially, intuition, along with trial and error, are two essential arrows in the quiver shared by teacher and assistant.

Note 3: Teachers and educational assistants must be prepared to offer instruction in what for most students would be skills normally acquired in the simple process of growing up. For example, it follows that a student who needs to be taught to pay attention to his name (not unusual in ASD) will likely find it difficult to follow simple instructions. This is not necessarily owing to diminished intelligence but more to a style of processing information. Usually a student with ASD needs more time to switch focus, to attach meaning to the words being tossed at him and to follow through on requests.

Note 4: A major challenge is getting a student with ASD to understand and accept the very ordinary, frequently occurring phenomena that characterize the behaviour of students in a classroom. Getting the student to understand, for example, that a classmate's movement from point A to point B is not necessarily an "invasion of his space" or that physical contact among peers is normal, is not something most classroom professionals have to encounter on an ordinary day. At the same time, a teacher or assistant who tries to educate the ASD student in these matters must realize that the aversive behaviours are real, not something to be punished but rather, a condition to be acknowledged so that alternatives can be taught. The suggestions below offer a few simple procedures that generally are helpful.

(1) Provide a safe haven. The noise and disorder of recess, a pep rally, an assembly, sometimes even normal classroom noise (such as on the day before a holiday break) may overwhelm. It may be advisable to have a quiet place for the student to go to, or to develop a routine response (e.g., by having him pair with a calm classmate) in these situations. Perhaps more important may be to anticipate and watch for signs that the student is approaching meltdown at these times. It may also be useful, if the student can be taught to recognize the signs himself, to teach him how to act accordingly. There may be a trusted adult (office personnel? nurse? other teacher or EA?) for the student to go to. Some students find it helpful to overcome stress by listening to music for a brief period.

(2) Prepare for changes in routine. Until the student develops the appropriate skills it may be necessary for the teacher/EA to be at her side when change is imminent, to quietly coach and help her through.

(3) Structure group work very deliberately.

(4) Seating plans are useful. Because of the potential for intense reactions to stimuli and for unusual behaviours, where the student sits, relative to the entrance, work areas, etc., and relative to who sits near him, may pre-empt "situations".

(5) The internet may help. Some students find the internet an ideal medium of communication because it offers the opportunity for interaction, cognition and language use without the impact of nearby human presence. The key for the teacher/EA of course, is to use the tool judiciously lest it become an escape.

(6) Be a positive interlocutor. The teacher or educational assistant, especially at first, may be the only one in a classroom who understands that the student with ASD lacks the intuition necessary for successful social and intellectual exchange. It will probably be necessary to coach both the autistic student and his classmates in this reality; the special stu-

dent on what impact he is having and the classmates to realize they should not take abruptness personally.

(7) Capitalize on special interests. Having an autistic student in a class, especially one with Asperger's, often means having a "geek". There may be reward for everyone if the "geek" is allowed to educate others on his latest passion. (But "geeks" are prime targets for bullies. If that is a problem in the school, teachers/EAs will need to plan ahead.)

(8) A caring community. As much as it sounds like an overbeaten cliché, there's no substitute for a classroom where understanding, accommodation and forgiveness prevail. It takes the professionals in the room to make it happen.

(9) (The following is from an adult diagnosed autistic at age three.)

- My head is like a video. The only way I learn is to see things. That's why nouns and verbs are easier to learn than other words. When you teach an autistic kid things, *show* him.

- You need blocks and sticks and things like that for math.

- Use art a lot.

- Phonics is best for reading. So are poems. And music and songs.

- Autistic kids stick with special things they like. I loved trains. Still do. My best teacher used math trains. We had train records and we read train stories. Ms. King was so cool.

- When you talk, don't say so much at once. Don't talk *slow*. We're not idiots! Just don't say so much at once! I wish we had computers when I was in school. With computers you control the information coming in.

READINGS & RESOURCES

Akshoomoff, N. (2000). *Neurological underpinnings of autism* (Vol. 9). Baltimore: Brookes.

Attwood, T. (1998). *Asperger's Syndrome: A Guide for parents and professionals.* London: Jessica Kingsley.

Baron-Cohen, S. (2003). *Essential Difference: The truth about the male and female brain.* Perseus.

Bauer, S. (1995). Autism and the pervasive developmental disorders. *Pediatrics in Review, 16,* 130-136.

Brownell, M.T., & Walther-Thomas, C., (2001). Steven Shore: Understanding the autism spectrum – what teachers need to know. *Intervention in School and Clinic, 36,* 293-305.

Cattell-Gordon, D., & Volkmar, F.R. (1998). The development of an effective applied behaviour analysis program for young children with autism: A parent's perspective. *Infants and Young Children, 10*(3), 79-85.

Cohen, D.J., & Volkmar, F.R. (1997). *Handbook of autism and pervasive developmental disorders.* New York: John Wiley & Sons.

Donnellan, A.M. (1999). Invented knowledge and autism: Highlighting our strengths and expanding the conversation. *The Journal of the Association for Persons with Severe Handicaps, 24*(3), 203-236.

Dunlap, G., & Fox, L. (1999). Supporting families of young children with autism. *Infants and Young Children, 12*(2), 48-54.

Gresham, F.L., & MacMillan, D.L. (1997). Autistic recovery? An analysis and critique of the empirical evidence on the early intervention project. *Behavioural Disorders, 22,* 185-201.

Gresham, F.L., & MacMillan, D.L. (1998). Early intervention project: Can its claims be substantiated and its effects replicated? *Journal of Autism and Developmental Disorders, 28*(1), 5-13.

Klin, A., Volkmar, F., & Sparrow, S.S. (2000). *Asperger Syndrome.* New Haven, CT: Child Study Center, Yale University.

Lovaas, I.O. (1987). "Behavioural Treatment of Normal Educational and Intellectual Functioning in Young Autistic Children", *Journal of Consulting & Clinical Psychology,* 55: 3-9.

Lovaas, I.O. (1981). *Teaching developmentally disabled children: The me book,* University Park Press.

Maurice, C. (1993). *Let me hear your voice,* Knopf.

Maurice, C. (1996). *Behavioural intervention for young children with autism: A manual for parents and professionals.* Austin, TX: Pro-Ed.

McGee, G.G., Morrier, M.J., & Daly, T. (1999). An incidental teaching approach to early intervention for toddlers with autism. *The Journal of the Association for Persons with Severe Handicaps, 24*(3), 133-146.

McLaughlin-Cheng, E. (1998). Asperger syndrome and autism: A literature and meta-analysis. *Focus on Autism and Other Developmental Disorders, 13*(4), 234-245.

Mostert, M.P. (2001). Facilitated communication since 1995: A review of published studies. *Journal of Autism and Developmental Disorders, 31,* 287-313.

Myles, B.S., & Simpson, R. (Eds.). (1998). *Educating children and youth with autism: Strategies for effective practice.* Austin, TX: Pro-Ed.

Myles, B. et al. (2001). *Asperger Syndrome Diagnostic Scale,* Austin, TX: Pro-Ed.

Myles, B.S., & Simpson, R. L. (2001). Understanding the hidden curriculum: An essential social skill for children and youth with Asperger syndrome. *Intervention in School and Clinic, 36,* 279-386.

National Research Council. (2001). *Educating children with autism.* Washington D.C.: National Academy Press.

Prizant, B.M., & Rubin, E. (1999). Contemporary issues in interventions for autism spectrum disorders: A commentary. *The Journal of the Association for Persons with Severe Handicaps, 24*(3), 199-208.

Quill, K.A. (1995). *Teaching children with autism: strategies to enhance communication and socialization,* Baltimore: Brookes.

Rapin, I. (1997). Current concepts in autism. *New England Journal of Medicine. 337*(2), 97-104.

Rogers, S.J, (1998). Empirically supported comprehensive treatments for young children with autism. *Journal of Clinical Child Psychology, 27*(2), 168-179.

Ruble, L.A., & Dalrymple, M. J., (1996). An alternative view of outcome in autism. *Focus on autism and other developmental disabilities, 11*(1), 3-14.

Sacks, O. (1995). *An anthropologist from Mars,* Picador.

Safran, J.A. (2002). Supporting students with Asperger's syndrome in general education. *Teaching Exceptional Children, 34*(5), 67-70.

Schopler, E. et al. (1998). *Asperger syndrome or high-functioning autism?* Plenum.

Siegel, B. (2003). *Helping children with autism learn,* Oxford.

Siegel, B. (1998). *The world of the autistic child: understanding and treating autistic spectrum disorder,* Oxford.

Wilkinson, K.M., (1998). Profiles of language and communication skills in autism. *Mental Retardation and Developmental Disabilities Research Reviews, 4*(2), 73-79.

Williams, K. (2001). Understanding the student with Asperger syndrome: Guidelines for teachers. *Intervention in School and Clinic, 36,* 287-292.

Wing, L. (1988). "The continuum of autistic characteristics", in Schopler E. & Mesibov, G.B. (Eds.) *Diagnosis and Assessment in Autism*, Plenum.

Links

Autism Society (Canada)
www.autismsocietycanada.ca

Autism Society (Ontario)
www.autismsociety.on.ca

Autism Resources
www.autism-resources.com

Centre for the Study of Autism
www.autism.org

CHAPTER 11

Students with Neurological Disabilities
Chronic health needs • Musculoskeletal impairments • Acquired brain injury

What I don't get is, what's with everybody! *The way they* treat us! *I mean—
so I've got tics. And sometimes I hum. What's so bad about that? So I've got Tourettes.
Big deal! And Eddy ... he's got CP. So he jerks. So what? I mean,* what's the big deal?
*Why do people treat us like we're some kind of freaks or something?
It's not like they're perfect either, you know."*

Paulo, age 16.

Misconceptions About Neurological Disabilities and Chronic Health Needs

1. Students with special health conditions are automatic candidates for special education.

Very often the distribution of intelligence and abilities like hearing or vision among students with health needs is similar to that of the rest of the population. Medication may have side effects that make program delivery easier in a special setting. Also, students with chronic needs often miss a great deal of school and may benefit from a remedial program which special education is better equipped to deliver.

2. Students with Tourette syndrome swear and 'talk dirty'.

The characteristic is known as 'coprolalia'. Only about a third of individuals with the syndrome manifest this trait, which waxes, wanes, and often disappears altogether.

3. The physical condition of students with cerebral palsy cannot be remediated or improved.

Cerebral palsy is considered irreversible but therapy, prosthetic devices, and sometimes surgical procedures, can make a positive change, especially if intervention is begun early.

4. When disabling conditions are neurologically based, there is always a consequent diminishing of intellectual capacity.

There is a higher incidence of intellectual problems among people with cerebral palsy, but the connection is not absolute. Other conditions such as spina bifida, muscular dystrophy, or convulsive disorders, generally have no connection with levels of intelligence.

5. Conditions like epilepsy and Tourettes indicate mental illness.

People with these conditions are no more or less disposed to mental illness than anyone else.

6. People with spina bifida are incontinent.

Lack of bowel and bladder control is a genuine problem which accompanies the severer cases of spina bifida, but milder cases generally do not have this effect.

7. Arthritis is found only in elderly adults.

It is found in all ages.

8. Medical science is reducing the incidence of physical disabilities and chronic conditions.

The number of children with these conditions is increasing because medical advances, particularly in post-natal care, have increased the birth and early year survival rate.

Describing the Needs

The primary characteristics of students with a physical disability or other neurological or health needs are the proper concern of the health professions. Because the students attend schools—more and more of them neighbourhood schools—it follows that teachers and educational assistants should therefore have some information about them. From an educational perspective, some bio-medical knowledge can be useful for developing an appropriate program. Certainly the knowledge can be very helpful in understanding a student's emotional needs and learning patterns. In most cases (with the occasional exception of some neurologically-based conditions, like Tourette syndrome) a student with a physical or health need will arrive in class already defined and classified by health personnel, and will have been presented to an IPRC. Thus classroom personnel should get a fair amount of information in advance.

It is very important to recognize that a physical or health or neurological condition will manifest itself in a variety of ways, but even more important, when it does, the student with it is first and foremost, a *student*. Teachers should approach medical information therefore, from an educational and cooperative perspective, not from a diagnostic or treatment one. In addition to learning about a particular condition, it is also wise to seek out the specifics of the individual student's case, since epilepsy, for example, or Tourette syndrome or

acquired brain injury will manifest itself in a variety of ways.

The descriptions that follow here are quite brief and offer preliminary information only. The authors have scrupulously avoided presenting a catalogue of the very long list of conditions encountered in the schools of the province, for despite the drama implied by the conditions, they are of very low prevalence, and each case will, inevitably, be significantly different from others.

Cerebral Palsy

A condition caused by injury to the brain before, during, or after birth, chiefly characterized by motor disorder. It is not progressive but is not considered curable although therapy can be helpful in improving comfort and mobility.

Approximately fifty percent of people with cerebral palsy have *pyramidal (also called spastic)* palsy, characterized by slow, laborious, poorly coordinated voluntary movement, stiff, tense muscles, and in some cases a degree of involuntary movement. About twenty-five percent have *extrapyramidal (also called choreoathetoid, and atonic)* cerebral palsy, characterized by regular, involuntary, writhing movements, difficulty maintaining posture, and floppy muscle tone. *Ataxic* cerebral palsy, characterized by poor coordination, balance and posture, affects

---

Motor Disability ✍️

Motor disability and paralysis are typically classified according to the limbs involved in the condition. Although the extent of a student's limb involvement is not necessarily a fundamental issue for teachers and educational assistants, it will have an impact on classroom planning. These are the terms generally used.

➡ *Paraplegia:* both legs are involved

➡ *Quadriplegia:* all four limbs involved

➡ *Diplegia:* legs involved more than the arms

➡ *Hemiplegia:* one side of the body involved

approximately fifteen percent. People with ataxia may be ambulatory; most others generally require a wheelchair. Some people with cerebral palsy have a combination of these symptoms.

Other matters associated with cerebral palsy are intellectual and developmental delays (not an absolute connection but the incidence is higher than in the general population) speech and language problems, visual and auditory difficulties, and seizures. An ongoing debate over cerebral palsy arises from the fact that IQ test scores for children with this condition tend to be lower than the general average. However, appropriateness of IQ tests, their administration and interpretation, are often suspect in these situations.

In the classroom, students with cerebral palsy may present a range of challenges. Not only may they require special equipment and procedures, but co-occurring conditions often require teachers and EAs to develop competence in a number of areas.

Spina Bifida

Spina bifida occurs in the spinal column when one or more vertebrae do not close during pre-natal development. The resulting condition varies from minor to severe. The most severe condition is spina bifida with *mylemeningocele* which usually results in irreversible (so far) disability, the most obvious being lower body paralysis. Less severe conditions such as *spina bifida occulta* and *meningocele* do not necessarily involve lower body paralysis although people with these conditions may require crutches or leg braces to help them walk. Spina bifida is often accompanied by *hydrocephalus*, an enlargement of the head caused by pressure from cerebrospinal fluid which if not diagnosed and treated in time, can cause brain injury. Usually, the medical response to hydrocephalus is the installation of a shunt (a short tube) in the spinal column to help this fluid drain. Hydrocephalus and the presence of a shunt,

The Case of Matt

The car crash that seriously disabled Matt also caused serious injury to three of his friends and killed two others, but Matt is the only crash victim with permanent spinal injury. Although his condition was at first diagnosed as 'diplegic' (legs more involved than arms) after about six months of therapy, Matt had a stroke and went into a coma. Doctors are sure he had another stroke for he came to having developed extreme choreoathetosis (abrupt, involuntary writhing movements) in all four limbs. This condition was so intense and painful that after three months it was decided to relieve the condition with a non- reversible surgical procedure that has made Matt a quadriplegic.

The accident happened after a weekend field party when Matt was 15 years old in grade ten. At the time, he was identified gifted and had been placed part time in a self-contained class with gifted peers, and part time in advanced grade twelve language and math classes. Matt is now 19. He returned to school about a year ago and, to everyone's delight, demonstrated immediately that although his body was largely immobilized, his intellect was unimpaired.

An admirable piece of creative thinking on the part of a special education teacher solved a potentially serious obstruction to Matt's rehabilitation. Bioengineering staff at the hospital had fashioned a 'headstick' so that he can tap a computer keyboard. (Matt speaks normally; he uses a computer for writing, problem solving, and a range of activities.) But leaning over the keyboard with the headstick exhausted him after a brief time, so the teacher simply mounted the keyboard above the monitor so that Matt's neck brace supports most of his movements.

Matt has done exceptionally well since his return and will graduate with honors. Now he has asked his teachers for some career counseling. Given his exceptional abilities in language and math, given what technology can (and will) do for him, and recognizing the possible limitations imposed by his physical condition, should he seek a liberal arts degree? (He is a superb writer and editor with a highly developed sense of language.) Or should he pursue accountancy? (His math skills are very superior.) He enjoys both areas equally.

indeed spina bifida itself, usually do not preclude a student's normal progress through school. However, educational experience with children who have hydrocephalus is beginning to reveal that the condition may also produce a higher than average chance of learning disability, owing to possible anomalies in the structure of the brain. The connection, at this stage, is more suspected (through empiricism) than proven, but teachers should be sensitive to the possibility.

Acquired Brain Injury

Acquired brain injury (ABI) is any type of sudden injury that causes temporary or permanent damage to the brain after birth (or according to some definitions, after two years of age). Motor vehicle accidents, near drowning, violence related incidents and sports related injuries are among the leading causes.

ABI can have a serious effect on a student's cognitive, behavioural/emotional and physical well-being. The list of potential problems is intimidating. Cognitively, students may experience difficulties with attention, processing, judgment, anticipation, perception, problem solving, transfer of learning, memory initiation and fatigue. As for behaviour and emotion, students may experience agitation, disinhibition, sudden outbursts of anger, impulsivity, and have general difficulty controlling their emo-

tions. Students with ABI may become isolated and withdrawn or overly aggressive, difficulties that are often exacerbated by a lack of social awareness and ability to self-monitor. Physical difficulties may include central and peripheral nervous system disruption, as well as orthopedic complications. Students may experience difficulty in other areas such as: fine and gross motor, speech, hearing, vision, taste, olfaction, muscle spasticity, contracture, paresis or paralysis, and physical fatigue.

Students who experience an acquired brain injury usually need specialized help in a school setting. Often the period following the injury can be difficult due to the sudden change in the student's functioning but also due to the variability of performance during what is termed the recovery period, which can last for up to two years. A team approach, involving parents, school and medical personnel, is the most effective way of meeting the challenges.

Seizure Disorders (Epilepsy)

Epilepsy is not a disease but rather a symptom of a brain disorder that leads to seizures. It occurs in about 300,000 Canadians according to the Epilepsy Association; over half of these (55 percent) are diagnosed before age ten. In the majority of cases, the cause is unknown. There are several types of seizure, the two most commonly occurring being *tonic-clonic* and *absence*

Dealing with a Tonic-clonic (Grand-Mal) Seizure in the Classroom ✍

☞ Do not try to restrain the student; you cannot stop the seizure.

☞ Remove or try to protect the student from furniture and sharp objects.

☞ DO NOT force anything between the teeth.

☞ After the seizure, turn the student to one side to allow saliva to drain.

☞ Loosen the collar and other tight clothing.

☞ Put something soft under the student's head.

☞ Do not offer a drink until the student is fully awake.

☞ Let him or her rest afterward. (Often they will sleep.)

☞ If it is known that a student has epilepsy, it is useful to be prepared. Simple aids kept in the classroom—a blanket, for example—will be helpful.

N.B. If the seizure lasts beyond five minutes, or seems to pass from one seizure to another without the return of consciousness, it should be treated as a medical emergency.

seizure (formerly called 'grand-mal' and 'petit-mal'). In a tonic-clonic seizure, an individual loses consciousness, often convulses, and may fall. Breathing may stop temporarily. The individual may lose bowel and bladder control, or bite the tongue. After one to five minutes or so, the person regains consciousness, but may experience confusion and headache and often goes into deep sleep. Absence seizures, on the other hand, are very brief and often go unnoticed. They may occur several times a day, usually when the person is sedentary, and are characterized by what is often called a "clouding of the consciousness", during which the individual's eyes may stare blankly, or the hands will move aimlessly. Return to normal is usually abrupt. It is not unknown for teachers and educational assistants to be the first to suspect absence seizures, since one-on-one learning situations are good opportunities for observation, especially if there is an effort to find out why a particular student's style is marked by significant ups and downs of understanding.

Students with idiopathic epilepsy (of unknown origin) seem to function entirely normally between seizures. Those with symptomatic epilepsy (from brain injury) often have to cope with the consequences of a primary condition, of which epilepsy is one factor. Either way, epilepsy itself, is not usually the reason a student is referred to an IPRC. Very often, it is a primary condition, or the side effects of seizure-control medication, that lead to consideration for special education.

Many students who have tonic-clonic seizures seem to be extremely sensitive about the events, and teachers may find themselves more challenged by the emotional than by the physical consequences of seizure. How a teacher deals with a post-seizure classroom atmosphere can have a major impact. Reassurance and emotional support for the student who had the seizure is crucial; equally vital is how the teacher educates the other students about epilepsy. (The Epilepsy Association has excellent material to assist with this issue. It also has up-to-date information on new medications for seizure control.)

Tourette Syndrome (a.k.a. 'Tourettes' or TS)

Tourettes is a neurological disorder that usually manifests itself in childhood, and is frequently characterized by motor and/or vocal *tics*. In a small percentage of the cases, the sounds are obscenities or curses (called 'coprolalia'). Although the condition was long thought to be limited to these manifestations, recent and more careful study of Tourettes suggests that significant behavioural features may also be involved, such as hyperactivity, obsession and indiscriminate rage. Although Tourettes seems to be a lifelong disorder, symptoms have been known to disappear for long periods or even disappear altogether, with and without medication.

Numbers?

From the time it was first identified by Gilles de la Tourette in the nineteenth century until about thirty years ago, the syndrome was considered rare. Indeed, other than psychiatrists and a few very curious—and persistent—special educators, it was largely unknown. Thanks to commercial television and advocacy, Tourette syndrome has become relatively well-known and is now the subject of expanded research. One consequence is awareness that it is far more prevalent than once believed, although disagreement continues to swirl over just how many people, especially students, actually have the condition. As ever, disagreement over prevalence arises largely out of a lack of certainty about the symptoms, the most prominent of which is ticcing. A study by Kurlan et al. (2001) for example, found that 19 percent of children in regular classes have tics (as did 23 percent of those in special education classes) but that just under 4 percent meet the DSM diagnostic criteria for Tourettes (over 7 percent in special education classes). Whatever the true prevalence—claims vary from one in 2000, similar to blindness, to one in four—all teachers and educational assistants can be sure of is that Tourettes is far more common than was once believed.

Characteristics and Diagnosis

Although it is a neurological disorder, there is no test for Tourettes so that a diagnosis must be determined clinically, i.e., by observation. Most health professionals, guided by the DSM, consider the following criteria as necessary for a diagnosis.

A common problem is finding information on rare conditions and disorders that may have implications for the classroom. Mobius Syndrome and tuberous sclerosis are typical examples. Tuberous sclerosis is marked by lesions in the brain and other organs, often the skin, and is very frequently accompanied by serious developmental delay. Students frequently have seizures, and some manifest obsessive compulsive and rage behaviours not unlike those found in students with autism or Tourettes. With Mobius Syndrome, first described in 1888 as congenital facial diplegia, the muscles of the face gradually weaken, so much so that the individual cannot make facial expressions, even when crying or laughing. Atrophy of the tongue is common. In some cases, the forehead and eyebrows may even droop over the eyes making vision difficult. Although, there is no clear evidence of intellectual delay, Mobius is a condition that generates special needs both at home and in the classroom.

Although these conditions do not automatically force a need for special education, the circumstances accompanying them may mean that a special education placement is preferred for a variety of reasons. In such cases, both teacher and educational assistant will often find it useful to contact support groups—if they exist. There is such a group for tuberous sclerosis but not as yet for Mobius Syndrome. Usually access to support groups is available via the internet or through the community support department of larger hospitals. (See more on support groups in this chapter.)

- Multiple motor and vocal tics must have been present for some time, although not necessarily together.
- Tics occur often, usually in bouts, nearly daily for over a year.
- Other causes such as medication side effects are ruled out.
- The effort expended to suppress tics affects other aspects of the individual's life.

While parents and teachers are front and centre in pointing out the frequent presence of obsessive behaviour, hyperactivity, uncontrolled rages etc., in people with Tourettes, some health professionals seem uncertain about whether these constitute part of the syndrome.

Implications for the Classroom

Common learning difficulties associated with Tourettes are difficulty in getting started (or finished), problems with comprehending verbal instructions, and confusion over space-time directionality. Given those difficulties, it is not hard to understand why it is confused with learning disability, intellectual handicap, schizophrenia and other conditions. No one medication dominates in the way that Ritalin does with AD/HD management (although haloperidol is popular) but drugs are frequently used and side effects may have an impact.

The role of the teacher and assistant, as usual, is vital in the case of a student with Tourettes. Understanding, empathy, common sense support and remediation strategies are obvious needs. Perhaps the most vital matter in assuring the student's security and sense of well being is the way in which classroom professionals manage the effect of the syndrome on the student's peers. [Note that the Tourette Syndrome Foundation has some very helpful literature for teachers, and this resource should always be pursued, if only for its excellent advice on helping the student deal with tics.]

Multiple Disabilities

Students identified as multiple-disabled or multi-handicapped typically have more than one special need. There is limited evidence showing that certain single handicaps are more predisposed to be accompanied by others. In fact, a particularly vicious prevailing myth is that all multiple-disabled students are severely intellectually retarded. Another is that all multiple-disabled students have no oral language. Yet there does seem to be a higher prevalence of disability associated with certain exceptionalities. Children with cerebral palsy, for example, have a disproportionately high ratio of visual impairments. About a third of children with significant hearing loss also have additional special needs.

A case of multiple disability often requires considerable administrative attention. Establishing an appropriate placement, for example, may be difficult. A jurisdiction may have only one student diagnosed deaf/blind, physically disabled and developmentally delayed. And it may have a total of three students who are identified as severely autistic, one of whom also has a visual impairment. The tendency, in situations where these students are not integrated into regular classes, is to identify them as multiple-disabled and place them together in a single self-contained class, the rationale being that such congregation allows individualized programming, easy access to support services, that it can permit program overlap, and that it is economically feasible. Still, it is not uncommon for students with multiple, severe disabilities to be integrated into a regular class ideally with the support of an educational assistant or health aide (or both).

Whatever the identification and placement of a student with several distinct special needs, his or her program will usually be:

  i) highly individualized; with

 ii) a significant amount of specialized support; and

iii) marked by extensive communication and cooperation (at least attempted) with the student's home so that education and habilitation can be coordinated beyond the school day.

Chronic Health Needs

A chronic health care need does not automatically predestine a student for special education, especially in terms of placement. If a student's health need can be met in a regular school, there is no reason why it cannot be met as well in a regular classroom for a chronic health care situation of itself, does not usually generate the need for an individualized educational program. However, the *effects* of the health need (missed

time, frequent medical and/or therapeutic interventions) may indeed mean that both special programming and placement are required. Either way, chronic health needs have become a factor in neighbourhood schools today.

Modern medical science continues to improve the survival, growth and development rate among children who are born with profound needs. These children go on to attend school, where their special health care needs must be met, sometimes prior to their learning. Teachers and assistants today encounter students with cystic fibrosis, scoliosis, congenital malformations, muscular dystrophy, diabetes, cancer, allergies, asthma,* encephalitis and other chronic conditions that preceding generations had never even imagined. As a consequence, among items that distinguish modern classrooms, in addition to learning hardware, are things like oxygen tanks and epi-pens. And with that reality comes the necessity for some knowledge of health maintenance. Not that classroom professionals should be medical managers, but for obvious reasons it is important they have an understanding of both daily and emergency procedures. What makes this an even trickier challenge is that their primary responsibility is still to educate, with all this implies, not to treat. Attending school, simply being in school, is a crucial element in the normalization and growth of a student with a non-sensory physical exceptionality, and teachers and assistants have powerful roles to play in that process. Difficult ones too.

Some Issues in the Field

✦ A particular concern to teachers is *how to react in an emergency situation*. It is this concern that sometimes leads them to resist placement of high risk students in their classes. Usually the resistance can be overcome with information and education about the particular exceptionality. However, a constant—and justified—

• • • ———————

* Most teachers and educational assistants today will readily agree with the claim by V.Q. Getch and S. Newharth-Pritchett that at any given time there are at least two children with asthma in a classroom. (See *Teaching Exceptional Children*, 1999, 31, 30-36.)

——————— • • •

complaint of frontline classroom personnel is that they are not kept adequately informed about students with health needs. Changes in medication, environmental triggers (e.g., of a seizure incident), crucial times of day: all these factors can be very important to the accommodation of a student with special health needs, and teachers quite rightly argue that poor communication from health personnel, inefficient bureaucracy in a school or larger system, not to mention stringent privacy regulations, makes their jobs more difficult and even puts the student at risk. (All of which substantiates the wisdom of regular, direct communication with parents who, for obvious reasons, will likely be both helpful and informative.)

♦ *Families often experience practical and emotional havoc* when they have a child with physical disabilities, or neurological condition, or chronic health need. Such a child inevitably demands a disproportionate amount of the family's resources in love, energy, money and time. Needless to say, families react in different ways, and their feelings usually have a profound effect on the way the child reacts in turn to the world at large. In whatever way the family—and the child—react, the teacher, educational assistant and a wide number of personnel in a school are inevitably drawn into this reaction, so that relative to their other students, they almost invariably find themselves expending equally disproportionate amounts of love, energy, money, and time. How this is dealt with in a school, morally and practically, can become a matter of serious debate.

♦ *Responsibility by default* is not unusual in the case of severely disabled students. Most of the time it occurs when an educational assistant becomes the sole teacher, classroom caregiver, even, unfortunately, sole companion of a student with profound needs. The issue is a particularly difficult

The Case of Tamhana

The fourth grade teacher had met Tamhana two years ago while substituting in a grade two class for several months. At the time, the teacher had taken note of the young girl's persistent and unusual behaviour, but followed the advice of a colleague and did not pursue the matter. Now, as the fourth grade teacher, he regrets that decision, for Tamhana's apparent oddities are much more pronounced, and more obsessive to a marked degree. She has continued a grade two habit: returning from the schoolyard according to a very specific walking pattern. But whereas she would permit intervention two years ago, Tamhana blows into a frightening rage now, if interrupted. She enters the classroom by a patterned path as well (and her peers have learned not to get in way). Her lunch is eaten in specific sequence, and she has taken to counting aloud while chewing to ensure an identical number of 'chews' each time.

Tamhana's facial tics, very evident in grade two, have ceased, but she now makes strange sounds when sitting alone (which, regrettably, is most of the time) ranging from growls to oohs and eehs, and on one occasion, the teacher is certain, barking. Lately, Tamhana has taken to impulsively running from the room. She allows herself to be brought back and is very remorseful for causing a disturbance. However, she cannot explain why she runs out, and often, if questioned the following day, denies any knowledge of the event.

The teacher, like many of the staff, believes Tamhana has Tourette syndrome and wants the principal to refer her to an IPRC. Unfortunately, this was attempted in grade three and then abandoned after a friend of Tamhana's family told her parents that girls don't get Tourettes. As a result, the parents refused all requests from the IPRC for cooperation. The staff has now learned of an additional complication: that Tamhana's father does not want attention focused on a female child in any way that might bring disgrace on the family. What the teacher knows he must do is somehow convince the girl's parents that some kind of intervention is necessary, for Tamhana's behaviour is intensifying daily.

one to solve for the student's needs are usually very demanding and it is both realistic and sensible for the needs to be dealt with by the person most familiar and competent. Often this is the EA. Management like this runs counter to the purpose of an inclusive classroom placement. It is also antithetical to the objective behind placing a student in a self-contained class in a neighbourhood school, for even in a specialized setting like this, it is expected that the student will interact with as wide a variety of people as possible. The issue is a challenge for educational assistants for both their inclination and their professional training leans toward a wider use of their talents.

Some Implications for the Classroom

❖ North Americans live in a culture obsessed with beautiful bodies. Health and strength are not enough; we must be well formed and attractive. It is not surprising therefore that to the physically exceptional especially, there is not only a battle to overcome the limitations imposed by their own bodies, there is also a battle to be accepted by others without stigma. The same phenomenon applies to behaviour. To people with Tourette syndrome, for example, the band of acceptable or so-called normal behaviour in our culture appears very narrow, so that when their condition expresses itself, they feel very much singled out. Therefore a teacher with one or more of these students in his class often finds himself dealing as much with behaviours—the disabled students', his own, that of other students, the culture at large—as he does with curriculum and instruction. Exceptional students will have negative feelings about themselves if it is obvious that others around them do. Conversely, they may become independent

and self-sufficient in response to the expectations of others. Self-acceptance and self-awareness will develop in kind with the open and honest appraisal that significant people in their lives give to them.

Classroom personnel have an enormously important role to play in this. For example, people normally react with caution to someone who has a surgically implanted shunt, or who has a leg brace, or who may suddenly convulse or experience an asthma attack. Such caution is reasonable, but it is important that the caution be just that, and not fear. Fear and ignorance are potentially as great a threat to exceptional students as the primary handicaps themselves.

❖ Treatment of conditions like epilepsy or Tourette syndrome often involves the use of medication which has sedating side effects. Teachers sometimes find they are adjusting, not to an exceptionality, but to its treatment. It is not uncommon for a student to be placed in special education principally because of the effects of the medication used to control a primary condition.

❖ The normal adjustments that every teacher makes to accommodate her students' personal needs are often intensified in cases of chronic health need. The students often miss a great deal of instructional time through illness and absences for therapy, etc. Teachers also have to make allowances in scheduling and in monitoring so that matters of the students' personal hygiene can be addressed. As well, students with particularly serious disabilities often have attendant behavioural, even psychiatric problems that can call upon the full extent of one's patience and stamina.

❖ A disabling condition like cerebral palsy can affect progress through the natural stages of development, so teachers can safely anticipate that some students may not be working at the same academic level as their peers, and must therefore make adjustments in program.

(1) Students in both regular and self-contained classes — most especially younger children — will invariably take their cue from adults when seeking out how to react to and behave toward people with disabilities. Teachers and EAs must play a very positive leadership and modeling role, showing other students tactfully, how to be helpful without taking over, how to react with empathy not pity, and how to treat their peer's exceptionalities with common sense.

(2) Where there are no secondary exceptionalities to deal with, such as developmental delay for example, teachers of a student with non-sensory physical limitations, or neurological impairments or chronic conditions, will likely treat a student in the same way as she treats everyone else, making allowance only for special needs in day-to-day functioning. These might include help in the administration of medication, help in the effective use of a prosthesis (artificial replacement for a body part) or some other adaptive device necessary for daily living.

(3) Continuing developments in computer technology accelerate far ahead of the capacity of texts like this one to describe them, and of course, classroom professionals need to stay abreast as best as they can to utilize this progress on behalf of their students.

(4) Because many children with physical disabilities are absent from school frequently, cooperation in out-of-school assistance can be important to academic success. Some jurisdictions appoint what are called 'itinerant' teachers, or teachers of the home and hospital-bound, whose teaching load usually involves on-site instruction at home, in hospital, or in other institutions.

(5) It is rare but not unheard of, for the classroom teacher or EA to be a catalyst in the discovery of a condition such as absence seizures for example, which may go unnoticed in a large and chaotic family but in the more structured demands of school become evident. Such relatively unknown conditions like Tourette syndrome sometimes go undiagnosed even through adolescence.

(6) Effective communication among teachers, parents, and health care professionals is absolutely essential but is ignored with discouraging frequency. It is often incumbent upon the teacher or EA to initiate this, usually by direct and regular contact with the parents.

Help From Support and Advocacy Groups

Support and advocacy groups are helpful in a variety of ways. Members of organizations like The Epilepsy Association, The Learning Disabilities Association, The Association for Bright Children, The Tourette Syndrome Foundation, Association for Community Living, The Canadian Hearing Society, The Canadian National Institute for the Blind (there are many more) are usually well-informed and current, and quite aggressive in seeking out information, supporting innovative practice, or dealing with slow-moving bureaucrats, and reluctant, sometimes poorly informed health professionals. All of these are issues faced by classroom professionals, and most of the time, regular contact and help from the appropriate advocacy group can be quite helpful in addressing them. Associations, for example, have education programs in kit form or video useful to enlighten both students and adults. It is not unknown for an advocacy group to be prominent in getting service. Advocacy groups are also a remarkably effective first line of emotional support and information to a family which has just learned their child has been diagnosed.

Agnew, C.M., Nystul, M.S., & Connor, M. C. (1998). Seizure disorders: An alternative explanation for students' inattention. *Professional School Counseling, 2*(1), 54-60.

Appleton, R., & Baldwin, T. (1998). *Management of brain injured children.* New York: Oxford University Press.

Batshaw, M.L., & Perret, Y.M. (1992). *Children with disabilities: A medical primer* (3rd ed.). Baltimore, MD: Paul H. Brookes.

Blum, R.W., Resnick, M.D., Nelson, R., & St.Germaine, A. (1991). Family and peer issues among adolescents with spina bifida and cerebral palsy. *Pediatrics, 88*, 280-285.

Buyer, D.M. (1999). Neuropsychological assessment and schools. *The Brain Injury Source, 3*(3), 18-20.

Dormans, J.P., & Pellegrino, L. (Eds.). (1998). *Caring for children with cerebral palsy: A team approach.* Baltimore, PD: Paul H. Brookes.

Giangreco, M.F. (1997a). Persistent questions about curriculum for students with severe disabilities. *Physical Disabilities: Education and Related Services, 15*(2), 53-56.

Huntinger, P.L. (1996). Computer applications in programs for young children with disabilities: recurrent themes. *Focus on Autism and Other Developmental Disabilities, 11*(2), 105-114.

Kurlan, R. et al. (2001). "Prevalence of tics in schoolchildren", *American Academy of Neurology, 57*, 1383-88.

Lash, M. H. (2000). Resource Guide: *Children, adolescents, and young adults with brain injuries.* Wake Forest, NC: LA Publishing/Training.

Parette, H.P., Hourcade J.J., & Brimer, R.W. (1996). Degree of involvement and young children with cerebral palsy. Physical Disabilities: *Education and related Services, 14*(2), 33-59.

Rainforth, B., & York-Barr, J. (1997). *Collaborative teams for students with severe disabilities: Integrating therapy and educational services* (2nd ed.). Baltimore: Brookes.

Sandler, A, (1997). *Living with spina bifida: A guide for families and professionals.* Chapel Hill: University of North Carolina Press.

Shu-Li, L. (2000). Coping and adaptation in families of children with cerebral palsy./ *Exceptional Children, 66*(2), 187-199.

Turnbull A.P. & Turnbull, H.R. (1997). *Families, professionals, and exceptionality: A special partnership* (3rd ed.). Upper Saddle River, NJ: Merill/Prentice Hall.

Tyler, J.S., & Wilkerson, L. R. (1999). Planning school transition for students with TBI. *Brain Injury Source, 3*(3), 14-16, 54.

Links

Spina Bifida and Hydrocephalus Association of Ontario
http://www.sbhao.on.ca/

Spina Bifida and Hydrocephalus Association of Canada
http://www.sbhac.ca/

Cerebral Palsy Canada
http://www.cerebralpalsycanada.com/

Tourette Syndrome Foundation of Canada
http://www.tourette.ca/

Ontario Brain Injury Association
http://obia.on.ca/

Educating Educators about Acquired Brain Injury
http://www.abieducation.com

CHAPTER 12

Students Who are Deaf or Hard of Hearing

*If you can hear, you're at the centre of the world, right in the middle of what's going on,
but if you're deaf, you're always out at the edge.*

Charley B., deaf by injury at age 43

Misconceptions About Deafness

1. Deafness diminishes intellectual ability.

Intellectual ability is distributed among the deaf in the same way as it is for the hearing. Nevertheless, deaf students often lag academically because of their difficulties in communicating with people who hear and can use spoken language easily.

2. Deafness leads automatically to muteness or to inability to speak.

People who are born deaf or become deaf before acquiring speech (usually called prelingual deafness) sometimes have difficulty learning to speak clearly, but the connection between deafness and the inability to speak is not absolute.

3. Profoundly deaf people live in a world of total silence.

Profoundly deaf people can respond to some sounds, particularly to the vibrations.

4. Hearing aids restore normal hearing.

Hearing aids do not restore normal hearing, but the technology has become very sophisticated now and allows for extensive customizing to individual needs.

5. It is counterproductive and potentially harmful for deaf people to socialize almost exclusively with others who are also deaf.

Some members of the deaf community argue that an exclusive "Deaf Culture" is entirely natural and should be encouraged. Others argue the opposite with equal vigor. There is as yet no conclusive evidence that the desire of some deaf people to associate primarily with one another is anything but normal.

6. Teaching sign to the deaf will retard their development of spoken language.

The teaching of sign language does not of itself, retard the development of spoken language. However, if a deaf person chooses to learn or to use sign exclusively, the development of facility in spoken language may be affected.

7. Deaf people compensate by reading lips.

Many deaf persons use *speech reading* whereby the receiver notes facial expression, hand gestures, and other body language in addition to simple lip movement. This skill does not come more easily to deaf people than to anyone else. Reading lips alone is often not helpful because of similarities in the words of spoken language, and because of the inconsistencies in the lip movements of speakers.

8. American Sign Language (ASL) is a loose style of gesturing primarily used to convey concrete ideas.

ASL is a sophisticated language with its own set of grammatical rules, and it can be used to convey levels of abstraction just as oral languages do. (See more in this chapter.)

9. American Sign Language is a universal sign language.

ASL has become increasingly popular, but is one (sign) language among many. Just as there is no universal spoken language, there is also no universal sign language.

Types of Hearing Loss

Most hearing losses are conductive or sensorineural (and sometimes, but not frequently, both). In the case of *conductive* hearing loss, sound is reduced or blocked before it reaches the inner ear, and may occur as the result of infection, trauma, wax build-up or other cause. Sometimes the blockage can be cleared or the sound amplified to reduce the effects of conductive hearing loss.

In *sensorineural* hearing loss, the problem is in the reception of sound in the inner ear or in the transmission of electrical impulses along the auditory nerve. Sound may reach the inner ear but because of problems in the inner ear structures, it may not be transmitted meaningfully even with amplification. There are many possible causes for sensorineural hearing loss, including such apparently simple diseases as mumps or measles, along with more complex viral infections like meningitis, and a range of congenital disorders and types of trauma. Attempts to correct sensorineural loss tend to be more radical and the results less predictable.

Some specialists in the field distinguish a third type of hearing difficulty, which they call *central auditory dysfunction*. It is described as an inability to interpret correctly (i.e., in the brain) some sounds that travel along the auditory nerve, even though sensitivity to sound may be otherwise normal. Central auditory dysfunction is still pretty much a mystery and is not yet universally accepted as a valid explanation of hearing difficulty.

Classifications of Hearing Loss

Specialists in the field of hearing generally include four markers to classify an individual's hearing loss. These are

- *Site of loss:* whether the loss is conductive or sensorineural, or both.

- *Age of onset:* whether the loss is pre or post lingual.

- *Etiology:* whether the individual's loss was present at birth (congenital loss) or has arisen since birth (adventitious loss).

- *Severity:* acuity of hearing, measured by an individual's response to intensity, or loudness, measured in decibels (dB), across a range of frequencies, measured in hertz (Hz). A simple metaphor for the severity measure can be found in the controls on a

---

Possible Indications of Mild to Moderate Hearing Loss in Children ✍️

In primary classrooms especially, children who experience more than the usual frequency of colds, earaches, sore throats, etc. need to be watched carefully for signs of the hearing problems that often follow. The following signs merit attention if a teacher or educational assistant notices them consistently.

- Poor articulation, especially consonants, not attributable to a factor like age, or a different first language

- Loud speech (and singing) in situations that do not require it

- Physical signs (like constantly cocking the head)

- Trouble following directions or answering simple questions

- Unusually frequent requests for repetition

- Unusual inattentiveness

The possibility of a hearing loss should always be considered when assessing a student's behaviour problems and/or failure to meet academic potential.

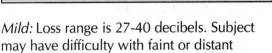
Mild: Loss range is 27-40 decibels. Subject may have difficulty with faint or distant sounds and with conversations; may have loss in groups, or settings with ambient noise.

Moderate: Loss range is 41-55 dB. Subject frequently has difficulty hearing normal speech, especially in groups, class discussions, etc.

Moderate/severe: Loss range is 56-70 dB. Subject frequently has difficulty comprehending speech. Voices must be loud or amplified to be understood.

Severe: Loss range is 71-90 dB. Subject has great difficulty understanding even loud or amplified speech. The latter may seem faint and distorted. Subject usually requires amplification and intensive speech and language training.

Profound (deaf): Loss range is 91 dB+. Subject may be aware of loud sounds and vibrations, but may not even comprehend amplified speech without training.

---

* A hearing loss is also described as *bilateral* (both ears) or *unilateral* (one ear) with the severity of loss indicated according to the better ear.

radio. The volume control of a radio increases or decreases the decibel rating of sound that issues from the speaker, while the frequency or pitch is modified by how carefully the tuner is set to the signal, and also by the degree of clarity achieved by adjusting the tenor/bass setting. Most of the speech in a typical classroom will range from 400 to 2500 Hz, often depending on whether one person is speaking or whether there is classroom buzz. The decibel rating in a classroom may vary from as low as 30 dB (a whisper) to as high as 80 or 90 dB (a shout). In most cases, comfortable human conversation has a dB rating of around 35-50, in a frequency or Hz range of about 400 to 1250. The severity classification is the one most frequently used by educators because it can be structured into functional clusters which imply some simple guidelines for the classroom.

A Caution About Severity

It is important to note that the characteristics used to describe the implications of hearing loss are by no means all there is to know about deaf or hard of hearing persons. Just like those who hear normally, deaf and hard of hearing persons are as completely individual as anyone else, and therefore attend or tune out like anyone else. Another difficulty with classification is that, despite a certain presumed level of function in a deaf or hard of hearing person, that function will invariably be affected by the style and expressive quality of the person *sending* the communication.

Some Issues in the Field

✦ Although several matters have a high profile, the single, most overwhelming and consuming issue is *communication method or style.* On the surface, the issue appears to be a simple one of oralism versus manualism: that is, should a deaf person learn to develop and fully use whatever residual hearing he has available in order to communicate as normally as possible with people who hear, or, should the emphasis and energy be devoted to learning how to sign in order to communicate with other signers (who, by and large, will be other deaf persons, family and teachers).

The Deaf Culture

Supporters of manualism argue that being deaf means being part of a culture that is distinguished by, among other things, its own language. They argue that because experience shows most deaf persons do not become comfortable participants in the hearing culture, to deny them their own language therefore denies them their own culture and forces them into one where they are at risk, or at the very least, are not full participants. Simple observation forces the conclusion that significant numbers of deaf people support this view. The phrase *deaf community* is frequently used (especially by the deaf) to describe deaf persons as a cohesive

> It happened in grade four. I was nine. I was concentrating on math—I love math; the numbers follow a pattern, not like words where the rules always change. I was aware other kids were moving. Nothing unusual about that. Class of thirty. But then the lights went out! I looked up. Everyone, including the teacher, had disappeared! I was so scared! I ran to the door and there was a class monitor waving at me. Probably yelling too. Looked like it anyway. It was a fire drill. Mustn't run, mustn't talk. But when I caught up with the class I was shaking and sobbing. Once again I felt ignored.
>
> *Vivienne T., profoundly deaf from birth*

group who share their own entertainment, activities—and language. This tendency toward self-exclusion does not prevail at all to the same degree among other groups with an equally apparent special need.

Supporters of oralism counter that the world is dominated by, and made up mostly of, hearing persons, and that deaf persons who do not avail themselves of the opportunity to be part of the dominant culture are denying reality and relegating themselves to what is in effect not a culture, but a sub-culture with all that this implies. Some advocates on this side of the issue suggest that it may be advantageous for deaf persons to develop skill in both styles, either simultaneously or separately, in order that they can make a choice. The issue of oralism versus manualism can present parents of a young child with an agonizing decision for it is advantageous to begin either method as early as possible.

Educators, too, are inevitably involved in this issue, both practically and ethically. Learning to read, for example, can be significantly affected if a student is using ASL (American Sign Language) as her predominant means of communication. For example, a phrase that in print is written, "Yesterday I went to the store." is typically signed in ASL as "Yesterday me store go." Because sensitivity to syntax is such a powerful component in learn-

ing to read, it follows that some deaf children using ASL may have an extra hurdle when learning to read English text.

Still another matter for educators is sensitivity to the intensity of this debate. While their primary role is to teach, that role can be more complex if the student (or her parents) is intensely committed to one side or the other of this communication and culture issue.

✦ Further complicating the matter of educating deaf and hard of hearing persons is the intensity of *debate inside the respective oralism and manualism philosophies* themselves. Even after a decision has been taken to emphasize one approach or the other, there is the potential for further disagreement over technique. For example, among supporters of manualism, American Sign Language has become an overwhelming, but not unanimous, choice. There are some who argue for manual methods like Signing Exact English (SEE) which, as the name implies, follows the syntactical and grammatical principles of English as it is written and spoken.

✦ In recent years, sophisticated *surgical implantation technology* has generated more possibilities—and difficult decisions—for dealing with significant hearing loss. One of the more vigorously debated technologies is the <u>cochlear implant</u>. In this procedure, a receiver is implanted either within or outside the cochlea (part of the inner ear) and an external component transmits signals to this receiver. The present state of cochlear implant technology does not restore normal hearing, but there is evidence to suggest that it can dramatically improve a subject's ability to interpret speech and to make sense of environmental sounds, both natural and artificial. Controversy about the procedure and the technology arises over the suitability of candidates, the type of implant to use, and the impact on the subject.

Somewhat less controversial is an at-the-ear, skullbone-anchored hearing aid system, which stimulates the inner ear by transmitting signals to the skull. This implantation technology was initially limited to subjects with conductive hearing loss, and has enjoyed a significant level of success.

Research is now being extended to subjects with sensorineural loss.

♦ An issue that plagues researchers, and one that has more than a peripheral impact on educators, is determining the *true prevalence* of hearing loss in Canadian populations. Inconsistent definitions across jurisdictions, differences in the style of collecting and reporting data, and difficulties in assessing hearing loss among individuals with other disabilities (especially if these are multiple) lead to some confusing numbers in the field. In a study published in 1994, Schein noted that the prevalence rate in the U.S. is reported as 86 per 1000 while in Canada, it is 41 per 1000. He also showed wide variations among the reported rates in Canadian provinces (e.g., 34/1000 in NWT vs. 61/1000 in MB). The uncertainties implied by these differences in data affect funding, research and even the degree of importance given to the matter by administrators.

Typical School Placements

• Special residential schools. There are four such schools in Ontario, each of which offers day programs as well. The Whitney school in Belleville, the Robarts school in London, and the Drury school in Milton are well known and highly regarded. Also held in high repute is the unique program at the MacDonald school in Brantford for the deaf and blind. Interestingly, over the past decade and more, the population of deaf students at these schools has declined somewhat, leading to the inference that more students with hearing loss are being educated in their neighbourhood schools.

• Special classes within regular elementary or secondary schools. (Self-contained classes of deaf and hard of hearing students are not uncommon.)

• Part-time inclusion programs. Students may attend some regular classes in a regular school. A signing interpreter, or an FM communication system or other support might be used. This type of program may have a resource room component, especially if a

trained teacher of the deaf is available to work directly with the student and to consult with the regular class teachers.

• Itinerant teacher programs. Specialist teachers offer assistance in classrooms. In this program, the student is usually in a regular class full time (and more often than not, has a hearing loss of lesser severity).

Communication Approaches and Supports

Oral Approaches

A deaf or hard of hearing child who learns via an oral approach typically is taught to take advantage of auditory, visual and tactile input. Much attention is given to auditory training, talking, speechreading, and amplification. Usually, oral programs emphasize the development of intelligible speech. Research suggests that significant successes in this type of program tend to occur in fully integrated school programs, and in students with above-average IQ test scores, whose parents are fully involved and supportive, and who have above-average socio-economic status. Some of the methods used under the rubric of oralism are described below. Educators and parents who wish to investigate further, usually begin with information available from the Canadian Hearing Society.

Speechreading

This is a process wherein a person receives a message principally by observing a speaker's face, paying special attention to the lips and expressions and gestures in the face, body and hands. Speechreading is enhanced if the receiver is aware of and familiar with the context of the speech. Complications make this method only one of several avenues for deaf persons to receive information. Very few deaf persons rely on speechreading exclusively.

Auditory Training

This process teaches a child to use what residual hearing she has. Also called the *auditory method* and *auditory learning*, it operates on the principle of teaching a child to learn how to listen rather than just learning how to hear. Advocates argue

(Frequently in this situation, the interpreter will sit with the class and face the instructor, while the deaf student will sit with the class and face the interpreter.)

☞ Be prepared for significant distraction at first.

☞ Both interpreter and student will benefit from getting lesson summaries in advance.

☞ Be conscious of the lag between oral speech and its translation into sign.

☞ A visual aid (e.g., a transparency) means the deaf student has two stimuli to process with one sensory organ. (Not dissimilar, in the case of a hearing person, to being addressed by two people at once.)

---

that only a very few children are unable to benefit from this training especially if it is begun as early as possible. Essentially, the method involves first the development of awareness of sound, then the ability to make gross discriminations among sounds in the environment, and finally the ability to discriminate among speech sounds. Supporters argue for the earliest possible use of amplifications, as well as simultaneous training in speech production.

Specialized Approaches

There are a number of individual and unique ideas appearing in the field from time to time, some of which attract attention because of active support—and active criticism. Two that have attained a high profile even though they are not widely used, are the *cued speech method* and the *acoupedic method*. The first uses a combination of oral and manual styles. Attempts to develop the individual's residual hearing capacity and the capacity for speech are supported by eight manual configurations and four hand positions to supplement the visual manifestations of speech. The originator of cued speech, Orin Cornett, claims it can be learned in 12 to 15 hours by anyone of average intelligence. The acoupedic method, on the other hand, excludes all visual clues in order to encourage the individual to use residual hearing to the maximum extent possible.

Manual Approaches

American Sign Language (ASL)

In May 1993, Ontario became the first Canadian province to authorize the use of ASL (and LSQ, Langue de Signes Quebecoise) as a language of instruction for deaf students. Ontario schools for the deaf now use ASL, and written English, and allow students opportunities to use and develop their auditory and speech potential.

ASL is a true language in itself, quite different from spoken language and most emphatically not a translation of English into manually communicated words. ASL has its own vocabulary, its own grammar, its own word order, and its own history. American Sign Language is founded on combinations of symbolic gestures produced by the shape, the location, and the movement of the hands. Whereas methods like *Total Communication* (see below) very often employ iconic signs, in which the shape of the sign encodes English as much as possible, the signs of ASL are unique. Many of the ASL signs symbolize concepts rather than individual words. ASL has no signs for the grammatical markers, such as *ed* and *ing* that express verb tense and condition. Rather, users depend on facial expression and body language to replace voice intonation and enhance meaning. ASL tends to be learned by deaf children in special settings like schools, rather than being passed on by parents in the way that language is learned by most hearing people. (The predecessor of ASL is FSL, French Sign Language, developed as a one hand signing system by Abbé Charles Michel de l'Epee (1712-1784) who founded an institution for the deaf in Paris, in 1770.)

Fingerspelling

This method spells out the letters of the English alphabet by using various finger positions on one hand. As a technique, it is often used as one part of the *Total Communication* method. Members of the Canadian Hearing Society have varied in their endorsement of fingerspelling. Critics generally hold that it is exceptionally inefficient and time consuming and requires an inordinate amount of attention for a style that has large potential for error. Supporters, especially those who are competent in the use of the method say that it is ideal for "fill-in", those times when a communication doesn't "get through", and the communicator must resort to spelling out a word or words (just as hearing people sometime feel the need to do).

Combination Approaches

Although a deaf or hard of hearing person's communication approach is likely to emphasize one rather than several methods, he will invariably avail himself of other sources for information (like facial expressions, body language, etc.) in the same way as a hearing person. Within the taxonomy of communication styles advocated for the deaf, there are approaches that operate from this multi-source position both practically and philosophically. Two of these approaches are the *Rochester Method* and *Total Communication*. The Rochester Method uses fingerspelling in conjunction with speech, speechreading, and amplification. Total Communication may be defined as the use of speech, speechreading, fingerspelling and amplification, along with the simultaneous use of a school-based manual system. In a school-based total communication system, signs are usually taught in the same order as language. This teaches the child to communicate manually using English syntax. Also, unlike ASL, the signs tend to attempt to reflect English syntax. Worth noting is that some classrooms use ASL as part of a Total Communication approach. As well, even advocates who strongly support ASL to the exclusion of all else acknowledge the potential usefulness of other support like speech-reading and hearing aid technology.

Hearing Aid Technology

There was a time not long ago when fitting someone with a hearing aid meant installing a device that simply amplified incoming sound. While the basic advantage of such a system is obvious, the accompanying drawbacks were often significant. Although straight amplification is still available today and in some cases is entirely adequate for a user, the technology has become far more sophisticated and versatile. In most cases, the professionals who assess hearing (audiologists and audiometrists) can not only point to where on the decibel and hertz range an individual has hearing problems, they can identify assistive devices that can be customized to address those problems. This technological step represents somewhat of a revolution for people with a hearing loss for it means that, in many cases, they are able to acquire hearing aids, although often at significant expense, which compensate for loss without adding new problems by amplifying other sounds unnecessarily.

In the classroom, technology can be generalized across a very wide spectrum. One example, and there are many, is a system that uses FM radio band technology. In this system, the

Common Sounds	dB Rating	Usual Effect
rustling leaves	20	pleasant
whisper	30	barely audible
2-3 people conversing	40-65	varies
hair dryer on high	70	interferes, disrupts
occupied cafeteria food blender motorcycle 5 m. away	80-95	annoying (85 dB for 8 hrs begins hearing damage)
chain saw, snowmobile jet flyby 300 m. away	105-110	regular exposure without protection can damage
sound system at 100+ watts rock concert or jet takeoff	120 110-140	pain threshold is 125 dB

teacher (and/or other students) wears a transmitter and the deaf student(s) a receiver. For the deaf student, the amount of classroom ambient noise is usually less obtrusive, with sounds coming principally from whoever is wearing the transmitter. The system—between speaker and listener—is usually wireless. This is only one of many systems recently developed primarily for classroom use, and educators involved in choosing technological support for students who are deaf or who have a hearing loss, need to investigate the options thoroughly, particularly in seeking out recent developments, and in seeking out the possibilities for customization of the support. Ironically, in an age that turns readily to technology in almost every facet of life, less than one-third of people who could be helped by hearing aids, actually own and use one.

Educational Implications of Hearing Loss

❖ Deaf and hard of hearing students often do not have an easy time in school, mostly because of what is in effect, a language barrier. Studies over several decades suggest that their academic achievement is affected by five specific factors more than any other. These are the severity of the hearing loss, the chronological age at onset, intelligence, socioeconomic status of the family, and hearing status of the parents; (a deaf student of deaf parents is considered to have a better chance for academic success than if the parents are hearing).

❖ Achievement test scores for the deaf are often significantly lower than the scores of students who hear, even on adapted test instruments. However, it behooves educators to consider whether this lower performance is simply the result of a bad fit between the real abilities of deaf students and the way achievement is measured. Even though deaf students may lag in reading and other language skills, teachers must be on guard against interpreting a difficulty with language as an inherent lack of ability. Yet the issue of language development and

its effective use is inevitably a principal consideration in any evaluation of ability.

❖ The difficulties deaf students have in communicating often lead to exaggerated compensatory behaviours or to frustration that is expressed in ways which cause them to be unfairly labeled as disturbed, or odd, or even developmentally disabled. In the past it was not unusual to find deaf students of normal intellectual and emotional mien placed in segregated classes because of this. There has even developed over time, a so-called 'psychology of the deaf', in which the characteristics of deaf people are sometimes described in very unflattering language. One result of this perception of the deaf, no matter what its accuracy or its origins, is reinforcement of the isolation that deaf students frequently describe as the worst part of living in a hearing world. Being aware of and responding to this factor is very important for teachers and educational assistants.

❖ Classroom environment plays a major role in accommodating the needs of a student who has a hearing loss. Although matters such as locating the student's desk are always taken into immediate account by most teachers and educational assistants, there are other issues that recent findings have shown to be important. One of these is the amount of echo in the classroom, technically referred to as reverberation (the amount of time it takes for a sound to decrease to 60 dB after it is turned off). Naturally, the more reverberation can be reduced, the less likely a student with hearing loss will experience interference. Interestingly, the impact of reverberation on students with normal hearing can be very significant too, a fact which makes reverberation reduction through the use of carpeting, acoustical ceiling tiles, and drapes*, a matter for serious consideration.

❖ Yet another issue is signal-to-noise ratio. This is the dB level of the speaker divided by the dB level of the ambient sounds in the room. The higher the latter, the lower the

●●● ───────
* Which may introduce allergy considerations. Nothing is simple!

─────── ●●●

ratio and, naturally, the lower the ratio, the more difficulty a deaf or hard of hearing student will experience. Signal-to-noise ratio is a powerful argument for advocates who support self-contained classrooms for deaf and hard of hearing.

❖ Whether a deaf student has an interpreter, or has amplification devices, or uses total communication—whatever the approach—communicating is very hard work, both as a consequence of the concentration needed to receive information and of the effort needed to send it. Deaf students get very tired, usually moreso than their hearing peers, and

teachers must recognize this. (It is important for hearing people to realize too, that signing is very tiring work; an interpreter has an intensely energy-consuming job.)

❖ Meaningful cooperation with the hearing world can be difficult to achieve. Deaf persons often describe their experiences with others in societal control (e.g., police, and other officialdom) as unsatisfactory. An important responsibility of educators because of their potential for extensive contact with deaf and hard of hearing persons is to sensitize the hearing public to this matter.

The Case of Nils

Nils' thirteenth birthday was more dramatic, if not traumatic, than most such days for a young adolescent. To begin with, on that day he boarded a plane in Stockholm, with his mother, to come to Canada. She had accepted a three-year diplomatic posting, with an option of a three-year extension.

On the day of their arrival, Nils and his mother learned their first lesson in Canadian geography: the school for deaf students that had agreed to accept him was too far away from his new home for him to be a day student. Even more distressing, they learned that the school used a communication style quite different from that which Nils used. From age six, Nils had attended a private, residential school for the deaf that uses sign exclusively. Moreover, the style of signing is one the school has developed, and it is quite significantly different from any form of sign used in any general way in North America. This difference might not have been an issue for Nils in his home country, for the school provides personal interpreters for students who leave to enroll in neighbourhood schools. However, with Nils' move to Canada, the matter has become far more complicated.

Over a series of meetings during the first month of his life in Canada, (during the summer vacation) Nils and his mother have decided, and the local (Ontario) board has agreed, that he will enroll in the neighbourhood school. At this point, however, the boy and his mother have a further decision to make, choosing from among one, or a combination, of the following options.

1. The Swedish diplomatic service will provide and pay for a personal, in-class, signing interpreter trained in the signing style used by Nils' former school.

2. Given that Nils has some residual hearing (his loss is severe to profound but he wears two powerful aids) a type of Total Communication can be used.

3. Nils is already familiar with sign; continue sign but use ASL.

One piece of good news for Nils is that the teacher of the class where he will attend is both qualified and interested in special education. She acknowledges that she has preferences in the matter of communication, but has pointed out in meetings with Nils and his mother, that she will happily accommodate whatever decision is made.

Nils' school career has demonstrated that he is very bright and very resourceful, and although his language skills are typically lagging behind those of his hearing peers, his superiority in subject areas like mathematics suggest that he would likely respond to any or all of the above. The question to be solved: what is best for him?

✔ STRATEGIES FOR THE CLASSROOM

The following suggestions are collected from deaf and hard of hearing students who were asked to offer advice to teachers and educational assistants in regular classes.

(1) Seat her toward the front of the room and to one side with the better ear toward the teacher and class. Otherwise seat in the second seat from the front, second row from the window, or similar setting, but always with light on the teacher's face.

(2) Permit the student to move his seat if the teaching centre moves to another part of the room.

(3) A deaf student needs to see the speaker's face. Seat him two to three metres away from the place where you do most of your talking. Keep your hands away from your face.

(4) From time to time attempt to keep your mouth near the level of the student's eyes. For example, instead of always standing, sit at your desk at certain times.

(5) Be sure to have the student's visual and aural attention before giving assignments or announcements.

(6) Make a practice of asking both hearing and hard of hearing students to repeat directions for the benefit of the whole class. Ask the student to repeat instructions to ensure she understands.

(7) Do not turn your back while talking. Do not talk while writing on the chalkboard. A moving speaker is impossible to speech read. Do not walk around the room while talking about important things.

(8) Don't use loud tones or exaggerated mouth movements. Use the same tone of voice and the same inflection you use for everyone else. Avoid gestures. Excessive gestures draw attention away from the face and lips. They're embarrassing too.

(9) Many words sound the same—blue, blew; tax, tacks. This is confusing enough. But many words that do not sound the same look the same on the lips; e.g., bat, pat, mat look alike as do bad, pad, mad.

(10) It may be helpful to explain to other students that many words look alike. Let the class try to speech read a few sentences. This procedure will help others in the class to understand. Understanding helps eliminate teasing and unfair judgments.

(11) During a discussion, ask questions to ensure that the person with hearing loss understands. If she does not understand, restate the material in a different way. Perhaps she was not familiar with the key words that you used, or some of them may have looked like other words.

(12) Names of people and places, especially new ones, are very difficult to understand. It is well to place new words or terms on the chalkboard and discuss new material from this vocabulary.

(13) A buddy can explain things. (A buddy can be a great fallback, but there is potential for too much dependence.)

(14) Try rephrasing rather than repeating, but be sure a rephrase does not add confusion.

(15) If the person with a hearing loss is completely lost, say quietly "I'm talking about..." This often gives her a fresh start. But be discreet!

(16) If the student seems to have trouble with certain words repeatedly, use these words often in as many ways as possible.

(17) Find out if he has a good ear and speak to that side.

(18) If your class has group discussions or cooperative learning activities, a round table is better for a deaf student than a rectangular one.

(19) If you have a good relationship with your deaf student, you can tell him when his voice is too loud or when it's getting on other students' nerves.

(20) *Encourage participation* in extra-curricular activities. Deaf students are like any others. They take their lead from their teachers.

(21) *If a visit is being planned,* or a visitor is coming, prepare for it. Write new and unusual words on the chalkboard; help the deaf student become familiar with the names of persons or objects she will be seeing. Explain any special rules ahead of time when you can be sure that she understands them. The brief discussion will help her associate lip movements with new words and promote her understanding of their meaning. By telling the student in advance what unit of activity will be studied, she has an opportunity to find material on the subject and will be able to follow along much better because she will be more familiar with the vocabulary. Always, in history, or science, and geography lessons where there will be new vocabulary or new concepts, try to give the student a brief written statement, e.g., "Today's topic is the Introduction of The War of 1812. Key words are Niagara Frontier, Sir Isaac Brock, York, James Madison", etc.

(22) *Deaf students tire more easily* than others do. You can help by planning the day's work so the periods when they must pay careful attention are interspersed with other activities.

(23) *Encourage the student* to keep trying. Please be patient. Repeat instructions as often as necessary.

(24) *If possible, try to help* the student learn to use a dictionary pronunciation key.

(25) *Many students hear* better on some days than others.

(26) *Talk with the deaf students* every day. Talk often rather than for a long time. Ask questions about movies, T.V. programs, hobbies, travel, work, etc.

(27) *A regular hearing aid* makes speech louder, not always clearer. It often amplifies all other noise too. See if some of the other noise can be reduced.

(28) *If it has not already been investigated,* look into the possibility of using an FM system. This system can be more effective in a classroom than a hearing aid.

(29) *There is a lot of helpful computer software* and a computer doesn't get tired of repeating something. If the student controls the keyboard, then the number of repeats will be just what is needed. Not too many. Not too few. While you are at it, most computers with sound capacity will have earphones. Earphones are always better for people with a hearing loss. They concentrate the sound and block out all the background. Half the time it's the background that's the problem anyway.

(30) (Author's note: The following is verbatim (orally) from a very bright twelve-year old student with a severe hearing loss.)
"Our teaching assistant this year was the best help I ever had. And she wasn't a hearing specialist. Couldn't sign or nothing. But she was helpful. You don't always need a specialist. Just a good T.A."

Calderon, R., & Naidu, S. (2000). Further support for the benefits of early identification and intervention for children with hearing loss. *The Volta Review, 100*(5), 53-84.

Clark, G.M., Tong, Y., & Patrick, J.F. (1990). *Cochlea prosthesis.* New York: Churchill Livingstone.

Cole, E.G. (1992). *Listening and talking: A guide to promoting spoken language in young hearing-impaired children.* Washington DC: Alexander Graham Bell Association for the Deaf.

Feher-Prout, T. (1996). Stress and coping in families with deaf children. *Journal of Deaf Studies and Deaf Education. 1*, 155-166.

Gaty, J.C. (1992). Teaching speech to hearing impaired children. *The Volta Review, 94*, 49-61.

Greer, A.E., & Tobey, E. (1992). Effects of cochlear implants and tactile aids on the development of speech production skills in children with profound hearing impairment. *The Volta Review, 94*, 135-163.

Holt, J., & Marshall, W. (1994). *Classroom attributes and achievement scores for deaf and hard of hearing students.* Silver Speng MD: Registry of interpreters of the deaf.

Luetke-Stahlman, B., & Luckner, J. (1991). *Effectively educating students with hearing impairments.* New York: Longman.

Mayer, C., Akamatsu, C.T. (2000). Deaf children creating written texts: Contribution of American Sign Language and signed forms of English. *American Annals of the Deaf, 145*, 394-403.

Mayer, C., Akamatsu, C.T., & Stewart, D. (2002). A model for effective practice: Dialogic inquiry with students who are deaf. *Exceptional Children, 68*(4), 485-502.

Moores, D.F. (2001). *Educating the deaf: Psychology, principles, and practices* (5th ed.). Boston: Houghton Mifflin.

Roberts, K. (1997). A preliminary account of the effects of otitis media on 15-month-olds' categorization and some implications for early language learning. *Journal of Speech, Language and Hearing Research, 40*, 508-518.

Salend, S.J., & Longo, M. (1994). The role of the educational interpreter in mainstreaming. *Teaching Exceptional Children, 26*, 22-28.

Schein, J. (1994). Deafness in Canada and the United States, *Deaf American monographs*, 93-99.

Schirmer, B.R. (2000). *Language and literacy development in children who are deaf.* Boston: Allyn & Bacon.

Schirmer, B.R., & Woolsey, M.L. (1997). Effect of teacher questions on the reading comprehension of deaf children. *Journal of Deaf Studies and Deaf Education, 2*, 47-56.

Schildroth, A.N., & Hontto, S.A. (1994). Inclusion or exclusion? Deaf students and the inclusion movement. *American Annals of the Deaf, 139*, 239-243.

Weber, J. (1997). *Teacher support in mainstreaming deaf and hard of hearing students in rural Saskatchewan, Canada: A pilot project.* CAEDHH, 23(1), 40-48.

Links

Ontario Association of the Deaf
http://www.deafontario.org/

Canadian Hearing Society
www.chs.ca

Gallaudet College Bookstore
http://bookstore.gallaudet.edu

Hearing Foundation of Canada
http://www.chsf.ca/press.html

Goverment of British Columbia
http://www.bced.gov.bc.ca/specialed/hearimpair/

Special Needs Opportunity Windows
http://snow.utoronto.ca/best/accommodate/deaf.html

CHAPTER 13

Students Who Are Blind or Partially Sighted

If there was only one thing about sighted people that I could change, it would be to make them think of me as just a normal person who can't see. So that when I do something normal, like find a CD and slip into the player and turn it on—stuff like that—nobody will say "Isn't he something?" When we blind people do ordinary things, it's because we're ordinary people. It's not like we should be in a circus."

Corey P-N., age 29, blind from birth

Misconceptions About Blindness and Partial Sight

1. Blind people have no sight at all.

Only a small percentage of legally blind people have absolutely no vision. The majority has a useful amount of functional vision.

2. Blind people use braille as their primary method of reading.

The majority use print—often large type—as a primary source of reading. An increasing trend among blind people who cannot see print is to use audio technology rather than braille.

3. An extra sense enables blind people to detect obstacles.

Blind people do not possess an extra sense, but often develop a strong sensitivity to nearby objects especially if they have the ability to hear.

4. The blind automatically develop better acuity in their other senses.

Through concentration and attention, blind persons often learn to make very fine discriminations in the sensations they obtain. This is not automatic but rather, represents a better use of received sensations.

5. If partially sighted students use their eyes too much, their sight will deteriorate.

Only in rare conditions is this true; visual discrimination ability can actually improve through training and use. Strong lenses, holding books close to the eyes, and using the eyes usually does not harm vision.

6. Blind children automatically become good listeners.

Good listening is primarily a learned skill. Although many blind people develop good listening skills, it is the result of effort because they depend on these skills for so much of their information.

7. Instructing children in mobility techniques should wait until elementary or even secondary school age.

The adage of "earlier the better" applies to blind children as well as to their sighted peers. Even the use of a cane at an early age has been shown to have advantages.

8. Using the long cane is simple and natural.

The task is not simple. There are specifications not just for using the cane but for its manufacture as well.

Definitions of Blindness

Legal blindness in Canada is defined as distance acuity of 6/60 m or 20/200 ft. or less in the better eye after the best available correction. That means the person must stand at six meters or less to see an object, which would normally be seen at sixty meters. Persons whose visual field is reduced to an angle of twenty degrees or less at its widest diameter are also legally blind. (Normally sighted people have a visual field of 180 degrees.) A partially sighted person is one whose distance acuity is 6/13 or less in the better eye. It is important to recognize that someone with visual acuity of 6/60 can probably read, or a least see, print. Total blindness, i.e., inability to see anything at all, is actually uncommon.

Prevalence of Blindness

For educators, three important facts underline the matter of prevalence. The first of these is that blindness and visual impairments are both low-incidence conditions. Secondly, they are conditions which affect adults at significantly greater rates than children and teenagers. A third is that while the conditions do not appear with high frequency in North America, their prevalence in many Asian, African and South American countries is much greater. Lack of sanitation, vitamin deficiency (particularly Vitamin A), poor sanitation and the high potential for water borne blindness raise the numbers in these countries.

Classifications

Near normal vision: able to function without special training, but will use corrective lenses.

Moderate functional impairment: requires specialized aids and lighting.

Reduction in central vision: moderate field loss; may qualify for special services as legally blind.

Low vision: even after correction, vision is lower than normal, although correction is usually helpful.

Poor functional vision (and possible poor central vision with marked field loss): Standard correction is of little or no benefit. Usually strong reading aids and other technologies are needed.

Blind: total field loss as well as total detail loss; may distinguish between light and dark.

Some Typical Causes of Blindness

Retinal detachment: The retina can become separated through injury or disease, making it incapable of receiving images.

Retinoblastoma: a known genetic disease that presents with malignant tumors. Treatment usually involves chemotherapy and localized eye-saving measures. According to the Ontario Cancer Institute, the majority of eyes are saved. The Institute advises genetic counseling for the families involved.

Retinopathy of Prematurity (formerly known as *Retrolental fibroplasia*): a condition occurring in babies who are exposed to a greater than normal concentration of oxygen post-natally.

Rubella: a syndrome occurring as a result of maternal rubella infection during the first months of pregnancy.

Sympathetic ophthalmia: When there is a penetrating wound to one eye, the other eye may reflect the same characteristics as the injured eye.

Some Typical Causes of Partial Sight

Albinism: A genetically transmitted disease in which the eyes are light sensitive. Minimum illumination is needed, and tinted glasses are usually prescribed.

Astigmatism: This defect causes an error in refraction. Images are blurred and there is generally poor visual discrimination. Glasses are prescribed,

> Sighted people have all these ways of saying shut up without actually saying it—you know? Like—they turn away, or they stand up suddenly. Stuff like that. I never interpreted that as shut up even when I knew it was happening, until someone told me about it. I'm glad I was told though. Helps to know. That's one of the things about being blind. Everybody treats you with kid gloves. We don't need that. We've got to be told to shut up too just like everybody else."
>
> *Ginny de, V. aged 17*

usually with positive results. Good illumination usually helps too.

Cataracts: Any lens opacity is a cataract. Such opacity causes blank areas in what is seen. Depending upon the nature of the opacity, adjustments in lighting are usually necessary.

Colour deficiency (a.k.a. *colour blindness*): Unable to distinguish colours. More boys than girls are affected.

Glaucoma: a problem caused by increased intraocular pressure. Glaucoma patients require regular medical attention and sometimes suffer headaches. Quite often peripheral vision is poor. Good illumination is recommended.

Hyperopia: The hyperopic eye is far-sighted. A student with this condition usually functions well in gross motor activity but finds reading and other near work difficult and tiring until correction is provided.

Macular degeneration: The centre of the field of vision blurs causing most detail to be lost. Some limited peripheral vision usually remains. There are two common forms: "wet", which usually progresses rapidly and "dry", which develops more slowly.

Monocular vision: Through disease, accident, or defect, a person is left with only one functioning eye.

Classroom Checklist of Possible Vision Problems

Although the ultimate diagnosis of a student's visual problem—or even its existence—would naturally be determined by an optometrist or ophthalmologist, teachers and educational assistants can play an important role in early detection. While this is a more common occurrence in the very early grades, teachers of older students should not exclude themselves since eye disease and poor vision can begin at any stage in life and grow serious rapidly. Any of the characteristics in the Classroom Checklist, especially if observed over time, might indicate real or potential visual impairment.

1. **Appearance of eyes**
   – One eye turns in or out at any time?
   – Reddened eyes or lids?
   – Encrusted eyelids?
   – Frequent sties on lids?
   – Eyes tear excessively?

2. **Complaints by student**
   – Headaches in forehead or temples?
   – Burning or itching of eyes after reading or deskwork?
   – Nausea or dizziness?
   – Print blurs or moves after reading a short time?

3. **Behavioural signs of visual problems**
   – Head turns while reading across the page?
   – Loses place often during reading?
   – Needs finger or marker to keep place?
   – Tilts head abnormally while working at desk?

   – Rereads or skips line unknowingly?
   – Too frequently omits or substitutes words?
   – Complains of seeing double (diplopia)?
   – Misaligns number columns regularly?
   – Squints, closes or covers one eye?
   – Consistently shows gross postural deviations?
   – Orients a worksheet unusually?
   – Must feel things to understand?
   – Disorderly placement of words or drawings on page?
   – Blinks to clear view of chalkboard after near task?
   – Squints to see chalkboard?
   – Holds book too closely?
   – Avoids all possible near-centred tasks?
   – Closes or covers one eye when reading?
   – Rubs eyes a great deal?

Myopia: Distance vision is blurred so that gross activities can be difficult. A student with this condition is more comfortable with reading and other close work.

Nystagmus: The involuntary movement of the eyeball caused by this problem makes focusing and fixation difficult.

Optic atrophy: The optic nerve sustains permanent loss of its ability to carry clear images to the brain. May result in restricted fields of vision. Visual behaviour may be inconsistent.

Peripheral vision: This is the ability to see only those activities and objects outside of the direct line of vision. Because of defective central vision, the student may have to tilt the head or raise or lower the eyes in order to read.

Retinitis pigmentosa: Pigment deposits in the retina cause loss of peripheral fields resulting in tunnel vision. Major difficulties occur in dim light. Good illumination is needed.

Strabismus: An imbalance of the eye muscles causes failure of the two eyes to focus on the same object. The eyes can cross or deviate upward or downward. Early treatment is vital, or a "lazy eye" condition (amblyopia) can result.

Tunnel vision: The field of vision is so reduced that a child sees only what is directly in front. It creates the same visual image that others see when looking through a tube, severely affecting mobility and the collection of information from the environment.

Problem solving

The Case of Lori

At age three, Lori seemed to bump into things and fall over her playmates far more frequently than seemed normal for her age. Both parents suspected a vision problem. That suspicion was reinforced two years later by a very observant kindergarten teacher and an equally perceptive educational assistant. After the first week of school, both instructors began to keep an "Events Journal" on Lori, noting specifically those behaviours that suggested Lori had impaired vision. Within ten days they were both convinced that their young student was using peripheral vision to accomplish what other students did by focusing face on. A conference with Lori's parents led to a visit with an ophthalmologist and then, confirmation of what the two suspected: that Lori had macular degeneration.

The quick and careful thinking by Lori's kindergarten teacher and educational assistant made a huge difference in her life. Macular degeneration usually means that the individual has blurred or completely obscured centre-of-field vision, while retaining some vision at the edges of the field. Very often it is progressive and intensifies over time. The early intervention in Lori's case meant that she was able to receive special training at a crucial time in her development. Lori's average to above-average ability, and what every adult in her life calls "high-profile spunk", along with this training, meant that she was able to progress quite smoothly through the next years of her school career. She was in a regular class in her neighbourhood school for this time.

Now, in the seventh grade, a problem has arisen. Lori's condition has worsened over time so that essentially, she has lost all of her vision. For several years now, she has been identified as legally blind for funding purposes. None of this has denied her full participation in all class activities, something she and her parents insist on, even though her mishaps have increased in number and seriousness—most recently a broken arm in gym. Other difficulties have arisen as well. Lori is in the school band, but she does not have a natural ear, cannot see the notes, and plays her trombone badly—and loudly. The dropout rate from the band has now reached a crisis level. Because of an incident during a natural science field trip last year (Lori fell over an embankment and pulled two other students down with her; no one was hurt) this year's cross-country skiing trip (an overnighter) can't attract enough volunteer parent supervisors and may be cancelled.

A meeting of Lori's teachers, assistants and parents has been called for next week by school officials. The agenda specifically sets aside the legal issues involved. What the administration wishes to discuss is what is best for Lori and her schoolmates in terms of their education and social development. Should her program be restricted?

Some Issues in the Field

✦ A most significant issue for blind and partially sighted people is *successful adjustment to the world at large*. This adjustment calls for mobility and a sensitivity to the environment that is natural in sighted persons but not so in those whose vision is limited. Much of a blind person's energy, life force, education, and time, are devoted to this matter, especially when they are young. At the same time, because they are normal human beings in every other respect, blind people naturally wish to live the lives that the rest of the world does. A great deal of the initial social exchange between visually disabled people and the sighted people in their lives is devoted to finding a mutually comfortable, appropriate and effective means of associating.

✦ *The failure of individuals and families to have regular eyesight examinations* continues to be a nagging concern of health care professionals and educators. Infants as young as three months can now be tested with considerable accuracy. Optometrists urge that all children be examined by three years of age and again at school entrance. This is because many vision problems are more correctable if a response is made early. It is also important to begin teaching visual *efficiency* early, if visual *acuity* is poor or weakening. Testing is especially important if there is a familial pattern of such problems as strabismus, cataracts, etc. Despite the logical and impassioned arguments of both educators and health professionals, the response of families and even educational jurisdictions is, surprisingly, less intense than one might expect, given the ease and limited expense with which these examinations can be conducted.

✦ *Treating learning disability as a vision problem* was not uncommon in the early to mid-1970's and still has some residual currency today, even though evidence of the connection is hard to find. A student presumed to have learning disabilities should always have his vision checked, but only to determine whether his academic difficulties are being caused by poor vision, not to find a visual/learning disability connection.

Some Educational Implications of Special Visual Needs

❖ Empirical evidence suggests that in the classroom, especially among younger students, cognitive abilities in the blind and partially sighted tend to develop more slowly than the norm. There is a good deal of support for the view, however, that this apparent lag is owing more to differentiated early learning experiences rather than to any inherent intellectual difference. Blind children simply have not had the opportunity to experience some of the things that sighted children have.

❖ It is difficult for students with serious vision problems to develop a spatial map of their environment. However, it is possible to develop the concept of space with other senses, such as noting the time it takes to walk various distances, or feeling the dimensions between objects. Because the amount of information that can be taken in at one time is limited, the process is understandably slower. This fact makes the time to acquire learning an important factor—as it is with almost all students with exceptionalities.

❖ For students who cannot see, or who see poorly, it is often difficult to understand abstract concepts without the aid of concrete materials. Such students will benefit from three-dimensional models, exaggerated bas-relief maps and globes, manipulative games and materials.

❖ Blind and partially sighted students are often overprotected by the adults in their lives and treated over-delicately by fellow students. Although this is not an unnatural response, it is important that independence be a prominent and continuing objective in the education of students with vision problems. Fostering this independence calls for frequent and delicate judgments by the teacher and educational assistant.

❖ Blind students must be taught social and communicative skills that many sighted persons acquire naturally. Most cultures, for example, attach great importance to whether or not a speaker looks at her listener, and many advocates for the blind urge that this habit be taught. However, some so-called natural skills are much more difficult to teach. For example, sighted people make constant use, subconsciously, of body language, important markers that indicate responses like reinforcement, enthusiasm, reluctance, disagreement, uneasiness, etc. Body language can alert a speaker to modify a particular communication and sometimes even indicates whether or not a communication is finished—or should be! For obvious reasons, the very notion of body language, and the means of dealing with it is something that blind and partially sighted students cannot be expected to acquire naturally.

❖ The less a person is able to know the world through sight, the more important it becomes that he be a good listener. Although it was once assumed that good listening skills automatically develop as a consequence of sight deprivation, it is now known that such skills must be taught.

❖ Professionals dealing with the very young must be particularly conscious of the fact that many children are not aware of a visual problem if they have one. Or if they are aware, they often do not understand its extent or its implications. This is important for classroom professionals, not just in discovering the presence of the problem, but in helping the child to deal with it.

❖ Academic success is more closely related to social, cultural, and familial factors than to degree of visual impairment.

Visual Stimulation

As recently as the 1960s, students with low vision were encouraged to "save" their visual capacity, to keep it from "wearing out". Today, the belief is that the more one's residual vision is used the stronger and fitter it may become. Thus educators now encourage students with low vision to attend to light and objects, to use tracing and scanning techniques, and to exercise their residual vision in a variety of ways. (E.g., a popular technique with younger and even older children is to sort, classify, sequence and creatively rearrange pictures.) With students who have low vision, many of the technical devices mentioned in this chapter can be very useful but they must be trained to use them.

Guide Dogs ✍

The popular term 'seeing eye dog' is misleading because it suggests that the animal undertakes sole responsibility for leading a blind person about. The term 'guide dog'(sometimes 'dog guide') more accurately describes its principal function of guiding a person around objects and ideally, preventing him or her from walking into a dangerous situation. The dogs are also excellent companions and many users describe them as important in connecting them socially to their communities. However, because management and control of the animal requires special training and special ability, (and is very expensive) only a small percentage of blind persons can use a guide dog. In addition, a dog and person must be carefully matched so that they can work as a team. Children almost never have a guide dog, although it is not uncommon now in older blind teenagers.

The choice of an animal for training is usually based on the level of placidity, steadiness, and intelligence (although a too-intelligent dog may choose its own interests over loyalty in a dangerous situation). When a dog is "working" it will almost always be in a harness and bystanders should not pet or otherwise pay it attention. Most guide dogs have a relatively short working life.

Assistive Technology

Braille

This well-known writing system is named for Louis Braille but originated in the hands of Charles Barbier, an officer in the army of Napoleon Bonaparte. Barbier devised a system of raised dot writing that could be read by touch in the dark. Braille published his modified system in 1834. Within twenty years it was adopted by the Paris School for the Blind, but took another half century to penetrate North America. By the mid 1950s, more than half of all blind and seriously visually impaired persons were braille users but then by the end of the century the number had dropped to below ten percent. More recently, there is a resurgence in the use of braille, partly in recognition of its usefulness as a means of communication but also because it is an identity feature for people who are blind.

Braille is a tactile communication method. Cells of from one to six raised dots on paper represent the letters of the alphabet (and numbers). Although it is a direct transliteration of English (or other language) braille resorts to contractions regularly to save time and space. (For example, in English braille, the letter 'r' by itself means 'rather'.) Although it has been established that braille is easier to read than raised letters of the alphabet, it is still a much slower process than reading print is for the average sighted reader.

Students can begin learning braille in the first grade or earlier, and have a number of technologies available to them, beginning with braille books. A brailler is a six key device not unlike a typewriter. (Integrated classrooms where a brailler is used must become accustomed to its noise.) There is also the *Optacon** which converts print into Braille electronically.

Computer-Assisted Technology

Computer technology continues to develop at a rate that almost outpaces the capacity of special education to use it effectively. Some examples are the *Versabraille II+** a laptop computer that combines brailler and word processor technology, the *Kurzweil Reading Machine** which con-verts print to audio output, the *DragonDictate** a speech-activated word processor, and the *Braille Blazer** which prints braille at 10-15 characters per second.

Optical Aids

Teachers and their blind and partially sighted students are assisted by still other devices, which, although they may appear simple in comparison to computer technology, are remarkable examples of technical common sense. These include items like large print materials, embossed rulers and tape measures, braille watches, three dimensional maps, hand-held and stand mounted magnifiers, special lighting, etc.

Mobility Assists

The *long cane* is one of the most effective and simplest devices yet devised for safe, efficient mobility. It's important to note that although the use of one seems simple to sighted people, learning to use it effectively requires some training and practice. For very young children the *Connecticut Pre-cane* has been developed but is still in the early stages of proving itself. (For more information, see Foy, C.J., et al, (1992) *Journal of Visual Impairment and Blindness*, 86 (4), pp. 178-81.) *Guide dogs* are reported by those who can use them as extremely helpful in alerting them to changes in the immediate environment, to potential dangers, and in guiding them through complex situations. *Electronic devices* like laser canes and sonic guides (worn on the head) are still experimental and very expensive.

Educational Placement

Increasingly, and with marked success, blind and partially sighted students are being educated in the regular classroom. Special assistance may be delivered by an itinerant specialist teacher who provides advice on strategy, materials,

● ● ● ────────

* Brand names are used in these descriptions. Further information about these devices and competing brands are available from provincial ministries and from the Canadian National Institute for the Blind. Also, web search engines regularly list both updated and new technologies.

──────── ● ● ●

and possibly on curricular modification. Such modification may be intense instruction on how to listen, how to make "mental mobility maps", etc. The assistance may also take the form of one of the educational aids listed above, or it may be a combination of aid from several sources. As they have in all other areas of special education, educational assistants in the classroom have proven to be invaluable for blind and partially sighted students.

For some students, a resource room is their primary placement. This arrangement may offer a more certain guarantee of the specialized instruction they may need, but still permits a high degree of integration.

A more specialized placement, used particularly for students whose vision problems are quite seriously disabling, is an entirely self-contained classroom, or even a residential school devoted to blind students (and students who are blind with other special needs as well). In these environments, where there are usually very low pupil-teacher ratios, students receive regular school curriculum adapted to their needs, along with very specialized instruction related to their blindness.

✔ STRATEGIES FOR THE CLASSROOM

(1) *It is usually very beneficial* for a teacher of a regular class with a blind or partially sighted student to establish the practice of holding regular, informal, and private discussions with that student to work out special means of communication.*

(2) *It may be necessary for a teacher* to set up the classroom with the expectation that physical arrangements will not be altered, at least for a significant period of time. While this may contradict the style a teacher likes to follow, it may be a necessity for simple reasons of safety.

(3) *At the same time* there is the student's normal need to be physically mobile, to explore, to expand her capacity, as well as the need to perceive the self as both part of and separate from the environment. A great deal of professional skill is demanded of teachers and educational assistants in marrying this need with the obvious requirements of safety and efficient function described above. The key phrase is responsible independence.

(4) *Common sense.* A student with partial sight for example, should always be permitted to sit near the chalkboard, to borrow notes, to have another student take carbon-paper notes. (Yet the exceptionality need not be emphasized. If other students are blindfolded in an activity, the blind student should be too.) An overhead transparency can be photocopied

for someone who cannot see the screen. Partially sighted students almost always respond to better lighting. Additional time may be necessary for tests or a variety of other activities. Doors should always be fully open or fully closed. Name students being addressed; if an instruction is given to another child, a blind child may automatically follow it with perhaps disastrous results. By the same token, be explicit in giving instructions, particularly those involving movement from one place to another. A blind student cannot be expected to compensate for obstacles. If told to "come here", he may well come in a straight line regardless of hazards, because of his trust in the teacher.

(5) *Teachers, assistants, and sighted fellow students* often have to make allowances for communication style. Blind and partially blind students usually do not reinforce others with eye contact or facial expression—a phenomenon that takes some getting used to. In the same vein, the students often place great interpretive value on the expression and tone of their teacher's voice. This can be very important in some situations. Also, when a

• • • ───────

* A quite loquacious blind student in one of my classes did not sense that her extensive contributions to class discussions often wore out her classmates' receptivity. We worked out a simple and very subtle pencil tap so that she would know when to quit. — K.W.

─────── • • •

blind person responds to a communication with total silence, it may be because he is taking in and interpreting available cues. This too, requires adjustment from the teacher.

(6) "Blindisms" are characteristic mannerisms such as rocking, head shaking, hand shaking and eye poking. Most advocates suggest that teacher and educational assistants adroitly discourage these behaviours for they may isolate the student as irremediably different in a way that goes beyond merely being blind.

(7) Many blind people have grown to associate physical contact with being guided. Gestures such as patting and hugging may have negative connotations for some students, or may be misinterpreted. When a blind person is being guided, let her be the one who maintains and controls the physical contact. Don't grab her arm and steer; let her hold your arm.

(8) A blind person who is lost or disoriented needs position in order to work out direction. If a sighted person has occasion to help a blind person in this situation, it is important to make the blind person understand where he is first. Once he is oriented as best as possible, then explanation about direction can follow. A subset of this issue is the matter of snow-covered surfaces. Blind people often describe snow as their fog because the snow covers the surface references they use to orient their position. It follows then that they will often need more assistance in winter.

(9) A tactful classroom buddy or advocate is always helpful, but this should never be an unnaturally long-term arrangement.

(10) Perhaps the single most important role a teacher plays is being the classroom leader in developing a positive attitude. Sighted students will take their cue from their teacher in determining how to react to and inter-relate with a blind student in their midst. An accepting atmosphere for this student, with realistic expectations, will build his self-esteem, his sense of success, and his willingness to deal with the world. It will also contribute in a major way to the maturing of all students in the class.

READINGS & RESOURCES

Bishop, V.E. (1996). *Teaching visually impaired children.* (2nd ed.). Springfield, IL: Charles C. Thomas.

Canadian National Institute for the Blind (*CNIB*). (1993). *History of the CNIB.*

Erin, J. (1996). Children with multiple and visual disabilities. In *Children with visual impairments: A parent's guide* (pp. 287-316). Bethesda, MD: Woodbine House.

Hill, E.W., & Snook-Hill, M. (1996). Orientation and Mobility. In M.C. Holdbrook (Ed.). *Children with visual impairments: A parents guide* (pp. 259-286). Bethesda, MD: Woodbine House.

Kirchner, C., & Diament, S. (1999). Estimates of the number of visually impaired students, their teachers, and orientation and mobility specialists. *Journal of Visual Impairment and Blindness, 93*(9), 600-606.

Minor, R.J. (2001). The experience of living with and using a guide dog. *RE:view, 32,* 183-190.

Rosenblum, L.P. (1998). Best friendships of adolescents with visual impairments: A descriptive study. *Journal of Visual Impairment and Blindness, 92,* 593-608.

Sacks, S.Z. & Kekelis, L.S. (1992). Guidelines for mainstreaming blind and visually impaired children. In S.Z. Sacks, L.S. Kekelelis, & R.J. Gaylord-Ross (Eds.). *The development of social skills by blind and visually impaired students* (pp. 83-102). New York: American Foundation for the Blind.

Sacks, S.Z., & Wolffe, K.E. (1998). Lifestyles of adolescents with visual impairments: An ethnographic analysis. *Journal of Visual Impairment and Blindness, 92*(1), 7-17.

Tuttle, D.W., & Tuttle, T.N. (1996). *Self esteem and adjusting with blindness: The process of responding to life's demands.* (2nd ed.). Springfield, IL: Charles C. Thomas.

Uslan, M.M. (1992). Barriers to acquiring assistive technology. Cost and lack of information. *Journal of Visual Impairment and Blindness, 86*(9), 465-478.

Links

Canadian National Institute for the Blind
http://www.cnib.ca/

American Foundation for the Blind
http://www.afb.org/

World Health Organization
http://www.who.int/health_topics/ blindness/en/

CHAPTER 14

Students with Speech and Language Disorders

Try this. Just for a day, or even an hour. Stop in the middle of each sentence.
But leave your mouth open and make it clear you're trying to talk but can't.
Then watch how people look at you. Like you've got two heads.
Now think of living your life like that.

Ronnie K., diagnosed with aphasia at age 11

Misconceptions About Speech and Language Disorders

1. Stuttering affects all ages and both genders equally.

Stuttering affects more boys than girls and more children than adults. The child over adult ratio is usually ascribed to the fact that by adulthood, many people with a stutter have been helped by speech and language specialists.

2. Speech and language disorders are not related to intelligence.

Prevalence data show that although the disorders may occur among very intelligent individuals, they are found more frequently among persons with lower intellectual ability.

3. Articulation disorders in very young children especially, are not serious, and correction is rarely worth the effort or the risk of trauma.

Many small children have unique speech patterns but articulation disorders should never be dismissed as insignificant. "He'll grow out of it." is often an inappropriate substitute for remedial action.

4. If an individual has a speech or language disorder, she also has a learning disability.

The connection is not an absolute one, although difficulties with language affect both areas. Speech and language disorders also overlap other areas of special need, such as deafness. Some estimates say up to 50 percent of students in special education receive speech and language intervention.

5. Speech disorders and language disorders are really the same thing.

Most people with language disorders, especially children, also have speech problems. Yet it is not uncommon for a person to speak clearly without making sense.

Defining Speech and Language Disorders

For most children, the process of acquiring language, though seemingly complex, follows a relatively straightforward path. From birth, children are exposed to a language-rich environment. Parents and caregivers are responsive, motivating teachers and so for a majority of children, language develops naturally. The successful acquisition of language can have a dramatic effect on a child's ability to understand and function in both the social and academic world. Communication, the exchange of ideas, can take many forms; a word, an expression, a movement of the body. When a child lacks the ability to engage effectively in this interactive exchange of information, her learning capacity is compromised and socialization potentially limited. Without such learning and socializing opportunities, the acquisition of language becomes more difficult and the opportunities to improve more limited. Because of this, it is essential that students with speech and language difficulties receive some type of structured intervention to assist them in the development of effective communication skills.

An Important Distinction

The distinction between a speech and a language disorder is an important one. Speech disorders are characterized by impairments of voice, articulation of sounds, or fluency. In essence, a student who has difficulty with the *oral production* of language is considered to have a speech disorder. Language disorders, on the other hand, encompass both receptive and expressive language and therefore may result in a problem receiving information and/or formulating an acceptable and adequate response.

Clues to a Speech or Language Disorder

◆ Does he follow simple directions?

◆ Does she understand the meanings of words that others understand?

◆ Does he have a limited vocabulary compared with age peers?

◆ Does she understand longer, more complex sentences?

◆ Does he follow the general rules of grammar?

◆ Does she have more than normal difficulty finding the correct word?

Types of Speech Disorders

Speech disorders, while more common in particular types of populations, are not exclusive to those populations and can be found across a wide range of students. Diagnosis and treatment are generally the province of professionals in the field, in particular speech and language pathologists, although it can often be a teacher or educational assistant who first notices that something may be amiss. Students with speech disorders have difficulty with the production of sound. This can be a result of a number of factors such as inability to manipulate the tongue, lips and jaw, breath irregularities and damage to the vocal chords. Speech disorders are generally divided into three distinct yet related categories: articulation, voice and fluency.

Articulation disorders

By far the most common type of speech disorder, articulation disorders are characterized by atypical production of speech sounds in a language. These vary from omissions (e.g., 'numer' for number) to substitutions (e.g., 'tack' for back) additions (e.g., 'sawl' for saw) and distortions (e.g., 'thleep' for sleep). For obvious reasons, an articulation anomaly must be a regular and typical element in the student's speech before it is regarded as a disorder.

Voice disorders:

Everyone's voice is unique. Individuals may have a quiet or loud voice, one with a nasal quality, or one with variations in pitch. All of these variations of speech can be considered normal. When the variations become so pronounced they cause the speaker difficulty in communicating successfully, they are considered voice disorders. Voice disorders are characterized by atypical production of vocal quality, pitch (high/low), loudness and resonance, (e.g., a harsh or whispery vocal quality).

Fluency disorder:

When a person's flow of speech is unusually irregular, marked by stoppages, repetitions, unusual pauses, and atypical rhythms, a fluency disorder may be present. Stuttering is the most common type of fluency disorder and is characterized by the repetition of a particular syllable or sound of a word, or by the inability to express a word or sound for a noticeably long time.

Articulation Expectations ✍

By age eight most children have a repertoire of the sounds that they will use for adult speech and most acquire these sounds in a similar sequence. In a normal population distribution, for example, 9 out of 10 will master these sounds:

By the end of age 3	/m/, /n/, /ng/, /p/, /f/, /h/, /w/
By the end of age 3 $1/2$	/y/
By the end of age 4	/b/, /d/, /gl, /k/, /r/
By the end of age 4 $1/2$	/s/, /sh/, /ch/
By the end of age 6	/t/, /l/, /v/, /th (as in then)
By the end of age 7	/z/, /zh/ (treasure) /j/, /th/ (three)

An average three-year-old will say 50 percent of the sounds in English correctly and will be 90 percent intelligible.

Types of Language Disorders

Language disorders are characterized by difficulty in the use and understanding of language. As with disorders of speech, they are found across a wide spectrum of the population. Students with language disorders can be at risk in the development of literacy. In the very early stages of infancy, children begin to acquire language skills. Small infants respond to voice by turning their heads and smiling. At two to three months, they start to coo and by the age of four have approximately 1,000 to 1,500 words. By the time a child starts grade one, more complex parts of language, such as the use of irregular verbs, are being mastered. Not all children reach these milestones for a variety of reasons. They may have difficulty hearing; some do not have the intellectual ability; others are not sufficiently exposed to language.

Some children may experience difficulty with expressive language, as in the use of incorrect tenses: *"I go to the store yesterday."* Others may have difficulty with receptive language (the ability to comprehend spoken, written or other symbol systems). A set of directions such as, *"Get your red jacket from the closet and make sure to put on your scarf and mittens"*, may overwhelm. (In the latter situation, it is not hard to understand why the complication intensifies in a school setting where a student may be told to: *"Discuss the impact of urban society as a root cause for the Civil War."*)

Some Common Language Problems

Language is comprised of a variety of components including morphology, phonology, syntax, semantics and pragmatics. These components, when impaired or not developed in any way, result in language disorders. Someone having a problem with the *morphology* of language, for example, may have difficulty understanding and using sections of words that have meaning. (The dog *bark* when the car went by.) With problems in *phonology* (combining sounds to form words and manipulating sound sequences to form coherent speech) the person may say 'bwush' instead of brush. *Syntax*, the rules that govern the combining of words to

For Students Who May Have Difficulty Processing Auditory Information

☞ Reduce distractions.

☞ Offer preferential seating, away from pencil sharpeners, open windows, doorways.

☞ Be aware of your delivery style. Decrease rate of speech; use repetition, simple explanations and short sentences.

☞ Use visual support to supplement information.

☞ Verify regularly that students have (and are) comprehending.

form coherent sentences can be a challenge (What he is doing?), while problems with the *semantics* of a language (combining words and sentences to convey meaning) often mean the individual just doesn't "get it", particularly if an expression is idiomatic or metaphorical. The baseball metaphor, for example, "I'll go to bat for him", in reference to defending a person, may well be interpreted literally as an actual baseball game situation. Problems with *pragmatics*, using language socially to greet others, to request needs or information, to protest, pretend, and respond mean that an individual may be unresponsive to normal social interchange.

Central Auditory Processing Disorders

Some students seem not to be listening although their hearing may be perfectly intact. More and more professionals in the speech and language field believe this is owing to a 'central auditory processing' (CAP) disorder: an inability to recognize as meaningful, acoustic signals sent to auditory areas of the brain. Normally, people use both ears to fuse information, and to "tune out" auditory distractions (selective attention). People who demonstrate CAP difficulties may lose messages, mix them up, or fail to integrate the information coming in via both ears. According to specialists in speech and language, students with CAP disorders generally exhibit the following types of behaviours. (However, it should be noted that these behaviours might also be associated with many students who have other types of difficulties, likely a reason why the notion of central auditory processing disorder has not yet been fully accepted across the broad area of special education.)

- Inconsistent response to oral speech.
- Better response to oral speech in quiet environments than in noisy environments.

The Case of Brent

Brent, in senior kindergarten, is the eldest of five children. For the first two months of school, his only form of communication was a slight nodding of the head. Brent seemed unwilling to follow class routines, did not socialize with other children, and refused to comply with direct requests by the teacher. While Brent eventually did begin to speak, his utterances were mumbled and scant. At times, it seemed as though his answers were designed to cause difficulty or mock the teacher.

Following kindergarten, Brent was placed in a self-contained class that emphasized behaviour modification. In the new setting his disruptive and non-compliant behaviour persisted. Brent's special class teacher suggested to the in-school team that he be assessed by the board's speech and language pathologist, a request supported by the principal and Brent's parents. Test results showed that, in both expressive and receptive language, Brent was functioning at the age level of a two and a half-year-old, results with profound implications.

An IPRC is to be held next week to discuss Brent's situation. Neither the teacher nor educational assistant in the behaviour class has any special training in areas of speech and language, but both are willing to undertake any program to help Brent, as long as they are given professional advice and supervision. The school board has one full time speech and language specialist with a very busy schedule. She visits the school twice weekly where she works with two children in a regular grade one class. If Brent were placed here, she would include him in her twice-weekly sessions. The grade one class, though, is a very busy and somewhat noisy setting, in a pod-style room with three other primary classes. The specialist feels that given the intensity of Brent's language needs, this may not be as helpful a setting as the behaviour class where things are much quieter and more controlled. The principal is now seeking opinions from other teachers on staff.

- Poor response to speech in environments that distort speech, such as a gym.
- Better response to speech when the speaker is close.
- Frequent communication checks such as "what?" or "huh?"

Getting Help

Most students with speech and language difficulties are in regular classroom settings. To assist them and their teachers, many school boards either employ or retain the services of speech and language specialists. The availability of these professionals to provide direct intervention on an ongoing basis varies from board to board. Often, there are just too many students requiring support. Thus a special education teacher or classroom teacher or educational assistant, under specific direction from a speech and language specialist may be enlisted to work directly with students. Intervention may involve working on a particular sound, or playing a word game to develop expressive language skills, or other relatively straightforward activities. Where more extensive assistance is required but unavailable at the school board level, a speech and language specialist may refer cases to support services outside the jurisdiction of the board. Some parents may also choose to get support privately.

Vital Roles for the Teacher and Educational Assistant

Very often, in fact in most cases, a specialist in speech and language will determine and manage the needs of the student. The more severe the case, the more likely the teacher and educational assistant will be part of a team, collaborating to develop programming ideas. However, since nothing in practice is as straightforward as it appears in theory, it will still be incumbent upon regular classroom personnel to provide leadership in several ways. These would include providing extended opportunities for the student to talk, making the classroom an enjoyable place for him to work on his speech and language, and modeling an appropriate response to abnormal language for peers to follow. In short, the teacher's role with speech and language disorders is similar to that which she fills with all students: to be a compassionate professional who takes responsibility for developing the whole individual. An essential difference in the speech and language area lies in the tradition that considerable expert help is usually available.

Helpful Hints for the Classroom

▶ Restate a student's phrases in a more grammatically correct way.

▶ Structure the environment to increase opportunities for interaction.

▶ Check for comprehension by asking the child to repeat what has been said.

▶ Gain attention before speaking (eye contact, tap on the shoulder).

▶ Don't turn away while speaking. Monitor that the student is listening.

▶ Speak in a clear voice.

▶ Be sensitive to the student's current level of language.

▶ Paraphrase your own ideas after speaking to ensure comprehension.

Asher, S., & Gazelle, H. (1999). Loneliness, peer relations, and language disorders in childhood. *Topics in Language Disorders, 19*(2), 16-33.

Battle, D. (1998). *Communication disorders in multicultural populations* (2nd ed.). Boston, MA: Butterworth-Heinemann.

Bauman Waengler, J. (2000). *Articulator and phonological impairments: A clinical focus.* Boston: Allyn & Bacon.

Berstein, D.K., & Bankson, N.W. (1997). *Language and communication disorders in children* (4th ed.). Boston: Allyn & Bacon.

Bobrick, B. (1995). *Knotted tongues: Stuttering in history and the quest for a cure.* New York: Simon & Schuster.

Butler, K.G. (Ed.). (1999). Children's language, behaviour, and emotional problems. (Special issue). *Topics in Language Disorders, 19*(2).

Calandrella, A.M., & Wilcox, M.J. (2000). Predicting language outcomes for young prelinguistic children with developmental delay. *Journal of Speech, Language and Hearing Research, 43,* 1061-1071.

Filla, A., Wolery, W., & Anthony, L. (1999). Promoting children's conversations during play with adult prompts. *Journal of Early Intervention, 22*(3), 93-108.

Hatnes, W.O., Moran, M.J., & Pindzola, R.H. (1994). *Communication disorders in the classroom* (2nd ed.). Dubuque IA: Kendall/Hunt.

Hedge, M.L., & Kaiser, A.P. (1994). *Introduction to communicative disorders.* Austin, TX: Pro-Ed.

Hulit, L.M. & Howard, M.R. (1993).*Born to talk.* New York: Macmillan.

La Blance, G.R. Steckol, K.F., & Smith, V.L. (1994). Stuttering: The role of the classroom teacher. *Teaching Exceptional Children, 26*(2), 10-12.

Morrison, J. & Shriberg, L. (1992). Articulation testing versus conversational speech sampling. *Journal of Speech and Hearing Research, 35*(2), 259-273.

Ownes, R. (1996). *Language development: An introduction* (4th ed.). Boston: Allyn & Bacon.

Palmer, J.M. & Yantis, P.A. (1990). *Survey of communication disorders.* Baltimore: Williams & Wilkins.

Schraeder, T., Quinn, M., Stockman, I., & Miller, J. (1999). Authentic assessment as an approach to preschool speech-language screening. *American Journal of Speech-Language Pathology, 8*(3), 195-200.

Shames, G., Wiig, E., & Secord, W. (1993). *Human communication disorders* (4th ed.). New York: Macmillan.

Stark, R.E., Bernstein, L. E. & Demorest, M.E. (1993). Vocal communication in the first 18 months of life. *Journal of Speech and Hearing Research, 36,* 548-558.

Wang, P.P., & Baron, M.A. (1997). Language and communication: Development and disorders. In M.L. Batshaw (Ed.), *Children with disabilities* (4th ed. pp. 275-292) Baltimore: Brookes.

Ward-Leeper, G. (1991). *Disorders of speech and language.* London, ON: The Department of Communicative Disorders.

Links

Speech/Language
http://home.ica.net/~fred/index.htm

Kids Health for parents
http://kidshealth.org/parent/medical/ears/central_auditory.html

Ontario Assoc. of S.L.P. and Audiologists
http://www.osla.on.ca/con_info/child.html

CHAPTER 15

Assessment
Identifying Strengths and Needs

"When you hear hoof beats you first look for a horse, not a zebra."

Medical school adage

The Role of Assessment

When students are assessed, relevant information is gathered and interpreted from a variety of sources that may include teacher-made tests, observation, curriculum-based assessment, peer evaluation, portfolio development and commercially available standardized test instruments. The results, at least theoretically, reveal some insights into the abilities, intelligence, strengths, needs, and behaviours of the students in question. The discoveries help in making informed evaluations about their present status and informed decisions about the future. Without a way to measure the progress of students, it would be impossible to program effectively within a school setting.

For students deemed exceptional in some way, the path of assessment, while similar to that taken for all students, can be more complicated and far more influential in determining program and placement. The assessment instruments used, the personnel required, indeed the depth and breadth of the assessment process itself will often vary from that used for more general evaluations. Ideally, the assessment process collects information, refines insight into an exceptionality, and then sets the table for both programming and follow-up evaluations.

Once regarded as the exclusive realm of specialists, assessment has moved toward a more team-oriented approach with participation, responsibility and accountability being shared by a number of key people, especially the classroom teacher who is most likely to deliver the program. Others involved include the student's parents (and occasionally, in the case of some adolescents, the student himself) the teaching assistant, the school's special education teacher (who may be responsible for some of the more formal investigations) and, if need demands and the personnel are available, various individuals with special expertise such as psychologists and speech and language pathologists.

The Reality of 'Loose Probability'

No matter how keenly we may seek specialized information about students, and no matter how acculturated we may be to the belief that such truth can be revealed, the simple fact is that the very best an educational assessment can produce is a kind of loose probability. However loose though, it is still an important probability. Education itself is not an exact science, and effective teaching is more art than the mere mechanics of instruction. An assessment provides information gathered in an organized way that, at the very least, confirms in a presumably unbiased way, the view of the people working with the student. At the very best, it reveals factors that no one had known or possibly even expected.

Granted, there are reasons to harbour doubts about some of the procedures and components in an assessment and, quite possibly, reasons to be wary of the results, but to ignore the possible contribution of an effective assessment to an exceptional student's case would be a disservice indeed. Assessment has an important role to play. What shapes the quality of that role is the quality of the assessment procedures, and the way the results are interpreted and applied.

When Are Assessments Completed?

Arguably, assessment happens at every moment in a school day. Whether they are monitoring a student's behaviour in the halls, or observing while she shoots baskets in the gym or writes a spelling test, teachers are always presented with opportunity to collect data that will identify needs and strengths. Assessment, quite simply, is an integral part of teaching. Choosing when to assess, what to observe, which piece of work to add to a portfolio, or whom to listen to in reading—these are all part of the daily challenges for classroom teachers.

Almost without exception, every student in every school setting will be subject to a *screening* at some time or another. A common practice, screening is a relatively formal but broad procedure that determines if more intrusive testing is needed. Usually, groups of students are screened via an achievement test or test of cognitive abilities or other instrument. (Some boards have their own systems of screening to be used along with or in place of, commercially published tests.) The purpose is to discover, in a general way, whether there are any students at risk—or potentially gifted. These students are usually assessed then, in a more formal and extensive way to confirm (or dismiss) their suspected risk or giftedness. Screenings often take place at the preschool level where children entering school are assessed for vision, hearing

The Case of Kyeesha

Kyeesha's parents call her their "divine gift". She was born to them when they were in their mid-forties after they had experienced several unsuccessful pregnancies over a period of years. Both have successful academic careers (in art history and microbiology) and their home is intellectually and culturally stimulating.

When Kyeesha was four years old, the parents had her assessed for intelligence and general ability in a private clinic. The clinic's test results placed Kyeesha in the Very Superior range intellectually, and for the next two years her parents enrolled her in a private pre-school. Prior to enrolling her in grade one of their neighbourhood elementary school, the parents requested an IPRC. The committee, having little information available to it except the clinic's test results as provided by the parents, along with anecdotal accounts from them, quite readily accepted their opinion that Kyeesha should be identified gifted and placed in a primary gifted program.

After considerable success initially, Kyeesha began to lag behind her colleagues in achievement seriously enough that by the end of grade two, the school requested, and was granted by the parents, permission to conduct an assessment. The school board's chief psychologist somewhat reluctantly reported his conclusion that, intellectually, Kyeesha is in the Average to High Average range. Not unexpectedly, her parents find this difficult to believe. Because they are naturally disposed to cooperate, and no matter what, wish to make decisions that are in their little girl's best interests, they have asked for a meeting with the school. What they want to have explained to them is: how can results of two assessments of the same child differ so greatly? And, is there other information the school can provide that would help make clear to them what Kyeesha's real status might be?

and general readiness. Further along in the school grades, screening helps to identify students who fall outside what is judged to be normal performance criteria. These students are tested further to assess the nature and possibly the basis of the discrepancy.

The Extra Challenge of Special Needs

In the case of students who may be exceptional, the assessment process is usually more extensive. Initially, a teacher who has concerns about a student may choose to seek assistance through the forum of the in-school team. At this level, often referred to as the 'pre-referral intervention level' because the student has not yet been referred for more formalized assessment and identification, the teacher is seeking assistance and direction from colleagues. Generally, the teacher will prepare for a pre-referral by conducting an initial assessment based on observation, classroom performance, samples of the student's work and, possibly, a rating scale/checklist (especially in potential behaviour cases). It is not unusual for the teacher to do a curriculum-based assessment, gathering information over a period of time of the student's performance in a particular curriculum area (like reading, or mathematics).

With the assistance of the team, a number of suggestions may be attempted within the classroom setting. This type of intervention, e.g., moving the student to a different reading group, chunking work, allowing for differing modes of information presentation, is often described as 'intervention focused assessment'. Intervention focused assessment examines the effectiveness of an intervention: Did the move to the front of the room work? Can the student complete a task better if done orally? Does the introduction of frequent breaks reduce the incidence of misbehaviours?

When a student's situation is more complicated or demanding, then in addition to the assessment described above, more intensive, formal, and specialized procedures (perhaps an IQ test or standardized achievement test, or even in some cases, a diagnostic test) will be carried out. One point when a fairly extensive assessment is sure to be carried out is prior to the development of an individual education plan (IEP).

In cases where a student is formally identified as exceptional, assessment tends to be very thorough. Usually, information is collected through a number of sources and a variety of assessment strategies are used. The data aid in the identification of the student as exceptional, help to decide on appropriate placement, and will be utilized in the development of the IEP. At the follow-up or review stage, the data will be used again with more current and perhaps additional information being added.

Who Does Assessments?

The process, quite naturally, begins in the classroom. It is the teacher who can best observe a student's response to text, reaction to physical environment, and relationship to peers and adults. Teachers collect samples of student's work: journal entries, recordings, tests, and portfolios to name a few. These are the materials which, along with the teacher's own professional opinions and views, establish the initial, basic, and often, most important information. Further testing (and observation) may then be done by a special education teacher. The combination has distinct advantages in that the two (or more) teachers can then cooperate in the next step: designing the program implied by the assessment.

At the school board level, there is often a separate unit responsible for assessment, known by descriptors such as psychological or support services. This unit does almost all the assessing for special education outside the classroom setting. Psychologists, or personnel working under their guidance and direct supervision, conduct standardized assessments measuring cognitive strengths, for example, or analyzing behaviour patterns. In jurisdictions where psychological services are not directly available, outside expertise may be hired and, where possible, classroom and special education teachers may be given more responsibility in formal types of assessment. Most boards though, even the smaller ones, have formal assessments done by a person for whom this is a primary role.

Some larger school boards may employ speech and language pathologists to assess children with language difficulties. Physical screening for vision and hearing is generally under the jurisdiction of the public health nurse. Assessments done by physiotherapists and occupational therapists are also outside the jurisdiction of the school boards, though schools may, with the cooperation of the parents, request such assessments. Parents sometimes obtain an assessment privately, even though, by law, they have access to any data the school has. If they choose, they may offer these data to the school.

Components of an Assessment

A majority, if not all of the assessment information collected about a student, revolves around

- what the student is seen to be doing (observation)

- a systematic collection of student work products

- discussions and information sharing by key persons (including parents)

- and finally, testing.

Historically, in special education, emphasis has been placed on the latter element. Indeed, the mystique of testing has often overshadowed and even delayed action on behalf of an exceptional student. The phrase "We are getting him tested" was—and still is— an oft-heard one, and it's not unusual for a teacher to be caught in the frustrating position of waiting on results before modifying a program. The benefits of more formalized types of testing can indeed inform the process of program planning. But for some time now, the experience of special education has made clear that formal tests are but one component in a much more complex process; one that starts with teachers in the classroom suspecting something, acting on that suspicion, and trying out possible strategies to ameliorate the difficulty before more formal steps are taken.

The 'Battery'

Curiously, the pieces that make up a formal assessment are often described collectively by an artillery term: 'assessment battery'. What follows here is a description of components that may be used in a battery, although certain of them will almost always be included. (It is difficult, for example, to conceive of an assessment being useful and valid without the observations of the teacher and assistant.)

The decision regarding what components to use is typically governed in part by school and board policy. For example, many boards have complex and stringent requirements for identifying students as gifted and specify that certain test instruments be used as part of the identification procedures. Some boards discourage or even forbid the use of certain components. However, once the school and board policies are met—and on the matter of components these matters are flexible for the most part—how an assessment is actually conducted, and what is used, will typically be the choice of the professional personnel involved. That choice will vary according to their knowledge, competence and personal preference.

Informal (Teacher Made) Tests

A growing awareness of the benefits of assessments conducted by someone working directly with the student on an ongoing basis, has led to an increasing acceptance of informal measures designed by classroom teachers to meet their own immediate purposes. A disadvantage to these measures is that there are no norms for them so they usually do not have acceptance beyond the immediate situation. But then, that is not their purpose. Their advantage is that they can be truly tailored to meet specific needs. For example, an informal test can be designed to reveal the presence or absence of a very specific skill, and may well provide a picture of why and when a student fails to grasp a skill (like subtraction) instead of simply confirming that he has not grasped it (which the teacher already knows in any case).

Informal measures may include a teacher using parts of rating scales and checklists so that she can be more certain to have covered all the points. Informal inventories are used here as well. Still another practice (albeit of questionable legality and efficacy) is to use parts of different formal tests to put together the desired information about a student.

Formal Tests

Intelligence tests

Generally, IQ tests give a relatively accurate assessment of what an individual has been taught (and what he remembers) and of what he has been exposed to thus far in his life. In this sense an IQ test is a measure of current performance. What continues to be hotly debated is whether the test measures intellectual potential and can thereby be legitimately regarded as a *predictor* of future school performance. Despite this concern these instruments continue to be used for the purpose. Among the several commercially available IQ tests, the most widely used one by far in Ontario has been the *Wechsler Intelligence Scale for Children III* (1991) known colloquially as the 'WISC III'.

Projective Tests

Gestalt psychology and psychoanalytic method propose that an individual will project her inner life, especially her inner feelings, when presented with an ambiguous stimulus like a

> The thing that surprised me most when I made the switch from private clinical practice to working for a school board was the faith so many teachers have in tests. Faith isn't surprising in clinical practice because you're dealing with the general public mostly. But teachers are professionals. I rather expected them to be a bit more—how shall I say it—*agnostic*? I mean, a test can help, but it's really only as good as the person who gives it.
>
> *Ed Seip*

picture of an inkblot. When asked to draw pictures of a situation or an object (e.g., her family or a tree) or when asked to describe "What is going on here?", while being shown a picture, according to this theory an individual will expose more of her deeper self than she would if asked directly. Projective tests have been fiercely criticized for lack of norms, insufficient standardization, entirely subjective interpretation, and even for revealing more about the examiner than the subject! Although their use has declined significantly in schools, they still appear in some assessments. Some examples are the *Rorschach Inkblot Test* (1932) and the *Human Figure Drawing Test* (1968).

Tests of Academic Achievement

These are the most widely used formal test instruments of all. There are achievement tests for large groups, e.g., the *Canadian Achievement Tests* (1981-2002)* and there are individual tests as well, e.g., the *Peabody Individual Achievement Test, Revised* (1998). Administrators of achievement tests can be anyone from a classroom teacher to a professional psychometrist. Publishers provide detailed administration manuals and recommend that examiners attend training seminars. Very often in special education, achievement tests are used as screening tests. Other uses include general comparison, since individual test results are calculated in terms of the results—called *norms*—developed across a wide, randomly selected population. In other words, the test takers reveal where they stand *in terms of the test*, compared to a general population.

Diagnostic Tests

The term is misleading. These tests do not diagnose in any absolute sense but rather, present specific information about a student's perform-

••• ⎯⎯⎯⎯
* See comment about test-aging in 'Issues' in this chapter.
⎯⎯⎯⎯ •••

Keys to an Effective Assessment

For reasons of economy, availability of personnel and appropriate instruments, and because of politics and the chronic problem of special education, lack of time, not all educational assessments will meet every one of the following criteria every time. But when these criteria are not met as a basic standard, the results of any assessment should be weighed accordingly.

1 Has the assessment used a broad spectrum of sources (e.g., teacher, parents, other professionals if appropriate, test instruments if appropriate)?

2 If test instruments have been used, are they known to be *valid* and *reliable*? Is the examiner adequately trained in the administration of the tests and the interpretation of the results?

3 Was the assessment individually tailored: did it take into account matters like the subject's culture, his language, age, school experience, physical abilities?

4 Was the assessment ecological: did it examine the *whole* student in relation to her whole environment, her program, classroom situation, home situation?

5 Does the assessment imply or recommend responses: avenues of remediation or enrichment (as opposed to presenting only an enumeration of deficiencies)?

6 Do key persons in the life of the subject—teacher, educational assistant, parent—acknowledge that the assessment has sampled genuinely representative factors?

---

ance in a specific area. Their true purpose is to suggest areas for remediation. Subtests of the *Woodcock Reading Mastery tests – Revised* (1977-2001), for example, deal with specific areas like 'Word Attack' 'Word Identification', and 'Word Comprehension', presumably giving indication about the extent to which a student is competent in these areas. Critics of this and other similar tests question the value and even the validity of this kind of subskill breakdown in an area like reading . However, they acknowledge it may have value in areas like mathematics, where steps in the process of subtraction, for example, can be broken down and illuminated more clearly.

Tests of Cognitive Ability

Judgments about cognitive strengths and needs are inferred from a student's response to items on these tests. Memory, problem solving, and reasoning are examples of the types of skills they attempt to measure; the inference being that the better developed these cognitive skills are, the more successfully a student will perform in school-related tasks. The jury is still very much out on the issue of whether or not testing for cognitive abilities is any different from testing for intelligence with the IQ instru-

ments already in use. Cognition is about thinking. Whether testing for thinking is any different from testing for IQ is moot. In Canada, supporters of the distinction generally opt for the *Canadian Cognitive Abilities Test* (1970-97).

Developmental and Readiness Tests

These are primarily administered by classroom teachers—especially teachers of primary grades—to determine the level of ability of students. For exceptional students, their purpose is generally for screening. Very often these instruments are used along with checklists and skill inventories. Two popular examples in Canada, are the *Boehm Test of Basic Concepts—Revised* (2000) and the *Brigance Inventories* (1976-99).

Rating Scales, Inventories and Checklists

These instruments offer descriptive statements about areas like attitude, self-esteem, self-care, etc., in lists. Each item in a list is followed by a frequency ranking like 'almost all the time, frequently, sometimes, occasionally, rarely', or sometimes just by 'yes' or 'no'. Responses are entered by the student's teacher, educational assistant, parent, social worker, or childcare worker (sometimes all of these for comparison and time/place/situation diagnosis). A reasonably popular example of this type is the *Child Behavior Checklist* (1986-94).

Some rating scales are designed to be completed by the student. The *Coopersmith Self-Esteem Inventory* (1983) for example, presents statements to the student like "I often wish I were someone else" followed by "like me ____' and "unlike me ____'.

Most often, the results of these scales are used to determine a developmental profile from which educational or social or self-care objectives are developed. Occasionally, the information may be used to indicate a developmental level and sometimes decisions about placement will be influenced by the level indicated. The *AAMD Adaptive Behavior Scale: School Edition* (1981-93) often called an adaptive behaviour 'test', is frequently used this way. Rating scale instruments invite considerable subjectivity and are both praised and criticized for this factor.

Interviews and Informal Commentary: Teachers and Parents

Any effective assessment procedure will seek opinions from the responsible adults who associate with, and have responsibility for the student most directly. Most school boards invite the classroom teacher, and ideally the educational assistant, to present information. Very often this face-to-face discussion is preceded by written information that may vary from a simple referral form, to anecdotal information, to a fully developed case study. Parents have vital information for an assessment or evaluation team. Their information is invariably current and intimate (if biased sometimes); they also have the advantage of knowing the student's full history. Ontario Regulation 181 requires that parents be an integral part of the IPRC process in which a child is being considered for special education.

Medical Information

This becomes part of an assessment only when it is germane, and it often is in the case of a student with special needs. Information may range from data about hearing, sight, and physical ability, to the general health and neurological

conditions relevant to a student's situation. These data, if available, will come from the appropriate health professionals; they are almost never prepared by school board personnel. Experience has demonstrated that without cooperation and impetus from parents, medical information, along with useful advice, is often hard to come by. Health professionals are understandably wary of privacy regulations but at the same time, often show a curious reluctance to share more than sketchy information with schools.

Reports and Analyses: Other Professionals

For reasons that require no elaboration here, members of the behavioural science professions can offer very helpful insights into the situations of certain students. What educators must weigh, however, when receiving information from these sources, is the amount of time any one of them has been able to spend with a

---

Involve the Parents

What parents have to offer an assessment about a student's abilities is essential for obvious reasons. Answers to the following questions are always useful.

- What are your concerns regarding your child's learning/behaviour at school?

- How does what we do at school affect him at home (reaction to homework, frustration level, general attitude to coming to school)?

- Has she had particular success in the past, with a strategy or program?

- What other reports do you have that we may need to be aware of?

- What goals do you have for your child?

- Do you have a preference in method of communication from home to school?

- What questions do you have of us?

Some Important Terms In Assessment

Bands of Confidence: because of the Standard Error of Measurement factor, a test score can never be considered as absolutely correct. Thus some test manuals offer a range *around* a given score about which there can be some confidence.

Criterion Referenced Test: a number of specific behaviours or performances are stated (e.g., Subject knows the alphabet. Can count from 1-20.) These are the criteria. The subject's ability in this particular area is then assessed.

Grade Equivalent: a subject's raw score on a test is applied statistically to produce the school grade he would be in if he were in the sample groups of students used to determine the norms for the test. (A subject's grade equivalent of 6.2 means that if he were in the group sampled to produce the norms, he would stand at the second month of the sixth grade.)

Norms: the results obtained by representative populations when a particular test was developed. Students who write a test have their results compared to these norms to produce scores like Percentile, Stanine, Grade Equivalent, etc.

Norm Referenced Test: a test which rates a subject's performance relative to the results obtained in a known comparison group (or norm group).

Percentile Rank: a subject's percentile rank of 82 means that she scored higher than about 82 percent of the norm group.

Reliability: the level of consistency and dependability of a test. (Will it produce similar results over variable conditions?)

Split Half Procedure: involves administering the same subject(s) half of a test instrument (e.g., the odd numbered questions) at a different time from the other half (e.g., the even numbered questions).

Standard Error of Measurement: the extent to which a subject's score is "out". These data are reported (or should be!) in the technical manual that accompanies a test. (See more in this chapter.)

Stanine: a reporting scheme for test results based on an equal interval scale of 1-9. (5 is average; 6 is slightly above etc.).

Validity: the degree to which a test measures what it purports to measure.

See Appendix for more terms.

---

student and, of that time, the amount in an actual classroom situation. Because of this factor, together with what seems to be a somewhat weak track record for predicting behaviour on the part of these professionals, educators often find it more helpful to use information from these sources for general understanding of a syndrome rather than for specific program planning.

Alternative Assessment Procedures

Curriculum-Based Assessment (CBA)

Curriculum-based assessment (CBA) involves measuring a student's performance according to curricular expectations the school has estab-lished. Academic abilities and achievement can be systematically examined using this type of assessment. While many different variations exist, two basic components of CBA are probes of basic academic skills and content-area strategy assessment. Probing, which may be done across subject areas, involves ascertaining the skill and accuracy level of a student's knowledge of curriculum, e.g., letter recognition and arithmetic skills. Content-area assessment uses probes to establish knowledge level and also examines learning skills like note taking.

Many observers suggest that curriculum-based assessment, despite the extensive explication and argument that surround it, does not differ very much from the way evaluation in schools was conducted well before special education became commonplace. In the case of an exceptional student, they go on to say, curriculum-based measurement is not really a true alternative since all it really does is confirm that the student is not responding appropriately to the curriculum, a fact already evident. Supporters argue that curriculum-based assessment peers into a student's personal, unique and complex characteristics as they relate directly to the curriculum, and that this insight is superior to the type of assessment that merely establishes the presence of some disability.

To be effective, curriculum-based assessment must be carried out frequently; it should be specific (i.e., directed exactly at what has been taught); the results should be considered as a reason for possibly adjusting the instruction in addition to just determining how the student is doing; and assessment should consider small, subskill gains in addition to the acquisition of more global matters.

Authentic Assessment

Based on the premise that traditional types of assessment instruments fail to measure a student's performance in an authentic way, this type of assessment focuses on forming a "complete and realistic" picture of what a child can or cannot do. Authentic assessment allows for a collection of data based on real situations in which the students can be engaged in an interactive way, and during which they can access help from teachers and peers as they supposedly would in any normal situation. *Very* unlike a formal test situation. The focus is on allowing students to integrate information taught in a classroom situation, and to apply it in a problem solving way. At its best, authentic assessment calls on a learner's best performance based on interaction and practice.

Portfolio Assessment

Portfolios are a collection of student's work that represents growth and development over a specified period of time. Rather than a haphazard collection of work samples periodically collected, a portfolio is a specifically representative sampling. The goal of portfolio development is twofold: first, to provide a vehicle for the teacher to measure progress, and secondly (and perhaps more importantly) to allow the student himself to monitor and evaluate his academic growth and thereby make informed decisions

on how to proceed. Salend (1998) suggests the following guidelines for effective use of portfolio assessment in the classroom:

- ☞ Determine the portfolio to be used (showcase, reflective, cumulative, goal based).
- ☞ Establish procedures for organizing the portfolio.
- ☞ Choose a range of authentic classroom products that reflect the objectives of the portfolio.
- ☞ Record the significance of items included in student's portfolios.
- ☞ Review and evaluate portfolios periodically.

Ecological Assessment

This concept includes an amalgam of formal and informal methods, along with careful evaluation of the teaching-learning variables in the student's case. The idea is to examine the context in which the student learns, as well as the student himself. Thus, matters like the teacher's management style, the curriculum, teaching strategies, and instructional materials are examined; work samples produced by the student are evaluated, as is his success and error patterns inside and outside of school. Ecological assessment is attractive in principle but management factors make it difficult to do.

Learning Style Assessment

In the 1980's, a proposal that was initially well-received, offered the idea that by examining how a student learns, by discovering under what conditions or through what style of presentation her learning is most natural and effective, remediation then becomes a relatively straightforward case of making appropriate adjustments when she does not learn. While the idea was successful in promoting attention to individualized programming, as an assessment method it has proven very complex for the rewards it generates. Another problem is that in the development stages of their growth, students' styles are not necessarily stable and thereby accessible to reliable measurement.

Dynamic Assessment

Feuerstein (1979) and his colleagues propose an alternative that conceptually, should be most appealing to special education. Generally critical of traditional assessment procedure for its habit of assessing a student *statically*, i.e., at a single point in time with all the attendant drawbacks, Feuerstein argues for *dynamic* assessment: in essence a test-teach-test model that stipulates the subject first be assessed to reveal needs. Then it directs the examiner to address the needs by interacting with the subject, teaching him the content and concepts that were first assessed; and third, to then re-assess to see if the subject has learned and to identify what strategies were the most successful in the process. Feuerstein's thesis is that it is more valuable to discover whether and what and how a student can be taught (his word is 'modified') and what strategies work best in the teaching, than it is to simply learn or have confirmed what he cannot do. Although dynamic assessment has a minority of firm converts in Canada, it has not gained the attention it perhaps deserves, an indication of how fixed are traditional testing methods in the educational universe.

Some Issues in the Use of Formal Tests

✦ The power of test *mystique*. Educators, including those who should know better, seem strangely willing to ascribe to tests a kind of mystical capacity to open a window into a student's inner being and the workings of his mind. As a result they will often defer to test results even if those results contradict their own observations and conclusions arrived at over months of on-site observations and analyses. Ironically, the professionals who administer and interpret the tests rarely push for this; in fact they are usually the ones who point out that a formal test instrument is just one of several looks at the subject. Yet so strong is the effect of a test result that almost everyone involved in a student's case will, however tacitly, acknowledge its superiority. As a consequence the relative importance of a test in the general assessment of a student can be strongly, even shockingly disproportionate.

✦ *The aging of published tests* is a serious problem. A quick review of the publication dates of any number of tests still in common use reveals disturbing results. Some standardized tests in use today were developed as early as the 1940's and '50s—before television! Many were produced in the 1970's and '80s—before the internet. Thus, even though some tests are regularly updated* it is very important for teachers and administrators to be aware of which version is being used. Given that most of the time, the norms of a test are generated at the time of a test's *original* development, it often happens that the results achieved by students today are being compared against norms established with children who went to school decades ago. It is ironic in the extreme that educators are invariably first to declare that our culture and our children are changing constantly and rapidly; yet they seem to accept test results based at least in part on the performance of people from their parents', even their grandparents' era!

✦ *Bias and tacit discrimination* against lower socio-economic groups and those of diverse cultures persists in testing. In older tests, normed groups may not be representative of current populations so current scores can be misleading. As well, many test items suggest that the questions, pictures, expected knowledge base and required skills do not take into account the diverse nature of many of today's classrooms. Producers of commercial tests claim to have addressed this matter in their revisions, but estimates of their success, as published in academic reviews, are conservative at best.

✦ In tests administered to groups, questions are typically phrased so that answers can be machine-scored, with multiple-choice format being the most popular. Almost every question therefore, must be responded to with a single, confined answer, a structure that invites a great many *dull and simplistic*

• • • ───────

* Publication dates for test instruments typically show the last date an addition or revision was made. However the change (and therefore the date) may indicate only a tiny adjustment to the content or even the layout. A publication date, therefore, does not necessarily mean the year when the instrument was last normed, updated or otherwise scientifically improved.

─────── • • •

questions and devotes an excessive amount of space, time, and effort to minutiae. Needless to say, it also leaves little room, if any, for the reflective or creative student.

✦ *Potential for misinterpretation.* It is not uncommon in tests of language and reading to find lists of single words, out of context, to be read aloud. (E.g., see the *Wide Range Achievement Test-Revised*, 1993.) These lists are often separated in subtests under titles like 'Word Recognition', with the results interpreted, not as just as a measure of word recognition, but as a measure of general reading ability. The practice also assumes that formally testing an unnatural idea like word recognition is possible and worth doing in the first place.

✦ In tests of achievement especially, *each item tends to be scored with the same value* (usually 1 or 0). School tasks typically increase in difficulty; thus also typically, students merit proportionately enhanced recognition for dealing with these tasks successfully. In most formal, published tests, Student A, who correctly answers only questions sixteen to twenty, earns the same score as Student B, who correctly answers questions one to five. Granted, a careful item by item

The Case of Larry

Each of Larry's eight years in the same elementary school has contributed to his reputation as a complete enigma. In fact, he is secretly (and kindly) known by the staff as "What Next Larry" because tales about him invariably attract that phrase.

In kindergarten and grade one, Larry did not seem to learn to read or write or even print his name. When he returned for grade two the next September, he immediately showed language skills well above grade level, and by Christmas was leading the class. By the end of the year he had begun to manifest odd behaviours, the most serious of which was eating chalk. That too, disappeared over the next summer, but when Larry returned in the fall, it appeared he had become an elective mute. Neither his teacher nor an educational assistant of whom he was very fond, could penetrate the mutism. His parents who were, then and now, as baffled as his teachers, reported the same behaviour at home, *and* that he was being emulated by his immediately younger brother! Like the previous mysteries, this too passed, and in grade four Larry took up music. The school has a grade 7-8 band, and Larry showed he could play the clarinet well enough to join this older group and even become a soloist. Again, his parents had no explanation. Larry never had lessons, they reported, and although they kept a clarinet in the attic, no one (except Larry, now) could play it.

Grade five saw sports enter the picture. Rather, sports*casting*. Larry's teacher scheduled a part of each morning for current events and media study, and two or three times a week, Larry, would report—pleasantly, but obsessively and in total detail—all the scoring from the previous night's NHL games. In grade six, Larry began his novel. He abandoned that venture before completion, but the writing took up almost all his time until winter break. A standardized achievement test that year showed Larry at grade in language but well behind in math. However, he had been completely absorbed in his novel, especially when math was being taught. In grade seven, Larry became officially eligible for the school band but then dropped out. Instead, he got permission to form a chess club. By the end of the year, it had a higher membership than the band.

It is now the first month of Larry's grade eight year. The principal (who is both fond of and protective of Larry—the affection is returned, fully) has held a meeting of all staff who have taught or otherwise dealt with Larry. What he has proposed, with the strong support of the boy's parents, is that, since Larry will go to a secondary school next year, it would be to his benefit if his arrival there were preceded by a confidential assessment. The principal wants the teachers to suggest to him, just what kind of information such an assessment should seek, and how it should be obtained.

analysis would reveal that Students A and B attained a raw score of five by different routes, but in practice, consumers of test information rarely see, or have time to see, an item analysis.

◆ Tests are usually *rigorously timed*, with all the difficulties that causes for slow not to mention deep, thinkers.

◆ *Misunderstanding 'standardized'*. Over time, commercially produced formal tests have come to be called 'standardized' (distinguishing them from teacher tests which by implication therefore, are *un*standardized). Many test consumers have come to accept 'standardized' to mean these tests are based on a standard against which students are judged. This is not at all the case. Test results are indeed compared to a scale of values or 'norms', but these norms are not an absolute standard; they are the scores obtained from the population samples used by the test publishers to establish the basis for comparison. Publishers usually contend that the norms they have established represent the range of results (in a perfect bell curve) that could be expected in a normal or typical population. That claim notwithstanding, the comparison is still relative; it is not standard. What *is* standard in formal tests are the procedures of administration and scoring. A 'standardized' test is one which is administered and scored the same way every time to reduce examiner interference. It is not a standard of evaluation.

◆ Another well established practice is to *generalize test results*. If student C takes test X in reading comprehension and scores a grade equivalent of say 4.2, those results are for that particular test. Yet it is regular practice by educators to make the assumption that the student's absolute reading level is 4.2

◆ *Ignoring the standard error of measurement*. One of the most misunderstood and ignored features of a formal test is the standard error of measurement (SEM). Because no test is absolutely accurate, a subject's true score is never known. The score that a subject gets—his 'obtained' score—is actually only an *estimate* of his true score. What the SEM does then, is give a statistical reflection of how close to a true score the subject's obtained score actually is. If, for example, he scores 110 on a test with an SEM of 3.8 then approximately two-thirds of the time, statistically, his true score would fall between 106.2 and 113.8 (his score of 110 plus or minus 3.8). The impact of the SEM can be very powerful (not least because it is so often ignored). If students are identified for a program on the basis of a cutoff in test scores, it is easy to see how the looseness implied by the SEM can be significant.

◆ Taken together, the problems with formal tests (not all of which by any means are the fault of the tests or the examiners) have led to a decrease in their use in assessing exceptional students. Although the testing tradition is still quite solidly established, alternative sources are more frequently being used, and tend to have increasing credibility. What still remains for special education, at least in some jurisdictions, is to narrow the gulf between the conducting of an assessment of an exceptional student and the developing of a program.

The Formal Case Study

A case study is an efficient executive summary that collates information from a number of sources into one document. In situations where an exceptional student's case has become complicated over time—and many do— and when it has involved a variety of personnel, some of whom may not know one another, or have never worked together, a case study brings together history, current status, and needs. If written with some care, it can be the most effective means by far, of bringing a group of professionals with diverse interests up to speed on a situation for which they share responsibility.

Ideally, an educational case study is prepared by the teacher nominally responsible for the student in question and is written according to two principal criteria:

✔ succinctness (Effective writers usually aim at a maximum of two pages.)

✔ a non-judgemental, non-evaluative statement of *facts*

and most often presents information under headings like these:

1. Demographic data
2. Description of the educational issue
3. Family history
4. Physical and health status
5. Social and behavioural matters
6. Supplementary reports
7. Assessment data
8. Current program and placement.

9. Recommendations (Most educational case studies do not include a recommendation component until *after* the meetings, discussions etc. for which it was initially prepared, have been concluded and decisions made for a next step.

Regrettably, case studies have pretty much fallen into disuse in education today, not because of any flaws in either the idea or the process, but largely because our contemporary system seems to deny the time needed to complete and use them.

READINGS & RESOURCES

Algozzine, B., & Ysseldyke, J. (1992). *Strategies and tactics for effective instruction.* Longmont, CO: Sopris West.

Bagnato, S.J., Neisworth, J.T., & Munson, S.M. (1997). Linking authentic assessment and early intervention: *Advances in curriculum based assessment* (3rd ed.). Baltimore: Paul H. Brooks.

Benner, S.M. (1992). *Assessing your children with special needs: An ecological perspective.* New York: Longman.

Bufkin, L.J., & Bryde, S.M. (1996). Young children at their best: Linking play to assessment and intervention. *Teaching Exceptional Children, 29,* 50-53.

Cole, E. & Brown. R. (1996). Multidisciplinary school teams: A five-year follow-up study. *Canadian Journal of School Psychology, 12,* 155-168.

Feuerstein, R. (1979). *The dynamic assessment of retarded performers: The learning potential assessment device, theory, instrument and techniques.* Baltimore: University Press Park.

Gajris, M., Salend, S.J. & Hemrick, M.A. (1994). Teacher acceptability of testing modifications for mainstreamed students. *Learning Disabilities Research and Practice, 9,* 236-243.

Howell, K. W., Fox, S. L., & Morehead, M.K. (1993). *Curriculum Based evaluation: Teaching and decision making* (2nd ed.). Pacific Grove CA: Brooks/Cole.

Kleinert, H.L., Haigh, J., Kearns, J.F., & Kennedy, S. (2000). Alternate assessments: Lessons learned and roads to be taken. *Exceptional Children, 67*(1), 51-66.

Kubiszyn, T. & Borich, G. (1996). *Educational testing and measurement: classroom application and practice* (5th ed.). New York: Harper Collins.

Neisworth, J.T., & Bagnato, S.J. (1996). Assessment for early intervention: Emerging themes and practices. In S.L. Odom & M.E. McLean (Eds.) *Early intervention/early childhood special education: recommended practices.* Austin TX: Pro-Ed.

Paulson, F.L., Paulson, P.R., & Meyer, C.A. (1991). What makes a portfolio a portfolio? *Educational Leadership, 48*(5), 60-63.

Pierangelo, G., & Giuliana, G. (1998). *Special educators complete guide to 109 diagnostic tests: How to select and interpret tests, use results in IEPs, and remediate specific difficulties.* West Nyack, NY: The Center for Applied Research in Education.

Popham, W.J. (1999). *Classroom assessment: What teachers need to know.* Needham Heights, MA: Allyn & Bacon.

Reed, L. C. (1993). Achieving the aims and purposes of schooling through authentic assessments. *Middle School Journal, 25*(2), 11-13.

Salend, S.J. (1998). In Assessment (Special Issue) (1998) *Teaching Exceptional Children, 31*(2) Nov/ Dec.

Sarouphim, K. (1999). Discovering multiple intelligences through a performance based assessment: Consistency with independent ratings. *Exceptional Children 65*(2)151-163.

Salvia, J., & Ysseldyke, J.E. (1995). *Assessment* (6th ed.). Boston: Houghton Mifflin.

Thurlow, M.L., Ysseldyke, J.E., & Silverstein, B. (1995). Testing accommodations for students with disabilities. *Remedial and Special Education, 16*(5), 260-270.

Tindal, G., McDonald, M., Tedesco, M., Glasow, A. Almond, P., Crawford, L., & Hollenbeck, K. (2003). Alternate assessments in reading and math: Development and validation of students with significant disabilities. *Exceptional Children, 69*(4), 481-494.

Valenca, S. (1990). A portfolio approach to classroom reading assignments: The whys, whats and hows. *The Reading Teacher, 43*(4). Pp. 38-40.

Weber, E. (1999). *Student assessment that works: A practical approach.* Needham Heights, MA: Allyn & Bacon.

Ysseldyke, J., & "Olsen, K. (1999). Putting alternative assessments into practice: What to measure and possible sources of data. *Exceptional Children, 65*(2), 175-185.

CHAPTER 16

The Individual Education Plan (IEP)
A Team Approach

Special education cannot be defined in a single statement. It is a process, a journey that takes different shapes for different students at different times in their educational careers. An IEP provides the roadmap for the completion of that journey.

Andrea J., principal

The Case of Ms. Kumar

When Ms. Kumar found out she would be having a grade two class in September (her first job since graduating), she immediately began to develop and collect materials for the new school year. She came into the school early to decorate her class and make the room feel welcoming. Ms. Kumar learned from her principal that she would be having 25 grade twos, all of whom had had little difficulty in the grade one program.

During the first two weeks of school, despite a few minor adjustments and the establishment of classroom practices, Ms. Kumar's class seemed to settle into an active and productive routine. At the beginning of the third week of school, a new child moved into the neighbourhood. Joey was of grade two age but had not yet attended regular school. He had spent senior kindergarten and grade one in a day treatment program for children with social/emotional difficulties. His mother had not informed the school of Joey's history and he began school on the Monday as number 26 in Ms. Kumar's room.

Within the first hour it became obvious that something was wrong. Joey had become very frustrated at journal writing time and got out of his desk frequently. At one point Joey decided that another child was bothering him, got out of his seat and spat on the child's desk. When Ms. Kumar reprimanded him, he responded by swearing at her and running from the room.

When Joey's mom came to get him at the end of the day, she confessed that she was extremely worried about her son. She had been afraid to tell the school too much about Joey's background in the hope that perhaps a new school meant a fresh start. The principal explained that Joey was now a member of their school and that in this school both teachers and she were willing to do everything in their power to plan and implement a program that would meet Joey's needs.

While Ms. Kumar agrees philosophically with the ideal espoused by the principal, she feels ill equipped to deal with a child with such complex problems. What she feels would be helpful, is some form of written guide with specific directions and ideas.

Everybody's Roadmap

Planning is an integral component of effective teaching practice. As a matter of course, teachers carefully consider how new learning is to be presented and absorbed and develop lesson and unit plans to meet that end. For a majority of students, those who fall within what, for lack of a better term is considered to be the normal range, lesson plans and goals are usually not differentiated to any significant degree. But in the case of exceptional students, planning becomes more complex because their needs, learning characteristics, and abilities are more diverse and challenging. A different, more individualized planning approach is usually necessary. Experience in special education has taught that this differentiated approach is best achieved in what educators know as an individual education plan, an 'IEP'. For a student with exceptionalities, an IEP encompasses both the goal of the teaching enterprise and the directions needed to meet it. A popular metaphor for the IEP—*roadmap*—seems apt, for without such a plan, such a *map*, the educational process can get off track and both student and teacher can become lost or end up in a place not intended.

A properly constructed and executed IEP provides consistency, continuity and clarity of purpose. It allows teachers to act within the requirements of their job, but permits them flexibility to adjust curriculum activities and assessments in a planned and systematic way to support the exceptional student. An IEP provides specific guidelines for the direction of a student's program, but always allows for the day-to-day adjustments required for any teaching-learning situation. And as a roadmap, an IEP ensures that everyone knows where to go, knows what direction to take, and is in agreement on how to get there.

The Roadmap As Policy

Until the late 1990s in Ontario, the development of an individual education plan for every exceptional student was not required (albeit implied in a Ministry document called Schools General). Yet for most Ontario teachers, as with their colleagues in other jurisdictions, using IEPs in various forms and designs had become pretty much standard practice by this time. Therefore when the province revised and reissued its regulation governing the identification and placement of students with special needs in 1998, making IEPs a clear and official requirement, most educators in the province were already experienced with them.

The Policy Requirements*

Ontario's Regulation 181/98 requires principals to ensure an individual education plan is developed for every student identified 'exceptional' by an Identification, Placement and Review Committee (IPRC). Also, students who require specialized funding for resources and equipment must have an IEP as supporting documentation for the funding claim. Finally, an IEP may be developed for students who have not been through the IPRC process but are experiencing difficulty meeting learning expectations, and are deemed by the school board to need special services or educational programs.

In each of the situations above, an IEP must include

- stated reason for developing it,

- specific educational expectations,

- an outline of the special education program and services to be provided to the student,

- a description of the methods that will be used to review the student's progress.

Principals must ensure the plan is developed within thirty school days after the student is placed in a special education program, *and must ensure it is completed in consultation with the parent* (and the student if 16 years or older). The plan must take into account recommendations by the IPRC that identified the student. A copy of the completed plan must be forwarded to parents (and to the 16-plus students) within the 30-day time frame. A copy of the plan must also be included in the student's Ontario Student Record (OSR).

• • • ─────────

* For specifics see *Individual Education Plans, Standards for Development, Program Planning and Implementation* (Ministry of Education, 2000).

───────── • • •

What an IEP *is...*

✔ a written plan of action for a student whose needs require modification of a regular school program.

✔ a document containing a summary of the student's strengths and needs, a statement of goals and expectations, and essential information regarding resources, program, teaching strategies, personnel, etc.

✔ an ongoing, flexible document, developed by a school staff, in collaboration with parents and the student where appropriate, usually under the leadership of one or two persons supported by a team,

✔ a document made available to teachers, assistants, resource personnel, administrators, parents, and the student so that all concerned can direct their energies to the same purposes.

What an IEP *is not...*

✘ a detailed account of every minute of a student's day. An overly detailed and minutely controlled plan would be impossible to implement in a classroom.

✘ an individual effort on the part of the special education teacher to fulfill Ministry requirements. An IEP created in isolation, without the input of personnel and family directly involved with the student, risks becoming merely a superfluous bureaucratic necessity rather than an effective and meaningful document.

✘ a document that, once completed, sits in a file unexamined until the next review. For an IEP to be effective it must be utilized and monitored. It is a living document that requires ongoing development and examination by everyone working with the student.

Preparing IEPs: Steps in the Process

The sequence presented here represents a pattern suggested by the Ministry of Education. For the most part, although individual boards in the province frequently add their own variations, all of them generally follow these steps.

I. Gathering information

II. Setting the direction

III. Developing the IEP

IV. Implementing the IEP

V. Reviewing and updating

I. Gathering information

From the OSR: For each student in the province, a continuing record called the Ontario Student Record (OSR) is maintained and continually updated. The OSR then, is a logical place to start gathering details for preparation of an IEP. Information such as previous report cards and reports by teachers and other professional staff, medical information, and—very important—*school history* are customarily available in this file. Especially useful documents often found in the OSR are a student's previous IEPs.

Among other details to be gathered in order to develop an IEP will be the reason(s) one is needed in the first place. This may come from a recent or even a past IPRC, from a special ed. teacher, a parent or school team. Additional information, e.g., whether the student requires specialized health support services will also be included if appropriate. Information on specialized equipment if applicable, listings of dates of consultations with parents, etc., may also be included. The information will vary case by case, and will range from specific details such as those recorded in an OSR to current, ongoing contributions like the following.

Insights from key persons: Information from people who have different insights and perspectives on a student is valuable in the development of the IEP. The classroom teacher has the most contact with a particular student and the information that she provides is essential. Yet she does not work alone and will not have all the answers. Parents, principals, special education teachers, previous teachers, other professionals, and indeed students themselves, where appropriate, can and should contribute. Parents, most of the time, have an in-depth understanding of their child..

Having seen progress (or lack of it) from year to year, they have a picture no one else has. The picture may have important features too, like updated medical information, likes and dislikes, other community involvement, relevant family information, etc.

Formal tests: If the appropriate professionals are available to administer standardized assessments (e.g., an IQ test, standardized achievement tests, etc.) and if the results from such tests will help inform the process, then these are a useful resource. In most cases, test results will not be as important, at least initially, as the careful, daily, in-the-classroom observations of teachers and educational assistants. Formal tests tend to be more important in situations that are at the relatively complex or intractable end of the scale. (Indeed it is not unheard of for students to be trapped in a sort of testing limbo where the school and parents see the need for differentiated programming but waiting lists for standardized assessments are staggeringly long. Therefore it is important that the use of formal tests be judicious, and administered in a timely fashion so that development of an effective plan does not stagnate.)

Classroom observations: For many years, special education suffered from an image as the realm of experts and specialists. Nowhere was this mystique more prevalent than in the area of assessment. Surprisingly, the perception persists. Special education teachers, just like teacher-librarians or computer specialists, do indeed possess some expert knowledge and training, but it does not replace the essential role that regular classroom teachers or educational assistants play in gathering crucial infor-

> A team is *everybody* and that is why we have such a diversity of people: so that they will come from different backgrounds in their teaching. I know I don't know everything and I don't think there is any one person who knows everything, but if we have a group, we can pool our knowledge and come up with the best for the student.
>
> *A. Walsh, Special Education Resource Teacher*

mation. Front-line personnel can assess things like the students' interaction with text, how they respond to new tasks, whether they work best in groups or individually, their response to authority and routines, and their response to environmental conditions such as lighting and noise level. Information like this may be recorded in a variety of formats: anecdotal records, checklists, interviews of students and others, even audio/visual recordings. No matter where or in what form this information is recorded, it is most valuable.

Student's work: Samples of a student's previous and current work reveals strengths, needs and rates of progress. Portfolios of student work, test papers, journal entries, assignments and artwork all contribute insights. Comparing samples of individual student's work throughout the year not only provides valuable information but much needed validation. In teaching, because the work is in such small units, progress is hard to discern at times and the perception that "we are getting nowhere" persists. A cumulative representative sampling of a student's work over time can not only demonstrate progress but also point out the direction to proceed.

In most cases, the types of information above will offer enough substance to develop an IEP. Naturally, there are situations where it is necessary to return to the sources and dig deeper or wider. In some cases, additional personnel and resources may be needed to conduct other types of assessments (e.g., diagnostic tests). As well, especially in the case of students with special physical or health needs, a school may seek information from medical professionals (although this is almost always done with the help, and certainly the permission, of parents).

II: Setting the Direction

The Strength of Team

Ideally, after the basic information is gathered, a collaborative approach involving staff, parents and the student (where appropriate) comes into play to establish the plan itself, for the simple reason that involving more than one person in the development of an IEP almost always produces a more thorough, relevant and creative plan. Most schools in Ontario already have in place some form of active school team* that meets on a regular basis to share information about students with special needs. Accordingly, these teams, with members added on an ad hoc basis (i.e., people with a stake in the case, like the classroom teacher, assistant, parent, etc.) are commonly used to shape and give direction to IEPs.

A school team generally includes the principal (or designate), certain classroom teachers appointed by the principal, and the school's special education teacher(s), along with ad hoc

• • • ————————

* Also known by other titles like In-School Team, School Support Team, Special Support Team, or just School Team. See below for more.

———————— • • •

members. The principal (or designate) is usually responsible for the establishment and maintenance of the team approach to IEP development but all members of the team play an important role. Each one has a perspective in terms of the information they can offer and the support or services they may be able to provide. This is where collaboration finds its strength. Once the different perspectives are aired and consolidated, with both the professional and the personal insights that everyone has to offer, the results invariably generate a more complete picture of the student's strengths and needs, along with a more informed and more creative set of strategies and actions for implementation.

Alternative Styles

Notwithstanding the creative power of a school team for developing IEPs, there are schools in the province where this style is not used. Although Ontario provincial policy specifically requires an IEP be prepared for all students

The Case of Mr. Pickett

Mr. Pickett has taught English to grades 9, 10, and 11 for some years now, and has always felt he does a good job. His peers would agree and note that Mr. Pickett always seems well prepared for his classes, has innovative ideas, and students seem to enjoy being in his class. In the past, under the direction of the previous principal, any students receiving special education support were withdrawn from Mr. Pickett's class and programmed for solely by the special education resource teacher. While Mr. Pickett has never objected to implementing some of the special education resource teacher's suggestions in his class, he has always been comfortable in the knowledge that the primary responsibility for an exceptional student's program rested elsewhere. This year, under a new principal, the focus of special education service delivery has shifted, with the primary responsibility of the programming for exceptional students now placed squarely on the shoulders of regular classroom teachers, assisted by the special education resource teacher.

This year, Mr. Pickett has two students identified as learning disabled. Both read far below grade level and require a great deal of assistance in completing any written work. He has been reluctant to take ownership for their program and is very resistant to altering his teaching practices in any significant way to accommodate their needs. Although he does not share this with the rest of the staff, Mr. Pickett has grave doubts about his ability to program for the two, fearing he lacks the necessary expertise. He is willing to help them, but does not feel he has the skills.

An in-school team meeting has been called this week to discuss the students. Mr. Pickett, while not a regular member of the in-school team, has been asked to provide in advance, some information about these students and then attend the meeting to discuss it. He is unsure of what kind of information he should provide; nor is he sure about how much he can or should tell the team about modifications and accommodations he has already tried with the students. Mr. Pickett is feeling very hesitant and would like some guidance.

What's On an IEP Form? ✍

Official forms vary, sometimes quite widely, from board to board, even from school to school. Fortunately, the majority of school boards now follow the template provided by the Ministry of Education. It requires the following information, even though headings may differ.

✓ Reason for development of IEP

✓ Student profile

✓ Assessment data

✓ Special supports and services required

✓ Student strengths and needs

✓ Accommodations (common to all subject areas)

✓ Annual program goals

✓ Current level of achievement for specific subject areas

✓ Learning expectations for specific subject areas

✓ Teaching strategies for specific subject areas

✓ Assessment methods for specific subject areas

✓ Personnel involved in the development of the IEP

✓ Transition plan (if required)

✓ Human resources

✓ Review and update information

(Except for demographics, not every section of a form will be filled in every time. The abiding problem of *available time* that confronts all teachers means that in practice, emphasis will likely be given to the issues that are most relevant in a particular case.)

identified exceptional, it does not stipulate that a team be used anywhere in the process (even though it is clear, in its support and explanatory materials, that the Ministry of Education strongly supports the team principle). Therefore in some schools the entire IEP process is begun, developed, written, implemented and monitored by one or two persons. Most frequently, where this approach is taken, that responsibility rests with the school's special education teacher(s). Nevertheless, because this teacher will be running a number of IEPs, what happens in practice is that he or she works very closely with the classroom teacher and assistant of the student concerned. And since the parent is involved too, in many cases, and possibly one or two supporting professionals (e.g., speech and language) even this "single-responsibility" style is in effect, collaborative.

III: Developing the IEP:

After the information is consolidated and checked for accuracy, and after any gaps are filled and possible discrepancies resolved, the material is then summarized on the IEP form that the board or school uses. Many school boards develop and use IEP forms tailored to their own practices. In Ontario, by far the majority of these forms follow the format suggested by the Ministry of Education. Formats are continually being tweaked but the most current information can always be found on the Ministry of Education web site **www.edu.gov.on.ca.** (The authors recommend that teachers and assistants be familiar with both the Ministry form and the form currently utilized in their own school board.) Whatever form a board uses, an IEP will almost always be developed with attention to these essential components.

List strengths and needs: (Much of this part will come from the observations gathered in the first phase of the process.) Including the student's strengths and needs is a prelude to understanding the program modifications that need to be set up. A strength might be expressed as "…has creative ideas for stories and has good story comprehension." A need might be expressed as "…to develop an understanding and application of mathematical concepts." Strengths listed in an IEP must reflect areas where a student has effective learning skills as well as those learning modalities or styles that contribute to his success in learning. Stated needs should be drawn directly from assessments and related directly to the areas for which the IEP is being developed. (In those cases where a student has been through an IPRC, strengths and needs listed in an IEP must be consistent with those listed in a student's IPRC statement.)

Establish goals and expectations: Goals state what a student would reasonably be expected to achieve by the end of a school year within a particular curriculum area or skill. Goals are considered more global targets for students (e.g., "The student will develop basic computational skills in mathematics.").

> An IEP is not a pristine piece of paper filed in the OSR and referred to only on occasion. Rather, it is a working document to be filled with crossed out expectations and remedial attempts, scribbled revisions and post-it reminders. It resides on the teacher's desk providing easy access to all concerned during the instructional day.
>
> R. Daigle, Superintendent

Expectations, on the other hand, are more specific about what the student will be doing (e.g., "The student will be able to recite subtraction facts between 1 and 18."). Expectations should reflect what a student is expected to attain within each reporting period and be written in a way that is observable and measurable. Both goals and expectations should be based directly on the Ontario Curriculum where academic performance is being modified. Alternative goals and expectations for such things as addressing the physical or behavioural needs of a student are also listed in IEP's and reviewed regularly.

Specify strategies and resources: Once goals and expectations are outlined, the task then becomes one of choosing strategies and identifying resources, including personnel, that will be used to help the student and teachers meet them. This section of an IEP stipulates what materials will be used, what programs and teaching methods will be employed, and who will work with the student, how often, and where.

Monitor the results: A crucial step in the development of an IEP is establishing the features of a monitoring cycle: student progress must be reviewed at least once every reporting period and the results of that progress indicated on the provincial report card. Decisions such as who will track the student's progress, how will the record keeping be handled, who will be responsible for communicating to whom, and what is the time frame for accomplishing the goals, need to be addressed.

Special Case: The Transition Plan

For students 14 and older, with the exception of students identified as gifted, regulations require schools to include a *transition plan* in his or her IEP. The plan is designed to allow for a smooth transition from school to school and/or school to workplace or training centre. It must include specific transition goals and actions required to achieve those goals (e.g., in the case of a deaf student who plans on post secondary education, a plan would identify those institutions especially geared to meeting that special need; in the case of a developmentally disabled student, the plan might identify work and community living options.) Under the regulation, the principal is responsible for consulting with appropriate community agencies and/or post-secondary institutions for purposes of completing a meaningful transition plan. For more information and samples of transition plans, access the Ministry of Education website **www.edu.gov.on.ca** for the document "Transition Planning: A Resource Guide 2002".

IV: Implementing the IEP:

Implementation of an IEP centres around communication and practical application. Teachers who will be delivering service to the exceptional student need to be informed and prepared for the upcoming changes (although, if a collaborative process has been used, it is very likely that key personnel will have been involved in the plan from the beginning). Parents need to be informed of changes and adjustments. The plan itself is translated into the day-to-day operation of the classroom with all practical considerations being taken into account. At the same time, a monitoring system is established, because even though an IEP will be updated at least once every reporting period, it must always be viewed as a working document, one that evolves and develops as new information arises. There are very few IEPs that do not require some modifications early on.

Once again, it is important to point out that the IEP does not cover every minute of every day in the exceptional student's school life. It is a document that records generally how a modified-from-regular program will be conducted and monitored.

V: Reviewing and Updating the IEP:

A student's IEP needs to be reviewed each reporting period. Considerations in such a review would include:

- Does the plan still reflect the student's needs?

- Are the strategies and resources still effective?

- Is the student progressing at the rate expected?

- Should changes be made to the assignment of responsibility?

- Has any new information emerged that means the plan should change?

- Is the student displaying responsibility and commitment to the learning process?

- Are family/student commitments in the plan being carried out?

Assigning Primary Responsibility

In most schools, IEPs are developed collaboratively, ideally by an 'In-school Team' or 'School Team' under the direction of the principal. However, because of the inevitable time constraints in a typical school, and for reasons of efficiency, the primary responsibility for preparation of an IEP is often undertaken by one person, or sometimes two. Very often, that primary person is the classroom teacher of the student under consideration, or one of the school's special education teachers, or the two of them in concert, along with the educational assistant. The teacher(s) having primary responsibility will almost certainly have been central in gathering the basic information and also, after consultation with the in-school team, will likely take responsibility for writing the plan, for seeing to its implementation, and may oversee or perhaps actually perform the monitoring of progress. In a well-run system, nevertheless, the primary persons do not work unsupported, for the school team is always there for consultation, assistance, and an insertion of fresh ideas.

The IEP: How Parents Can Help

✔ Communicate regularly with the student's teacher; attend meetings.

✔ Keep records of information that may be helpful, especially meetings or discussions that may have taken place outside the school.

✔ Share insights about the student's likes, dislikes, relevant medical information, assessments the school may not have.

✔ Ask questions. Clarify definitions, jargon, and the roles of those participating. Ask for an explanation of procedural issues that are unclear.

✔ Assume the best. Professionals share your goal to develop your child's full potential.

Dangers and Trouble Spots

Despite the appeal of IEPs, and even though experience has proven their value, there are some potential difficulties to be aware of, both in preparation and implementation. Some teachers feel they are ill equipped to develop what they consider a radical departure from their normal planning. Even teachers with training in special education may have little experience in coordinating a team and developing plans. There can often be confusion, if not tension, over who has responsibility for the various components of the process. And, even though a multidisciplinary approach is useful, a lack of systematic training for school personnel and sporadic attendance at meetings can make the approach difficult to maintain.

Some educators are concerned that the relatively formal nature of the IEP creates yet another level of bureaucracy, and thereby moves education even farther away from its intended recipient, the student. The use of computer programs to develop IEPs, and programs that spin out computer generated strategies to complete a plan, have raised legitimate concerns over weak paper compliance to the very important IEP process. Yet paper compliance is a natural response for teachers faced with increased workload, heavy demands from administration and parents, excessive paperwork, insufficient support and lack of training. One entirely legitimate criticism of the IEP form recommended by the Ministry of Education is that, notwithstanding its theoretical excellence, it is too demanding a document for the typically overwhelmed teacher to maintain well.

Ultimately, an IEP is only a tool. A proven one, but a tool nevertheless. To put it to effective use requires the same skills, resources, and above all, *willingness*, which any other educational tool requires. One way to circumvent the possible problems with an IEP and to ensure a more beneficial outcome is to manage its preparation and implementation through the power of a school team. Experience proves that a team approach to the IEP not only enhances the quality of an IEP, it also offers greater likelihood that its contents and its ideals will take effect.

The In-School Team

The Role a Team Plays

The role and the style of an in-school team vary from school to school and board to board. Some schools have teams that meet on a regular, scheduled basis; others meet only when a certain number of students have been referred for discussion. Some teams meet to help a teacher with ideas for students who are having only mild difficulty, while other teams meet only if a child is already identified as exceptional or at risk of being so. Team style and function depends on a variety of other factors too, like the expertise, experience and beliefs of the staff, the nature of the student population, and the needs of the school. There are some schools, for example, that organize the team role quite bureaucratically, making it official policy that any student being considered for presentation to an Identification, Placement and Review Committee or for the development of an IEP, must first be presented to the team. Other schools involve the team only after an IPRC has identified a student exceptional and therefore in need of an IEP. Still others use a combination of these two approaches. Still, although there is

wide variation in the types of in-school teams at work in Ontario, and an equally wide variation in the way their strengths are put to use, one very important, widespread, and effective role for this group is the collaborative development of individual education plans.

Who Is On the Team?

Usually, a team has a relatively permanent core of people, e.g., the principal (or designate), classroom teachers, and special education teacher. Other teachers, professionals, parents and advocates may be added to suit the needs of an individual case. The group works as a team, but each member usually has a particular role in the team process, a role defined by a variety of factors: their knowledge base, their experience with the student under consideration or, in general, their capacity to provide information or support at a particular level.

❖ *The principal* (or designate) is nominally the head of the team. From a purely practical perspective, administrative power is needed for scheduling, and for making personnel and resources available. Usually, it is the principal who assigns one team member to carry primary responsibility for a particular IEP. The principal is also officially responsible for meeting provincial requirements (timelines for developing a plan, notifying participants, storing information, etc.) Research on effective in-school teams suggests that strong administrative support is a key factor in the success of any in-school team.

❖ *A special education teacher* in a school is often the person assigned the responsibility for scheduling, chairing and maintaining the records for team meetings. Usually, he is the teacher on the team with skills and training in assessment, as well as the person with the readiest access to a multitude of program modification ideas and additional resources. In most cases, the special education teacher plays a direct role in the implementation of strategies, or else arranges for implementation. It may be the special education teacher who describes and models a new technique for a classroom teacher, arranges for support personnel, works with the student directly, etc.

The special education teacher is also a gatekeeper of sorts. He communicates regularly with other professionals (e.g., speech and language pathologists, counselors, assessment services) and is usually the one who can access these resources, depending on the decisions of the team.

> "It's not so much that I shell out advice, because if that were the case we would not hear the expertise of others. I more or less stimulate the discussion, try to encourage suggestions from other members of the team, bounce ideas off them. They bounce ideas off each other, so, in a way, I am a facilitator."
>
> *Joan C., Special Ed. Resource Teacher*

❖ Many teams have *classroom teachers* as regular members who attend every meeting whether or not the student being discussed is in their class. Their role is to help generate solutions for students in difficulty and to provide support for implementing these solutions. Regular classroom teachers provide information about curriculum expectations in particular grades; they are aware of combinations of students who may be appropriate for social interventions with students having difficulty; classroom teachers have the best line into school sports and clubs and other activities. They are also a creative source of ideas. Representation from each school division on an elementary team, or from subject areas in the case of secondary schools, provides a better-rounded

The Case of Ms. Wall

The grade 4/5 split that Ms. Wall was assigned this year presented quite a few challenges in classroom management. Like many experienced teachers, she has a repertoire of strategies to maintain class attention and, while they are effective for many of the students, the behaviour of one student, Audrey, has led her to seek extra support and ideas from the in-school team.

Audrey first came to the school at the beginning of grade three. She had been identified as developmentally delayed but had always been in a regular class. During the grade three year, many discussions were held with concerned individuals, including the parents, as to how to best meet Audrey's academic needs. A suggestion that she move to a segregated class was considered but rejected. Now, with the increasing academic demands in the grade four setting, Ms. Wall is seeing what she considers a dramatic change in Audrey's behaviour. Audrey has become extraordinarily quiet and withdrawn. She does not participate in class discussions and spends much of her time staring out the window. In music class, which used to be her favourite subject, Audrey keeps her head down and does not seem to have learned any of the songs.

At the first team meeting, attended by the principal, special education teacher, two regular classroom teachers and Ms. Wall, it was decided that Audrey's curriculum expectations be decreased with a focus on basic instruction. This instruction would be delivered in part by the special education teacher in a resource room but, for a majority of the program, Audrey would stay in the regular class with Ms. Wall getting planning help from the special education teacher. It was also decided that Audrey would join the grade one class for music as an assistant to the teacher and to help the students learn and sing the songs. The immediate result was that Audrey seemed to regain her interest in music. She relishes being "assistant teacher" and in her grade four class, Audrey has begun to participate, not just in music class, but in her other subjects as well.

As the team meets to review her case, there are several concerns. Ms. Wall is making every effort to incorporate the curriculum changes but sees a broadening gap between Audrey's achievements and what is expected of the rest of the class. Audrey's parents are encouraged by the progress but are also concerned about Audrey's ability to fit in academically and socially. They have accepted the school's invitation to attend the meeting, called to come up with what everyone feels would be the best plan to meet Audrey's academic and emotional needs.

pool from which to draw information and solutions.

❖ A *classroom teacher who is an ad hoc team member* because the student under consideration is in her class, will have similar, but slightly more onerous responsibilities. Usually, this teacher will collect much of the assessment data, often in collaboration with the special education teacher. She will bring in observations of the student's behaviour and work habits across a variety of settings and subject areas, samples of work, results of teacher made tests, and information gathered through discussions with family members or other involved persons. Perhaps most important, the regular classroom teacher will likely be the person to carry out instructional plans generated by the team, and she must therefore make sure the rest of the team understands clearly what can be accommodated reasonably in the real world of her classroom. One real world factor is that she will probably do most of the communicating with the parents.

❖ An *educational assistant* is often an ad hoc member in the case of a student he may know better than most, and can play a crucial part in the formation of an IEP. In the implementation of the developed plan, the educational assistant, under the direction of the teacher, may be responsible for particular types of instruction or assistance within the classroom setting. Along with the classroom teacher, he often takes on responsibility for monitoring.

❖ Other important team members may be the *parents* of the student being discussed, for they have a wealth of information to be considered. The reasonableness and practicality of interventions such as a behaviour plan that would require home support, is far easier to discuss productively if a parent is present. Perhaps most important, parent participation helps foster bonds of trust and communication. Naturally, parents are almost always ad hoc members. Experience has shown that parents often find it difficult to get to meetings, but the provincial regulations, not to mention effective teaching practice, means they are to be kept informed.

❖ By regulation, *students who are 16 years and older* may participate in a team meeting in which an IEP is being developed. If the student is a participant in the actual meeting, he may play a very special role in describing needs and perspectives, at the very least, offering some insights into what is possible and realistic.

❖ *Support personnel* may be involved in a team meeting, but usually are not permanent members. These individuals, physiotherapists or attendance counselors for example, attend meetings where their information, expertise, and intervention may be needed. Their role, as with all members of an in-school team, is to act as an information resource. Especially with secondary school students, who have considerably more independence and a wider circle of activity that is not necessarily known to their parents or classroom teachers, support personnel may be vital to the implementation and monitoring elements in a plan.

When Teachers Collaborate

Teachers collaborate naturally. Before and after and in-between classes, in the hall, over lunch, they share strategies they have found useful, seek opinions about their concerns for a student at risk, borrow materials, plan mutual projects for their classes; the exchanges are part of their day (and beyond). But a team situation is more formalized, and the process, as a consequence, requires a somewhat more formal structure. To put together an IEP, most teams follow a variation of this problem-solving technique.

1. identify/clarify the problem;

2. formulate a plan;

3. initiate the plan;

4. assess the success of the plan;

5. revise as necessary.

Yet even these steps can be more effectively and efficiently realized if members of a team consult and collaborate with some appreciation of team dynamics.

What Makes A Team Succeed?

For collaboration to be successful, all members of the team must, at the very least, share a common focus, a sense that they are each trying to achieve the same goal. But by itself, a mutually understood purpose is still not enough. Realistically, members of a team must be voluntary participants, with a sense of voluntarily shared responsibility and accountability. Above all, to function truly without impediment, team members should have parity. The latter issue can be awkward, particularly given the fact that teachers exist in a hierarchical structure in which parity, even on a philosophical level, can be difficult to establish. On the plus side, however, teachers are members of a profession, and as a team, they are professionals united to achieve a goal for which they are better equipped than any others.

There is a practical side too. No matter how professionally a team may approach its tasks, there are some simple but fundamental requirements to apply its collective strength effectively. Schools that have been benefiting from the team concept in special education for some time now, unanimously attest that to succeed, a team must

✔ have administrative support;

✔ meet at regularly scheduled intervals;

✔ keep group size manageable;

✔ receive pertinent information *prior* to meetings;

✔ set time limits;

✔ follow an agenda;

✔ set review dates;

✔ keep records;

✔ share accountability and responsibility.

Some Issues in Team Practice

Collaboration with colleagues in a school setting is sometimes a complex dance, and ensuring that everyone is in step can prove difficult. Here are a few of the issues that must be kept in mind.

Personal beliefs: In any group of individuals, there is bound to be a variety of perspectives and beliefs. This indeed is one of the strengths of a team: the multiplicity of perspectives. But perspectives and absolute commitment to an idea or ideal, if held to the exclusion of all else, can interfere with the problem-solving goal of an IEP. It is important to be aware and respectful of the beliefs of team members, and to remember that it is the needs of a student, not the power of a principle, that ultimately must rule.

Administrative support: Administrators, whether at the school level or at the school board level, hold the keys to a variety of resources and decision making powers that are not generally available to other members of the team. Within a school, the principal sets the tone for discipline and the delivery of curriculum. In team meetings, a principal's active participation as a member of the team lends a status and aura of responsibility to that team that it would otherwise not attain. Without administrative support from within the school and at the board level, in-school teams may continue to function, but do so with their hands tied.

Time: As any teacher will attest, there is never enough time—for anything! Thus team meetings can often be viewed as an unwelcome extra in a teacher's schedule. This is even more strongly the case when a team is run inefficiently, decisions are not made or followed up, communication is poor, procedures are not well established and there is no support. Given that time is a precious commodity, it is essential that team time be seen as worthwhile and, in the end, a time saving activity. When teams are run well and teachers are given the opportunity to work with their colleagues in an effective way, the benefits to the school far outweigh the time spent at the meeting.

Adams, L., & Cessna, K. (1991). Designing systems to facilitate collaboration: Collective wisdom from Colorado. *Preventing School Failure, 35*(4), 37-42.

Cole, E., & Brown, R. (1996). Multidisciplinary school teams: A five- year follow-up study. *Canadian Journal of School Psychology, 12,* 155-168.

Cook, L., & Friend, M. (1993). Educational leadership for teacher collaboration. In B. Billingsley (Ed.), *Program leadership for serving students with disabilities* (pp. 421-444). Richmond, VA: Virginia Department of Education.

Dettmer, P.A., Dyck, N.T. and Thurston, L.P. (1996). *Consultation, Collaboration and Team Work for Students with Special Needs.* Toronto: Allyn and Bacon.

Evans, S. B. (1991). A realistic look at the research base for collaboration in special education. *Preventing School Failure, 35*(4), 10-14.

Friend, M. & Cook, L. (1992). *Interactions: Collaboration Skills for School Professionals.* Toronto: Copp Clark Pitman.

Fuchs, D. & Fuchs, L.S. (1996). Consultation as a technology and the politics of school reform. *Remedial and Special Education, 17*(6), 386-392.

Idol, L., Nevin, A., & Paolucci-Whitcomb, P. (1994). *Collaborative consultation* (2nd ed.). Austin, TX: Pro-Ed.

Jordan, A. (1994). *Skills in Collaborative Classroom Consultation.* New York: TJ Press Padstow Ltd.

Mills, M. (1994). The consultative role of school based resource teachers. *B.C. Journal of Special Education, 18*(2), 181-189.

Napier, E. (1995). *Integrating students with special needs: Effective strategies to provide the most enabling education for all students.* Vancouver: EduServ.

Ontario Ministry of Education and Training (1998). *Individual Education Plan (IEP) Resource Guide.* Queens Printer for Ontario.

Ontario Ministry of Education (2000). *Individual Education Plans standards for development, program planning and implementation.* Queens Printer for Ontario.

Ontario Ministry of Education (2001). *Special education a guide for educators.* Queens Printer for Ontario.

Ontario Ministry of Education (2002). *Transition Planning: A resource guide.* Queens Printer for Ontario.

O'Shea, D. & O'Shea, L. (1997). Collaboration and school reform: A 21st century perspective. *Journal of Learning Disabilities, 30*(4), 449-462.

Pugach, M.C. & Johnson, L.J. (1995). A new framework for thinking about collaboration. In *Collaborative practitioners collaborative schools.* Denver, CO: Love.

Safran, S.P., & Safran, J.S. (1996). Intervention assistance programs and prereferral teams. *Remedial and Special Education, 17*(6), 363-369.

Shea, T. M., & Bauer, A. M. (1991). *Parents and teachers of children with exceptionalities: A handbook for collaboration.* (2nd ed.). Boston: Allyn and Bacon.

Sheridan, S.M., Welch, M., & Orme, S.F. (1996). Is consultation effective? A review of outcome research. *Remedial and Special Education, 17*(6), 341-354.

Stanovich, P. (1996). Collaboration—The key to successful inclusion in today's schools. *Intervention in School and Clinic, 32*(1), 39-42.

Westby, C. E., & Ford, V. (1993). The role of team culture in assessment and intervention. *Journal of Educational and Psychological Consultation, 4,* 319-341.

Whitten, E., & Dieker, L. (1993). Intervention assistance teams: A collaborative process to meet the needs of students at risk. *B.C. Journal of Special Education,17*(3), 275-283.

Wiener, J & Davidson, I. (1990). The in-school team: A prevention model of delivery in special education. *Canadian Journal of Education, 15*(4), 427-445.

APPENDIX

Categories and Definitions of Exceptionalities (Ontario)

The following five categories of exceptionalities are identified in the Education Act definition of exceptional pupil, and are current at publication (30/04/04):

• **Behaviour** • **Communication** • **Intellectual** • **Physical** • **Multiple**

These broad categories above include the following definitions, as clarified in a memo to school boards on January 15, 1999:

Behaviour

A learning disorder characterized by specific behaviour problems over such a period of time, and to such a marked degree, and of such a nature, as to adversely affect educational performance, and that may be accompanied by one or more of the following:

a) an inability to build or to maintain interpersonal relationships;

b) excessive fears or anxieties;

c) a tendency to compulsive reaction;

d) an inability to learn that cannot be traced to intellectual, sensory, or other health factors, or any combination thereof.

Communication

Autism

A severe learning disorder that is characterized by:

a) disturbances in: rate of educational development; ability to relate to the environment; mobility; perception, speech, and language;

b) lack of the representational symbolic behaviour that precedes language.

Deaf and Hard-of-Hearing

An impairment characterized by deficits in language and speech development because of a diminished or non-existent auditory response to sound.

Language Impairment

A learning disorder characterized by an impairment in comprehension and/or the use of verbal communication or the written or other symbol system of communication, which may be associated with neurological, psychological, physical, or sensory factors, and which may:

a) involve one or more of the form, content, and function of language in communication; and

b) include one or more of: language delay; dysfluency; voice and articulation development, which may or may not be organically or functionally based.

Speech Impairment

A disorder in language formulation that may be associated with neurological, psychological, physical, or sensory factors; that involves perceptual motor aspects of transmitting oral messages; and that may be characterized by impairment in articulation, rhythm, and stress.

Learning Disability

A learning disorder evident in both academic and social situations that involves one or more of the processes necessary for the proper use of spoken language or the symbols of communication, and that is characterized by a condition that:

a) is not primarily the result of: impairment of vision; impairment of hearing; physical disability; developmental disability; primary emotional disturbance; cultural difference;

b) results in a significant discrepancy between academic achievement and assessed intellectual ability, with deficits in one or more of the following: receptive language (listening, reading); language processing (thinking, conceptualizing, integrating); expressive language (talking, spelling, writing); mathematical computations; and

c) may be associated with one or more conditions diagnosed as: a perceptual handicap; a brain injury; minimal brain dysfunction; dyslexia; developmental aphasia.

Intellectual

Giftedness

An unusually advanced degree of general intellectual ability that requires differentiated learning experiences of a depth and breadth beyond those normally provided in the regular school program to satisfy the level of educational potential indicated.

Mild Intellectual Disability

A learning disorder characterized by:

a) an ability to profit educationally within a regular class with the aid of considerable curriculum modification and supportive service;

b) an inability to profit educationally within a regular class because of slow intellectual development;

c) a potential for academic learning, independent social adjustment, and economic self-support.

Developmental Disability

A severe learning disorder characterized by:

a) an inability to profit from a special education program for students with mild intellectual disabilities because of slow intellectual development;

b) an ability to profit from a special education program that is designed to accommodate slow intellectual development;

c) a limited potential for academic learning, independent social adjustment, and economic self-support.

Physical

Physical Disability

A condition of such severe physical limitation or deficiency as to require special assistance in learning situations to provide the opportunity for educational achievement equivalent to that of pupils without exceptionalities who are of the same age or development level.

Blind and Low Vision

A condition of partial or total impairment of sight or vision that even with correction affects educational performance adversely.

Multiple

Multiple Exceptionalities

A combination of learning or other disorders, impairments, or physical disabilities that is of such a nature as to require, for educational achievement, the services of one or more teachers holding qualifications in special education and the provision of support services appropriate for such disorders, impairments, or disabilities.

Some Assessment Instruments Popular in Ontario

Titles below appear in alphabetical order, and include the 'familiar' name. Each summary is brief; for in-depth reviews and information on test construction refer to the appropriate Mental Measurement Yearbook. Many test instruments show two publication dates. The first indicates original publication and approximate time of original norming (or in some cases, its most recent re-norming and/or complete revision). The second date indicates when the latest changes were made. Note:These changes may be as simple as a formatting change or design change. Some tests are updated regularly but many others carry on with only minor changes. *It is extremely important to be aware of the age of both the content and norms of any testing instrument.* Results based on content and norms established decades ago may produce misleading or irrelevant information that could affect appropriate programming.

AAMD Adaptive Behavior Scale, School Edition ("The ABS") (1981-1993): Pro-Ed Inc.

This individually completed scale is used principally to aid in classification, placement, and general programming decisions for individuals with developmental delay by assessing their adaptive functioning. There is some evidence to suggest that this scale may also be helpful in assessing the adaptive functioning of students with *autism*. Consisting of 21 scores encompassing subsections such as physical development, economic activity, social engagement and self-abusive behaviour, the test yields percentile ranks for individuals within the 3-69 age range. The rater (test completer) can be the parent, teacher, social worker, etc.

Strengths and Weaknesses:

The *ABS* enjoys popularity with educators and health professionals who emphasize adaptive behaviour in assessing mental handicap. It is used most frequently to assess an individual's ability to thrive in a particular placement (independent, group home, etc.). Validity and reliability are criticized. Generally it is not used for severely handicapped persons.

The Behavior Evaluation Scale ("The BES") (1993): Hawthorne Educational Services Inc.

The *BES* is a scale for evaluating behaviour in students K-12. It is filled out by the teacher or other adult, and covers areas like learning problems, interpersonal difficulties, unhappiness, depression, etc. Takes about 15 minutes to complete and produces a number that can be used to judge a student's behaviour comparatively.

Strengths and Weaknesses:

Useful for comparison purposes if it is completed by several significant adults in the subject's life. However, this or any evaluation scale should never be used as a sole determinant for identification or placement.

Boehm Test of Basic Concepts, Third Edition ("The Boehm") (2000): The Psychological Corporation.

A standardized, individual or group screening test of comprehension, quantity and time concepts designed to assess knowledge basic to early academic success. If used to assess school readiness, it may help identify students at risk for learning difficulties. The grade range is K-2; it takes 30-40 minutes to administer and produces a percentile score.

Strengths and Weaknesses:

Most young people find *The Boehm* interesting. Illustrations are clear and well organized. Has an excellent manual. Easy to administer. Unfortunately, no documentation is offered to support the concepts in the test as crucial to the early years of school.

Brigance Diagnostic Comprehensive Inventory of Basic Skills ("The Brigance") (1976-1999): Curriculum Associates.

An individual, non-standardized (but field-tested in Ontario and the U.S.) instrument, designed to assess pre-academic, academic, and vocational skills so that teachers can more easily define objectives and plan individual programs. The grade range is pre-school to 12; it takes 15-90 minutes to administer, and in some subtests produces a grade or age level score. Subtests consist of readiness, speech, listening, research and study skills, reading, spelling, writing and math. (There are several other similar instruments by Brigance.)

Strengths and Weaknesses:

Can be useful in record-keeping and planning student programs. Not suitable for comparisons between students but can serve as a useful and quick method of assessing student progress. Administered easily by paraprofessionals under supervision. The somewhat informal procedures tend to encourage carelessness but, properly used, this test can be a useful planning aid.

The Canadian Achievement Test ("The CAT") (1981-2002): Canadian Test Centre, Educational Assessment Services.

A standardized, norm-referenced *and* criterion-referenced group test to assess achievement. Grade range is 1-12; time to administer is flexible (depending on the number and combination of sub-tests); produces percentile, stanine, scaled, and grade equivalent scores.

Strengths and Weaknesses:

The major content areas are reading, spelling, language, mathematics, and reference skill. It has been sharply criticized as too unwieldy and threatening to both subjects and examiners, yet given the many pieces to it, the test is reasonably easy to administer. It produces a detailed Student Diagnostic Profile (SDP) that can be very useful if all personnel are prepared to take the time to interpret it.

Canadian Cognitive Abilities Test ("The C-Cat") (1970-1997): Thomas Nelson Learning (Canada).

This is a standardized, norm-referenced group test designed to measure cognitive abilities in the verbal, quantitative, non-verbal and problem solving areas. The grade range is 3-12; it takes 1-2 hours to administer and produces standard, percentile, and stanine scores for age groups, and percentile and stanine scores for grade groups.

Strengths and Weaknesses:

The *C-Cat* has high validity and reliability estimates and reviewers compliment it for careful norming and standardization. Supporters say it has better predictive value than IQ tests, although critics argue that cognitive ability by itself is not a straightforward entity to assess.

The Canadian Test of Basic Skills ("The CTBS") (1955-97): Thomas Nelson Learning, (Canada).

A Canadianization of the Iowa Test of Basic Skills, very popular in Ontario, the *CTBS* is a standardized, norm-referenced, group-administered achievement test for K-12 that produces mounds of data. It can be hand scored, although a computerized scoring system is preferred. Scores range from percentile to scale to grade equivalent. Intra-class data as well as other, extensive comparative data can be made available. The test examines 7 areas: vocabulary, reading, language, sources of information, mathematics, maps & diagrams and science.

Strengths and Weaknesses:

Although the *CTBS* can be extremely time-consuming to administer, many educators say it is worth the effort. Validity and reliability data are generally good and the test is well-received by reviewers. The most severe criticisms are not directed at the test itself but at the general abuse to which achievement tests especially, are subject.

Child Behavior Checklist (The "CBCL") (1986-1994): University Associates in Psychiatry, Burlington, VT.

Focuses on social relationships and general behaviour, using three forms. Uses a teacher or EA report form with 168 items rating behaviours, plus an item on academic performance and one on adaptive functioning. A second form is 'direct observation' which requires an evaluator to observe the subject in ten-minute time samples and then complete 96 items that provide a behaviour and an on-task score. The third is a 112 item 'youth report form', that the subject completes. Data produce a series of profiles that differ for boys and girls and for three different age levels (4-6, 6-11, 12-16).

Strengths and Weaknesses:

Reviewers consider the CBCL one of the better rating scales available. The test is carefully developed and has good reliability scores. It is not simple to administer, nor is the raw data conversion easy. Proponents of the instrument, however, insist results are worth the effort.

Detroit Tests of Learning Aptitude – Fourth Edition, ("The Detroit") (1935-1998): Pro-Ed.

This is a revision of a once popular standardized, individual test designed to measure general intelligence functions such as verbal ability, reasoning, time and everyday fact and knowledge. Age range is 6-18. Test takes 1-2 hours to administer and produces percentile scores and a General Intelligence or Overall Aptitude Score.

Strengths and Weaknesses:

Reviewers of the revised *Detroit* note that while it may be useful in examining various abilities associated with learning disabilities and other neurologically based learning difficulties, it should not substitute for better recognized and developed intelligence tests.

Gates-MacGinitie Silent Reading Tests ("The Gates-MacGinitie"), Third Edition, (1992): Riverside Publishing Company.

A standardized, norm-referenced, group test designed to measure silent reading skills. Grade range is 1-12; takes 50-60 minutes to administer; produces grade, standard, and percentile scores. *The Gates-MacGinitie* is offered at eight levels and gives two basic measures: vocabulary, comprehension. (The older, first edition also had a measure of speed and accuracy.) They are pen and paper tests completed by the subject(s) usually in groups.

Strengths and Weaknesses:

These tests can be useful for determining broad comparisons and are often used for test-retest procedures because alternate forms are available. But a test of silent reading offers little diagnostic information. The comprehension sub-tests are criticized as poor. The questions sometimes rely on factors not present in the passages to be read, and measure a very low level of comprehension. A most serious criticism is that the *Gates-MacGinitie* tests do not offer a teacher more than he or she already knows about a student, except a number with which to satisfy bureaucracy.

Kaufman Assessment Battery for Children ("The K-ABC") (1983): American Guidance Service.

A standardized, individual, norm-referenced test of intelligence and achievement for age range 2-12; it takes 30-90 minutes to administer and produces age level, standard, percentile, scaled, and grade level scores. Three dimensions—sequential processing (serial or temporal order problem-solving), simultaneous processing (a gestalt approach), and achievement—are assessed in 16 sub-tests, which in turn report four global scales: the three above plus a global estimate of intellectual functioning.

Strengths and Weaknesses:

The *K-ABC* is a complex and involved instrument requiring expertise, time, and patience in the examiner. The authors urge examiners to take training courses. A major claim made for the test is assessment of disabled and minority students and pre-schoolers, but as with the Woodcock-Johnson Psycho-Educational Battery (see below) neither the claim nor the test itself has widespread acceptance. Draws heavily on neuropsychology and cerebral specialization theory, and whether or not a test based on these elements can be educationally useful is still uncertain.

Keymath Revised: A Diagnostic Inventory of Essential Mathematics ("Keymath") (1971-1998): American Guidance Service.

This is a standardized, individual test designed to assess mathematics skills. Grade range is pre-school-6; it takes 30-45 minutes to administer, and produces grade level and percentile scores. Note that the *Keymath* is *criterion-referenced*, a relatively rare feature.

Strengths and Weaknesses:

Keymath is easy to administer; diverse, colourful, and widely applicable. It has some unique sub-tests (such as Missing Elements) and is generally very motivating. On balance, Keymath is an excellent screening instrument but is criticized for gaps in the continuum of difficulty. Another criticism is that grade level scores tend to be inflated.

Leiter International Performance Scale—Revised ("The Leiter") (1948-1998): C.H. Stoelting Co.

A non-verbal test producing mental age and IQ scores by assessing areas such as reasoning, memory and attention. Often used for individuals with hearing and language difficulties or severe disabilities, and for non-English speakers. Directions are pantomimed and gestured. Age range is 2-18.

Strengths and Weaknesses:

There are no time constraints and the scoring is very objective. Subjects usually enjoy the test process. There is no leeway for partial scoring, which seems contradictory given there is no guarantee the subjects have fully understood the tasks, or are fully capable of responding. *The Leiter* is heavy and awkward to use and store but is a popular and potentially useful instrument for certain subjects. (There is an adaptation known as the Arthur (1950) Adaptation.)

McCarthy Scales of Children's Abilities ("The McCarthy Scales") (1972): The Psychological Corporation.

A standardized, individual, norm-referenced test of general intellectual ability frequently offered as an instrument to identify children with possible learning disabilities. Age range is 2.5- 8.5 years; it takes an hour to administer and produces mental age, standard, and percentile scores.

Strengths and Weaknesses:

The McCarthy Scales include several verbal tasks appropriate for children with suspected learning disabilities and has good reliability support. Ironically, no exceptional children classified as exceptional were included in the norming sample! This test also has a very small age range, which makes re-testing comparisons difficult as the child grows. Not an easy test to interpret.

Peabody Individual Achievement Test-Revised ("The PIAT-R") (1988 -Normative Update in 1998): American Guidance Service.

An individual, norm-referenced, standardized test, designed to give a wide measure of general achievement, with particular emphasis on reading, spelling, and arithmetic achievement. The grade range is K-12; takes 50-70 minutes to administer; produces age level, grade level, standard and percentile scores.

Strengths and Weaknesses:

The PIAT-R uses a multiple choice answer format. It requires recognition of correct spelling and tests sentence comprehension as well as mathematical problem-solving skills. Provides a quick, overall, preliminary view, but should not be regarded as the last word. Nor should sub-test scores be regarded as absolutely indicative of a student's ability in a particular area like reading.

Peabody Picture Vocabulary Test — III ("The PPVT-III") (1959-1997): American Guidance Service.

A standardized, individual test of single word receptive vocabulary of standard (American) English. The age range is 2-90 years; it takes 10-20 minutes to administer and produces age level, standard, percentile and stanine scores.

Strengths and Weaknesses:

Because *The PPVT-R* format presents pictures to elicit a response to a word, it is non-threatening. A good *first* test in a battery; well-designed and normed. But not too much should be made of the results of a test of single word vocabulary. The fact a subject must understand a word and an image means more than vocabulary is being assessed.

Progressive Matrices ("The Ravens") (1935-2000): Oxford Psychologists Press Ltd. (England).

The test requires a subject to complete progressively complicated visual analogies. It is entirely non-verbal and is available in Standard and Advanced levels. There is a coloured version for younger children.

Strengths and Weaknesses:

The Ravens can be used very effectively for a test-teach-test approach (See Chapter 15) and because it is non-verbal, may reveal some cognitive strengths in poor readers.

Slingerland Screening Tests for Identifying Children With Specific Language Disability ("The Slingerland") (1962-1974): Educators' Publishing Service.

A non-standardized, informal group test of visual, auditory, and kinesthetic skills related to reading and spelling, designed to identify students with a specific language disability. The age range is 6-12; it takes 60-90 minutes to administer and it produces no scores but has guidelines for evaluating test performance.

Strengths and Weaknesses:

The tests are strictly informal and permit a great deal of subjectivity. Some students become very frustrated during administration because extensive writing is required. Administration procedures are complex and difficult. Lack of validity and reliability data, and strong criticism of the *Slingerland* has led to a decline in its popularity.

Spache Diagnostic Reading Scales ("The Spache") (1963; rev. 1972, 1981): McGraw-Hill.

This is an individual, standardized, criterion-referenced test designed to measure oral and silent reading, and listening comprehension. The grade range is 1 to 7; it takes 30-60 minutes to administer and the test produces grade level scores.

Strengths and Weaknesses:

The newer version of the *Spache* is considered to be an improvement over the original but reading levels it reports may not provide good information for placement as the test's definition of independent and diagnostic reading levels differ considerably from the ones typically used in schools.

Stanford-Binet Intelligence Scale, Fourth Edition ("The Binet") (1986): Riverside Publishing.

The fourth edition retains many features of previous editions. Its authors claim this edition is designed to help differentiate between mental handicap and learning disability, to identify giftedness, to understand why a student is having learning problems, and to study the development of cognitive skills from 2-adult. There are 15 subtests, not dissimilar from those in the WISC-III, including Vocabulary, Quantitative, Memory for Sentences, Pattern Analysis, Copying, Verbal Relations, Memory for Objects, and others.

Strengths and Weaknesses:

There is surprisingly little research or review material on this edition, perhaps because of the excellent reputation of its predecessors. The publishers claim to have responded to cultural-bias criticism directed at earlier versions. Some educators regard the *Binet* as a preferred alternative to the *WISC-III*.

Test of Reading Comprehension- Third Edition ("The TORC") (1978-1995): Pro-Ed.

A standardized, norm-referenced test for individual or group, designed to give a normed measure of silent reading comprehension independent of specific curriculum via nine sub-tests like Paragraph Reading, Syntactic Similarities, Social Studies Vocabulary, Reading the Directions of Schoolwork, etc. The age range is $6\text{-}^1/_2$ -$14\text{-}^1/_2$; it takes $1\text{-}^1/_2$-2 hours to administer and produces scaled (each sub-test) and standardized (total test) scores.

Strengths and Weaknesses:

The test has come to be used mostly at upper age ranges because of very specific, subject-based vocabulary. Several sub-tests measure abilities not taught in classrooms and therefore the value of the results for school purposes may be questionable. Because the theoretical constructs underlying *The TORC* are new and complex, the worth of the scores, not to mention their interpretation, may well be suspect, especially in light of the intricate psycholinguistic base from which the tests are developed.

The Wechsler Intelligence Scale For Children – Third Edition ("The WISC-III") (1991) The Psychological Corporation.

This is an individual, standardized, norm-referenced test designed to offer an ability score (IQ) and to offer information about a subject's skills in a variety of areas. Test results give three overall scores: *Verbal Scale, Performance Scale,* and *Full Scale.* The Verbal Scale is built on six subtests: (general) information, similarities, arithmetic, vocabulary, comprehension, and digit span. According to the publisher, these subtests evaluate such areas as attention span, analysis of relationships, social maturity, memory, and others. The Performance Scale has seven subtests: picture completion, picture arrangement, block design, object assembly, coding, symbol search, and mazes. Among the areas evaluated, according to the publisher, are attention to detail, visual sequencing, analysis of differences, etc. The Verbal Scale is much more closely correlated with classroom activities than the Performance Scale. *The Full Scale Score* is offered as an IQ score.

Classroom teachers usually do not administer a WISC, but they do (or should) receive results. Ideally, teachers will be given the sub test results as well as the Full Scale, Verbal, and Performance Scores, for these may have diagnostic information on which a plan of remediation can be based.

Strengths and Weaknesses:

The *WISC-III*, like its predecessors, has wide acceptance as a clinical and diagnostic tool. Although the manual for the test states that the instrument is intended for use with people aged 6 years 0 months through 16 years 11 months, it is not uncommon for the test to be used with students who are older or younger. (Adult and older students should theoretically be tested on the WAIS, the Wechsler Adult Intelligence Scale, and younger children on the WPPSI, the Wechsler Pre-Primer Scale of Intelligence.) Reliability and validity coefficients are high; it is particularly well standardized, and can produce some useful diagnostic information. Testing time is approximately 1-1/2 hours.

Wide Range Achievement Test – 3 ("The WRAT-3") (1940-1993): Jastak Associates.

This is an individual, norm-referenced, standardized test designed to assess skills in reading (actually, word recognition), written spelling, and arithmetic computation. Age range is 5 to adult; 20-30 minutes to administer; produces grade level, standard, percentile, and stanine scores.

Strengths and Weaknesses:

Easy and fast in administration and scoring, and can be a fairly efficient first step in an assessment. It should never be used as the sole

element in any evaluation, assessment or admission procedure (but often is!). The arithmetic computation sub-test does not test ability as much as it tests what the subject's curriculum offered. As well, the reading sub-test asks the subject merely to read a list of single words. There is no measure of sentence or paragraph reading, or of comprehension. Reviewers also point out that over-estimations of reading ability, at the primary level especially, are a weakness.

Woodcock-Johnson Psycho-Educational Battery- Revised ("The Woodcock") (1977-2001): Riverside Publishing Company.

An individual, standardized, norm-referenced test designed to measure cognitive ability, academic achievement and interests over a wide range. The age range is 3-adult; it takes 1-1/2-2 hours to administer and produces grade level, age level, percentile, and standard scores, along with scores the authors call 'functional level' and `relative performance index'.

This is a busy and involved instrument, with a large number of sub-tests. Areas covered consist of measures of "Cognitive Ability" (e.g., analysis-synthesis; memory for sentences, etc.) as well as an achievement battery (e.g., calculation, dictation, proofing, etc.). Provides a large amount of information.

Strengths and Weaknesses:

To make this instrument work its best requires a major commitment from the examiner. It is difficult, complex and time-consuming. This fact has restricted the popular use of the instrument, along with the concern over whether the scholastic aptitude clusters are reliable and valid measures of reading, math, written language, and knowledge.

Woodcock Reading Mastery Tests-Revised ("The Woodcock Reading") (1973- normative update in 1998): Guidance Service.

This is an individual, standardized, criterion and norm-referenced test designed to measure a wide range of reading skills. The grade range is K-12; it takes 30-45 minutes to administer; and it produces a wide set of scores including grade level, percentile, relative mastery, achievement index, and reading range.

Strengths and Weaknesses:

This test offers six sub-tests covering letters, words, and passages. The Word Comprehension sub-test uses analogy, and the Passage Comprehension makes use of the cloze procedures, both highly regarded techniques. A useful concept is the `relative mastery' which provides a useful indication of what can be expected of a student. Another useful point is the concept of instructional range in which the test gives indication of where a student can be expected to perform. Reliability and validity data are very good.

Some General Terms Used In Testing (See Chapter 15 for more)

Age Norm (Age Score) A score indicating average performance for students classified according to chronological age.

Base Level The level at which all items of a test are passed, just preceding the level where the first failure occurs. All items below the base level are assumed correct. Contrast with ceiling level.

Battery A group of selected tests administered to a student.

Ceiling Level The highest item of a sequence in which a certain number of items has been failed. All items above the ceiling item are assumed incorrect.

Chronological Age (CA) Age from birth expressed in years and months; e.g., 7 years, 6 months.

Correlation Coefficient (r) A statistical index that measures the degree of relationship between any two variables.

Diagnostic Testing An intensive, in-depth evaluation process using formal, standardized tests and informal tests designed to determine the nature and severity of specific learning problems.

Intelligence Quotient (IQ) An index of mental capacity, expressing a student's ability to perform on an intelligence test.

Mean (M) The sum of a set of scores divided by the number of scores.

Median (MD) The middle point in a set of ranked scores.

Mental Age (MA) A measure of a student's level of mental development, based on performance on a test of mental ability and determined by the level of difficulty of the test items passed.

Mode (MO) The score that occurs most frequently in a distribution. In the distribution 18, 14, 12, 11, 10, 10, 7, the mode is 10.

Percentile Rank A type of converted score that expresses a student's score relative to his or her group in percentile points. Indicates the percentage of students tested who made scores equal to or lower than the specified score.

Projective Technique A test situation in which the student responds to ambiguous stimulus materials, such as pictures, inkblots, or incomplete sentences, thereby supposedly projecting personality characteristics.

Protocol The original record of the test results.

Rank Ordering The arrangement of scores from highest to lowest.

Raw Score The score initially obtained by scoring a test according to directions in the manual.

Reliability The degree to which a student would obtain the same score if the test were re-administered assuming no further learning, practice effects, or other change.

Scaled Score a score used to measure students' growth from year to year.

Standard Deviation (SD) The most commonly used measure of variation. A statistic used to express the extent of the distribution's deviations from the mean.

Standardization In test construction, this refers to the process of trying the test out on a group of students to determine uniform or standard scoring procedures and methods of interpretation.

Standardized Test Contains empirically selected materials, with specific directions for administration, scoring, and interpretation. Provides data on validity and reliability, and has adequately derived norms.

Standard Score Derived score that transforms a raw score in such a manner that it has the same mean and the same standard deviation.

Stanine A weighted scale divided into nine equal units that represent nine levels of performance on any particular test. The stanine is a standard score.

Validity The extent to which a test measures what it is designated to measure. A test valid for one use may have negligible validity for another.

Ontario Legislation and Policies Affecting Special Education

The Education Act

Usually referred to as 'The Act', it governs the operation of schools and school boards in the province. The requirement mandating special education is now found in paragraph 170(1)7. Section 1(1) defines exceptional pupil, special education program and special education service. Other sections deal with various elements, e.g., subsections 57 (3), (4) and (5) deal with the Tribunal stage in appealing an IPRC decision. The obligations most immediately affecting day to day issues are usually covered in Regulations and Policy/Program Memoranda.

Key Regulations Affecting Special Education

<u>296</u> Ontario Schools for the Blind and the Deaf relates to the operation of the Ontario Schools for the Blind and the Deaf.

<u>298</u> Operation of Schools-General: *Subsection 3(3)* permits a reduction in the length of the instructional program for exceptional pupils below the required 5 hours per day. *Section 19* sets out qualifications teachers must hold to be placed in charge of or to teach in a special education program. *Section 26* sets out the relationship between principals and professional support staff, including psychiatrists, psychologists,and social workers. *Section 30* provides for special education programs for pre-school chil-

dren who are deaf or hard of hearing. *Section 31* sets out maximum enrolment for special education classes.

<u>181</u> Identification and Placement of Exceptional Pupils (See Chapter 5)

<u>306</u> Special Education Programs and Services requires each school board to maintain a special education plan for the delivery of special education programs and services.

<u>464</u> Special Education Advisory Committees governs the appointment to and operation of Special Education Advisory Committees (SEACs).

Policy / Program Memoranda

Policy/ program memoranda (PPMs) are statements of ministry policy and often include information about the Education Act and regulations made under the act. The PPMs listed here contain information about the education of exceptional pupils.

PPM1 Ontario Schools for the Blind and Deaf as Resource Centres.

PPM 8 Learning Disabilities.

PPM11 Early Identification of Children's Learning Needs.

PPM59 Psychological Testing and Assessment of Pupils.

PPM76C Alternative Educational Programs and Services for Deaf, Blind, and Deaf-Blind Exceptional Pupils.

PPM81 Provision of Health Support Services in School Settings.

PPM85 Educational Programs for Pupils in Government-Approved Care and/or Treatment Facilities.

PPM89 The Residential Demonstration Schools for Students With Learning Disabilities.

PPM127 Provincial Secondary School Literacy Test in English-Language Secondary Schools-Accommodations, Deferrals.

SUBJECT / CONTEXT INDEX

standard deviation (SD), 219
standard error of measurement, 190, 194
standard score, 219
standardization, 219
standardized test, 219
standards, 82
Stanford-Binet Intelligence Scale, 217
stanine, 190
Sternberg, Robert, 101-02
stigma, 82
Still, George, 90
stimulants, 88
strabismus, 170
strategies *see* classroom strategies
Straterra, 88
stuttering, 177
support, 39, 118, 153, 207, 208
Supreme Court of Canada, 14, 15
surgery, 121, 158
sympathetic ophthalmia, 168
syntax, 179
syphilis, 122

T
talent, 106
Talmud, 6
task analysis, 128-29
Tay-Sachs, 116
TEACCH program, 137
teams *see* school teams
teamwork, 67-68
Terman, Lewis, 106
terminology, 29-30, 81, 100, 116, 118-19, 190, 219
Test of Reading Comprehension (TORC), 217
test-teach-test model, 192
testing, 56, 107-08, 186-89, 192-94, 200
  terminology, 219
  see also achievement tests; assessment; IQ tests
thioridazine (Mellaril), 88
Thorazine, 88
time management, 65-66
Tofranil, 88
Tomatis Method, 137

tonic-clonic seizures, 147-48
Total Communication Method, 160, 161
Tourette, Gilles de la, 148
Tourette syndrome, 90, 144, 148-49, 152
trainable retarded, 12, 17, 121
tranquilizers, 88
transition plan, 39, 46, 203
treatments, 60, 69-70, 136-38
Treves, Frederick, 6
Triad model, 101
triad of impairments, 136
Triarchic theory, 101-02
Trillium School, 42
tuberous sclerosis, 122, 149
tunnel vision, 170

U
underachievers, gifted, 107

V
vaccination, 131
validity, 190

Versabraille II+, 173
video games, 83
violence, 75
Vistaril, 88
visual impairment, 168
  checklist, 169, *see also* blindness
visual stimulation, 172
vocational training, 121
voice disorders, 178

W
Wechsler Intelligence Scale for Children (WISC), 217-18
Whitney (Sir James) School, 42, 159
Wide Range Achievement Test (WRAT), 193, 218
Williams' syndrome, 124
Wolfensberger, Wolf, 10
Woodcock-Johnson Psycho-Educational Battery, 218
Woodcock Reading Mastery Tests, 188, 218-19

AUTHOR / RESOURCE INDEX